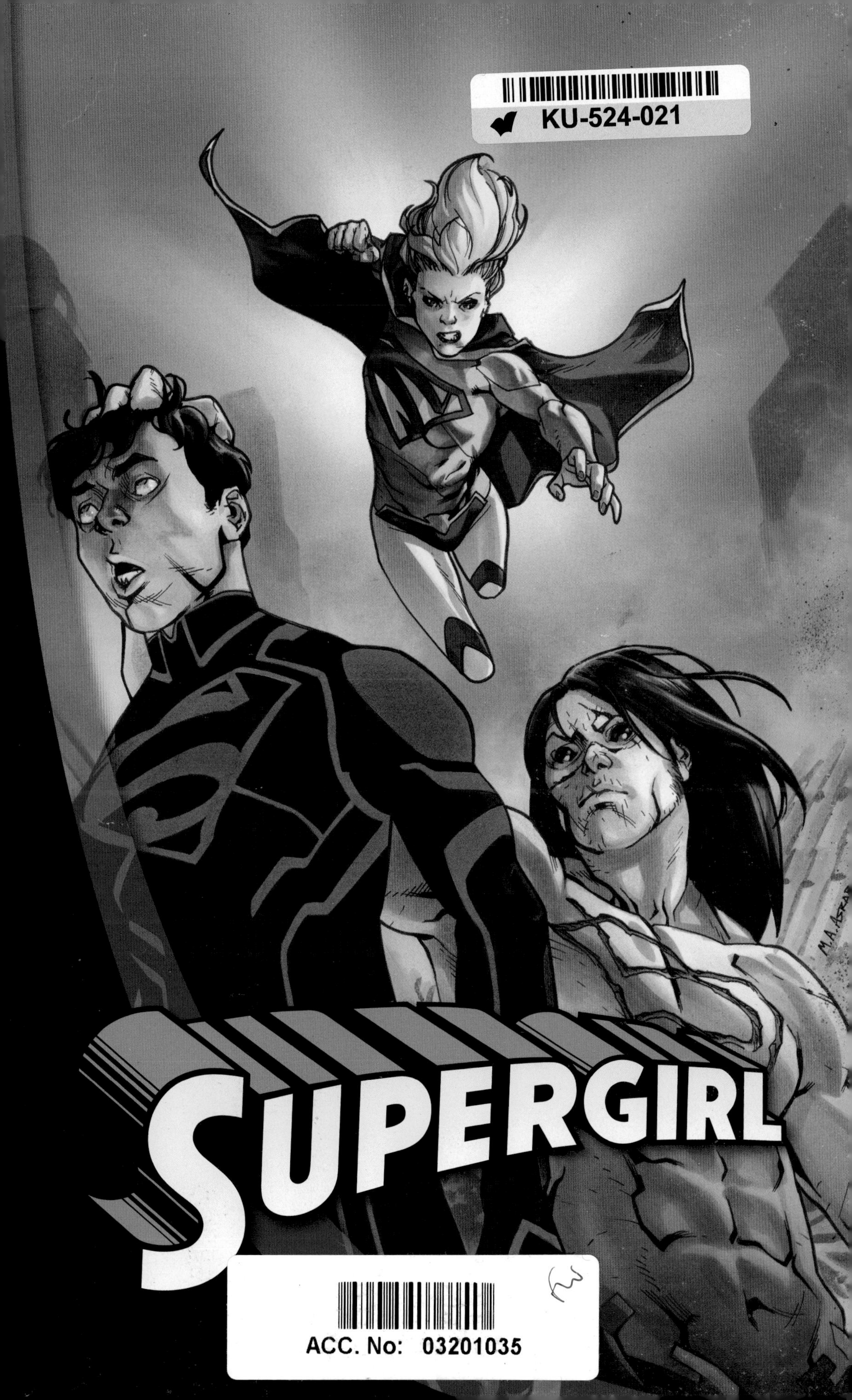
SUPERGIRL

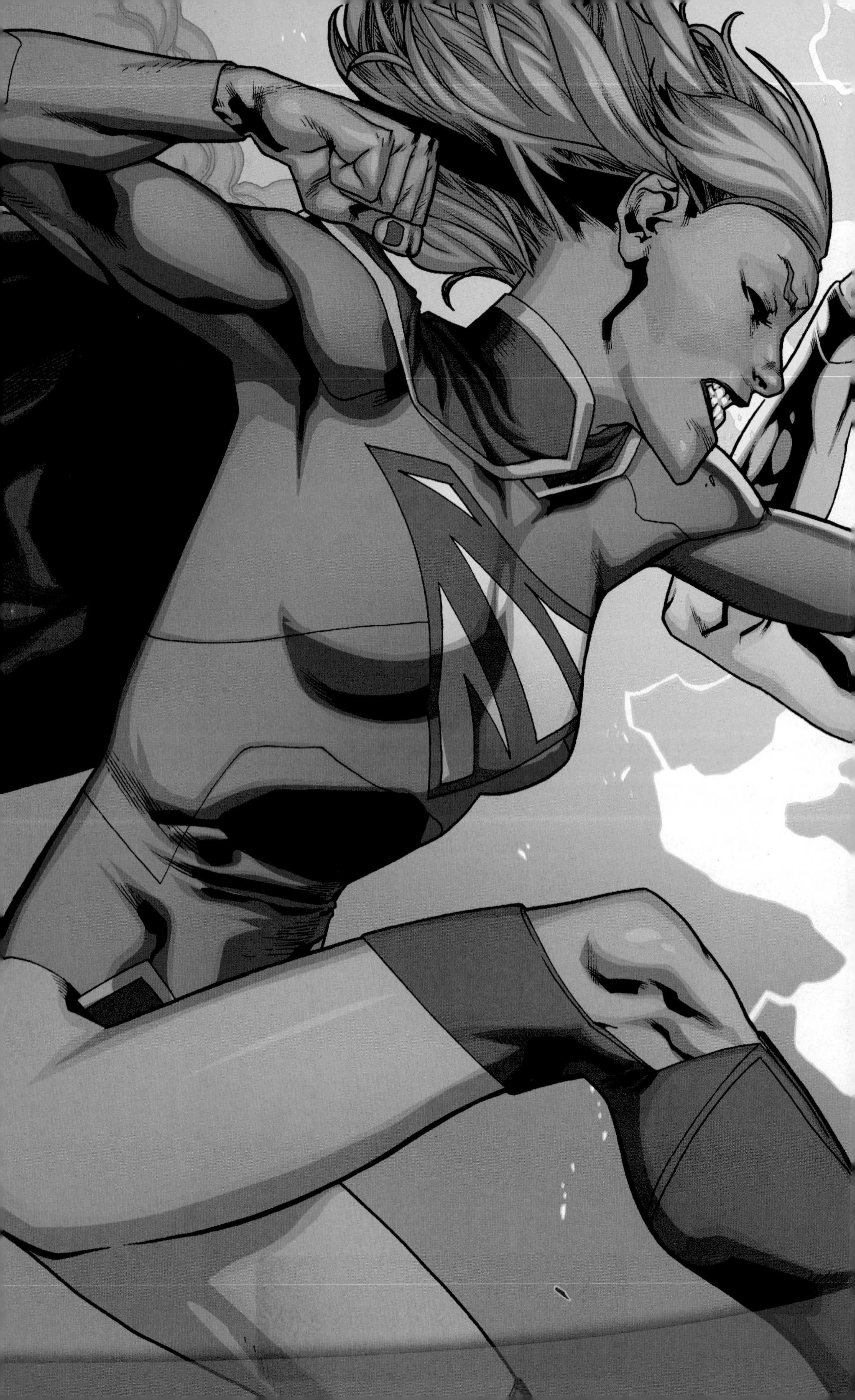

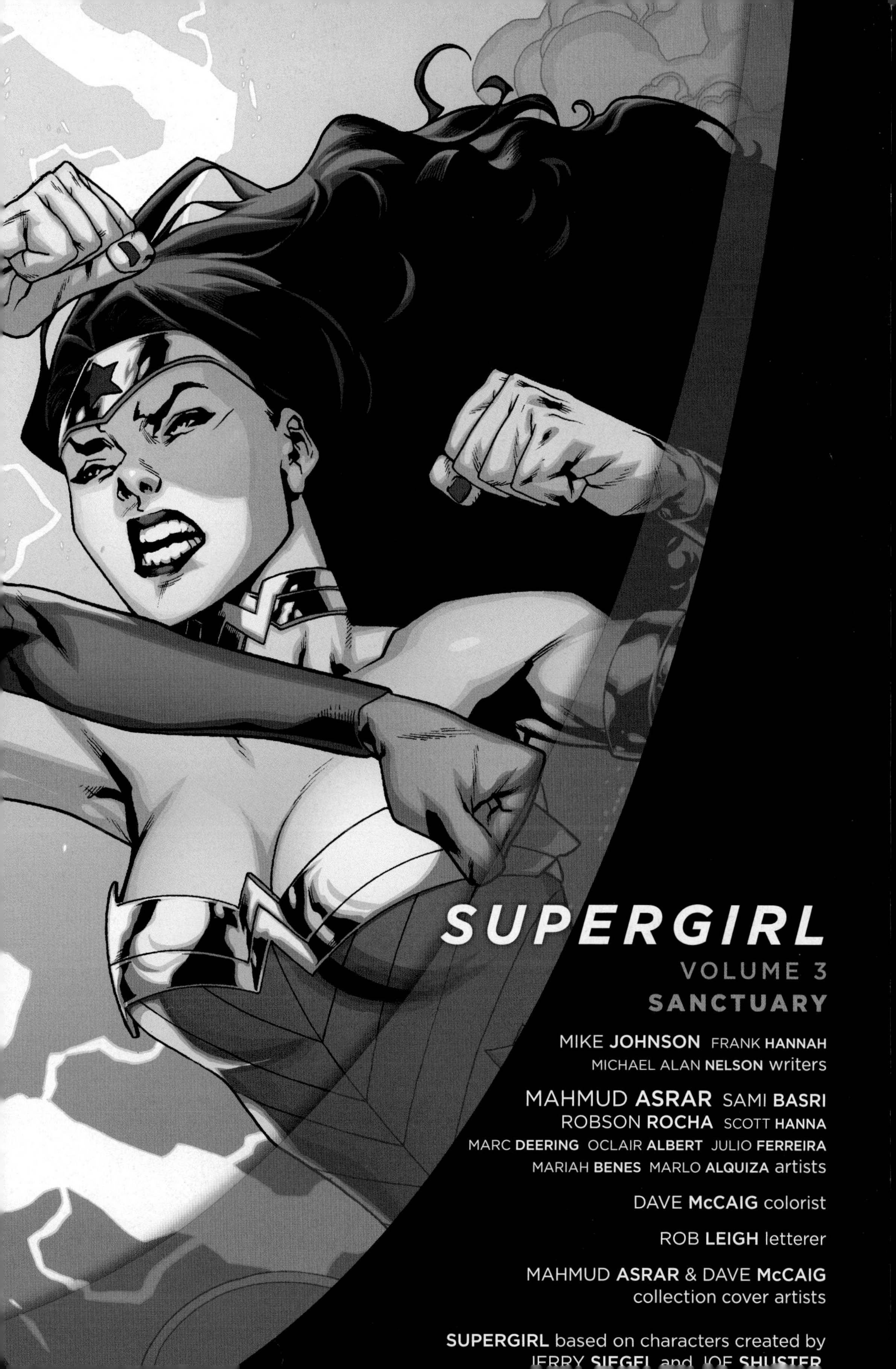

SUPERGIRL

VOLUME 3
SANCTUARY

MIKE **JOHNSON** FRANK **HANNAH**
MICHAEL ALAN **NELSON** writers

MAHMUD **ASRAR** SAMI **BASRI**
ROBSON **ROCHA** SCOTT **HANNA**
MARC **DEERING** OCLAIR **ALBERT** JULIO **FERREIRA**
MARIAH **BENES** MARLO **ALQUIZA** artists

DAVE **McCAIG** colorist

ROB **LEIGH** letterer

MAHMUD **ASRAR** & DAVE **McCAIG**
collection cover artists

SUPERGIRL based on characters created by
JERRY **SIEGEL** and JOE **SHUSTER**

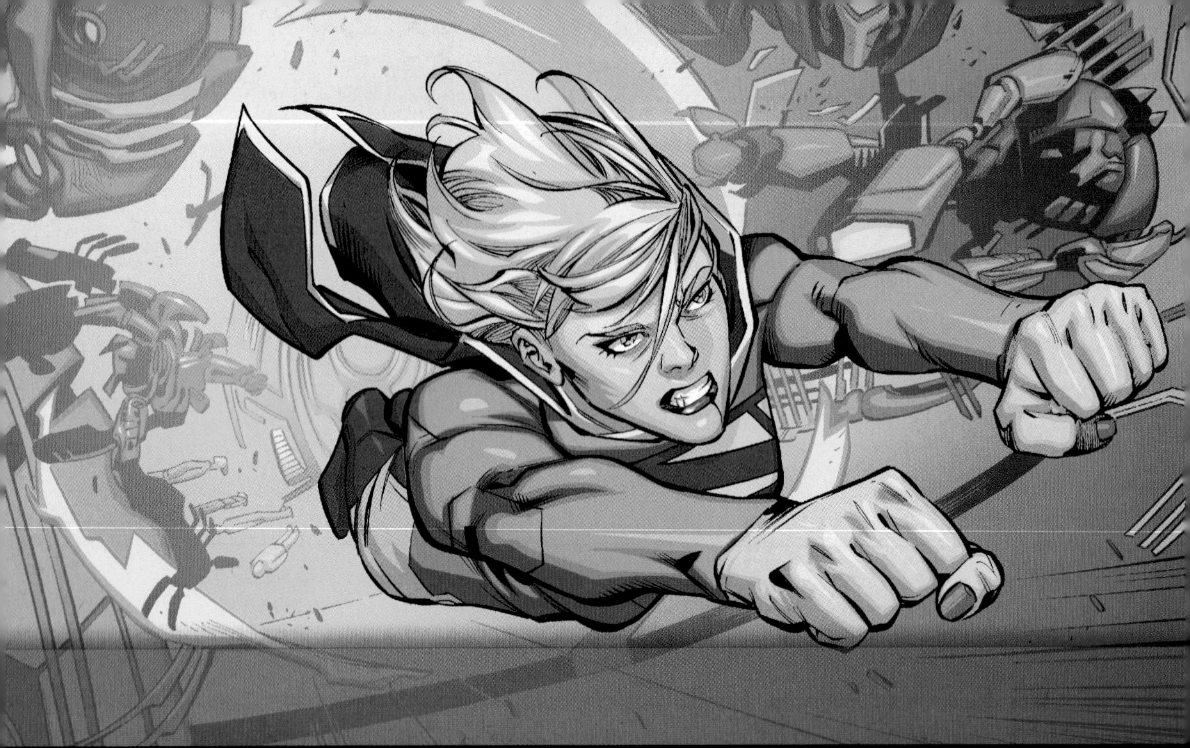

WIL MOSS EDDIE BERGANZA Editors - Original Series RICKEY PURDIN Associate Editor - Original Series
RACHEL PINNELAS Editor ROBBIN BROSTERMAN Design Director - Books ROBBIE BIEDERMAN Publication Design

BOB HARRAS Senior VP - Editor-in-Chief, DC Comics

DIANE NELSON President DAN DIDIO and JIM LEE Co-Publishers
GEOFF JOHNS Chief Creative Officer
JOHN ROOD Executive VP - Sales, Marketing and Business Development
AMY GENKINS Senior VP - Business and Legal Affairs NAIRI GARDINER Senior VP - Finance
JEFF BOISON VP - Publishing Planning MARK CHIARELLO VP - Art Direction and Design
JOHN CUNNINGHAM VP - Marketing TERRI CUNNINGHAM VP - Editorial Administration
ALISON GILL Senior VP - Manufacturing and Operations HANK KANALZ Senior VP - Vertigo and Integrated Publishing
JAY KOGAN VP - Business and Legal Affairs, Publishing JACK MAHAN VP - Business Affairs, Talent
NICK NAPOLITANO VP - Manufacturing Administration SUE POHJA VP - Book Sales
COURTNEY SIMMONS Senior VP - Publicity BOB WAYNE Senior VP - Sales

SUPERGIRL VOLUME 3: SANCTUARY

DC Comics, 1700 Broadway, New York, NY 10019
A Warner Bros. Entertainment Company.
Printed by RR Donnelley, Salem, VA, USA. 1/10/14. First Printing.

ISBN: 978-1-4012-4318-0

Library of Congress Cataloging-in-Publication Data

Johnson, Mike (Comic book author) author.
Supergirl. Volume 3, Sanctuary / Mike Johnson ; [illustrated by] Mahmud Asrar.
pages cm. -- (The New 52!)
ISBN 978-1-4012-4318-0 (pbk.)
1. Graphic novels. I. Asrar, Mahmud A., illustrator. II. Title. III. Title: Sanctuary.
PN6728.S89J64 2014
741.5'973--dc23
2013039600

SUSTAINABLE Certified Chain of Custody

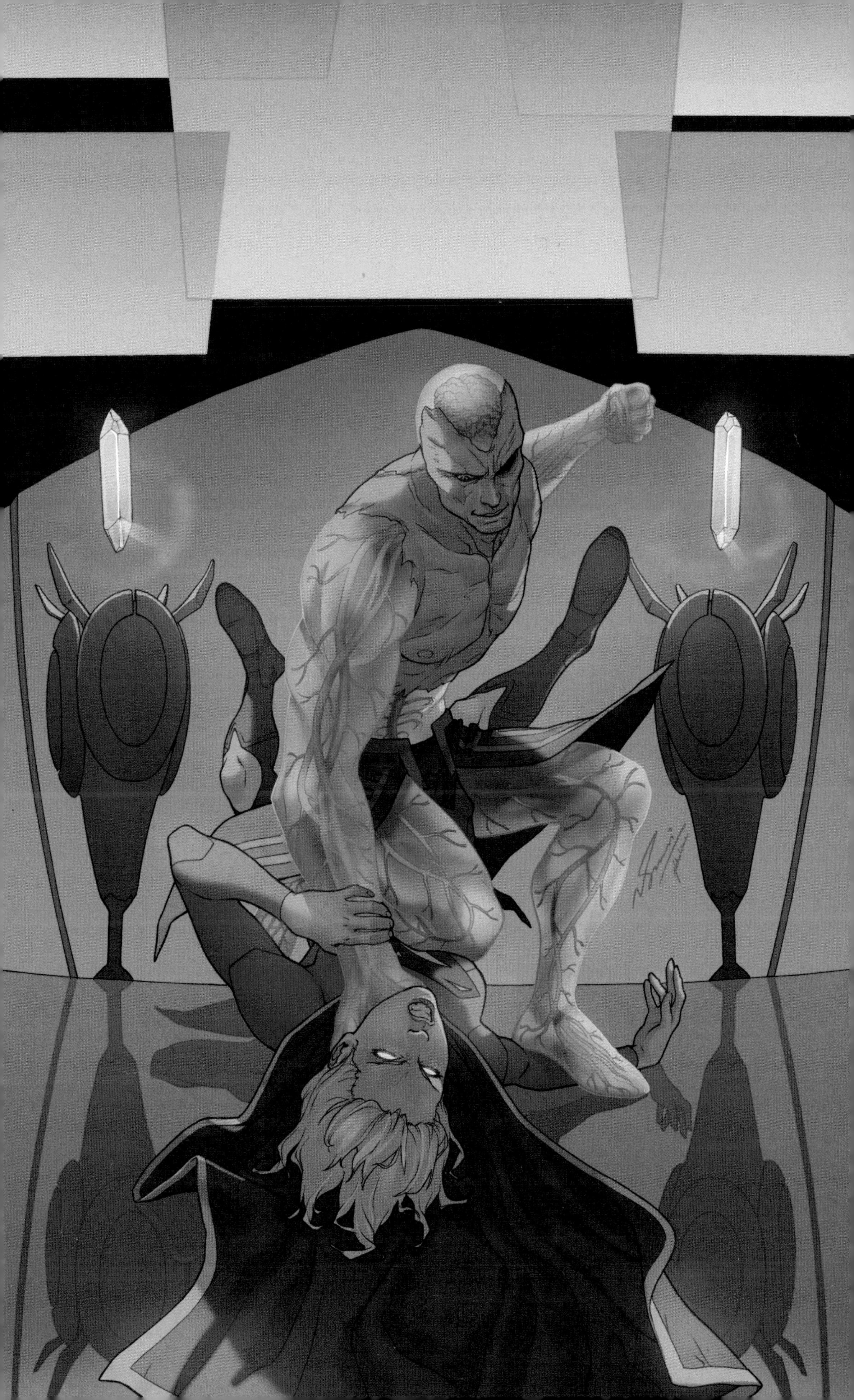

SANCTUARY

MIKE JOHNSON writer SAM BASRI artist cover art by SAM BASRI & JESSICA KHOLINNE

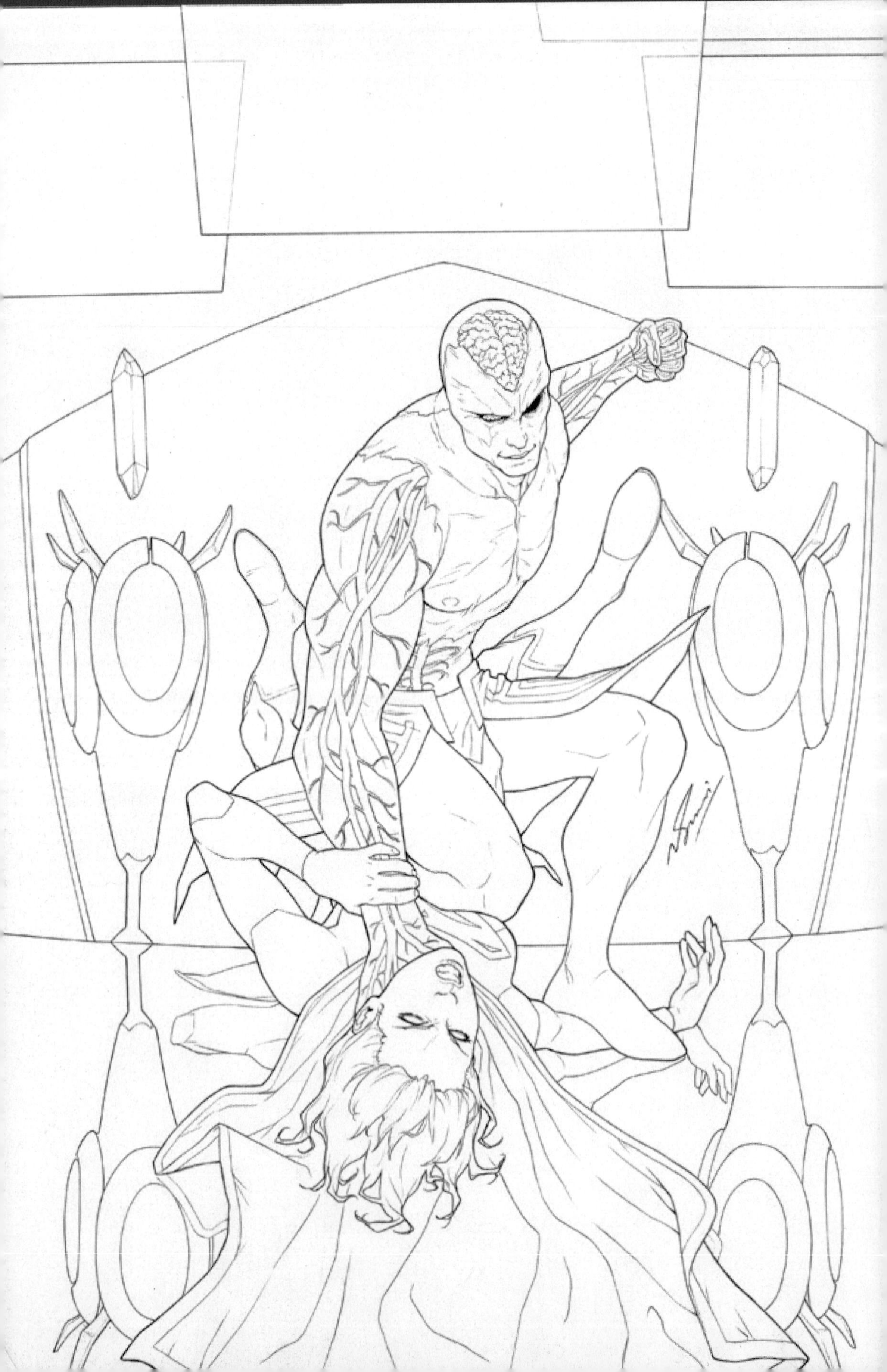

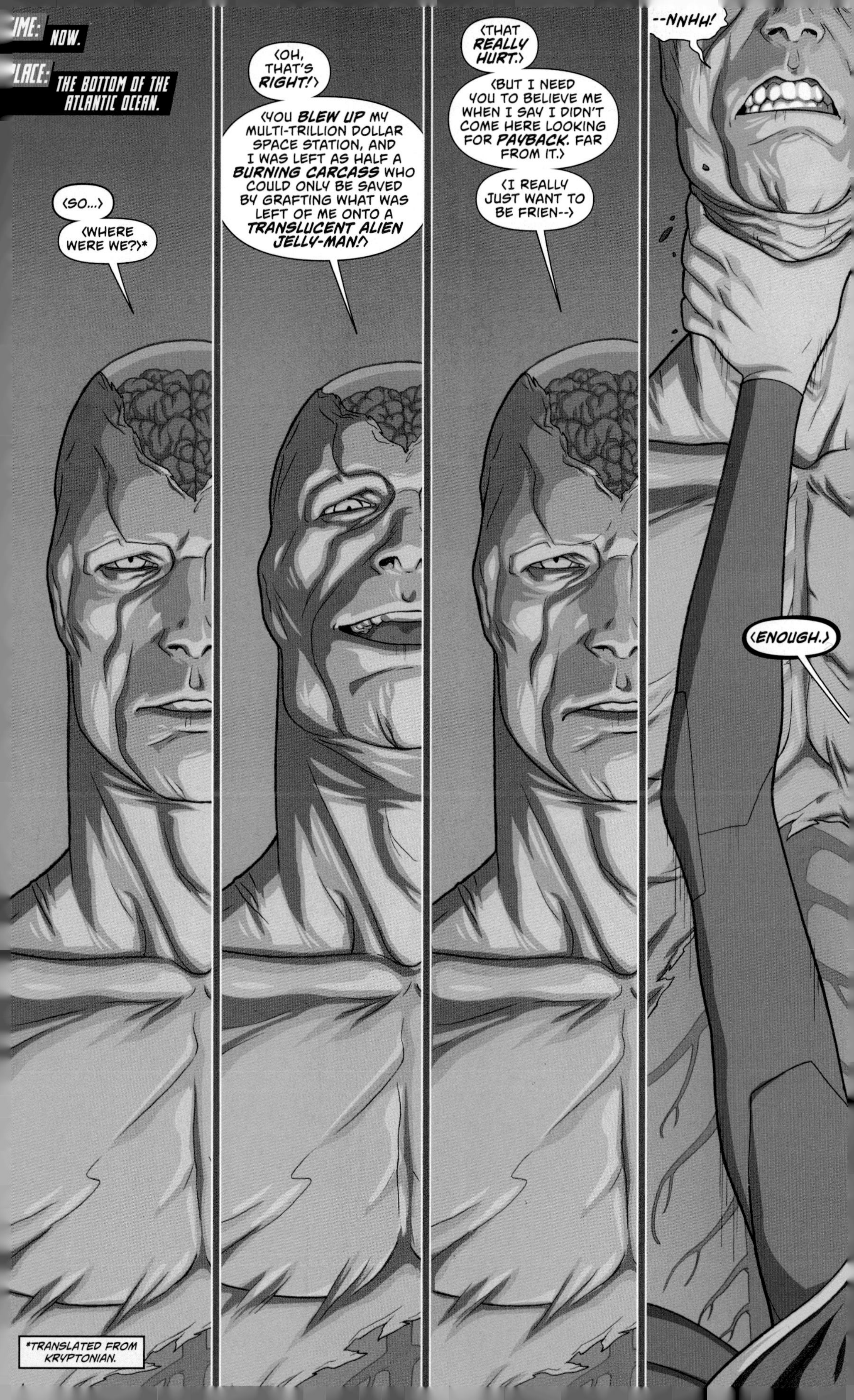
TIME: NOW.
PLACE: THE BOTTOM OF THE ATLANTIC OCEAN.
‹SO...›
‹WHERE WERE WE?›*
‹OH, THAT'S RIGHT!›
‹YOU BLEW UP MY MULTI-TRILLION DOLLAR SPACE STATION, AND I WAS LEFT AS HALF A BURNING CARCASS WHO COULD ONLY BE SAVED BY GRAFTING WHAT WAS LEFT OF ME ONTO A TRANSLUCENT ALIEN JELLY-MAN!›
‹THAT REALLY HURT.›
‹BUT I NEED YOU TO BELIEVE ME WHEN I SAY I DIDN'T COME HERE LOOKING FOR PAYBACK. FAR FROM IT.›
‹I REALLY JUST WANT TO BE FRIEN--›
--NNHH!
‹ENOUGH.›
*TRANSLATED FROM KRYPTONIAN.

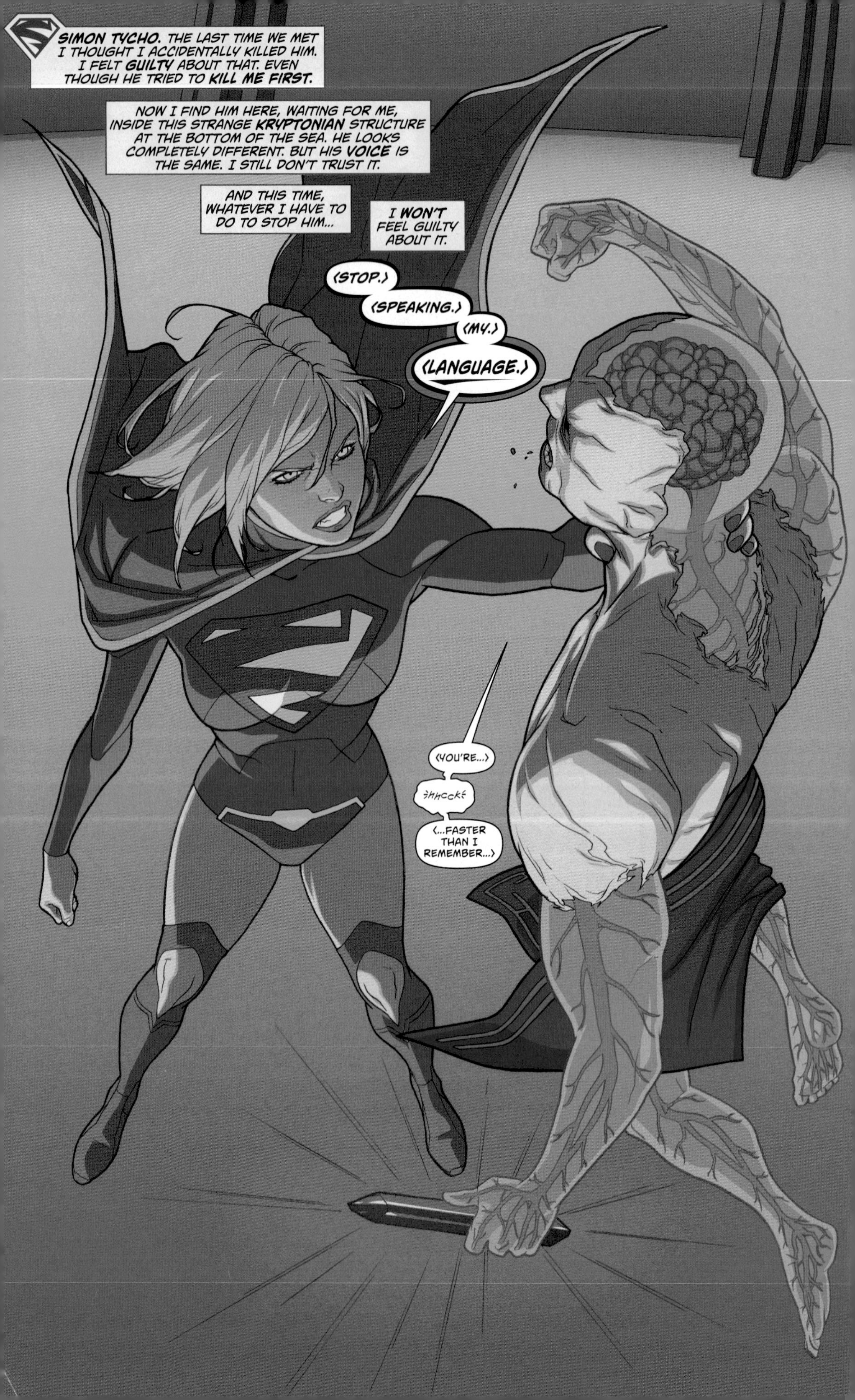
SIMON TYCHO. THE LAST TIME WE MET I THOUGHT I ACCIDENTALLY KILLED HIM. I FELT GUILTY ABOUT THAT. EVEN THOUGH HE TRIED TO KILL ME FIRST.
NOW I FIND HIM HERE, WAITING FOR ME, INSIDE THIS STRANGE KRYPTONIAN STRUCTURE AT THE BOTTOM OF THE SEA. HE LOOKS COMPLETELY DIFFERENT. BUT HIS VOICE IS THE SAME. I STILL DON'T TRUST IT.
AND THIS TIME, WHATEVER I HAVE TO DO TO STOP HIM...
I WON'T FEEL GUILTY ABOUT IT.
(STOP.)
(SPEAKING.)
(MY.)
(LANGUAGE.)
(YOU'RE...)
HHCCK
(...FASTER THAN I REMEMBER...)

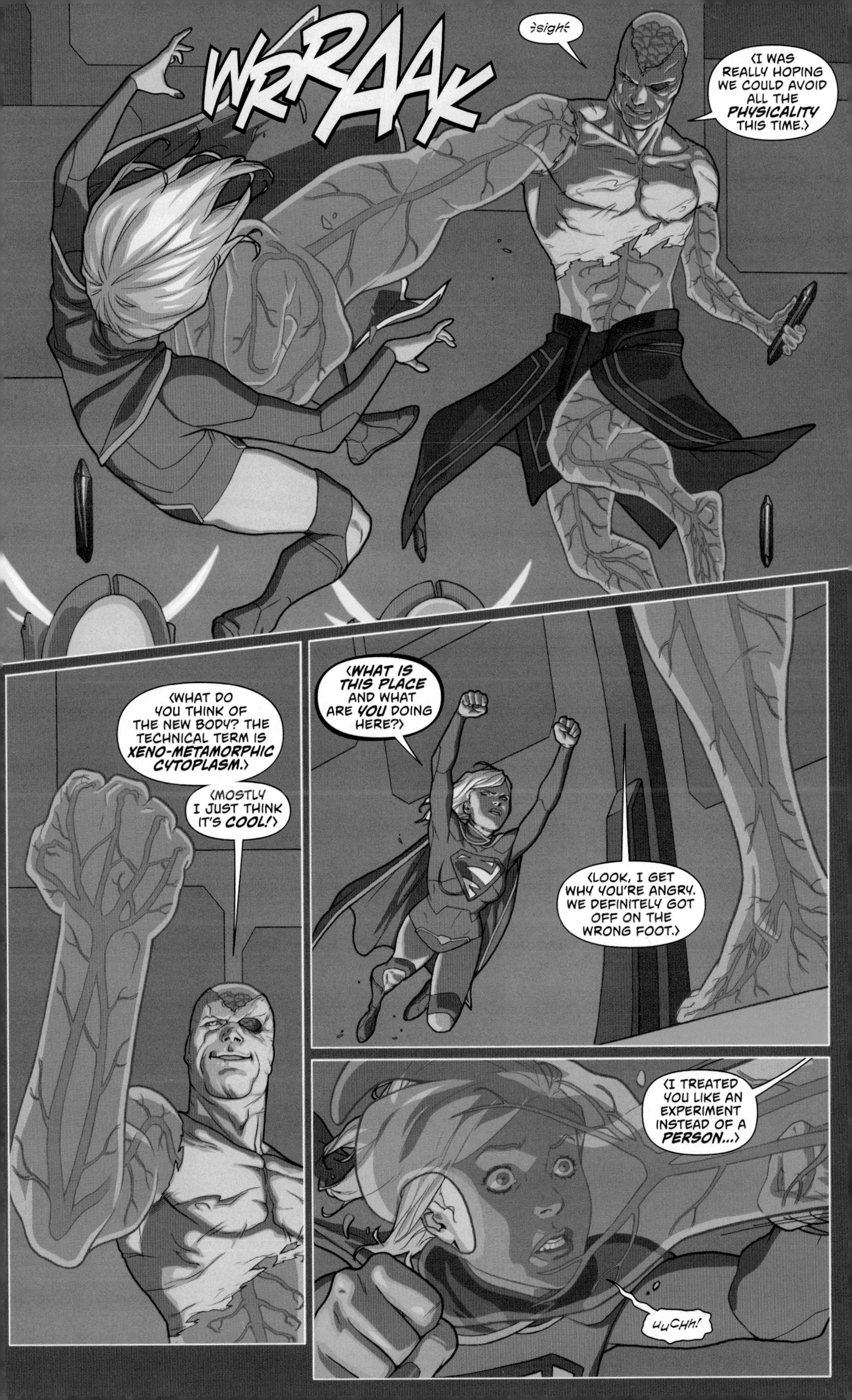
WRRAAK
⟩sigh⟨
⟨I WAS REALLY HOPING WE COULD AVOID ALL THE PHYSICALITY THIS TIME.⟩
⟨WHAT DO YOU THINK OF THE NEW BODY? THE TECHNICAL TERM IS XENO-METAMORPHIC CYTOPLASM.⟩
⟨MOSTLY I JUST THINK IT'S COOL!⟩
⟨WHAT IS THIS PLACE AND WHAT ARE YOU DOING HERE?⟩
⟨LOOK, I GET WHY YOU'RE ANGRY. WE DEFINITELY GOT OFF ON THE WRONG FOOT.⟩
⟨I TREATED YOU LIKE AN EXPERIMENT INSTEAD OF A PERSON...⟩
UUCHH!

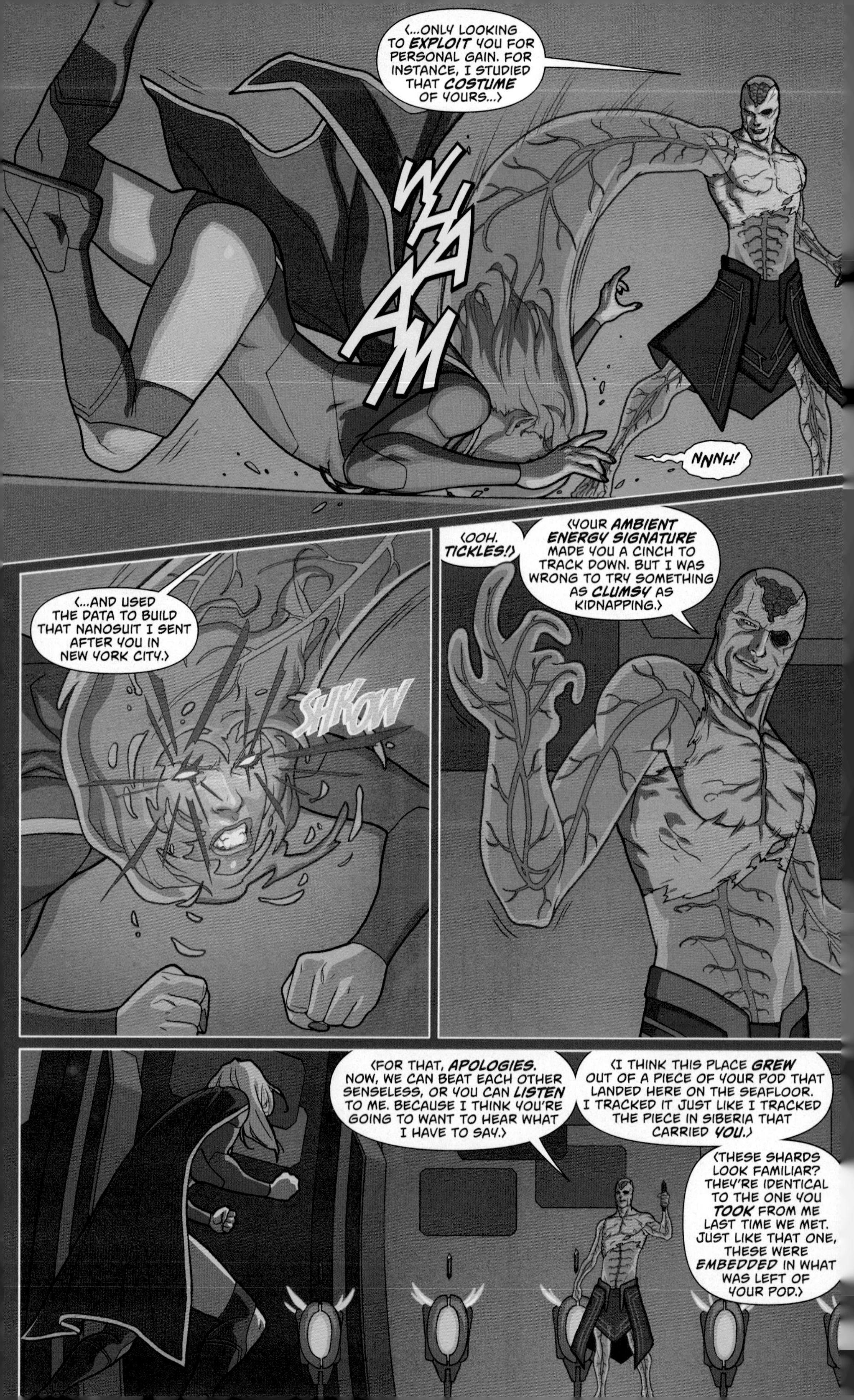
‹...ONLY LOOKING TO EXPLOIT YOU FOR PERSONAL GAIN. FOR INSTANCE, I STUDIED THAT COSTUME OF YOURS...›
WHAAM
NNNH!
‹...AND USED THE DATA TO BUILD THAT NANOSUIT I SENT AFTER YOU IN NEW YORK CITY.›
SHKOW
‹OOH. TICKLES!›
‹YOUR AMBIENT ENERGY SIGNATURE MADE YOU A CINCH TO TRACK DOWN. BUT I WAS WRONG TO TRY SOMETHING AS CLUMSY AS KIDNAPPING.›
‹FOR THAT, APOLOGIES. NOW, WE CAN BEAT EACH OTHER SENSELESS, OR YOU CAN LISTEN TO ME. BECAUSE I THINK YOU'RE GOING TO WANT TO HEAR WHAT I HAVE TO SAY.›
‹I THINK THIS PLACE GREW OUT OF A PIECE OF YOUR POD THAT LANDED HERE ON THE SEAFLOOR. I TRACKED IT JUST LIKE I TRACKED THE PIECE IN SIBERIA THAT CARRIED YOU.›
‹THESE SHARDS LOOK FAMILIAR? THEY'RE IDENTICAL TO THE ONE YOU TOOK FROM ME LAST TIME WE MET. JUST LIKE THAT ONE, THESE WERE EMBEDDED IN WHAT WAS LEFT OF YOUR POD.›

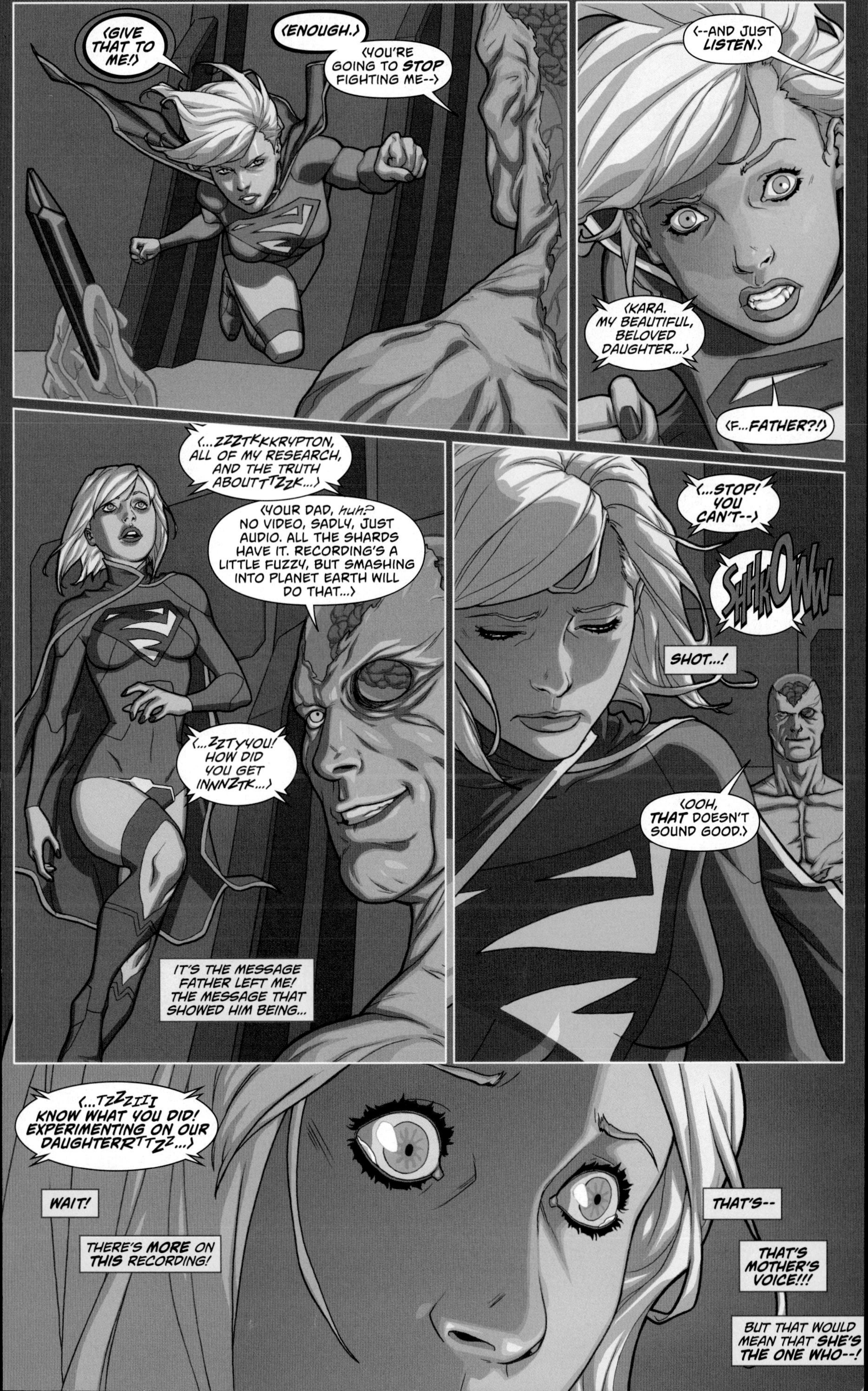
‹GIVE THAT TO ME!›
‹ENOUGH.›
‹YOU'RE GOING TO STOP FIGHTING ME--›
‹--AND JUST LISTEN.›
‹KARA. MY BEAUTIFUL, BELOVED DAUGHTER...›
‹F...FATHER?!›
‹...ZZZTKKKRYPTON, ALL OF MY RESEARCH, AND THE TRUTH ABOUTTTZZK...›
‹YOUR DAD, huh? NO VIDEO, SADLY, JUST AUDIO. ALL THE SHARDS HAVE IT. RECORDING'S A LITTLE FUZZY, BUT SMASHING INTO PLANET EARTH WILL DO THAT...›
‹...ZZTYYOU! HOW DID YOU GET INNNZTK...›
IT'S THE MESSAGE FATHER LEFT ME! THE MESSAGE THAT SHOWED HIM BEING...
‹...STOP! YOU CAN'T--›
SHHROWW
SHOT...!
‹OOH, THAT DOESN'T SOUND GOOD.›
‹...TZZZIII KNOW WHAT YOU DID! EXPERIMENTING ON OUR DAUGHTERRTTZZ...›
WAIT!
THERE'S MORE ON THIS RECORDING!
THAT'S--
THAT'S MOTHER'S VOICE!!!
BUT THAT WOULD MEAN THAT SHE'S THE ONE WHO--!

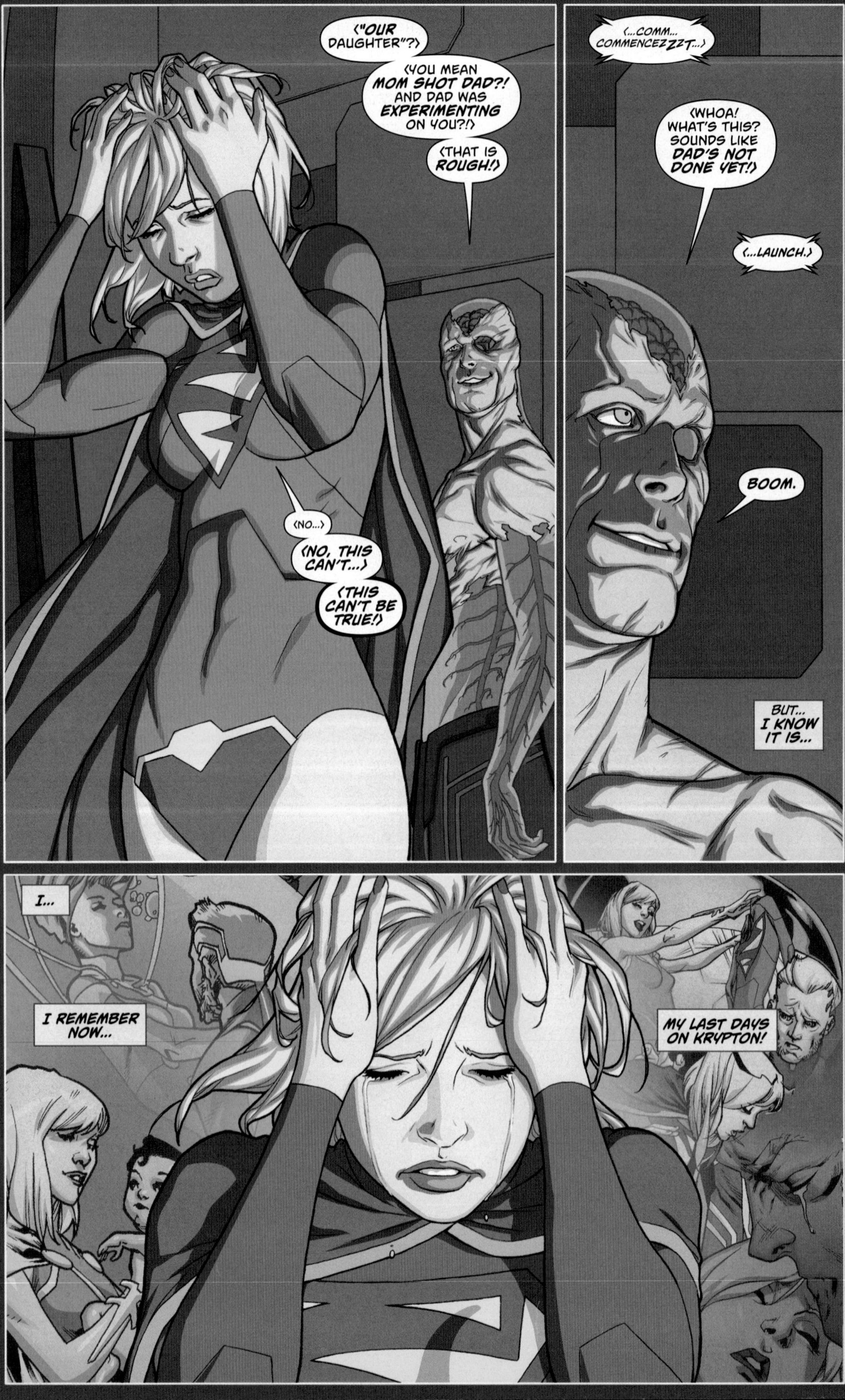

("OUR DAUGHTER"?)
(YOU MEAN MOM SHOT DAD?! AND DAD WAS EXPERIMENTING ON YOU?!)
(THAT IS ROUGH!)
(NO...)
(NO, THIS CAN'T...)
(THIS CAN'T BE TRUE!)
(...COMM... COMMENCEZZZT...)
(WHOA! WHAT'S THIS? SOUNDS LIKE DAD'S NOT DONE YET!)
(...LAUNCH.)
BOOM.
BUT... I KNOW IT IS...
I...
I REMEMBER NOW...
MY LAST DAYS ON KRYPTON!

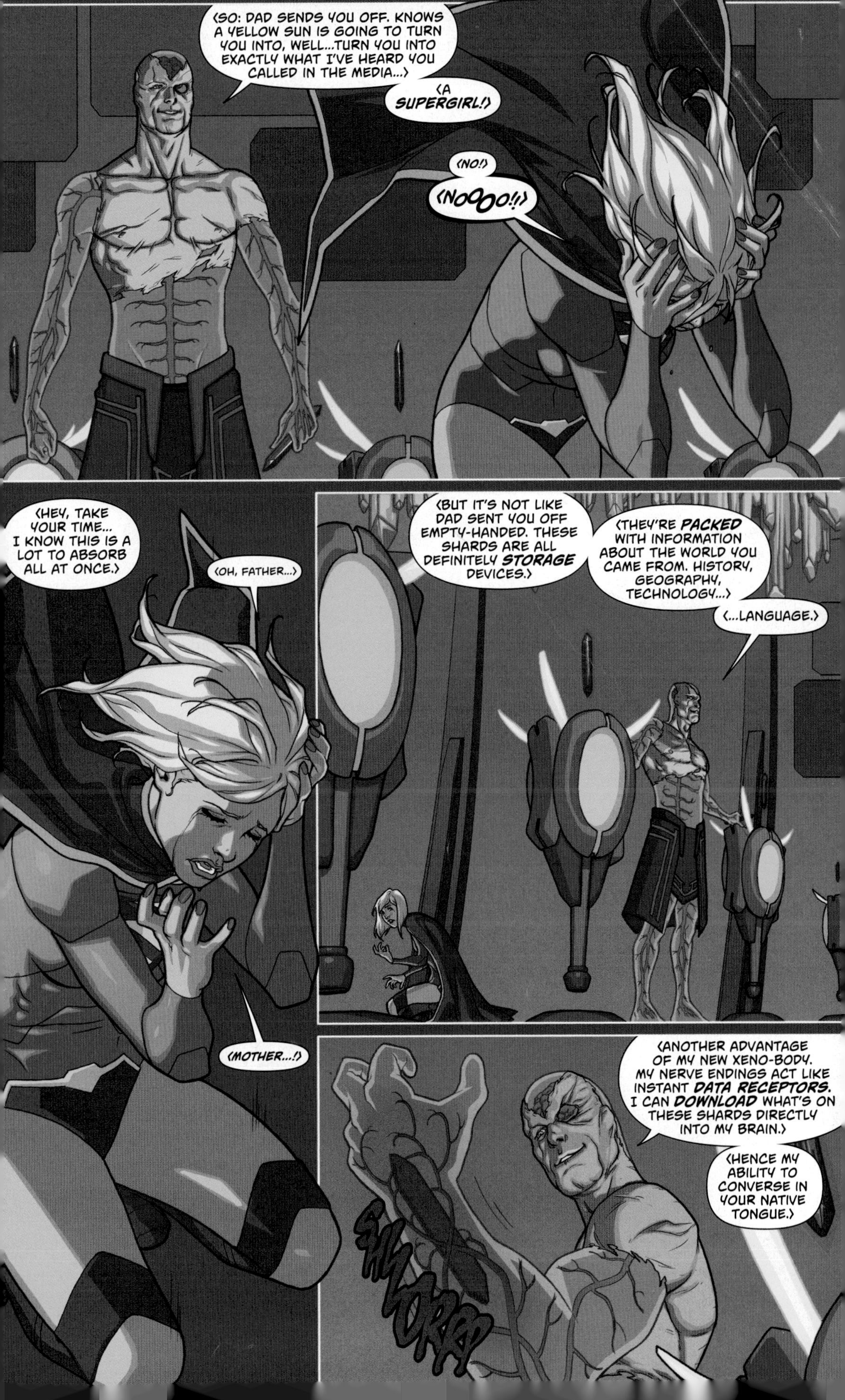
<SO: DAD SENDS YOU OFF. KNOWS A YELLOW SUN IS GOING TO TURN YOU INTO, WELL...TURN YOU INTO EXACTLY WHAT I'VE HEARD YOU CALLED IN THE MEDIA...>
<A SUPERGIRL!>
<NO!>
<NOOOO!!>
<HEY, TAKE YOUR TIME... I KNOW THIS IS A LOT TO ABSORB ALL AT ONCE.>
<OH, FATHER...>
<MOTHER...!>
<BUT IT'S NOT LIKE DAD SENT YOU OFF EMPTY-HANDED. THESE SHARDS ARE ALL DEFINITELY STORAGE DEVICES.>
<THEY'RE PACKED WITH INFORMATION ABOUT THE WORLD YOU CAME FROM. HISTORY, GEOGRAPHY, TECHNOLOGY...>
<...LANGUAGE.>
<ANOTHER ADVANTAGE OF MY NEW XENO-BODY. MY NERVE ENDINGS ACT LIKE INSTANT DATA RECEPTORS. I CAN DOWNLOAD WHAT'S ON THESE SHARDS DIRECTLY INTO MY BRAIN.>
<HENCE MY ABILITY TO CONVERSE IN YOUR NATIVE TONGUE.>

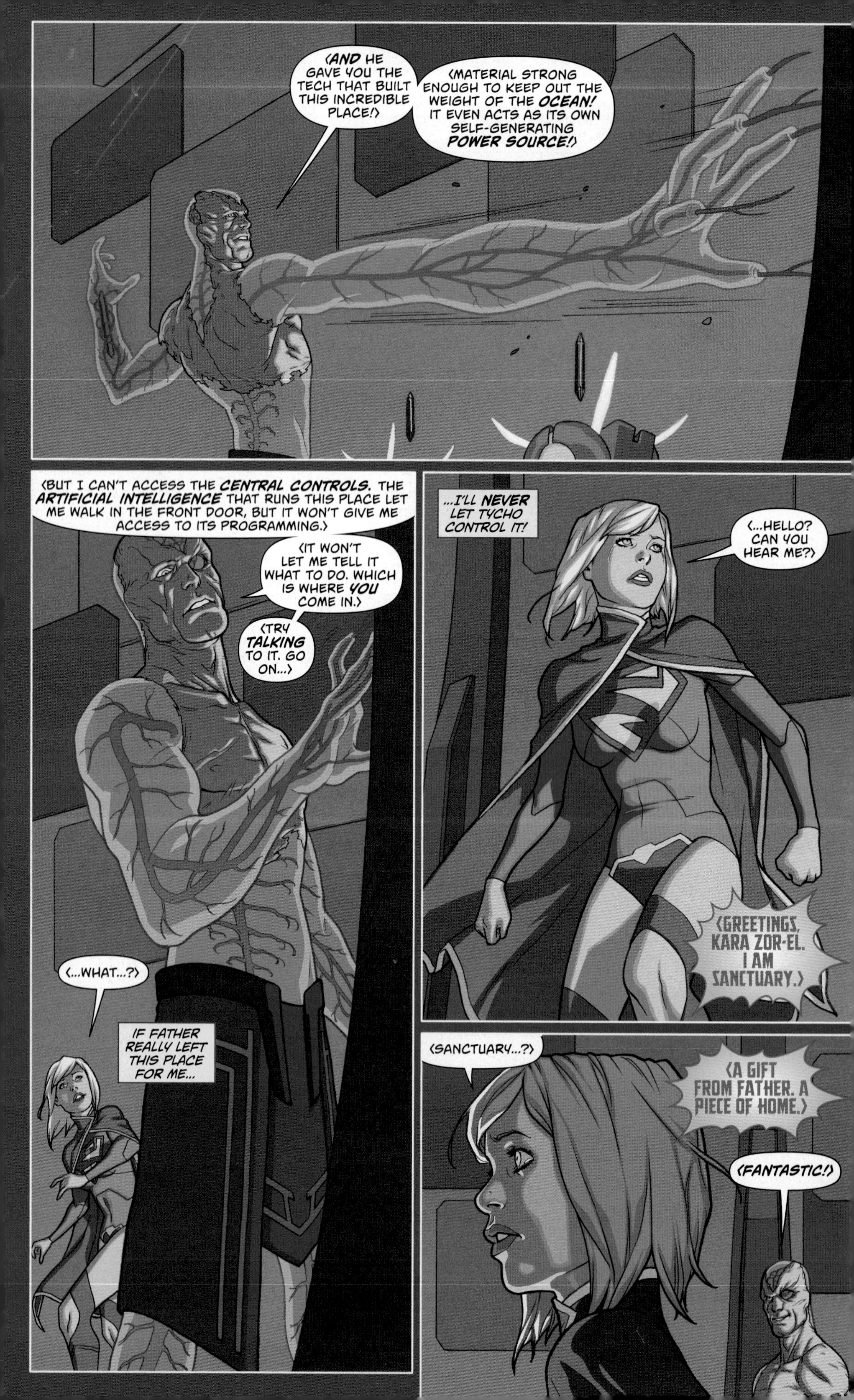

‹AND HE GAVE YOU THE TECH THAT BUILT THIS INCREDIBLE PLACE!›
‹MATERIAL STRONG ENOUGH TO KEEP OUT THE WEIGHT OF THE OCEAN! IT EVEN ACTS AS ITS OWN SELF-GENERATING POWER SOURCE!›
‹BUT I CAN'T ACCESS THE CENTRAL CONTROLS. THE ARTIFICIAL INTELLIGENCE THAT RUNS THIS PLACE LET ME WALK IN THE FRONT DOOR, BUT IT WON'T GIVE ME ACCESS TO ITS PROGRAMMING.›
‹IT WON'T LET ME TELL IT WHAT TO DO. WHICH IS WHERE YOU COME IN.›
‹TRY TALKING TO IT. GO ON...›
‹...WHAT...?›
IF FATHER REALLY LEFT THIS PLACE FOR ME...
...I'LL NEVER LET TYCHO CONTROL IT!
‹...HELLO? CAN YOU HEAR ME?›
‹GREETINGS, KARA ZOR-EL. I AM SANCTUARY.›
‹SANCTUARY...?›
‹A GIFT FROM FATHER. A PIECE OF HOME.›
‹FANTASTIC!›

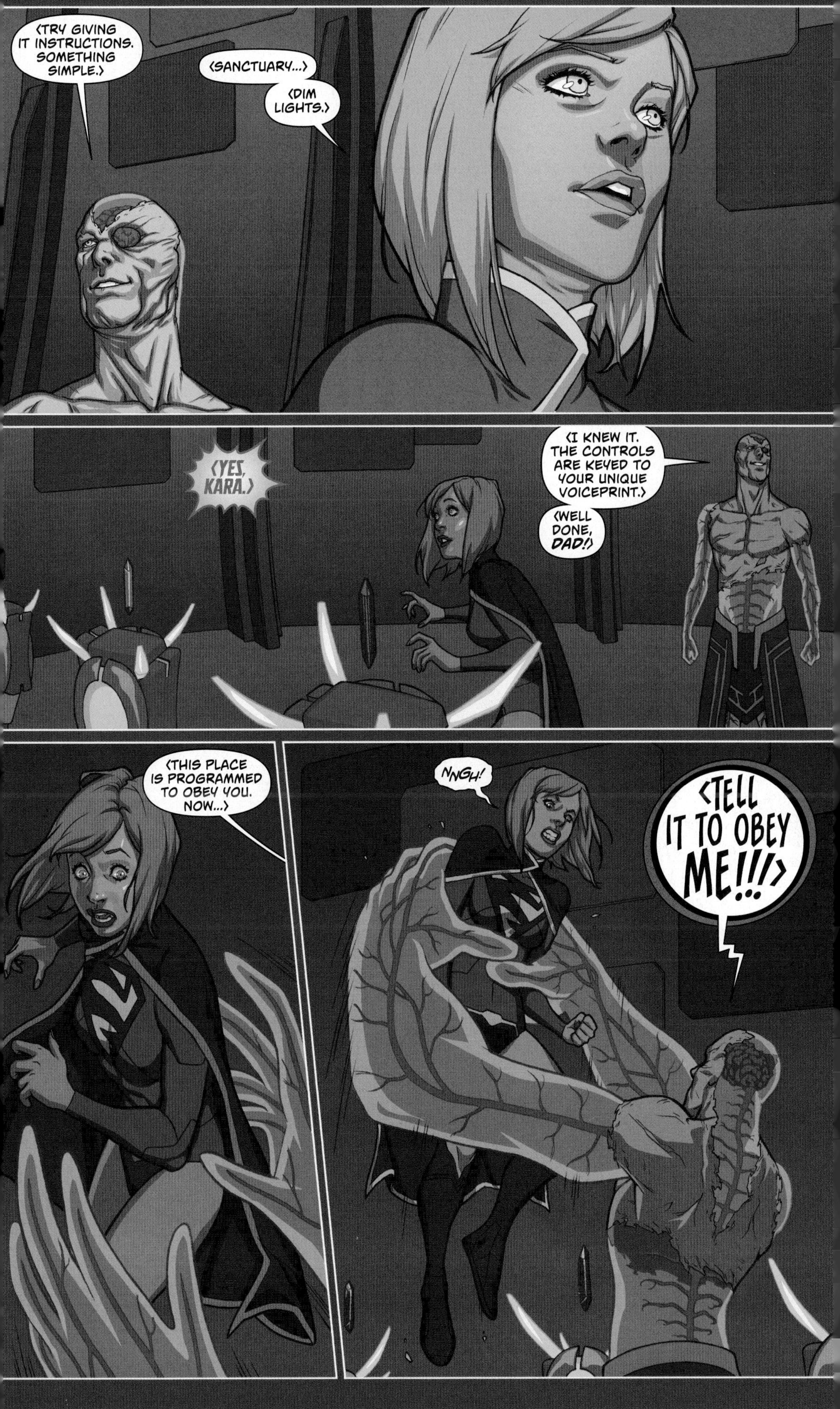
‹TRY GIVING IT INSTRUCTIONS. SOMETHING SIMPLE.›
‹SANCTUARY...›
‹DIM LIGHTS.›
‹YES, KARA.›
‹I KNEW IT. THE CONTROLS ARE KEYED TO YOUR UNIQUE VOICEPRINT.›
‹WELL DONE, DAD!›
‹THIS PLACE IS PROGRAMMED TO OBEY YOU. NOW...›
NNGH!
‹TELL IT TO OBEY ME!!!›

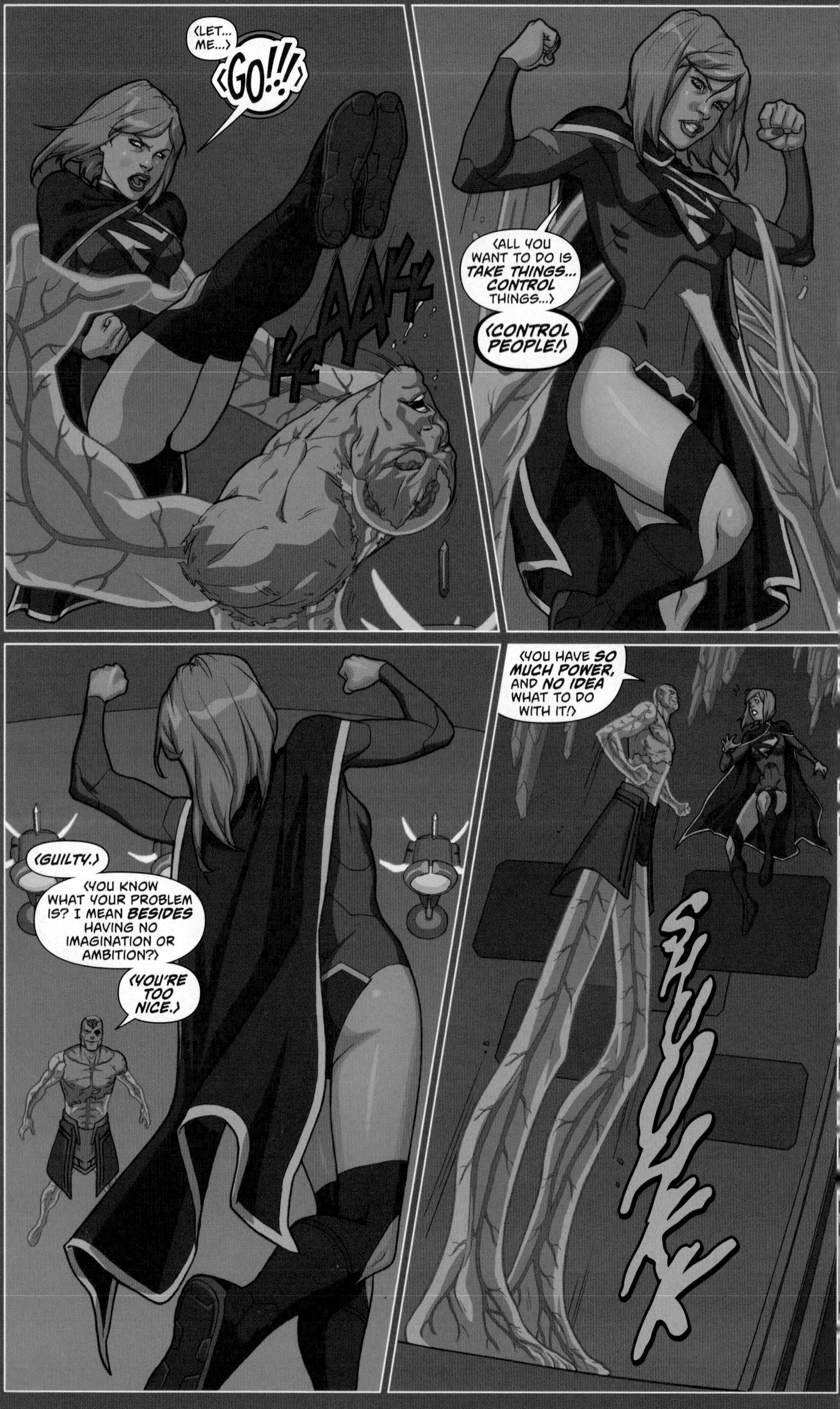

‹LET... ME...›
‹GO!!!›
AAHH
‹ALL YOU WANT TO DO IS TAKE THINGS... CONTROL THINGS...›
‹CONTROL PEOPLE!›
‹GUILTY.›
‹YOU KNOW WHAT YOUR PROBLEM IS? I MEAN BESIDES HAVING NO IMAGINATION OR AMBITION?›
‹YOU'RE TOO NICE.›
‹YOU HAVE SO MUCH POWER, AND NO IDEA WHAT TO DO WITH IT!›

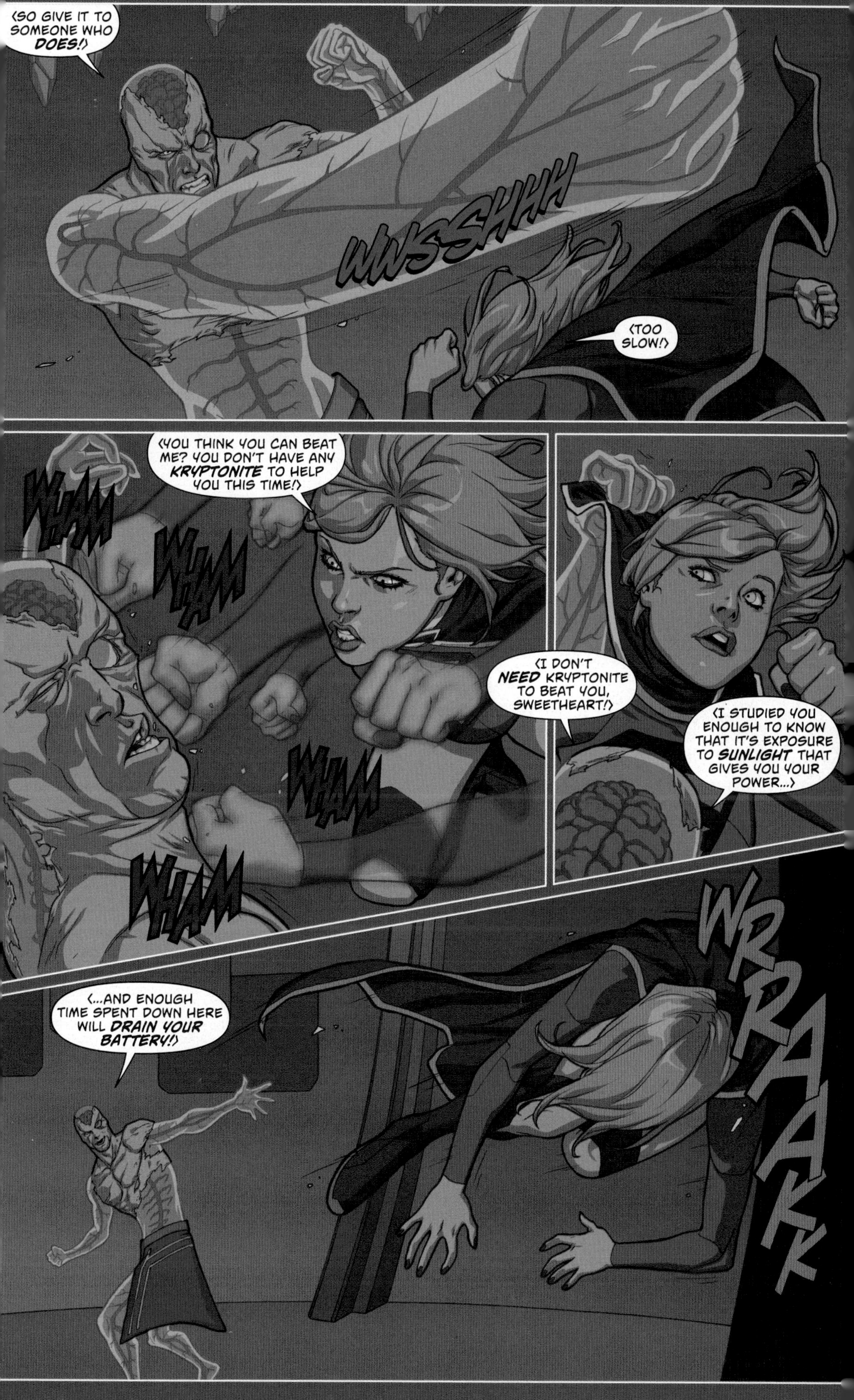
⟨SO GIVE IT TO SOMEONE WHO DOES!⟩
WWSSHHH
⟨TOO SLOW!⟩
⟨YOU THINK YOU CAN BEAT ME? YOU DON'T HAVE ANY KRYPTONITE TO HELP YOU THIS TIME!⟩
WHAM
WHAM
⟨I DON'T NEED KRYPTONITE TO BEAT YOU, SWEETHEART!⟩
WHAM
WHAM
⟨I STUDIED YOU ENOUGH TO KNOW THAT IT'S EXPOSURE TO SUNLIGHT THAT GIVES YOU YOUR POWER...⟩
WRRAAKK
⟨...AND ENOUGH TIME SPENT DOWN HERE WILL DRAIN YOUR BATTERY!⟩

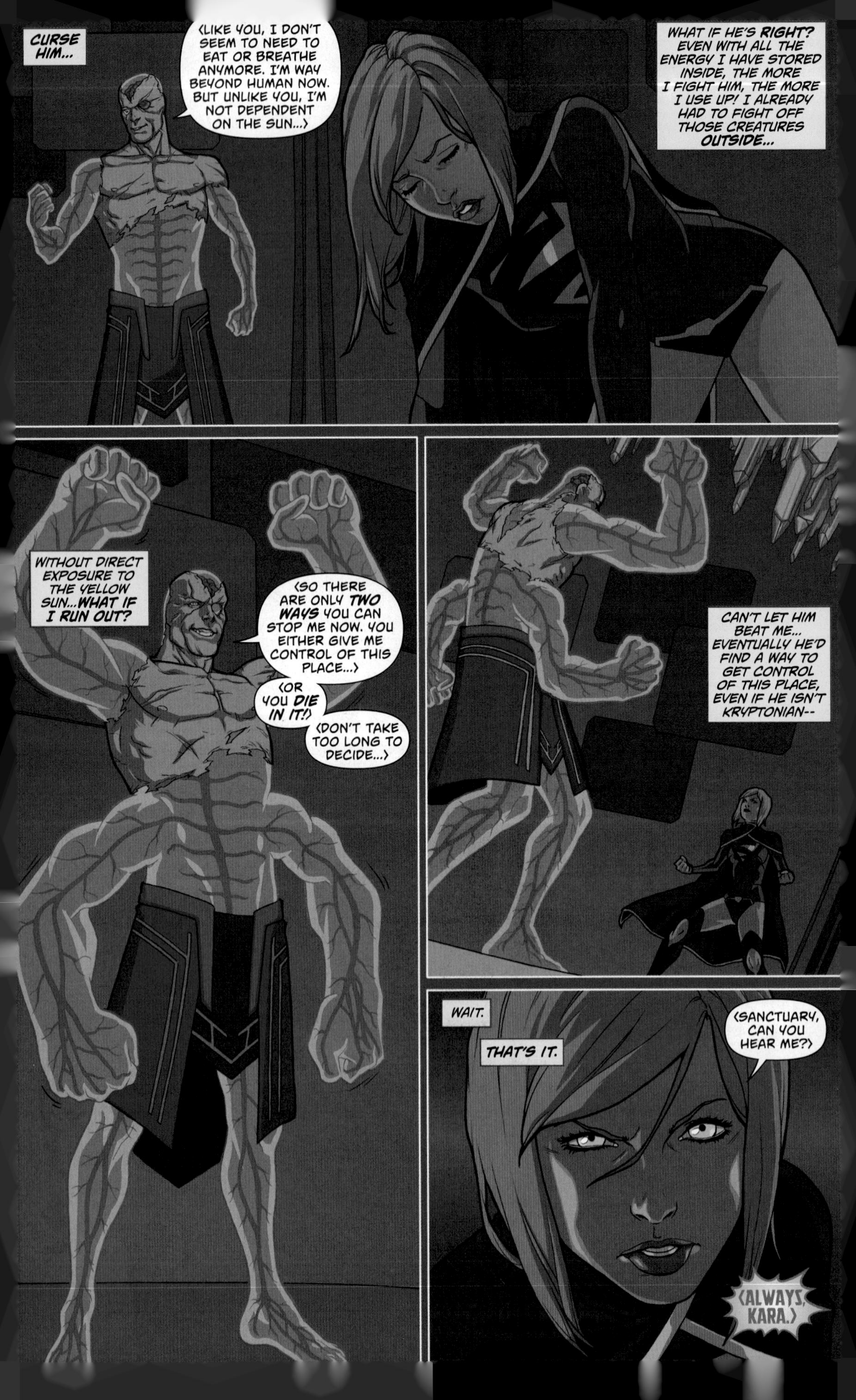
CURSE HIM...
<LIKE YOU, I DON'T SEEM TO NEED TO EAT OR BREATHE ANYMORE. I'M WAY BEYOND HUMAN NOW. BUT UNLIKE YOU, I'M NOT DEPENDENT ON THE SUN...>
WHAT IF HE'S RIGHT? EVEN WITH ALL THE ENERGY I HAVE STORED INSIDE, THE MORE I FIGHT HIM, THE MORE I USE UP! I ALREADY HAD TO FIGHT OFF THOSE CREATURES OUTSIDE...
WITHOUT DIRECT EXPOSURE TO THE YELLOW SUN...WHAT IF I RUN OUT?
<SO THERE ARE ONLY TWO WAYS YOU CAN STOP ME NOW. YOU EITHER GIVE ME CONTROL OF THIS PLACE...>
<OR YOU DIE IN IT!>
<DON'T TAKE TOO LONG TO DECIDE...>
CAN'T LET HIM BEAT ME... EVENTUALLY HE'D FIND A WAY TO GET CONTROL OF THIS PLACE, EVEN IF HE ISN'T KRYPTONIAN--
WAIT.
THAT'S IT.
<SANCTUARY, CAN YOU HEAR ME?>
<ALWAYS, KARA.>

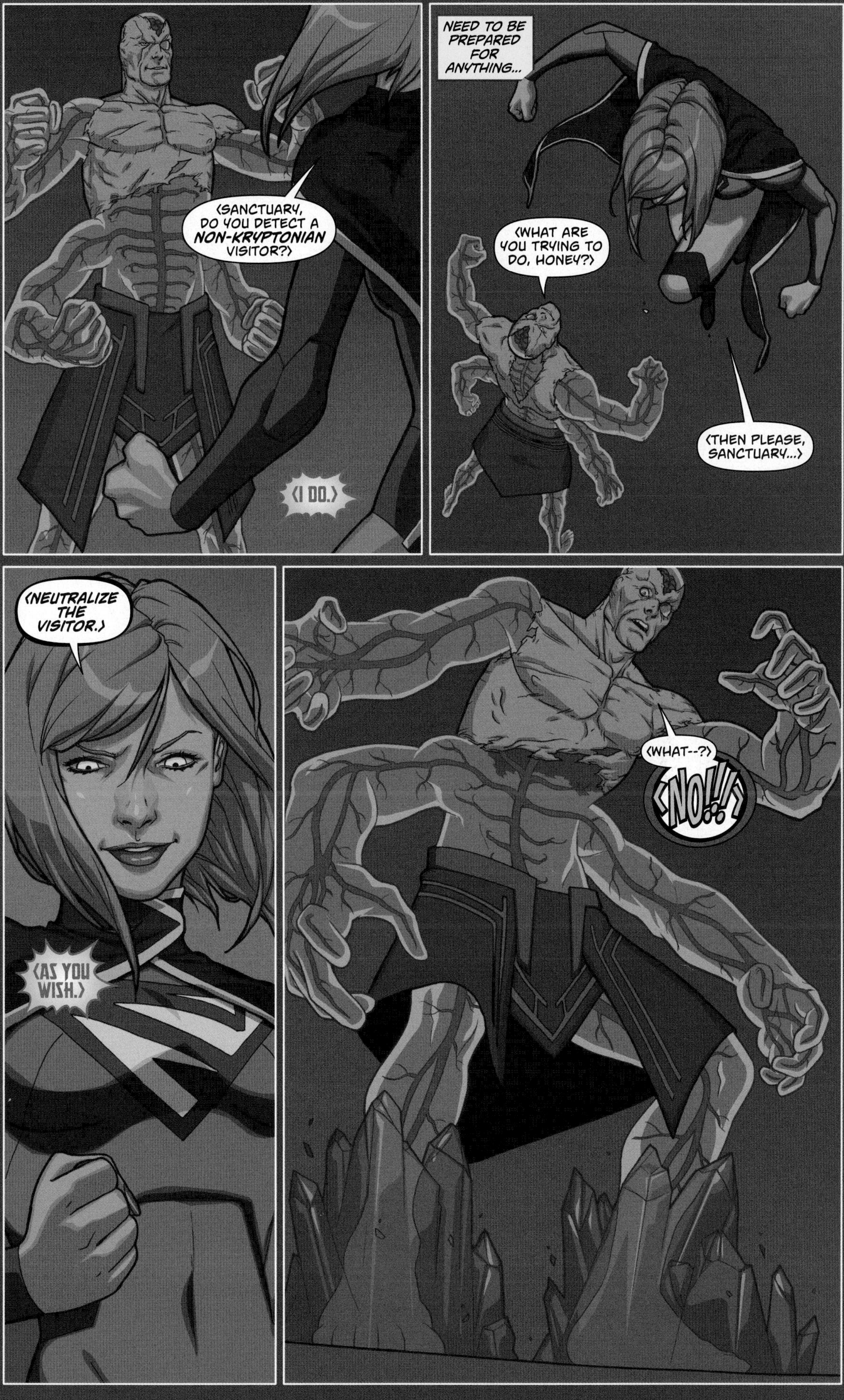

⟨SANCTUARY, DO YOU DETECT A NON-KRYPTONIAN VISITOR?⟩
⟨I DO.⟩
NEED TO BE PREPARED FOR ANYTHING...
⟨WHAT ARE YOU TRYING TO DO, HONEY?⟩
⟨THEN PLEASE, SANCTUARY...⟩
⟨NEUTRALIZE THE VISITOR.⟩
⟨AS YOU WISH.⟩
⟨WHAT--?⟩
⟨NO!!!⟩

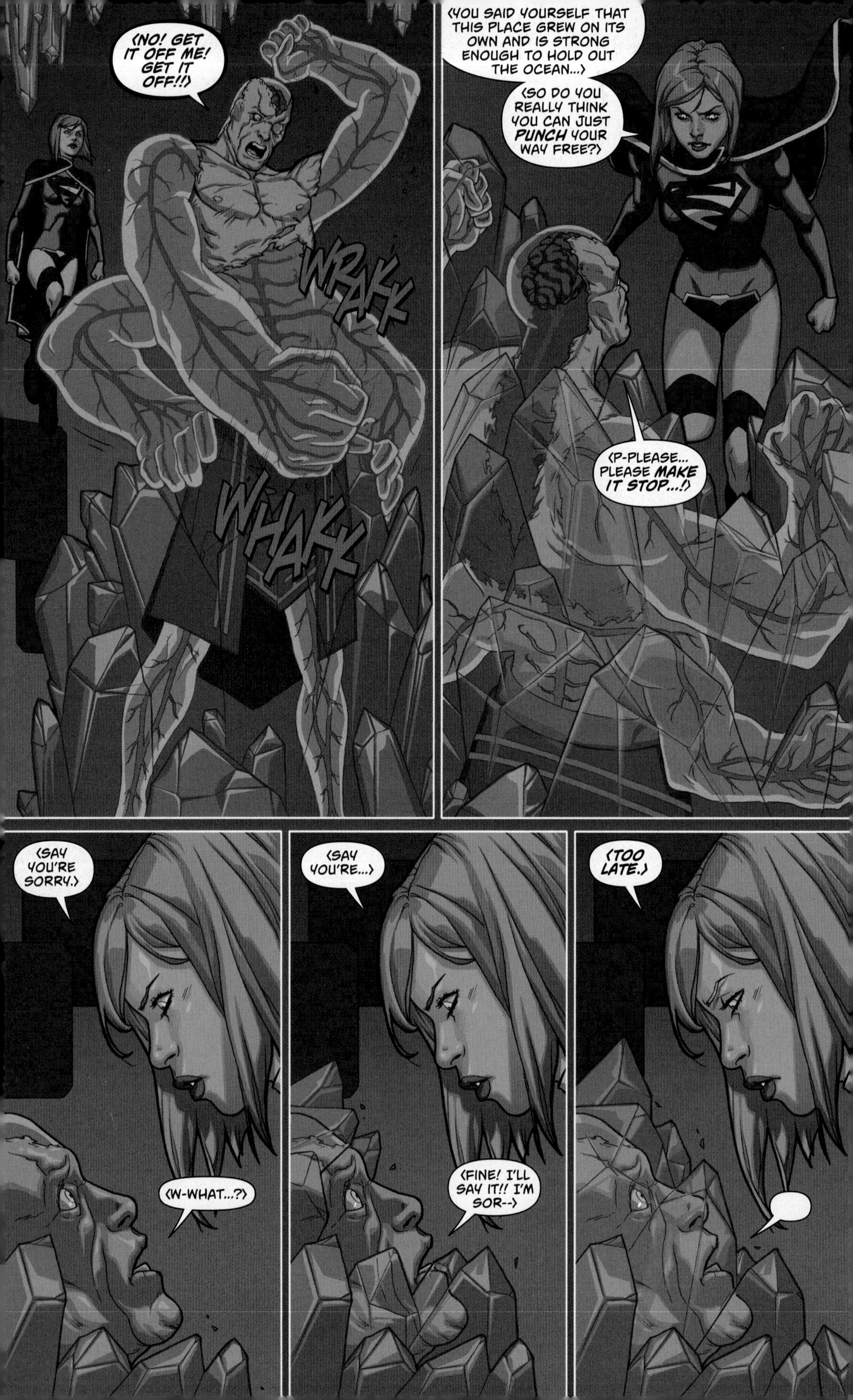
‹NO! GET IT OFF ME! GET IT OFF!!›
WRAKK
WHAKK
‹YOU SAID YOURSELF THAT THIS PLACE GREW ON ITS OWN AND IS STRONG ENOUGH TO HOLD OUT THE OCEAN...›
‹SO DO YOU REALLY THINK YOU CAN JUST PUNCH YOUR WAY FREE?›
‹P-PLEASE... PLEASE MAKE IT STOP...!›
‹SAY YOU'RE SORRY.›
‹W-WHAT...?›
‹SAY YOU'RE...›
‹FINE! I'LL SAY IT!! I'M SOR--›
‹TOO LATE.›

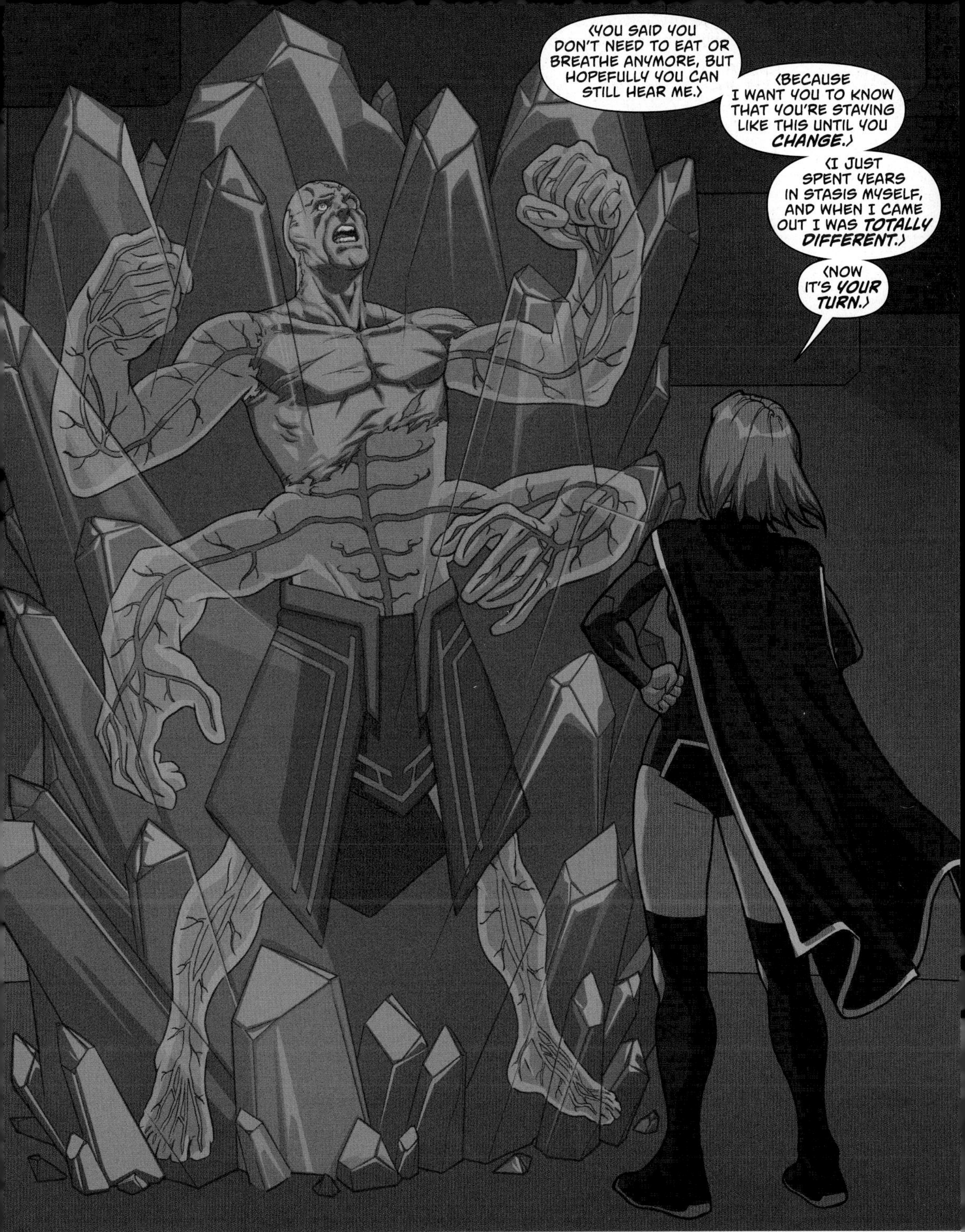
⟨YOU SAID YOU DON'T NEED TO EAT OR BREATHE ANYMORE, BUT HOPEFULLY YOU CAN STILL HEAR ME.⟩
⟨BECAUSE I WANT YOU TO KNOW THAT YOU'RE STAYING LIKE THIS UNTIL YOU **CHANGE.**⟩
⟨I JUST SPENT YEARS IN STASIS MYSELF, AND WHEN I CAME OUT I WAS **TOTALLY DIFFERENT.**⟩
⟨NOW IT'S **YOUR TURN.**⟩

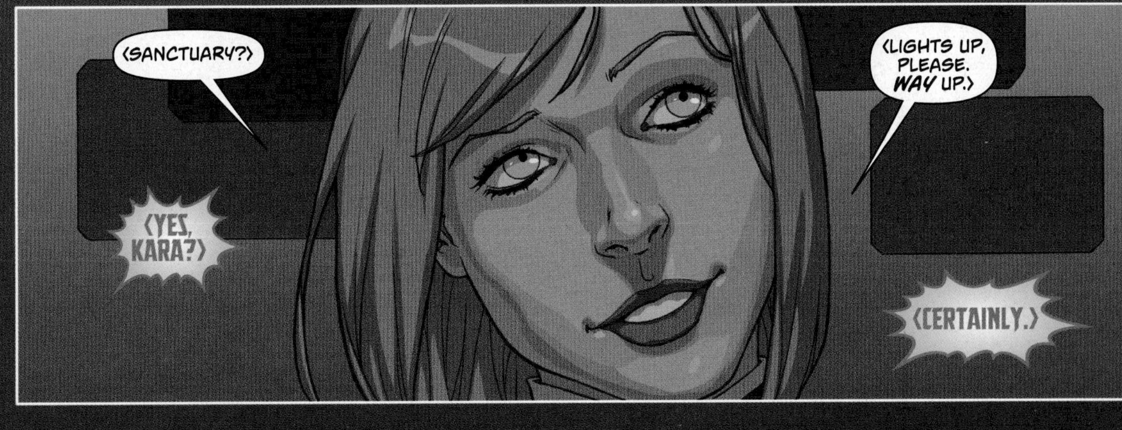
⟨SANCTUARY?⟩
⟨YES, KARA?⟩
⟨LIGHTS UP, PLEASE. **WAY** UP.⟩
⟨CERTAINLY.⟩

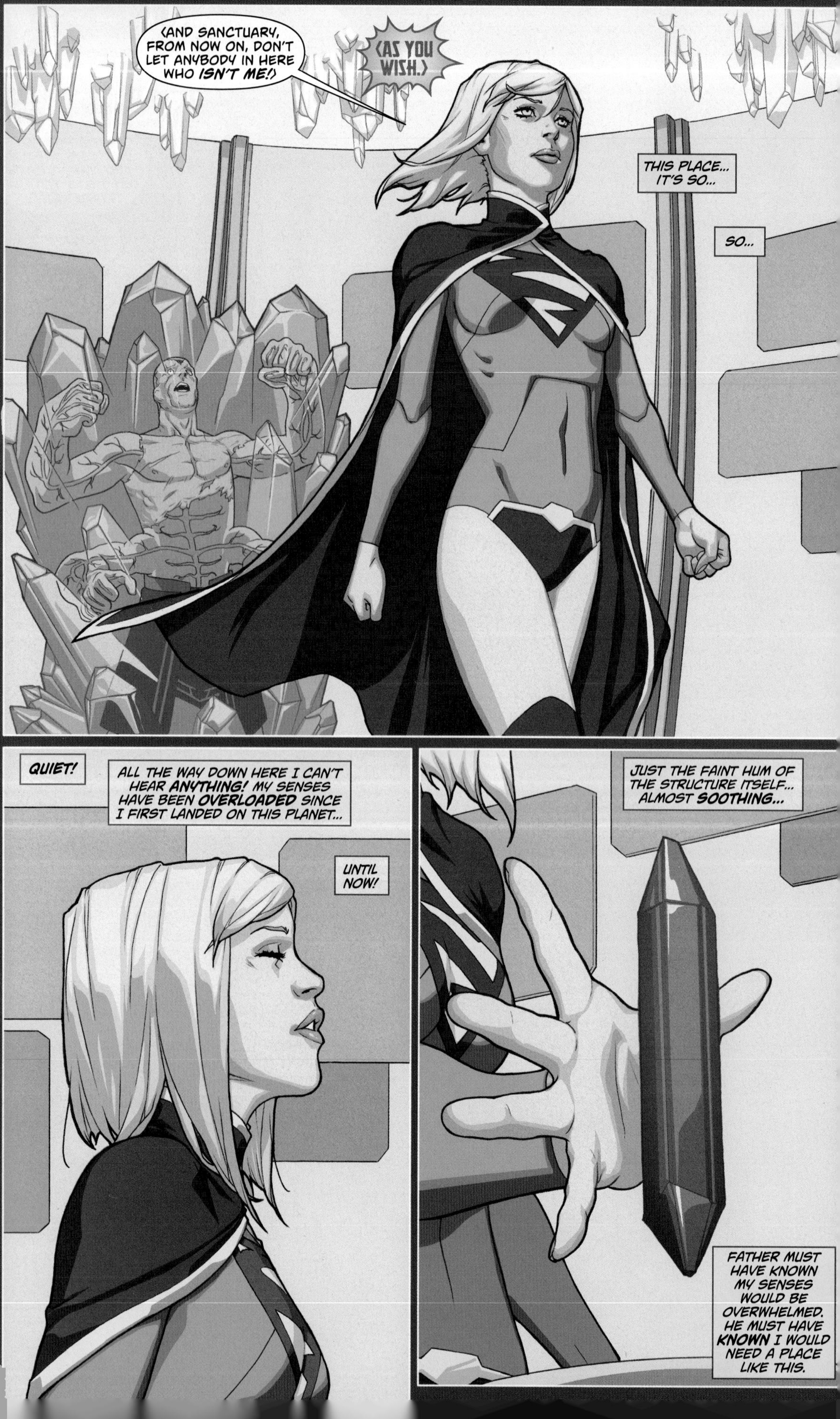
‹AND SANCTUARY, FROM NOW ON, DON'T LET ANYBODY IN HERE WHO ISN'T ME!›
‹AS YOU WISH.›
THIS PLACE... IT'S SO...
SO...
QUIET!
ALL THE WAY DOWN HERE I CAN'T HEAR ANYTHING! MY SENSES HAVE BEEN OVERLOADED SINCE I FIRST LANDED ON THIS PLANET...
UNTIL NOW!
JUST THE FAINT HUM OF THE STRUCTURE ITSELF... ALMOST SOOTHING...
FATHER MUST HAVE KNOWN MY SENSES WOULD BE OVERWHELMED. HE MUST HAVE KNOWN I WOULD NEED A PLACE LIKE THIS.

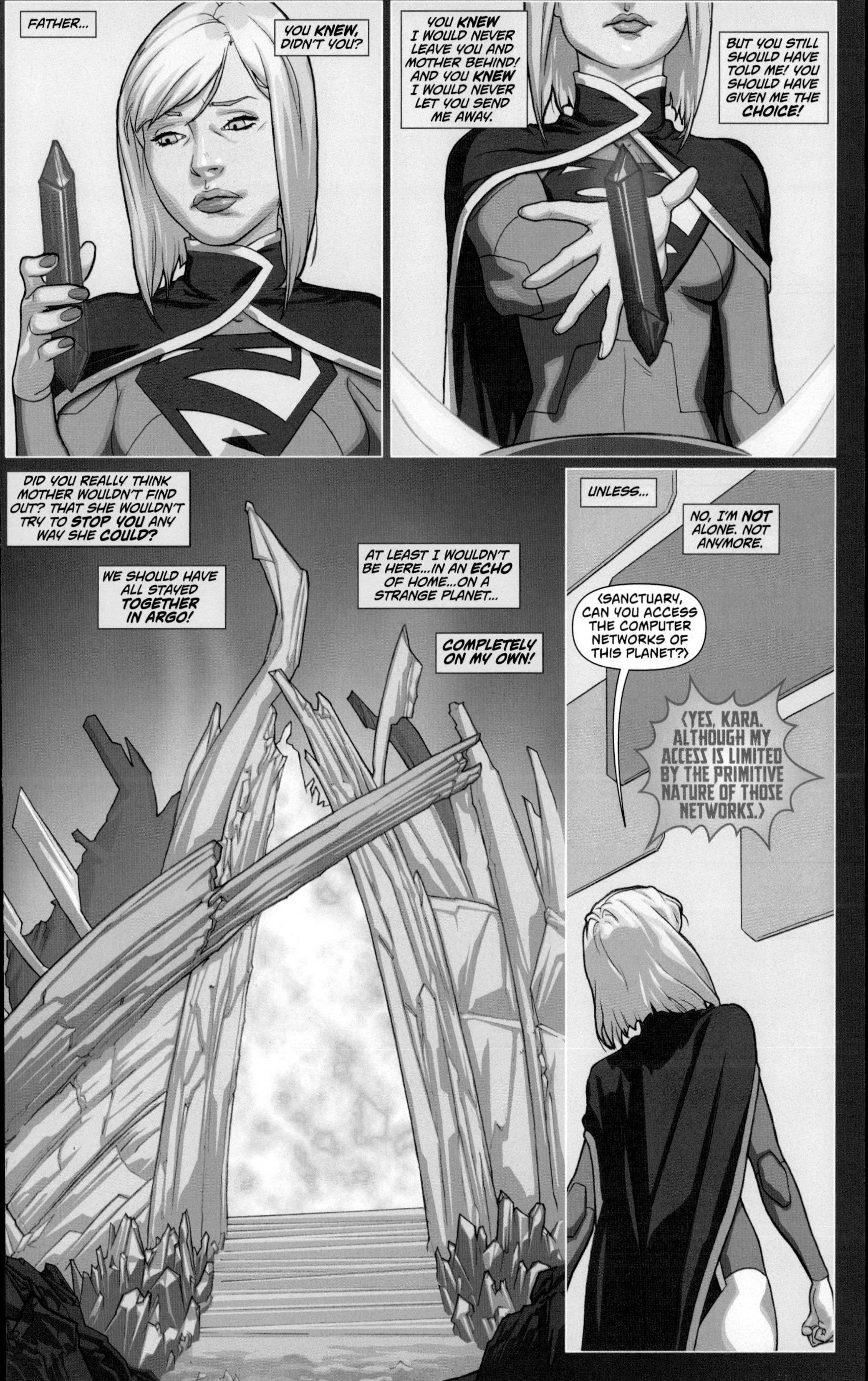
FATHER...
YOU KNEW, DIDN'T YOU?
YOU KNEW I WOULD NEVER LEAVE YOU AND MOTHER BEHIND! AND YOU KNEW I WOULD NEVER LET YOU SEND ME AWAY.
BUT YOU STILL SHOULD HAVE TOLD ME! YOU SHOULD HAVE GIVEN ME THE CHOICE!
DID YOU REALLY THINK MOTHER WOULDN'T FIND OUT? THAT SHE WOULDN'T TRY TO STOP YOU ANY WAY SHE COULD?
WE SHOULD HAVE ALL STAYED TOGETHER IN ARGO!
AT LEAST I WOULDN'T BE HERE...IN AN ECHO OF HOME...ON A STRANGE PLANET...
COMPLETELY ON MY OWN!
UNLESS...
NO, I'M NOT ALONE. NOT ANYMORE.
<SANCTUARY, CAN YOU ACCESS THE COMPUTER NETWORKS OF THIS PLANET?>
<YES, KARA. ALTHOUGH MY ACCESS IS LIMITED BY THE PRIMITIVE NATURE OF THOSE NETWORKS.>

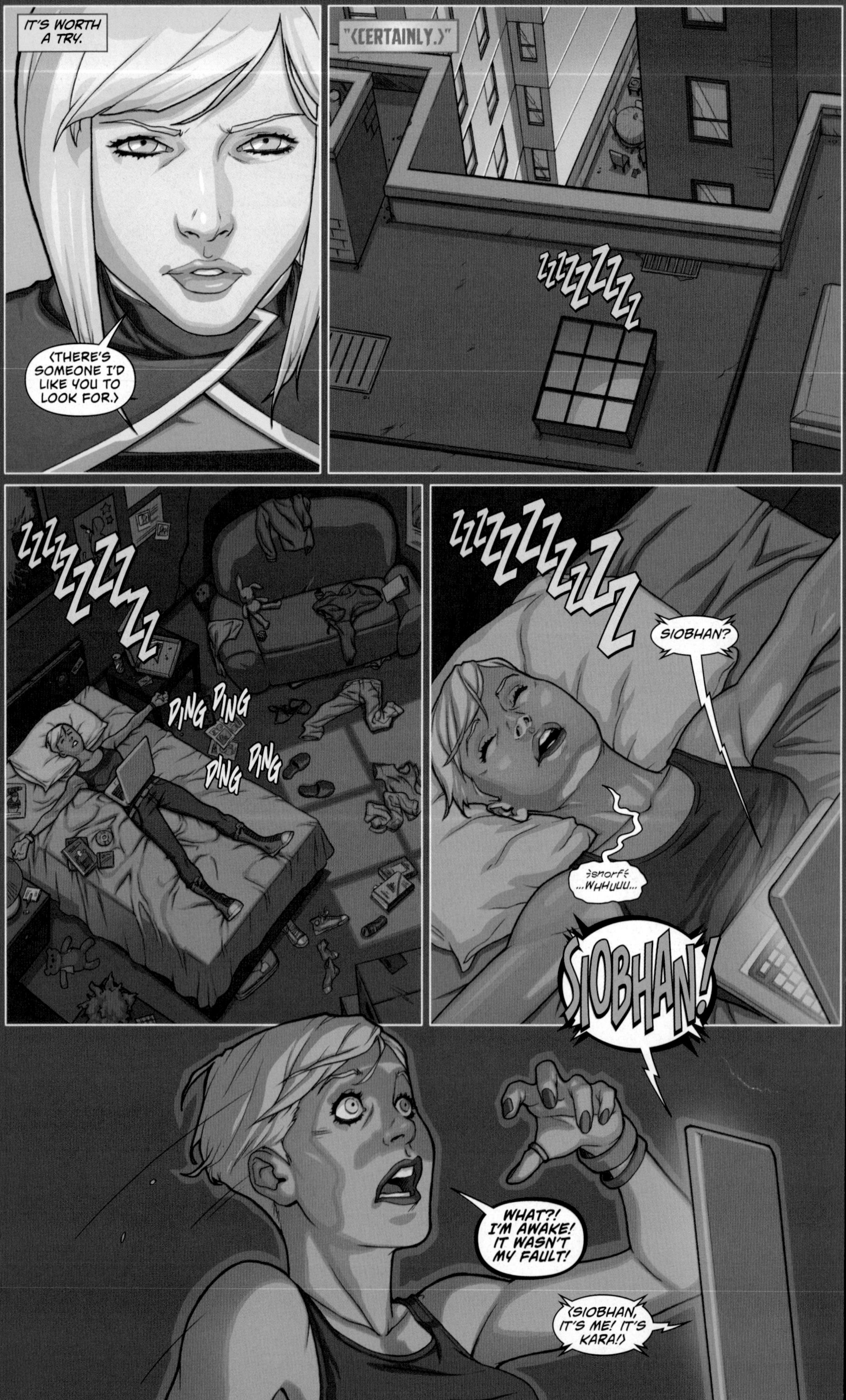
IT'S WORTH A TRY.
‹THERE'S SOMEONE I'D LIKE YOU TO LOOK FOR.›
"‹CERTAINLY.›"
ZZZZZZZZZ
ZZZZZZZZZZ
DING DING
DING DING
ZZZZZZZZZZZZ
SIOBHAN?
snorf ...WHHUUU...
SIOBHAN!
WHAT?! I'M AWAKE! IT WASN'T MY FAULT!
‹SIOBHAN, IT'S ME! IT'S KARA!›

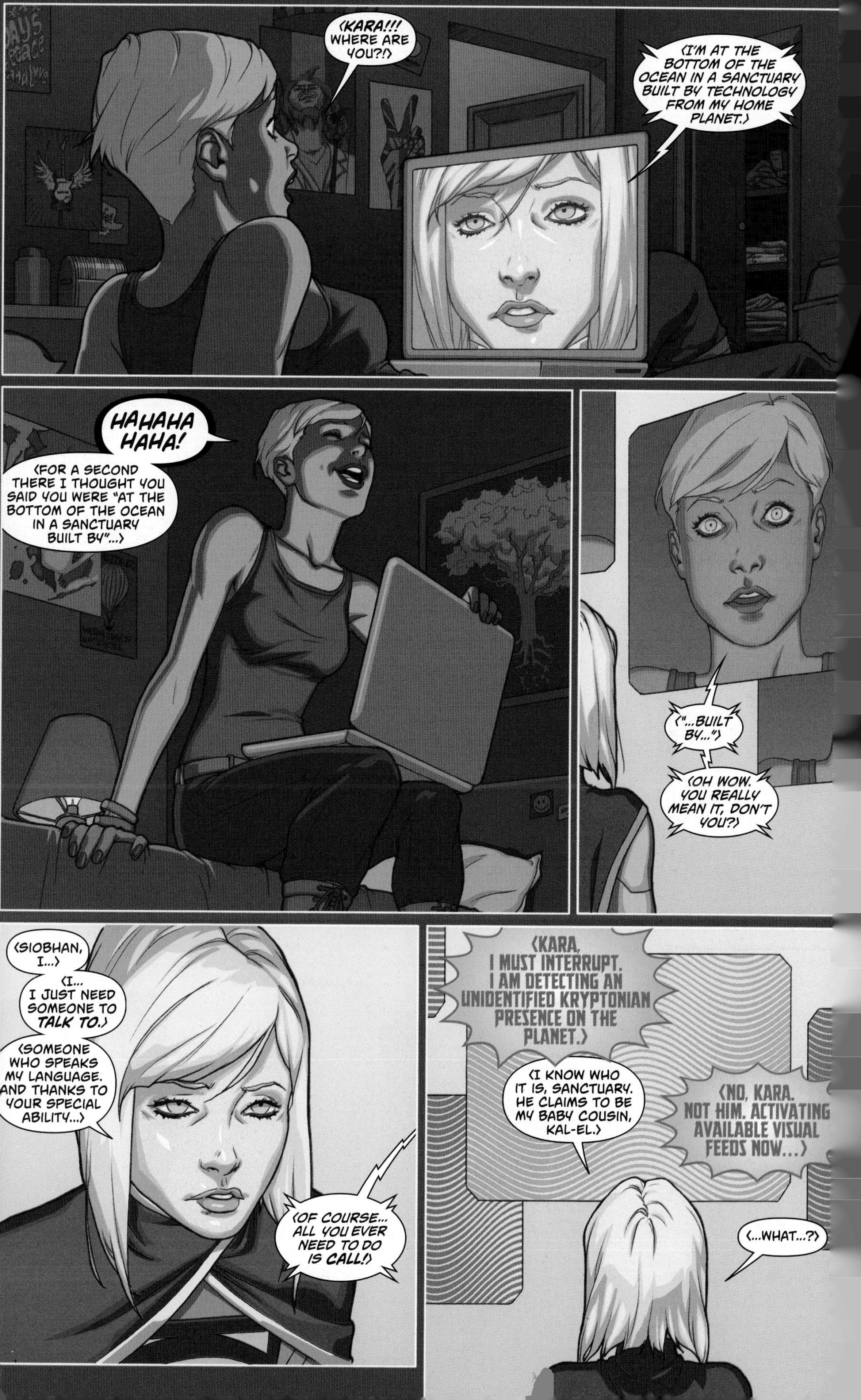

‹KARA!!! WHERE ARE YOU?!›
‹I'M AT THE BOTTOM OF THE OCEAN IN A SANCTUARY BUILT BY TECHNOLOGY FROM MY HOME PLANET.›
HAHAHA HAHA!
‹FOR A SECOND THERE I THOUGHT YOU SAID YOU WERE "AT THE BOTTOM OF THE OCEAN IN A SANCTUARY BUILT BY"...›
‹"...BUILT BY..."›
‹OH WOW. YOU REALLY MEAN IT, DON'T YOU?›
‹SIOBHAN, I...›
‹I... I JUST NEED SOMEONE TO TALK TO.›
‹SOMEONE WHO SPEAKS MY LANGUAGE. AND THANKS TO YOUR SPECIAL ABILITY...›
‹OF COURSE... ALL YOU EVER NEED TO DO IS CALL!›
‹KARA, I MUST INTERRUPT. I AM DETECTING AN UNIDENTIFIED KRYPTONIAN PRESENCE ON THE PLANET.›
‹I KNOW WHO IT IS, SANCTUARY. HE CLAIMS TO BE MY BABY COUSIN, KAL-EL.›
‹NO, KARA. NOT HIM. ACTIVATING AVAILABLE VISUAL FEEDS NOW...›
‹...WHAT...?›

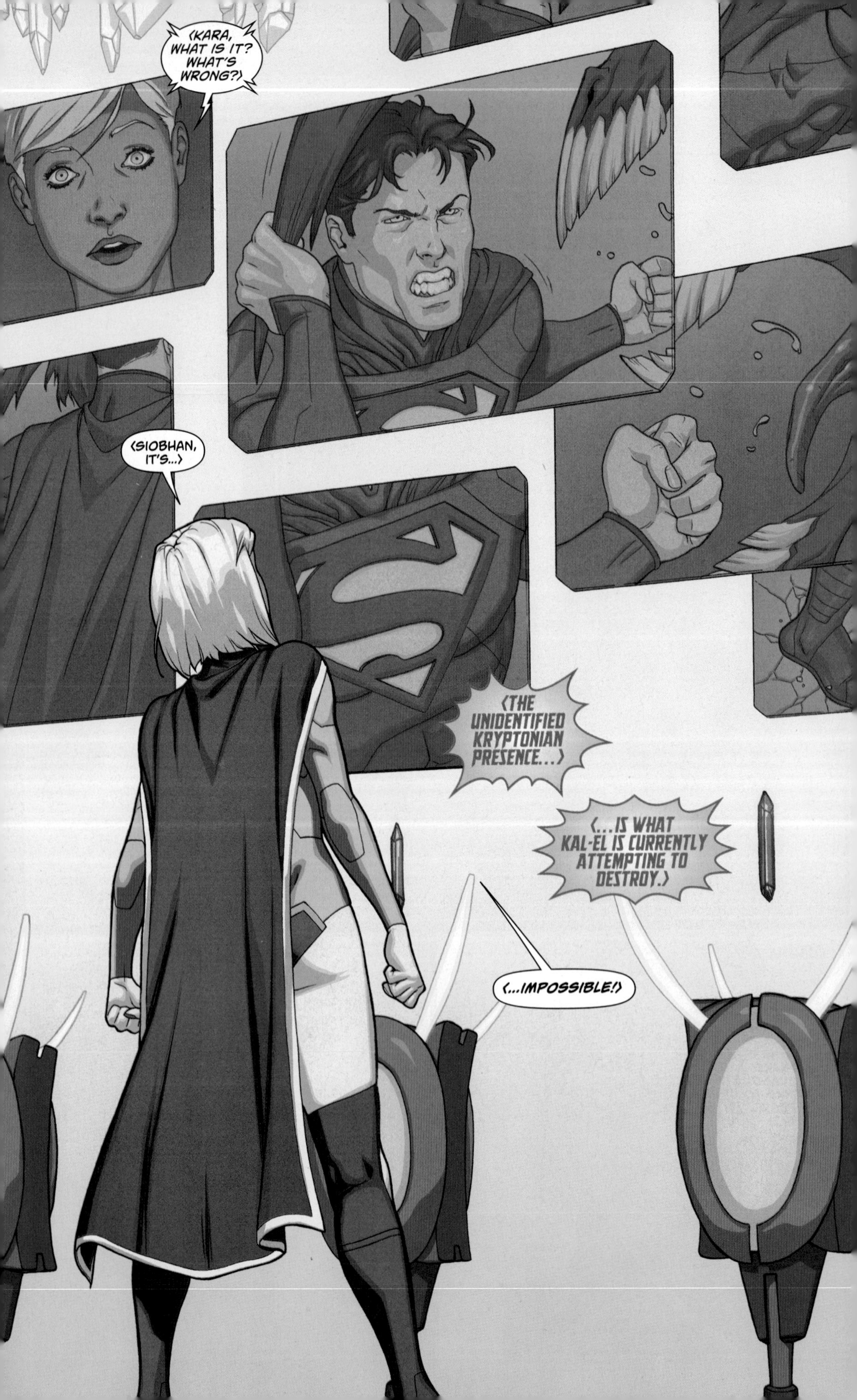
⟨KARA, WHAT IS IT? WHAT'S WRONG?⟩
⟨SIOBHAN, IT'S...⟩
⟨...IMPOSSIBLE!⟩
⟨THE UNIDENTIFIED KRYPTONIAN PRESENCE...⟩
⟨...IS WHAT KAL-EL IS CURRENTLY ATTEMPTING TO DESTROY.⟩

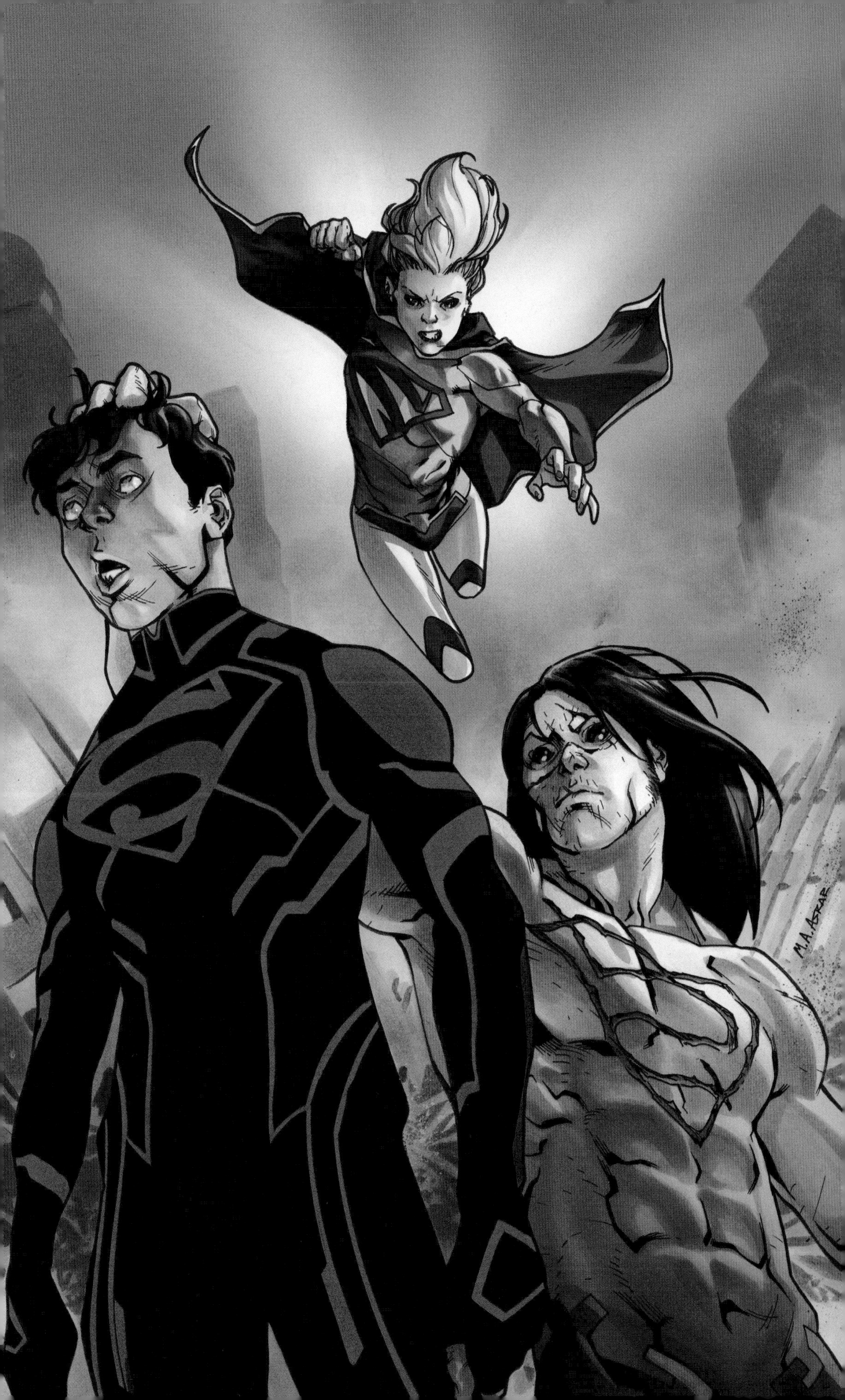
M.A. ASRAR

H'EL ON EARTH: LOST SON OF KRYPTON

MIKE JOHNSON writer **MAHMUD ASRAR** artist cover art by **MAHMUD ASRAR & DAVE McCAIG**

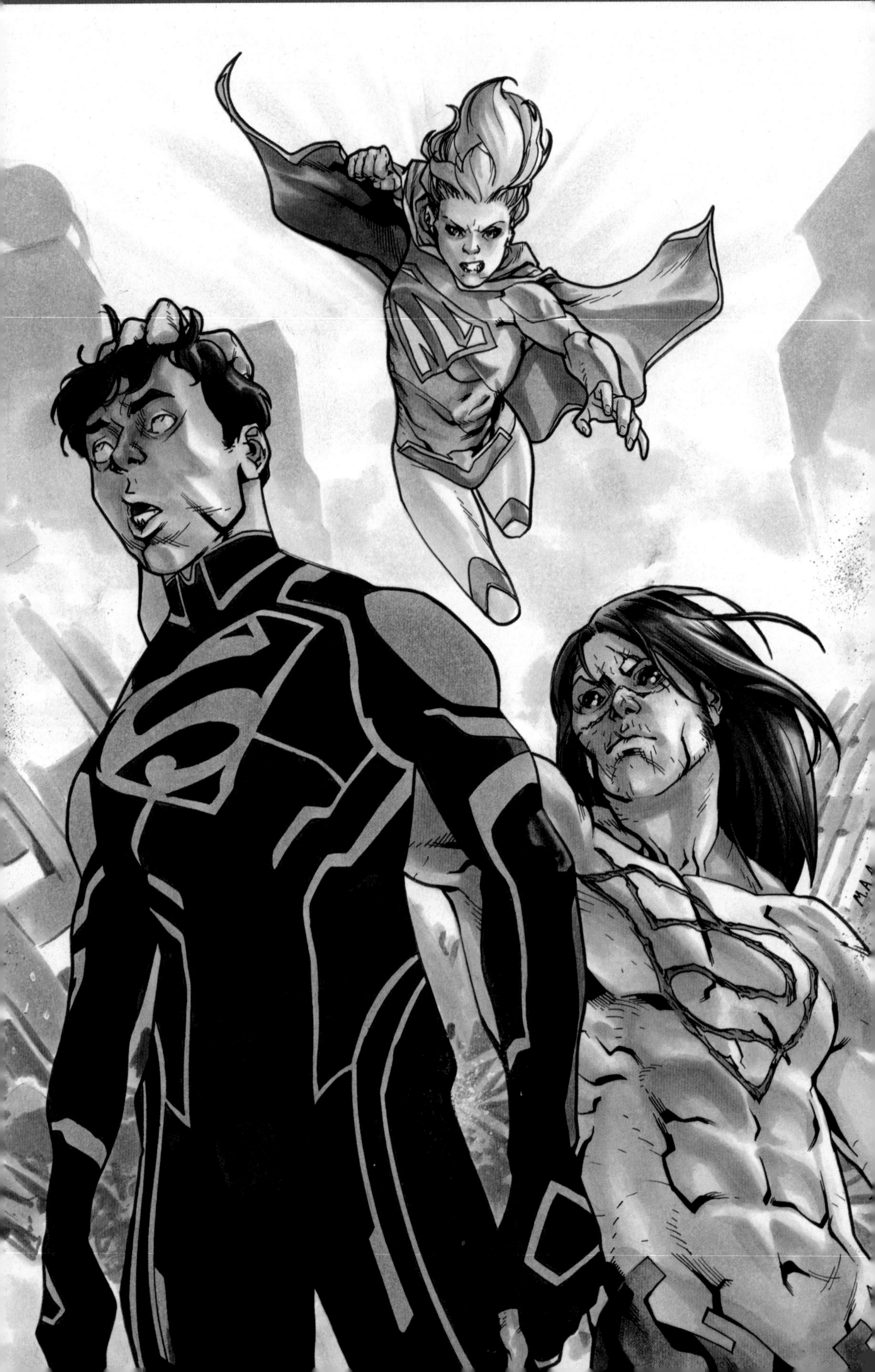

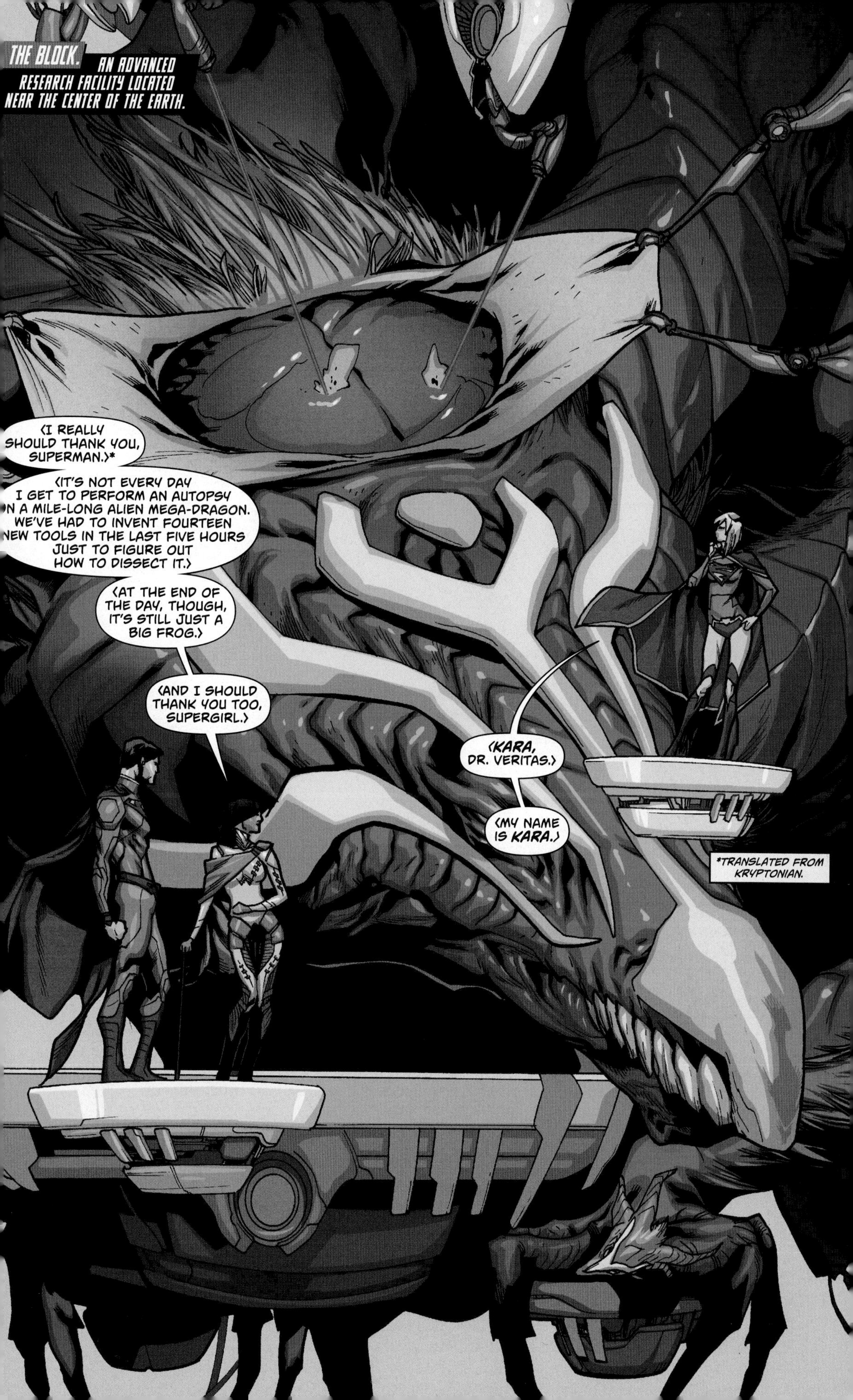
THE BLOCK. AN ADVANCED RESEARCH FACILITY LOCATED NEAR THE CENTER OF THE EARTH.
‹I REALLY SHOULD THANK YOU, SUPERMAN.›*
‹IT'S NOT EVERY DAY I GET TO PERFORM AN AUTOPSY ON A MILE-LONG ALIEN MEGA-DRAGON. WE'VE HAD TO INVENT FOURTEEN NEW TOOLS IN THE LAST FIVE HOURS JUST TO FIGURE OUT HOW TO DISSECT IT.›
‹AT THE END OF THE DAY, THOUGH, IT'S STILL JUST A BIG FROG.›
‹AND I SHOULD THANK YOU TOO, SUPERGIRL.›
‹KARA, DR. VERITAS.›
‹MY NAME IS KARA.›
*TRANSLATED FROM KRYPTONIAN.

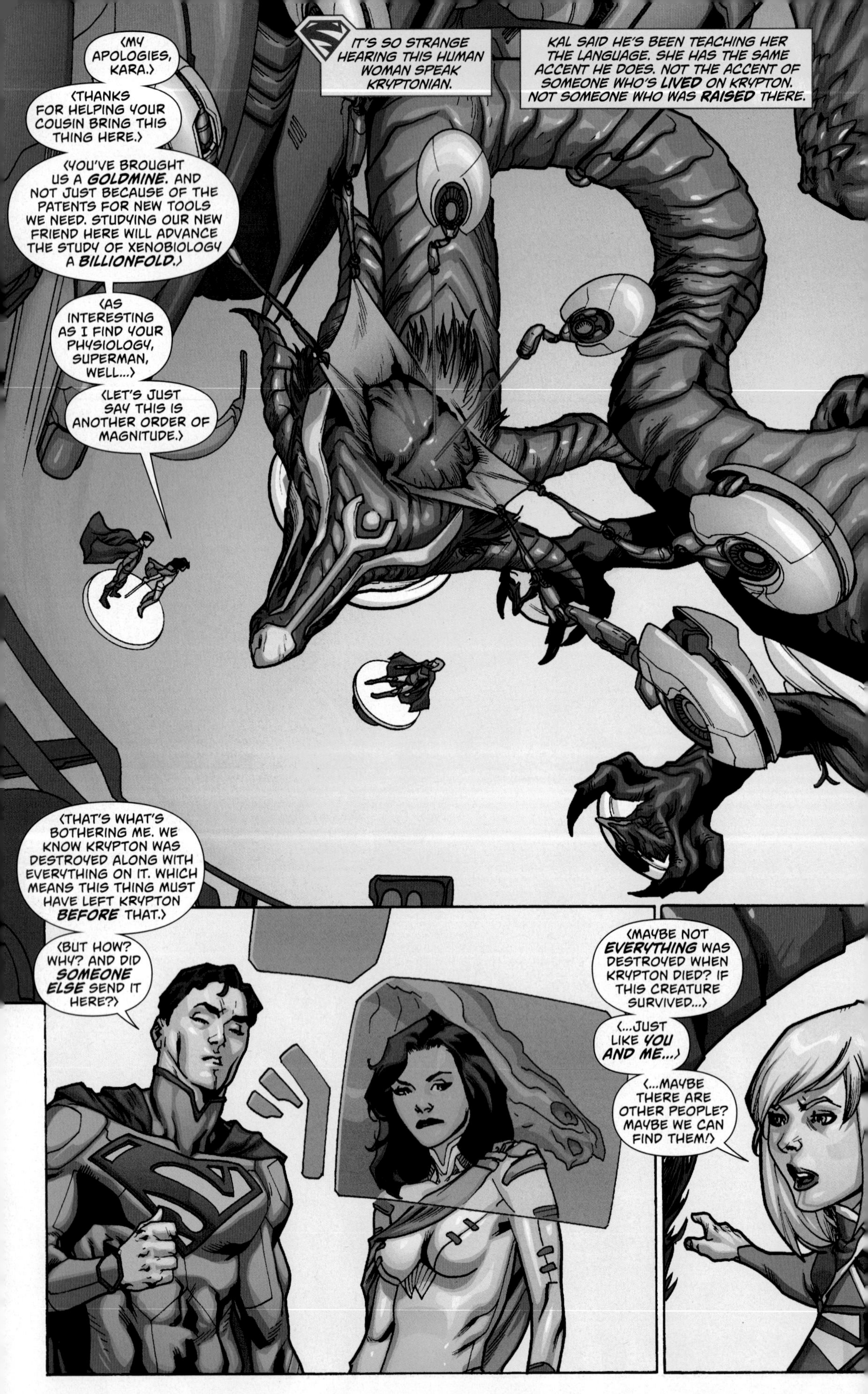

IT'S SO STRANGE HEARING THIS HUMAN WOMAN SPEAK KRYPTONIAN.
KAL SAID HE'S BEEN TEACHING HER THE LANGUAGE. SHE HAS THE SAME ACCENT HE DOES. NOT THE ACCENT OF SOMEONE WHO'S LIVED ON KRYPTON. NOT SOMEONE WHO WAS RAISED THERE.
‹MY APOLOGIES, KARA.›
‹THANKS FOR HELPING YOUR COUSIN BRING THIS THING HERE.›
‹YOU'VE BROUGHT US A GOLDMINE. AND NOT JUST BECAUSE OF THE PATENTS FOR NEW TOOLS WE NEED. STUDYING OUR NEW FRIEND HERE WILL ADVANCE THE STUDY OF XENOBIOLOGY A BILLIONFOLD.›
‹AS INTERESTING AS I FIND YOUR PHYSIOLOGY, SUPERMAN, WELL...›
‹LET'S JUST SAY THIS IS ANOTHER ORDER OF MAGNITUDE.›
‹THAT'S WHAT'S BOTHERING ME. WE KNOW KRYPTON WAS DESTROYED ALONG WITH EVERYTHING ON IT. WHICH MEANS THIS THING MUST HAVE LEFT KRYPTON BEFORE THAT.›
‹BUT HOW? WHY? AND DID SOMEONE ELSE SEND IT HERE?›
‹MAYBE NOT EVERYTHING WAS DESTROYED WHEN KRYPTON DIED? IF THIS CREATURE SURVIVED...›
‹...JUST LIKE YOU AND ME...›
‹...MAYBE THERE ARE OTHER PEOPLE? MAYBE WE CAN FIND THEM!›

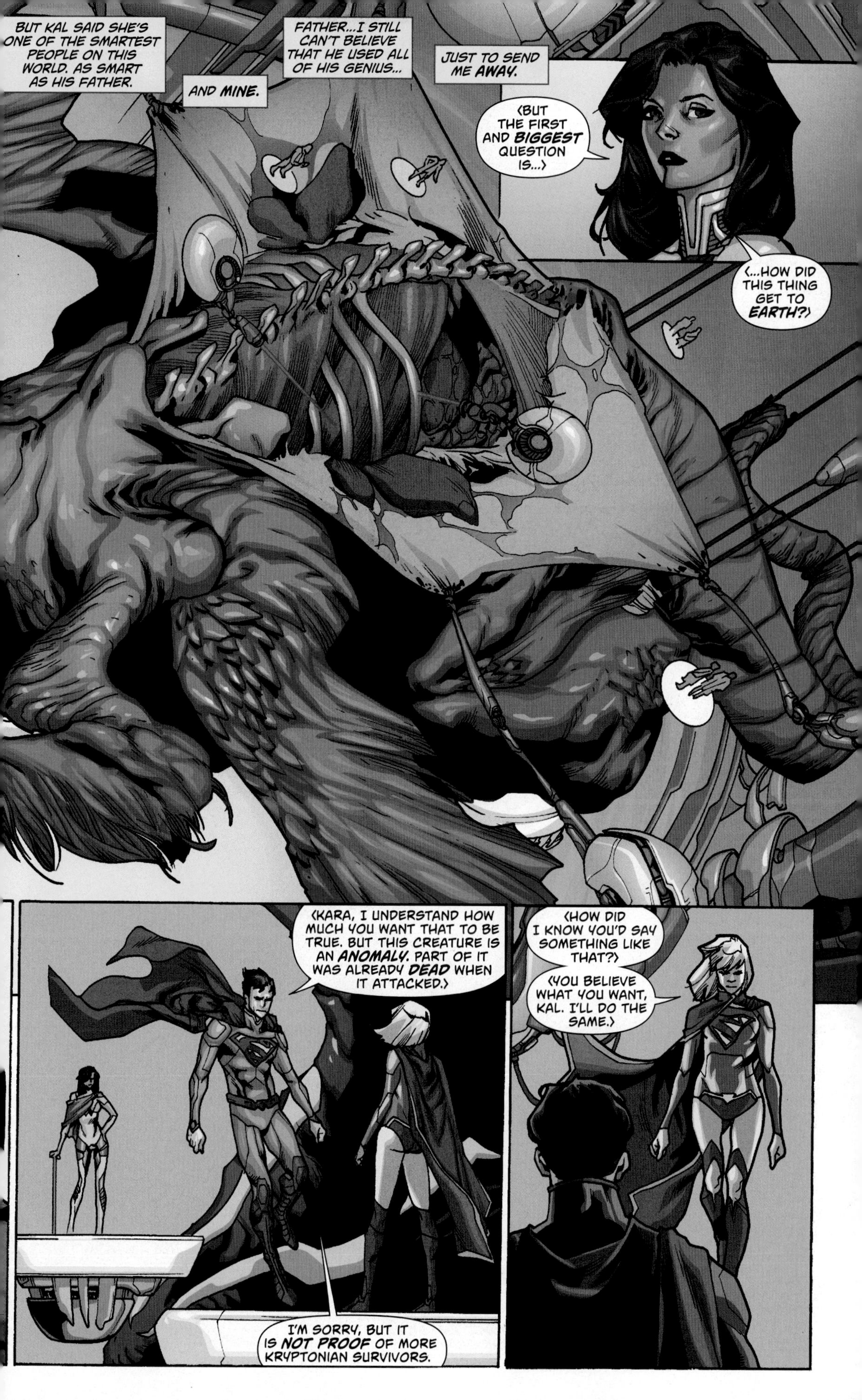
BUT KAL SAID SHE'S ONE OF THE SMARTEST PEOPLE ON THIS WORLD. AS SMART AS HIS FATHER.
AND MINE.
FATHER...I STILL CAN'T BELIEVE THAT HE USED ALL OF HIS GENIUS...
JUST TO SEND ME AWAY.
‹BUT THE FIRST AND BIGGEST QUESTION IS...›
‹...HOW DID THIS THING GET TO EARTH?›
‹KARA, I UNDERSTAND HOW MUCH YOU WANT THAT TO BE TRUE. BUT THIS CREATURE IS AN ANOMALY. PART OF IT WAS ALREADY DEAD WHEN IT ATTACKED.›
I'M SORRY, BUT IT IS NOT PROOF OF MORE KRYPTONIAN SURVIVORS.
‹HOW DID I KNOW YOU'D SAY SOMETHING LIKE THAT?›
‹YOU BELIEVE WHAT YOU WANT, KAL. I'LL DO THE SAME.›

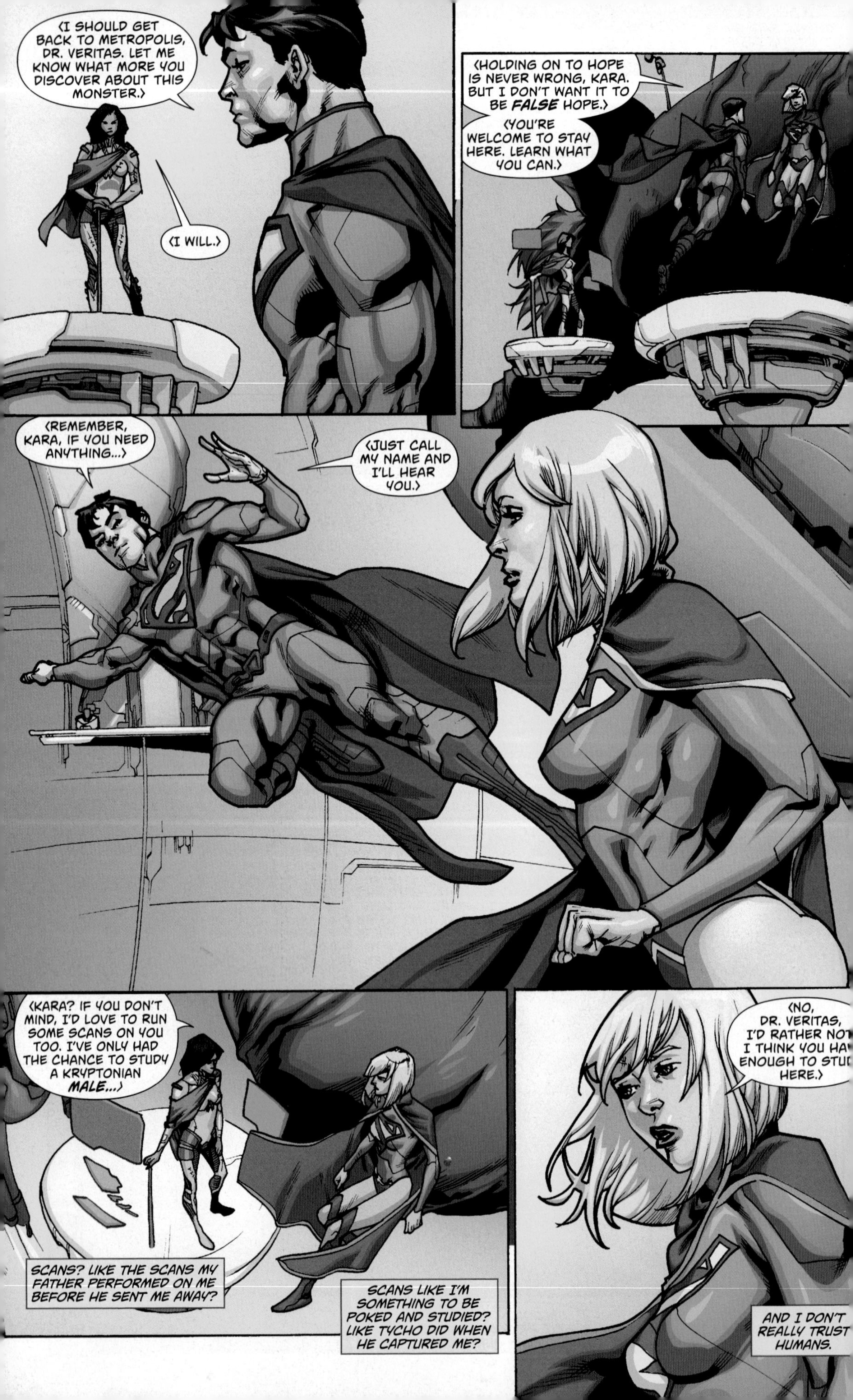
‹I SHOULD GET BACK TO METROPOLIS, DR. VERITAS. LET ME KNOW WHAT MORE YOU DISCOVER ABOUT THIS MONSTER.›
‹I WILL.›
‹HOLDING ON TO HOPE IS NEVER WRONG, KARA. BUT I DON'T WANT IT TO BE *FALSE* HOPE.›
‹YOU'RE WELCOME TO STAY HERE. LEARN WHAT YOU CAN.›
‹REMEMBER, KARA, IF YOU NEED ANYTHING...›
‹JUST CALL MY NAME AND I'LL HEAR YOU.›
‹KARA? IF YOU DON'T MIND, I'D LOVE TO RUN SOME SCANS ON YOU TOO. I'VE ONLY HAD THE CHANCE TO STUDY A KRYPTONIAN *MALE*...›
SCANS? LIKE THE SCANS MY FATHER PERFORMED ON ME BEFORE HE SENT ME AWAY?
SCANS LIKE I'M SOMETHING TO BE POKED AND STUDIED? LIKE TYCHO DID WHEN HE CAPTURED ME?
‹NO, DR. VERITAS, I'D RATHER NOT
AND I DON'T REALLY TRUST HUMANS.

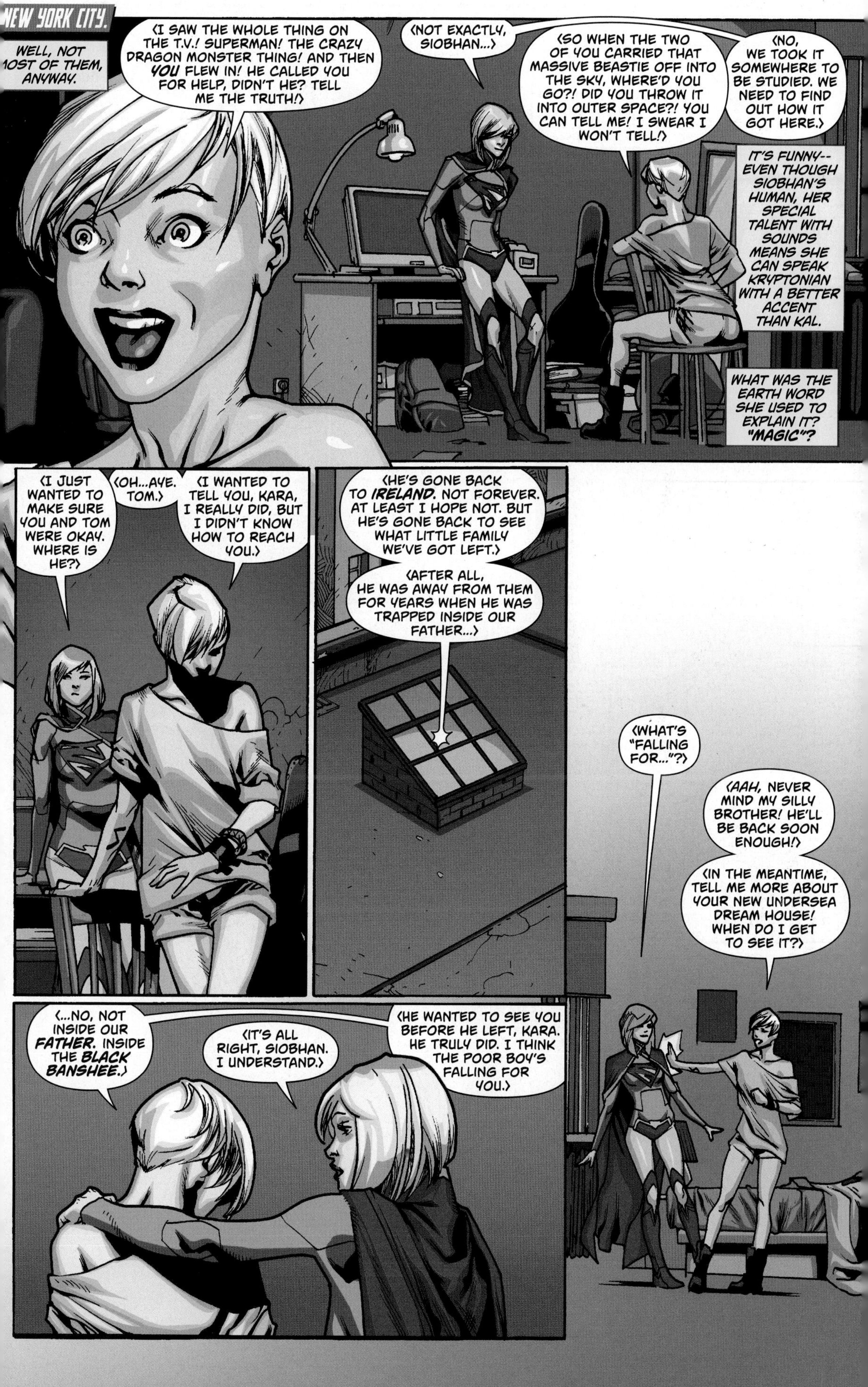
NEW YORK CITY.
WELL, NOT MOST OF THEM, ANYWAY.
‹I SAW THE WHOLE THING ON THE T.V.! SUPERMAN! THE CRAZY DRAGON MONSTER THING! AND THEN YOU FLEW IN! HE CALLED YOU FOR HELP, DIDN'T HE? TELL ME THE TRUTH!›
‹NOT EXACTLY, SIOBHAN...›
‹SO WHEN THE TWO OF YOU CARRIED THAT MASSIVE BEASTIE OFF INTO THE SKY, WHERE'D YOU GO?! DID YOU THROW IT INTO OUTER SPACE?! YOU CAN TELL ME! I SWEAR I WON'T TELL!›
‹NO, WE TOOK IT SOMEWHERE TO BE STUDIED. WE NEED TO FIND OUT HOW IT GOT HERE.›
IT'S FUNNY-- EVEN THOUGH SIOBHAN'S HUMAN, HER SPECIAL TALENT WITH SOUNDS MEANS SHE CAN SPEAK KRYPTONIAN WITH A BETTER ACCENT THAN KAL.
WHAT WAS THE EARTH WORD SHE USED TO EXPLAIN IT? "MAGIC"?
‹I JUST WANTED TO MAKE SURE YOU AND TOM WERE OKAY. WHERE IS HE?›
‹OH...AYE. TOM.›
‹I WANTED TO TELL YOU, KARA, I REALLY DID, BUT I DIDN'T KNOW HOW TO REACH YOU.›
‹HE'S GONE BACK TO IRELAND. NOT FOREVER. AT LEAST I HOPE NOT. BUT HE'S GONE BACK TO SEE WHAT LITTLE FAMILY WE'VE GOT LEFT.›
‹AFTER ALL, HE WAS AWAY FROM THEM FOR YEARS WHEN HE WAS TRAPPED INSIDE OUR FATHER...›
‹...NO, NOT INSIDE OUR FATHER. INSIDE THE BLACK BANSHEE.›
‹IT'S ALL RIGHT, SIOBHAN. I UNDERSTAND.›
‹HE WANTED TO SEE YOU BEFORE HE LEFT, KARA. HE TRULY DID. I THINK THE POOR BOY'S FALLING FOR YOU.›
‹WHAT'S "FALLING FOR..."?›
‹AAH, NEVER MIND MY SILLY BROTHER! HE'LL BE BACK SOON ENOUGH!›
‹IN THE MEANTIME, TELL ME MORE ABOUT YOUR NEW UNDERSEA DREAM HOUSE! WHEN DO I GET TO SEE IT?›

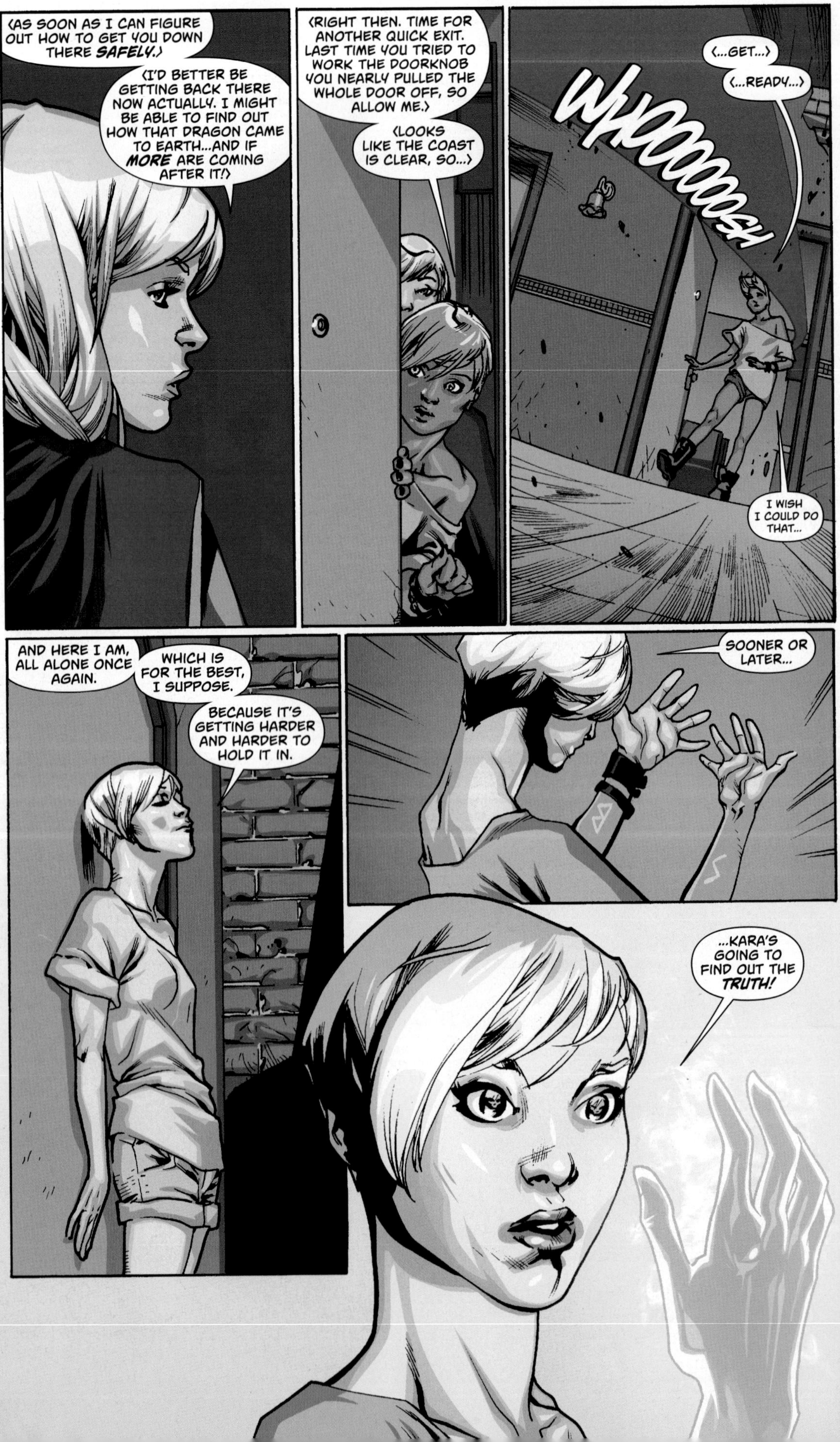
‹AS SOON AS I CAN FIGURE OUT HOW TO GET YOU DOWN THERE *SAFELY.*›
‹I'D BETTER BE GETTING BACK THERE NOW ACTUALLY. I MIGHT BE ABLE TO FIND OUT HOW THAT DRAGON CAME TO EARTH...AND IF *MORE* ARE COMING AFTER IT!›
‹RIGHT THEN. TIME FOR ANOTHER QUICK EXIT. LAST TIME YOU TRIED TO WORK THE DOORKNOB YOU NEARLY PULLED THE WHOLE DOOR OFF, SO ALLOW ME.›
‹LOOKS LIKE THE COAST IS CLEAR, SO...›
‹...GET...›
‹...READY...›
WHOOOOOOSH
I WISH I COULD DO THAT...
AND HERE I AM, ALL ALONE ONCE AGAIN.
WHICH IS FOR THE BEST, I SUPPOSE.
BECAUSE IT'S GETTING HARDER AND HARDER TO HOLD IT IN.
SOONER OR LATER...
...KARA'S GOING TO FIND OUT THE *TRUTH!*

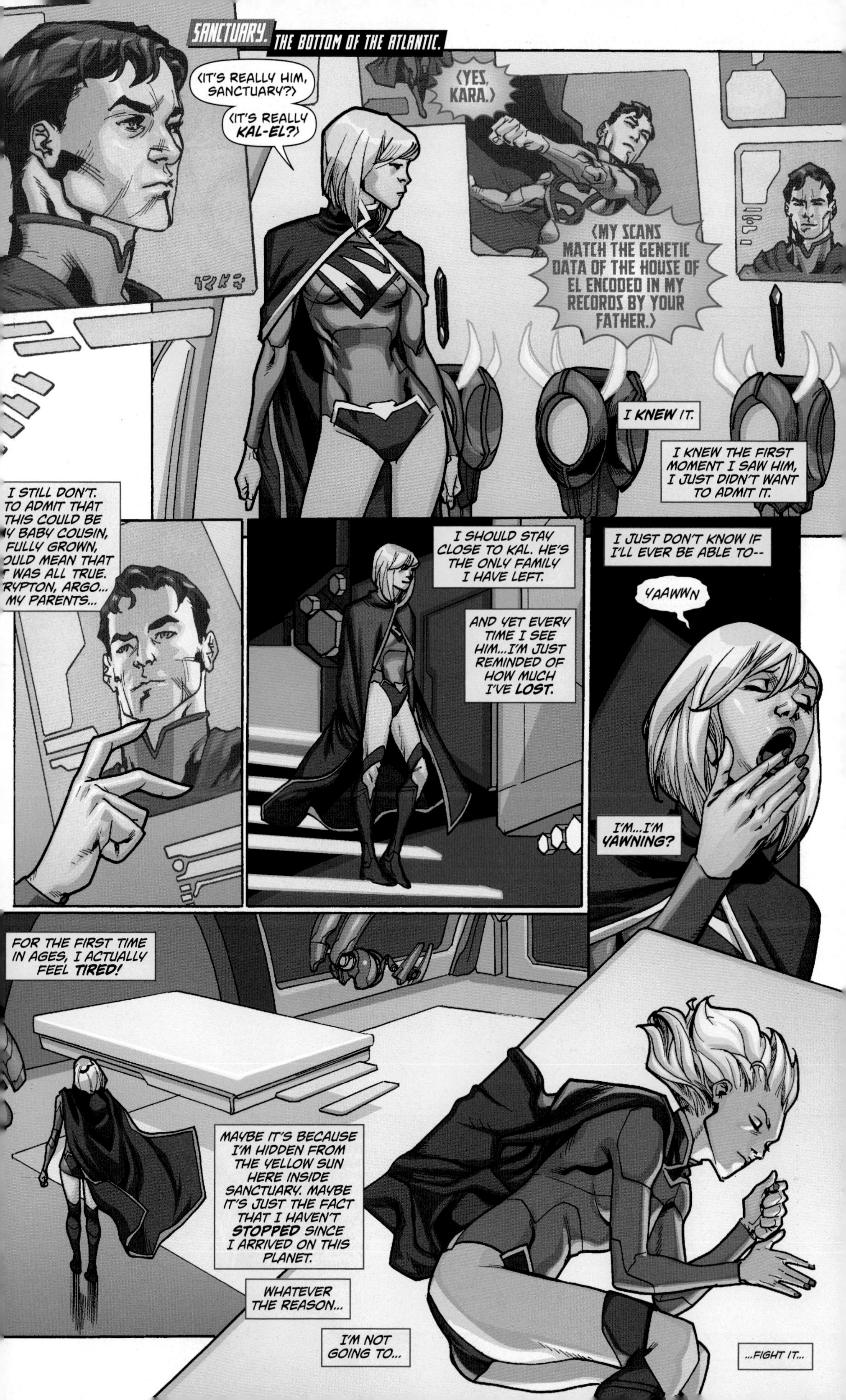
SANCTUARY.
THE BOTTOM OF THE ATLANTIC.
⟨IT'S REALLY HIM, SANCTUARY?⟩
⟨IT'S REALLY KAL-EL?⟩
⟨YES, KARA.⟩
⟨MY SCANS MATCH THE GENETIC DATA OF THE HOUSE OF EL ENCODED IN MY RECORDS BY YOUR FATHER.⟩
I KNEW IT.
I KNEW THE FIRST MOMENT I SAW HIM, I JUST DIDN'T WANT TO ADMIT IT.
I STILL DON'T.
TO ADMIT THAT THIS COULD BE
Y BABY COUSIN, FULLY GROWN,
OULD MEAN THAT
T WAS ALL TRUE.
RYPTON, ARGO... MY PARENTS...
I SHOULD STAY CLOSE TO KAL. HE'S THE ONLY FAMILY I HAVE LEFT.
AND YET EVERY TIME I SEE HIM...I'M JUST REMINDED OF HOW MUCH I'VE LOST.
I JUST DON'T KNOW IF I'LL EVER BE ABLE TO--
YAAWWN
I'M...I'M YAWNING?
FOR THE FIRST TIME IN AGES, I ACTUALLY FEEL TIRED!
MAYBE IT'S BECAUSE I'M HIDDEN FROM THE YELLOW SUN HERE INSIDE SANCTUARY. MAYBE IT'S JUST THE FACT THAT I HAVEN'T STOPPED SINCE I ARRIVED ON THIS PLANET.
WHATEVER THE REASON...
I'M NOT GOING TO...
...FIGHT IT...

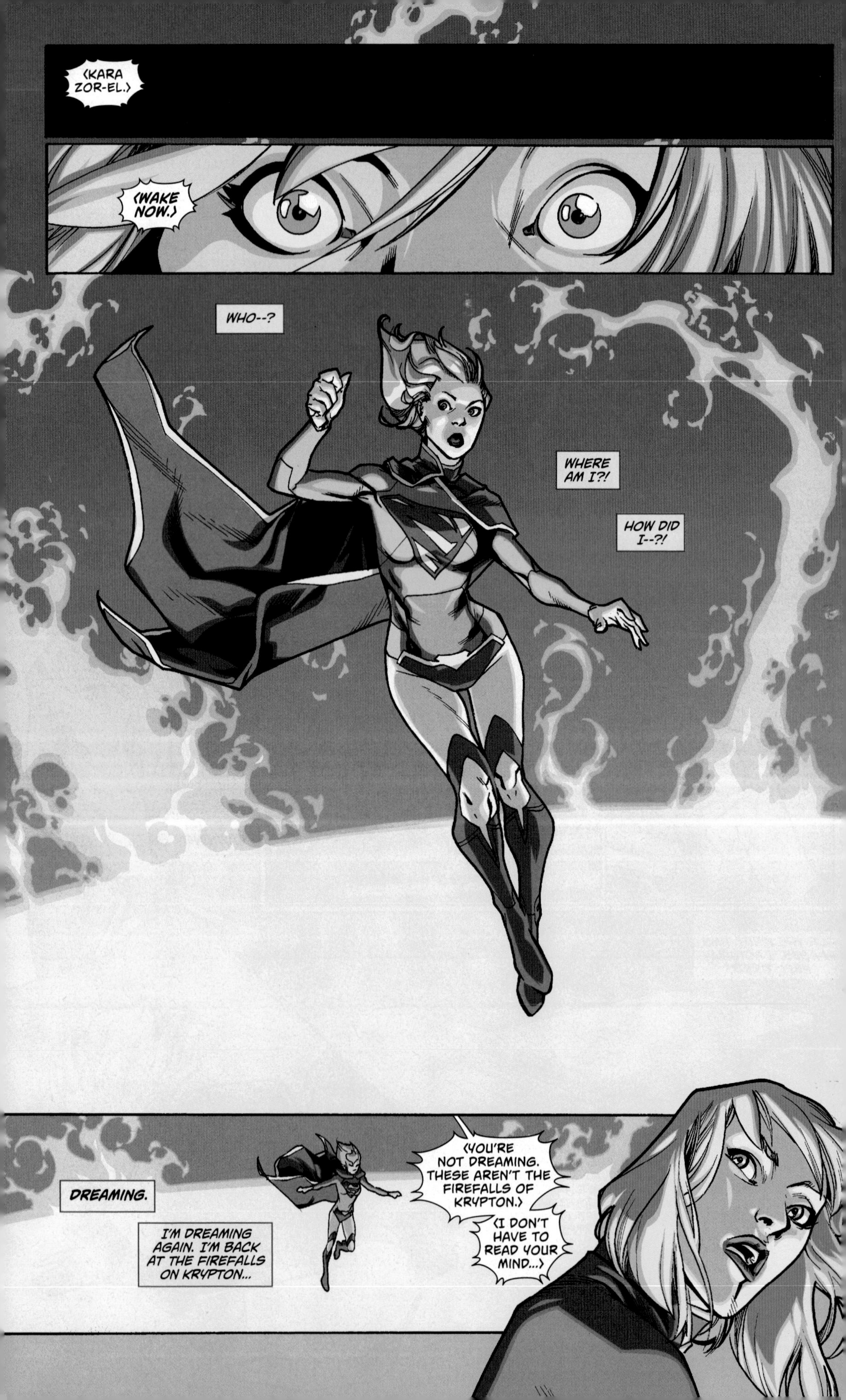
‹KARA ZOR-EL.›
‹WAKE NOW.›
WHO--?
WHERE AM I?!
HOW DID I--?!
DREAMING.
I'M DREAMING AGAIN. I'M BACK AT THE FIREFALLS ON KRYPTON...
‹YOU'RE NOT DREAMING. THESE AREN'T THE FIREFALLS OF KRYPTON.›
‹I DON'T HAVE TO READ YOUR MIND...›

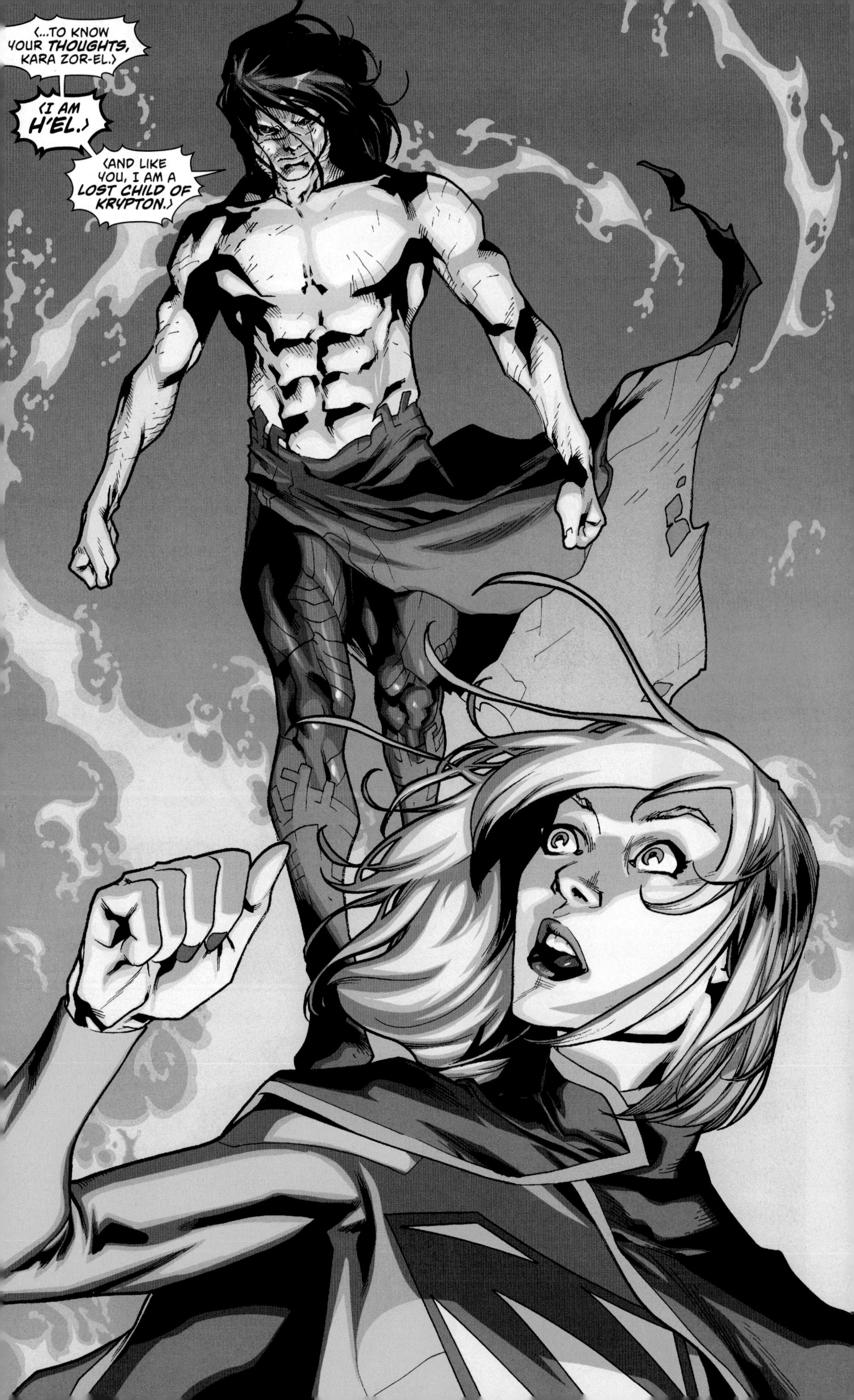

‹...TO KNOW YOUR THOUGHTS, KARA ZOR-EL.›
‹I AM H'EL.›
‹AND LIKE YOU, I AM A LOST CHILD OF KRYPTON.›

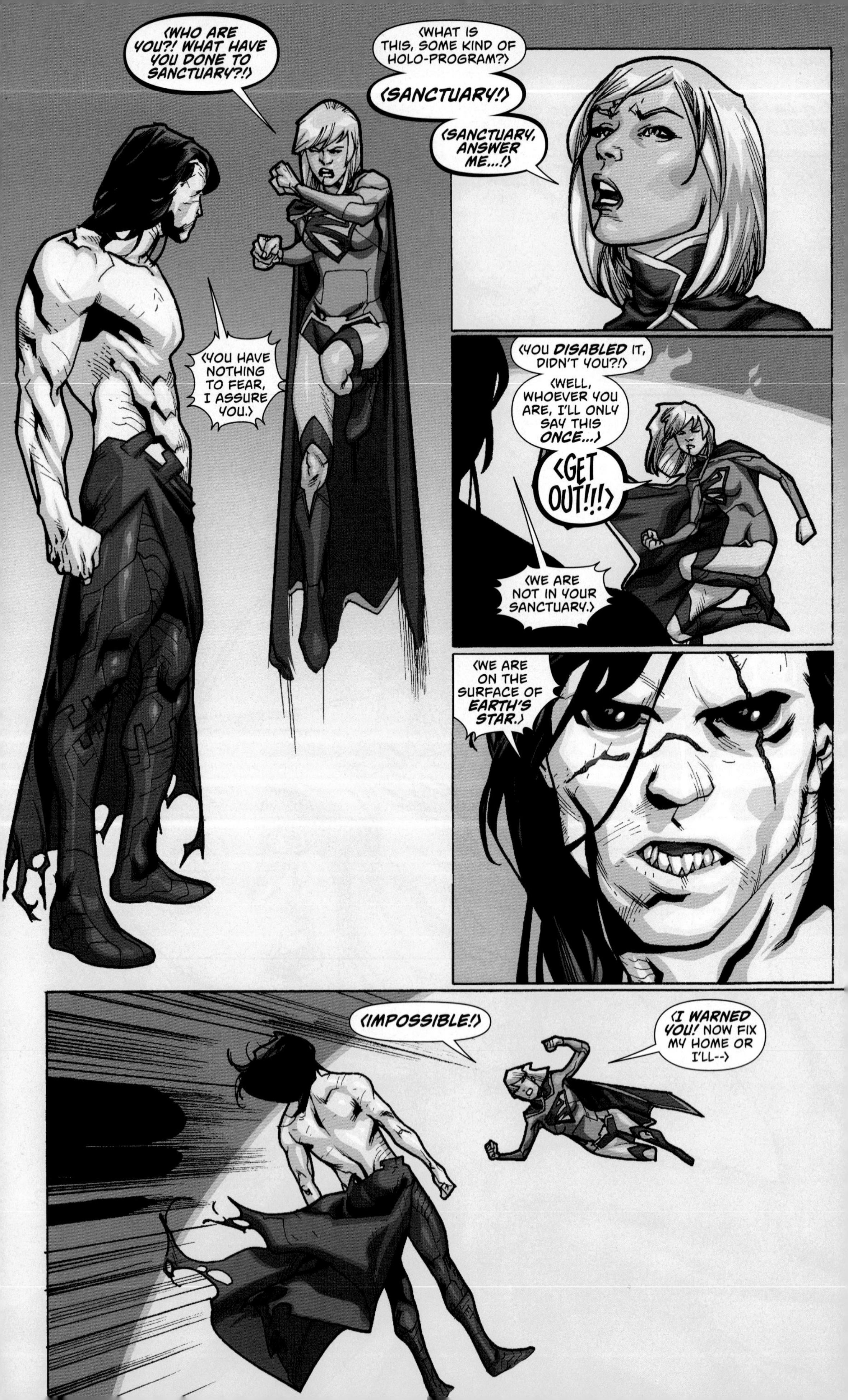
(WHO ARE YOU?! WHAT HAVE YOU DONE TO SANCTUARY?!)
(WHAT IS THIS, SOME KIND OF HOLO-PROGRAM?)
(SANCTUARY!)
(SANCTUARY, ANSWER ME...!)
(YOU HAVE NOTHING TO FEAR, I ASSURE YOU.)
(YOU DISABLED IT, DIDN'T YOU?!)
(WELL, WHOEVER YOU ARE, I'LL ONLY SAY THIS ONCE...)
(GET OUT!!!)
(WE ARE NOT IN YOUR SANCTUARY.)
(WE ARE ON THE SURFACE OF EARTH'S STAR.)
(IMPOSSIBLE!)
(I WARNED YOU! NOW FIX MY HOME OR I'LL--)

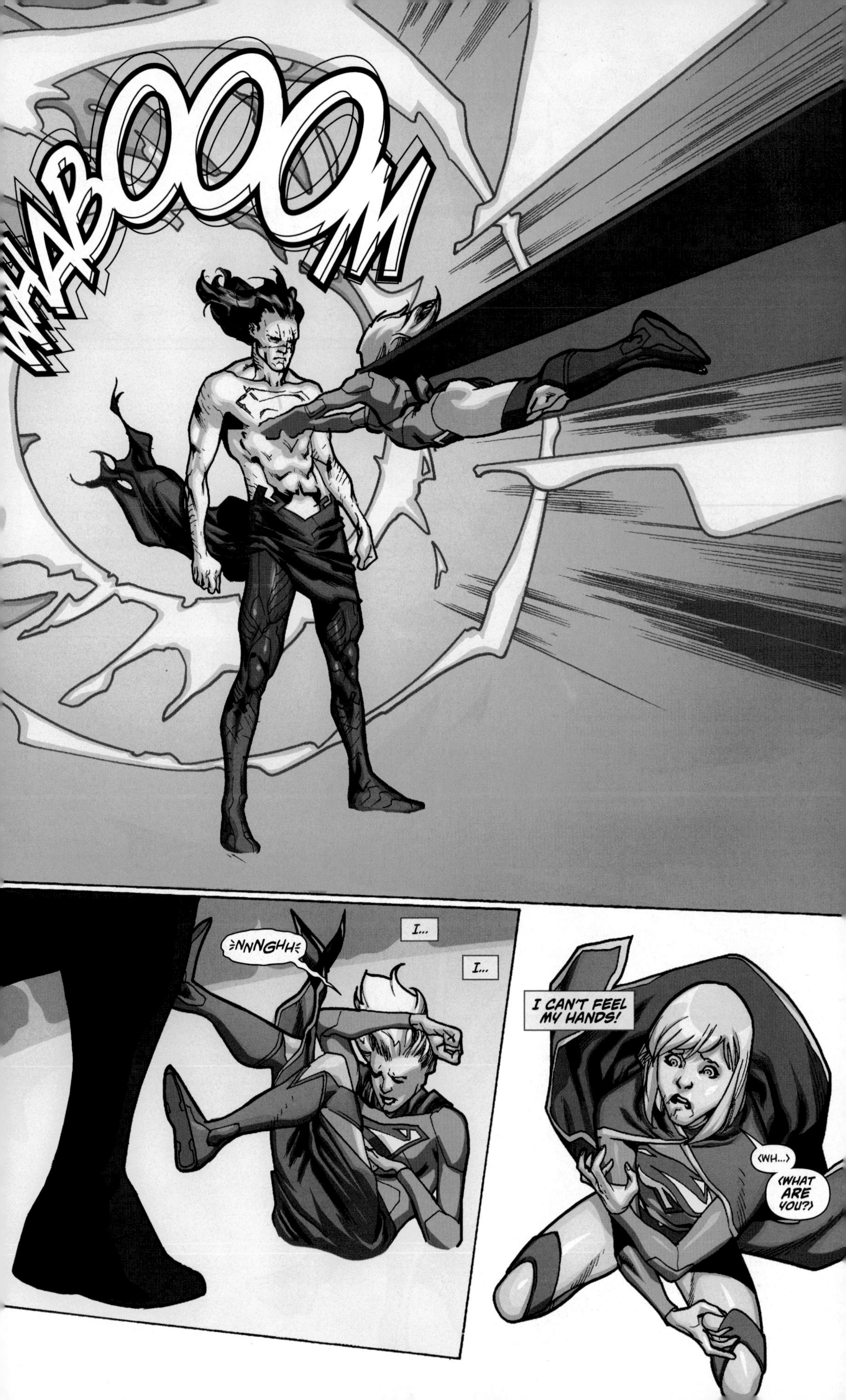
WHABOOOM
ƎNNNGHHƎ
I...
I...
I CAN'T FEEL MY HANDS!
‹WH...›
‹WHAT ARE YOU?›

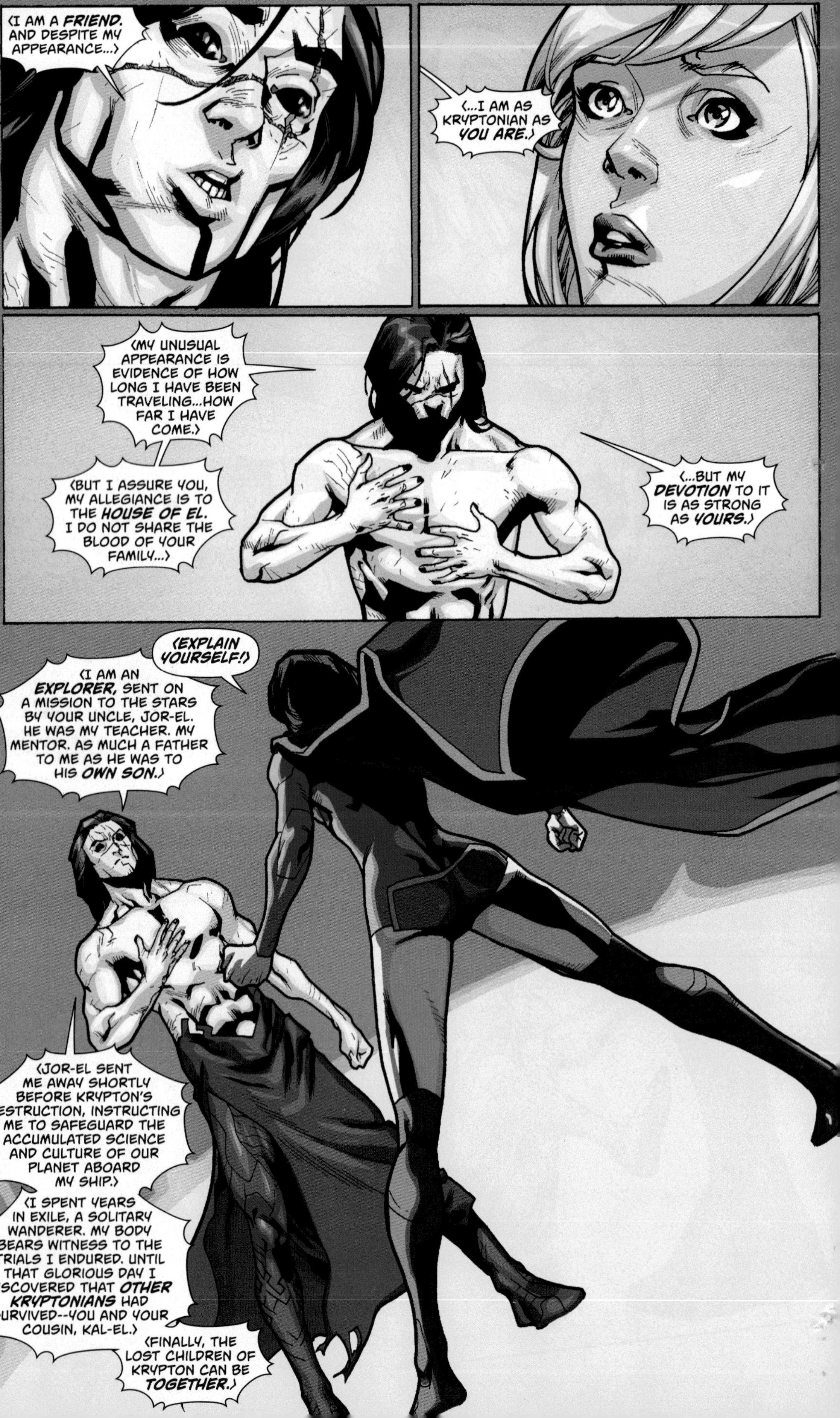

‹I AM A FRIEND. AND DESPITE MY APPEARANCE...›
‹...I AM AS KRYPTONIAN AS YOU ARE.›
‹MY UNUSUAL APPEARANCE IS EVIDENCE OF HOW LONG I HAVE BEEN TRAVELING...HOW FAR I HAVE COME.›
‹BUT I ASSURE YOU, MY ALLEGIANCE IS TO THE HOUSE OF EL. I DO NOT SHARE THE BLOOD OF YOUR FAMILY...›
‹...BUT MY DEVOTION TO IT IS AS STRONG AS YOURS.›
‹EXPLAIN YOURSELF!›
‹I AM AN EXPLORER, SENT ON A MISSION TO THE STARS BY YOUR UNCLE, JOR-EL. HE WAS MY TEACHER. MY MENTOR. AS MUCH A FATHER TO ME AS HE WAS TO HIS OWN SON.›
‹JOR-EL SENT ME AWAY SHORTLY BEFORE KRYPTON'S DESTRUCTION, INSTRUCTING ME TO SAFEGUARD THE ACCUMULATED SCIENCE AND CULTURE OF OUR PLANET ABOARD MY SHIP.›
‹I SPENT YEARS IN EXILE, A SOLITARY WANDERER. MY BODY BEARS WITNESS TO THE TRIALS I ENDURED. UNTIL THAT GLORIOUS DAY I DISCOVERED THAT OTHER KRYPTONIANS HAD SURVIVED--YOU AND YOUR COUSIN, KAL-EL.›
‹FINALLY, THE LOST CHILDREN OF KRYPTON CAN BE TOGETHER.›

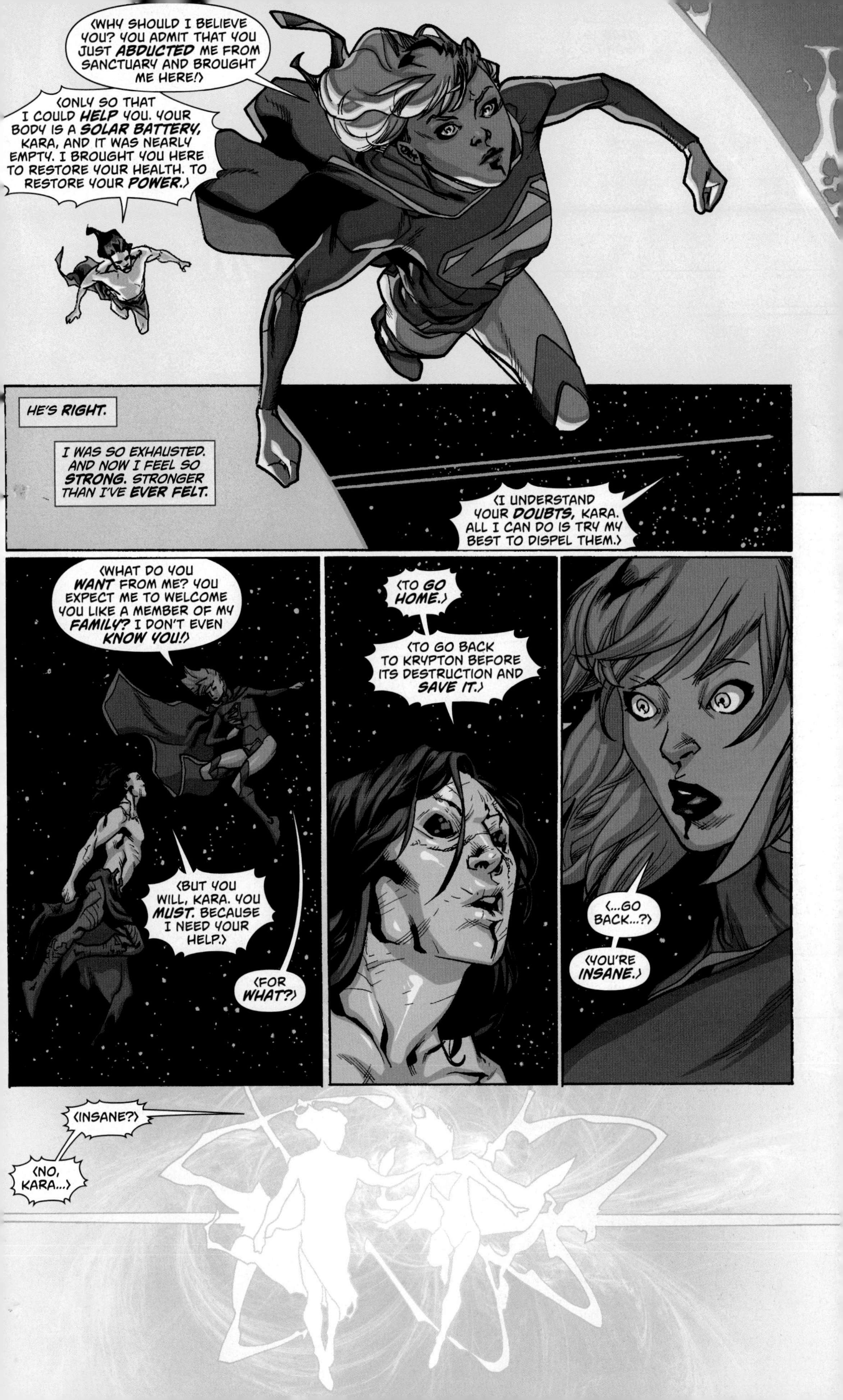

‹WHY SHOULD I BELIEVE YOU? YOU ADMIT THAT YOU JUST ABDUCTED ME FROM SANCTUARY AND BROUGHT ME HERE!›
‹ONLY SO THAT I COULD HELP YOU. YOUR BODY IS A SOLAR BATTERY, KARA, AND IT WAS NEARLY EMPTY. I BROUGHT YOU HERE TO RESTORE YOUR HEALTH. TO RESTORE YOUR POWER.›
HE'S RIGHT.
I WAS SO EXHAUSTED. AND NOW I FEEL SO STRONG. STRONGER THAN I'VE EVER FELT.
‹I UNDERSTAND YOUR DOUBTS, KARA. ALL I CAN DO IS TRY MY BEST TO DISPEL THEM.›
‹WHAT DO YOU WANT FROM ME? YOU EXPECT ME TO WELCOME YOU LIKE A MEMBER OF MY FAMILY? I DON'T EVEN KNOW YOU!›
‹BUT YOU WILL, KARA. YOU MUST. BECAUSE I NEED YOUR HELP.›
‹FOR WHAT?›
‹TO GO HOME.›
‹TO GO BACK TO KRYPTON BEFORE ITS DESTRUCTION AND SAVE IT.›
‹...GO BACK...?›
‹YOU'RE INSANE.›
‹INSANE?›
‹NO, KARA...›

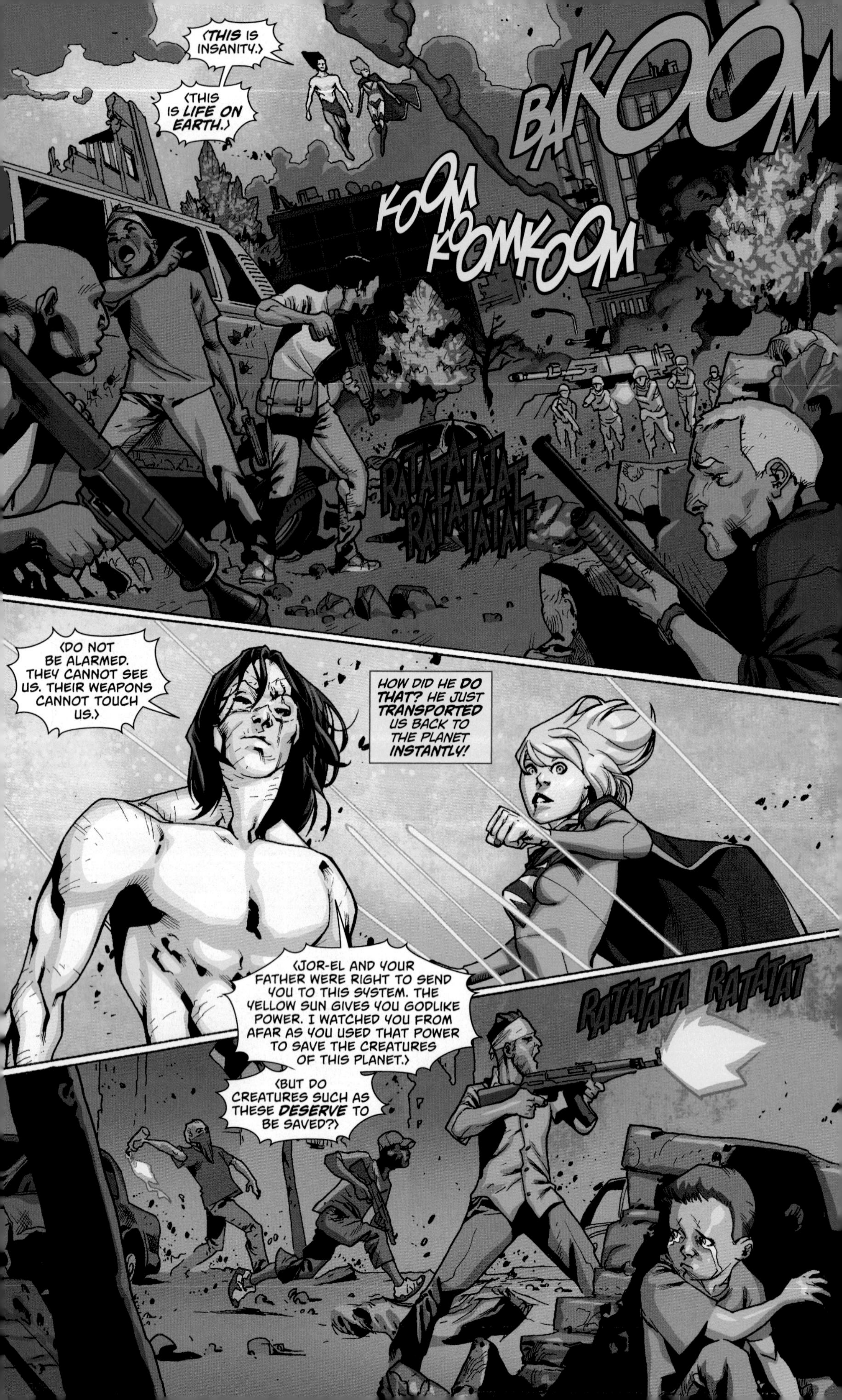

⟨THIS IS INSANITY.⟩
⟨THIS IS LIFE ON EARTH.⟩
BAKOOM
KOOM KOOMKOOM
RATATATATAT RATATATAT
⟨DO NOT BE ALARMED. THEY CANNOT SEE US. THEIR WEAPONS CANNOT TOUCH US.⟩
HOW DID HE DO THAT? HE JUST TRANSPORTED US BACK TO THE PLANET INSTANTLY!
⟨JOR-EL AND YOUR FATHER WERE RIGHT TO SEND YOU TO THIS SYSTEM. THE YELLOW SUN GIVES YOU GODLIKE POWER. I WATCHED YOU FROM AFAR AS YOU USED THAT POWER TO SAVE THE CREATURES OF THIS PLANET.⟩
RATATATA RATATAT
⟨BUT DO CREATURES SUCH AS THESE DESERVE TO BE SAVED?⟩

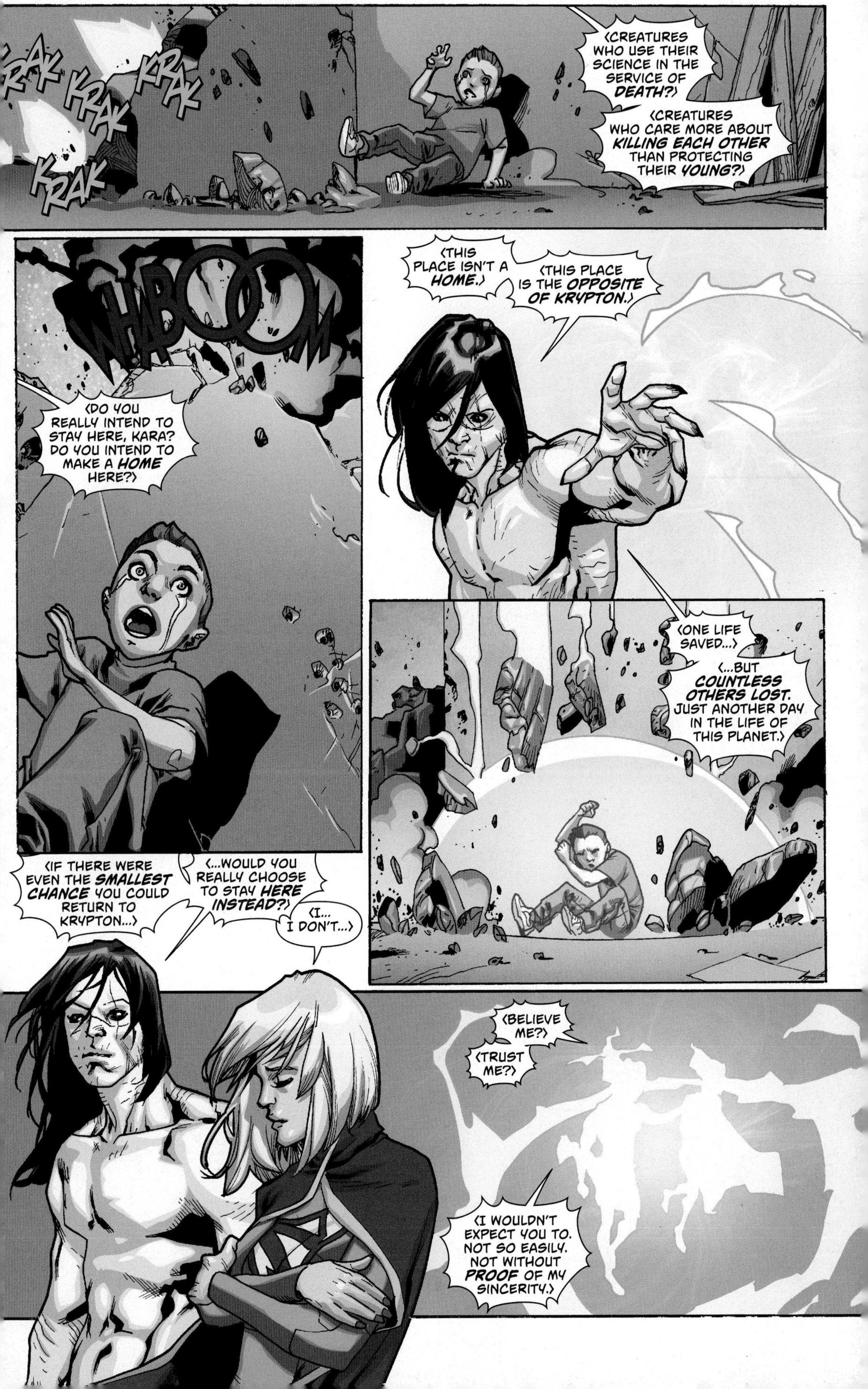
KRAK KRAK KRAK KRAK
⟨CREATURES WHO USE THEIR SCIENCE IN THE SERVICE OF DEATH?⟩
⟨CREATURES WHO CARE MORE ABOUT KILLING EACH OTHER THAN PROTECTING THEIR YOUNG?⟩
WHABOOM
⟨DO YOU REALLY INTEND TO STAY HERE, KARA? DO YOU INTEND TO MAKE A HOME HERE?⟩
⟨THIS PLACE ISN'T A HOME.⟩
⟨THIS PLACE IS THE OPPOSITE OF KRYPTON.⟩
⟨ONE LIFE SAVED...⟩
⟨...BUT COUNTLESS OTHERS LOST. JUST ANOTHER DAY IN THE LIFE OF THIS PLANET.⟩
⟨IF THERE WERE EVEN THE SMALLEST CHANCE YOU COULD RETURN TO KRYPTON...⟩
⟨...WOULD YOU REALLY CHOOSE TO STAY HERE INSTEAD?⟩
⟨I... I DON'T...⟩
⟨BELIEVE ME?⟩
⟨TRUST ME?⟩
⟨I WOULDN'T EXPECT YOU TO. NOT SO EASILY. NOT WITHOUT PROOF OF MY SINCERITY.⟩

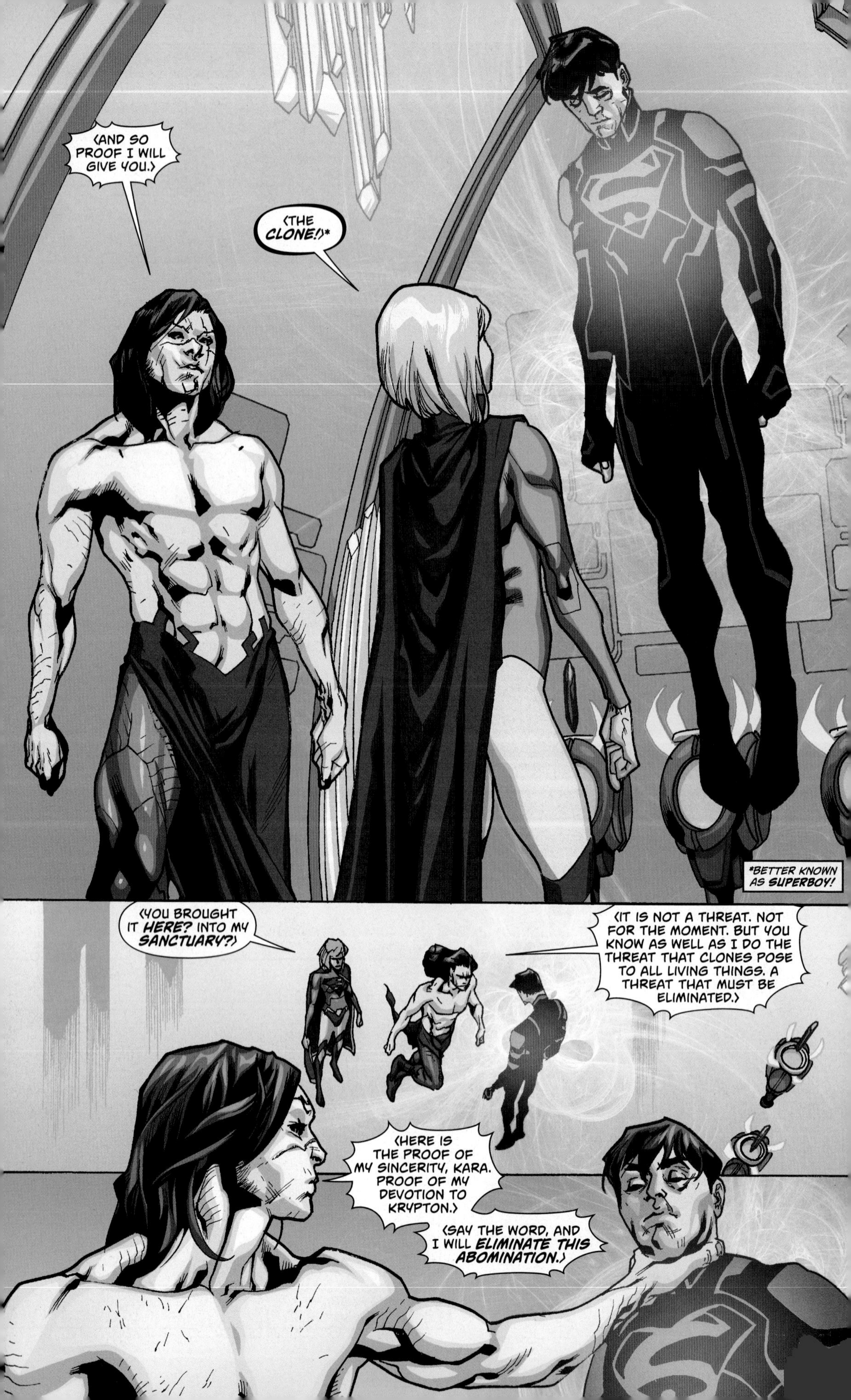

⟨AND SO PROOF I WILL GIVE YOU.⟩
⟨THE CLONE!⟩*
*BETTER KNOWN AS SUPERBOY!
⟨YOU BROUGHT IT HERE? INTO MY SANCTUARY?⟩
⟨IT IS NOT A THREAT. NOT FOR THE MOMENT. BUT YOU KNOW AS WELL AS I DO THE THREAT THAT CLONES POSE TO ALL LIVING THINGS. A THREAT THAT MUST BE ELIMINATED.⟩
⟨HERE IS THE PROOF OF MY SINCERITY, KARA. PROOF OF MY DEVOTION TO KRYPTON.⟩
⟨SAY THE WORD, AND I WILL ELIMINATE THIS ABOMINATION.⟩

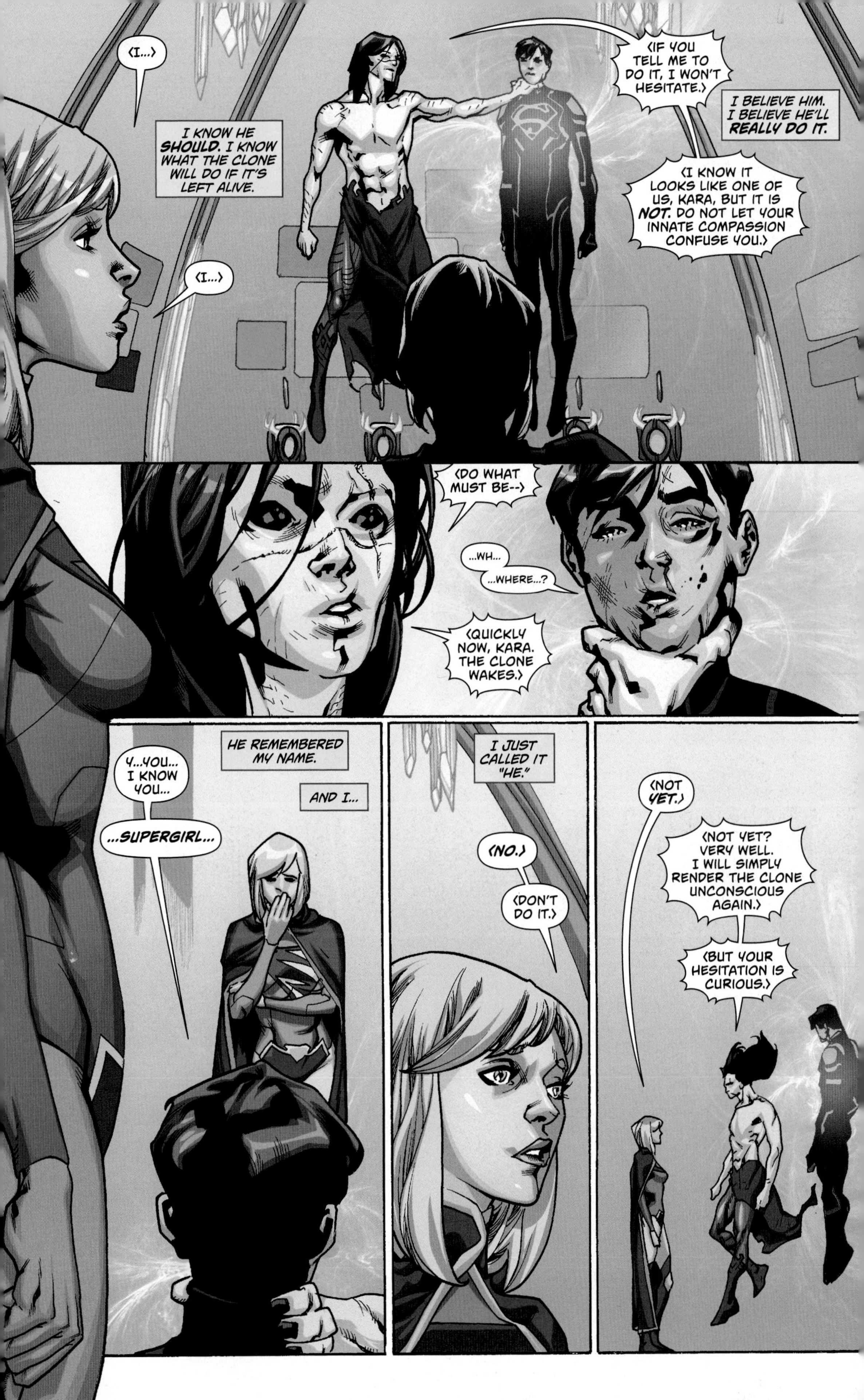

⟨I...⟩
I KNOW HE SHOULD. I KNOW WHAT THE CLONE WILL DO IF IT'S LEFT ALIVE.
⟨I...⟩
⟨IF YOU TELL ME TO DO IT, I WON'T HESITATE.⟩
I BELIEVE HIM. I BELIEVE HE'LL REALLY DO IT.
⟨I KNOW IT LOOKS LIKE ONE OF US, KARA, BUT IT IS NOT. DO NOT LET YOUR INNATE COMPASSION CONFUSE YOU.⟩
⟨DO WHAT MUST BE--⟩
...WH...
...WHERE...?
⟨QUICKLY NOW, KARA. THE CLONE WAKES.⟩
Y...YOU... I KNOW YOU...
...SUPERGIRL...
HE REMEMBERED MY NAME.
AND I...
I JUST CALLED IT "HE."
⟨NO.⟩
⟨DON'T DO IT.⟩
⟨NOT YET.⟩
⟨NOT YET? VERY WELL. I WILL SIMPLY RENDER THE CLONE UNCONSCIOUS AGAIN.⟩
⟨BUT YOUR HESITATION IS CURIOUS.⟩

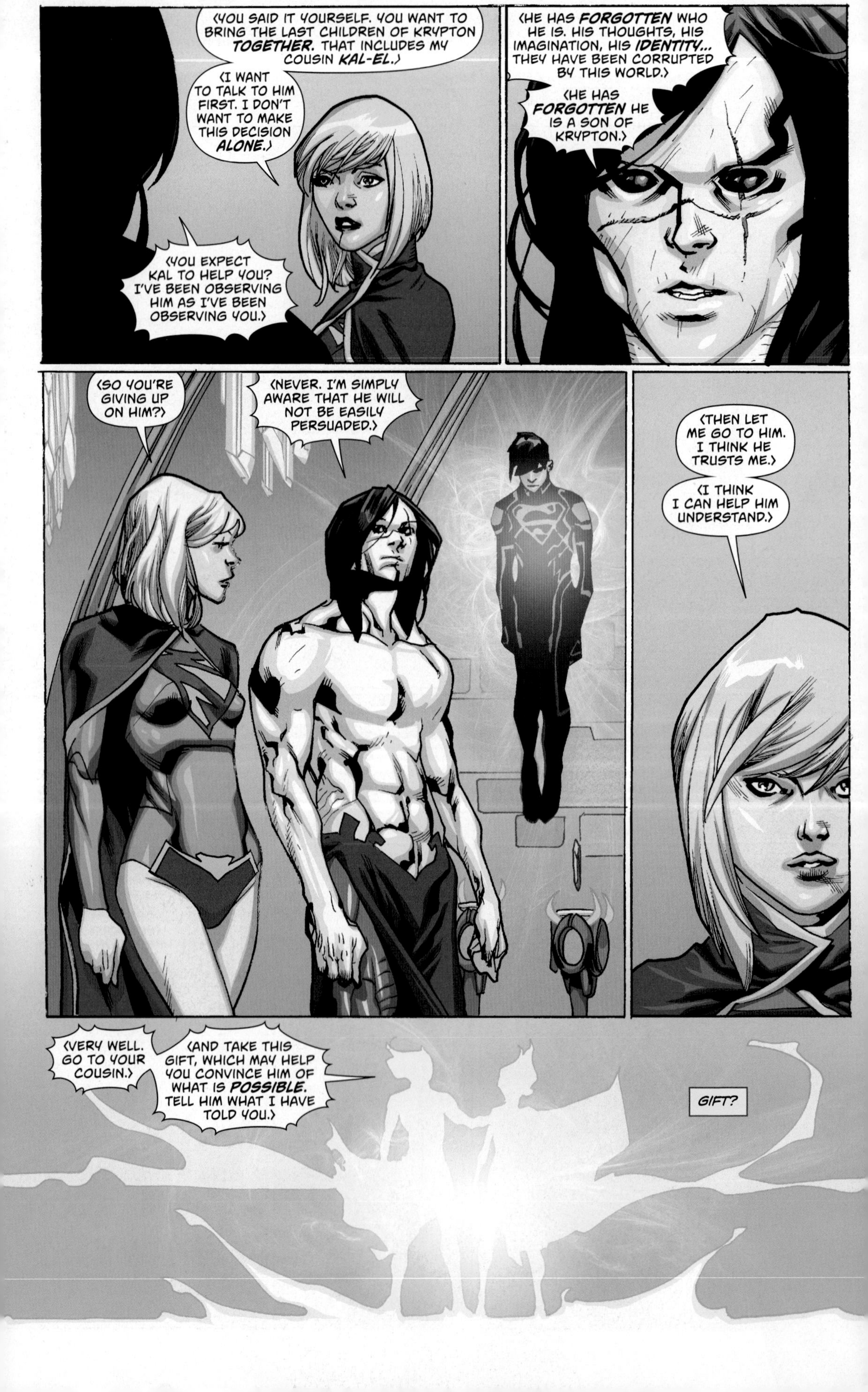

(YOU SAID IT YOURSELF. YOU WANT TO BRING THE LAST CHILDREN OF KRYPTON TOGETHER. THAT INCLUDES MY COUSIN KAL-EL.)
(I WANT TO TALK TO HIM FIRST. I DON'T WANT TO MAKE THIS DECISION ALONE.)
(YOU EXPECT KAL TO HELP YOU? I'VE BEEN OBSERVING HIM AS I'VE BEEN OBSERVING YOU.)
(HE HAS FORGOTTEN WHO HE IS. HIS THOUGHTS, HIS IMAGINATION, HIS IDENTITY... THEY HAVE BEEN CORRUPTED BY THIS WORLD.)
(HE HAS FORGOTTEN HE IS A SON OF KRYPTON.)
(SO YOU'RE GIVING UP ON HIM?)
(NEVER. I'M SIMPLY AWARE THAT HE WILL NOT BE EASILY PERSUADED.)
(THEN LET ME GO TO HIM. I THINK HE TRUSTS ME.)
(I THINK I CAN HELP HIM UNDERSTAND.)
(VERY WELL. GO TO YOUR COUSIN.)
(AND TAKE THIS GIFT, WHICH MAY HELP YOU CONVINCE HIM OF WHAT IS POSSIBLE. TELL HIM WHAT I HAVE TOLD YOU.)
GIFT?

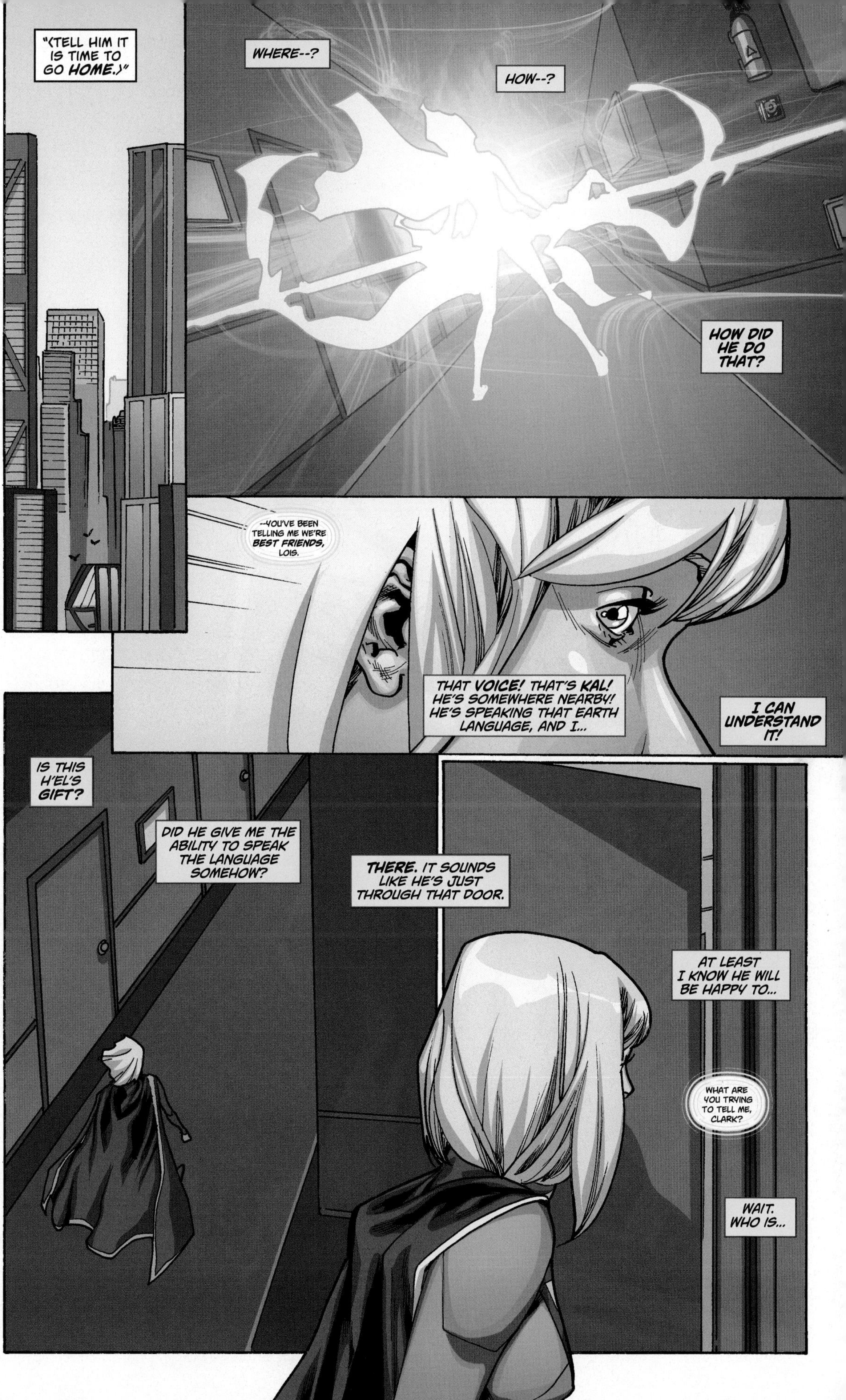
"⟨TELL HIM IT IS TIME TO GO HOME.⟩"
WHERE--?
HOW--?
HOW DID HE DO THAT?
--YOU'VE BEEN TELLING ME WE'RE BEST FRIENDS, LOIS.
THAT VOICE! THAT'S KAL! HE'S SOMEWHERE NEARBY! HE'S SPEAKING THAT EARTH LANGUAGE, AND I...
I CAN UNDERSTAND IT!
IS THIS H'EL'S GIFT?
DID HE GIVE ME THE ABILITY TO SPEAK THE LANGUAGE SOMEHOW?
THERE. IT SOUNDS LIKE HE'S JUST THROUGH THAT DOOR.
AT LEAST I KNOW HE WILL BE HAPPY TO...
WHAT ARE YOU TRYING TO TELL ME, CLARK?
WAIT. WHO IS...

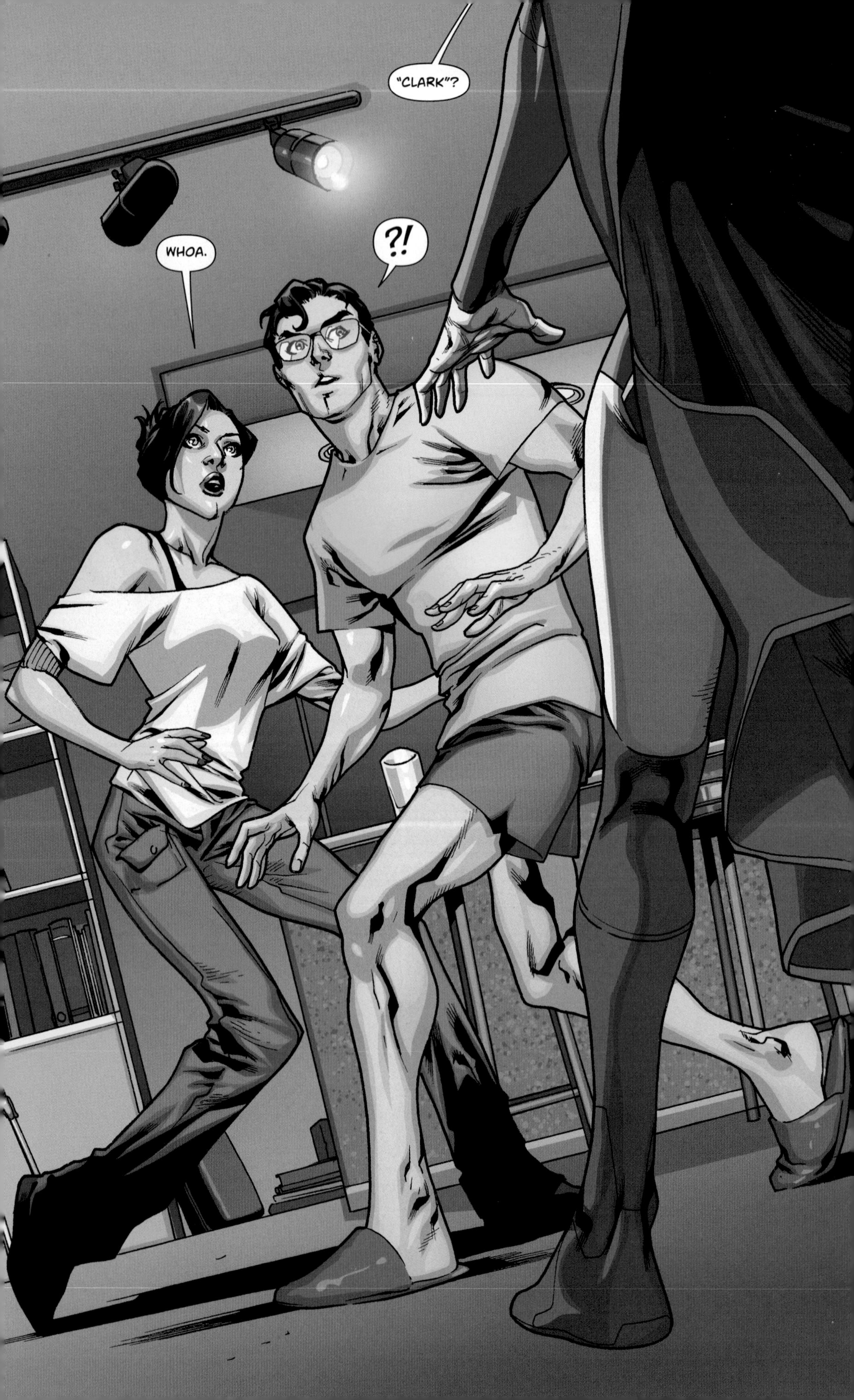
"CLARK"?
WHOA.
?!

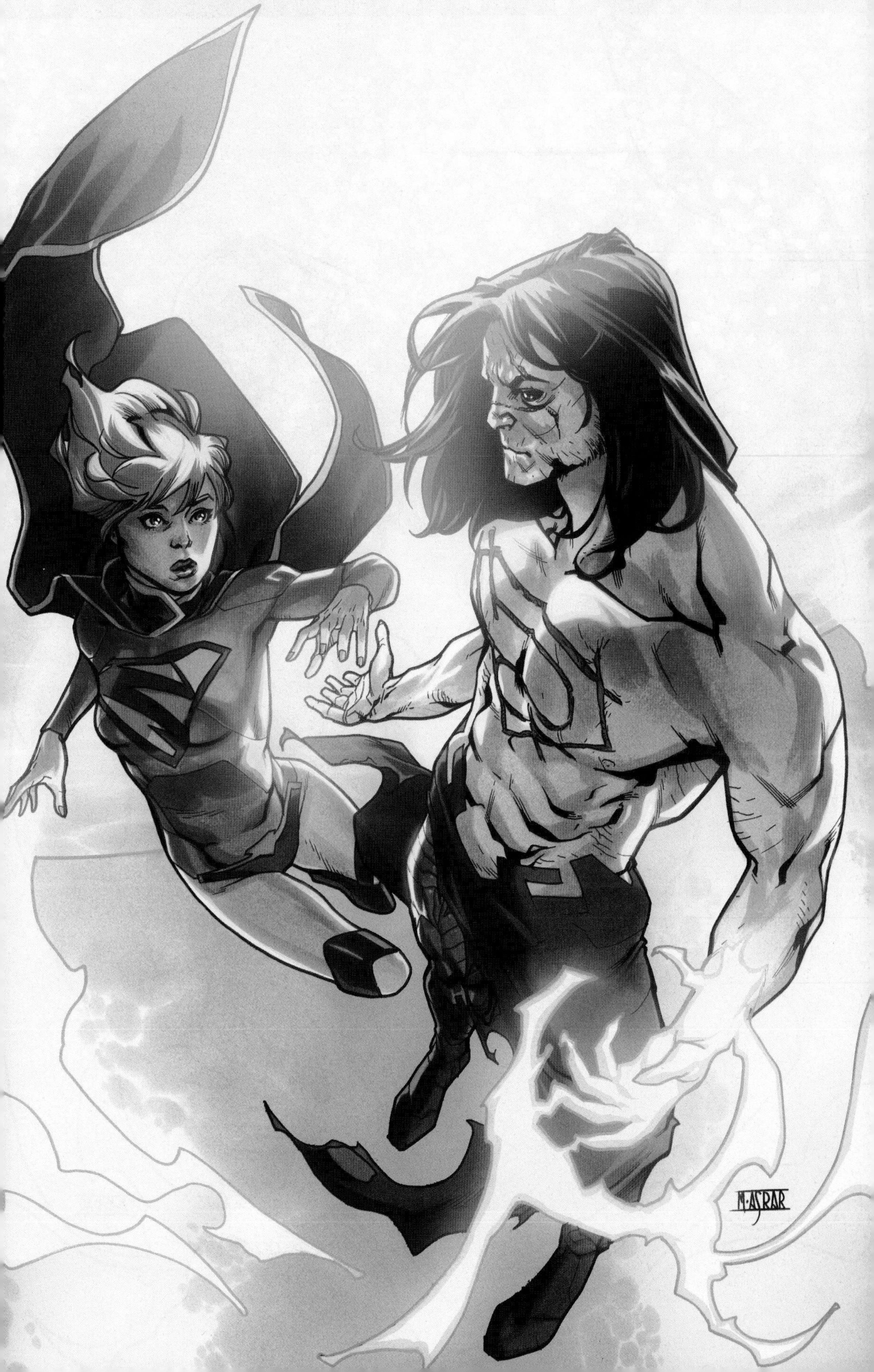
M·ASRAR

H'EL ON EARTH: INTO KANDOR

MIKE JOHNSON writer **MAHMUD ASRAR** penciller **MAHMUD ASRAR, SCOTT HANA & MARC DEERING** inkers
cover art by **MAHMUD ASRAR & DAVE McCAIG**

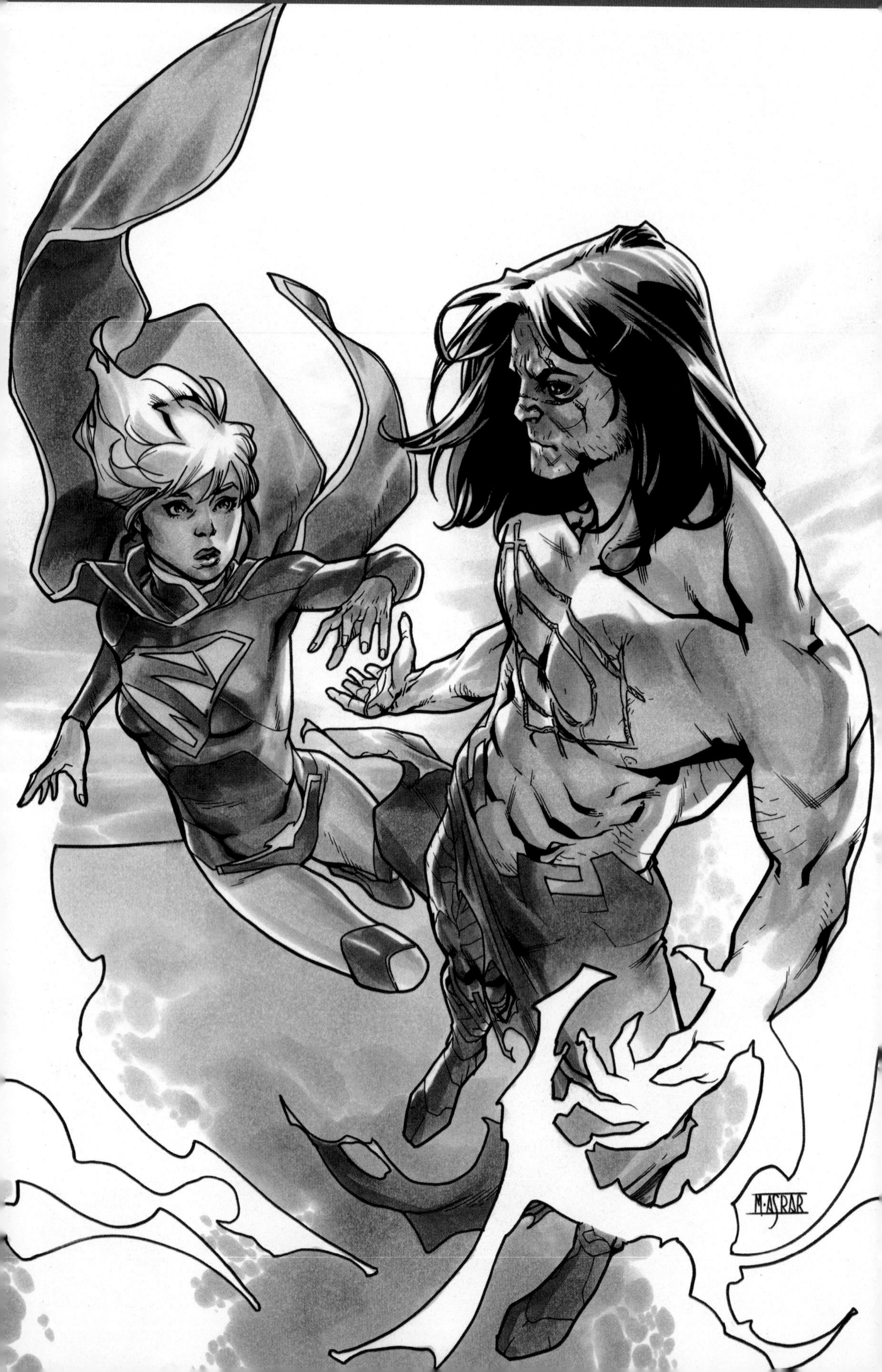
M.ASRAR

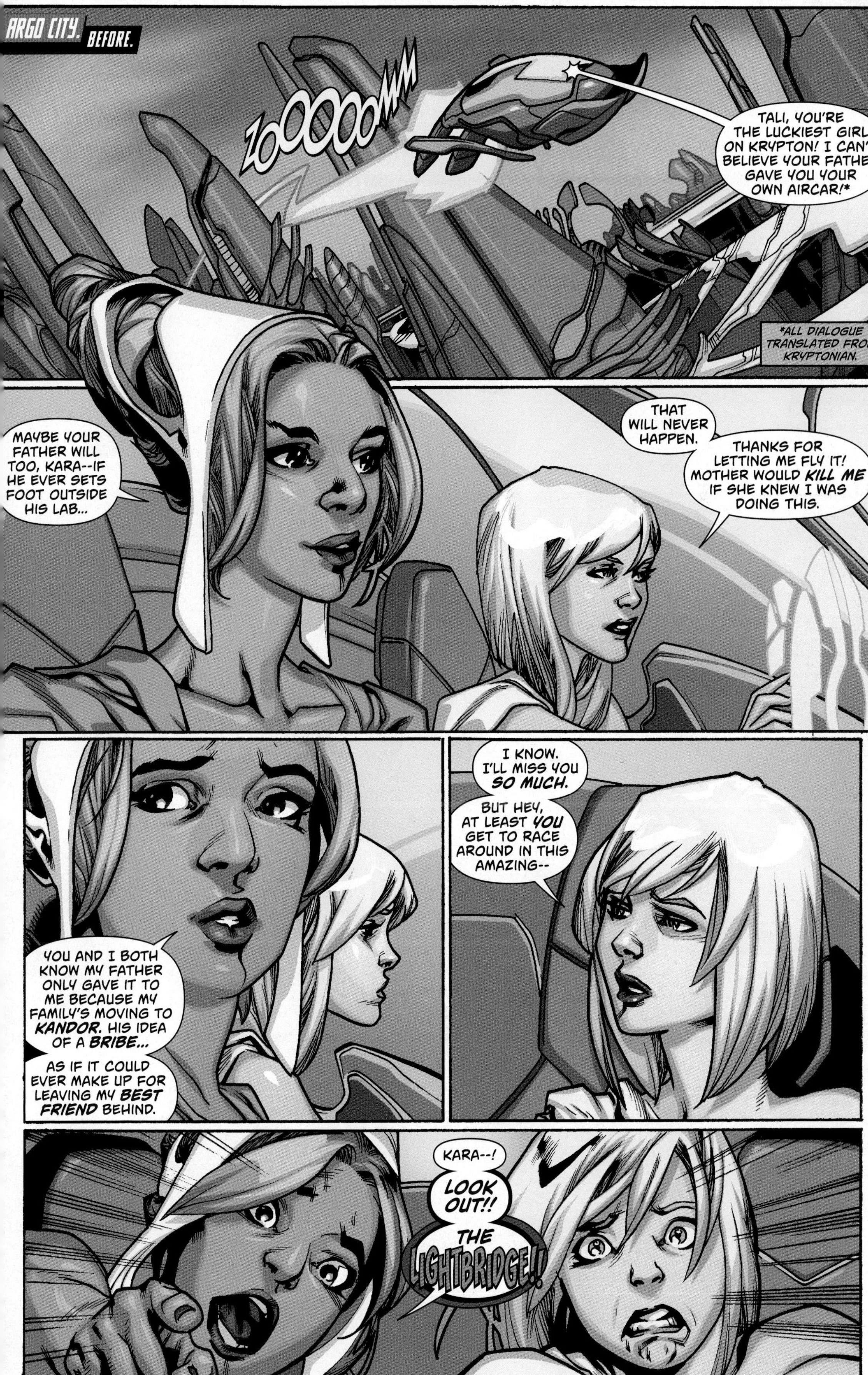
ARGO CITY. BEFORE.
ZOOOOOMM
TALI, YOU'RE THE LUCKIEST GIRL ON KRYPTON! I CAN'T BELIEVE YOUR FATHER GAVE YOU YOUR OWN AIRCAR!*
*ALL DIALOGUE TRANSLATED FROM KRYPTONIAN.
MAYBE YOUR FATHER WILL TOO, KARA--IF HE EVER SETS FOOT OUTSIDE HIS LAB...
THAT WILL NEVER HAPPEN.
THANKS FOR LETTING ME FLY IT! MOTHER WOULD KILL ME IF SHE KNEW I WAS DOING THIS.
YOU AND I BOTH KNOW MY FATHER ONLY GAVE IT TO ME BECAUSE MY FAMILY'S MOVING TO KANDOR. HIS IDEA OF A BRIBE...
AS IF IT COULD EVER MAKE UP FOR LEAVING MY BEST FRIEND BEHIND.
I KNOW. I'LL MISS YOU SO MUCH.
BUT HEY, AT LEAST YOU GET TO RACE AROUND IN THIS AMAZING--
KARA--!
LOOK OUT!!
THE LIGHTBRIDGE!!

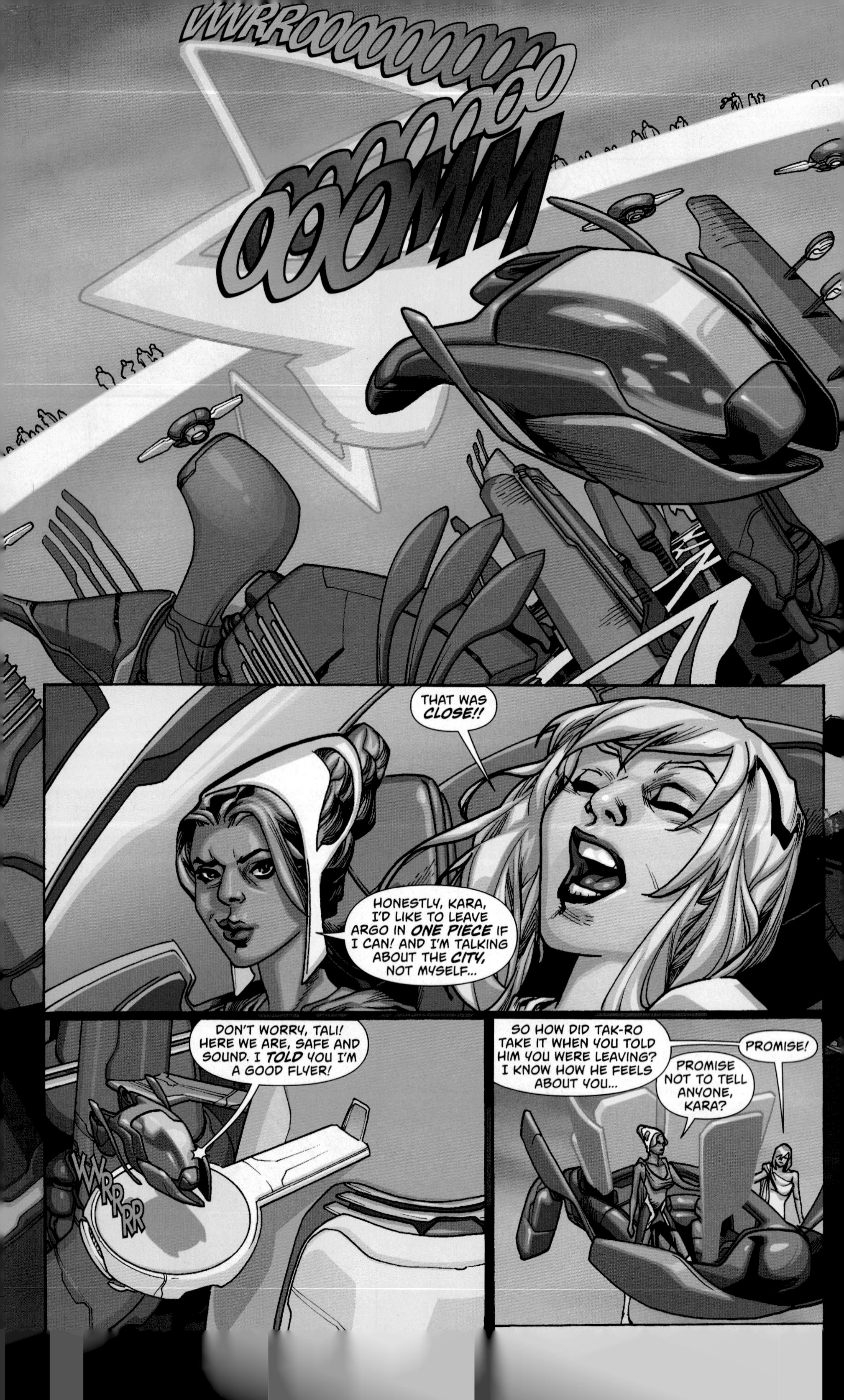
VWRROOOOOOOOOOOOOOOOMM
THAT WAS CLOSE!!
HONESTLY, KARA, I'D LIKE TO LEAVE ARGO IN ONE PIECE IF I CAN! AND I'M TALKING ABOUT THE CITY, NOT MYSELF...
DON'T WORRY, TALI! HERE WE ARE, SAFE AND SOUND. I TOLD YOU I'M A GOOD FLYER!
VWRRRR
SO HOW DID TAK-RO TAKE IT WHEN YOU TOLD HIM YOU WERE LEAVING? I KNOW HOW HE FEELS ABOUT YOU...
PROMISE NOT TO TELL ANYONE, KARA?
PROMISE!

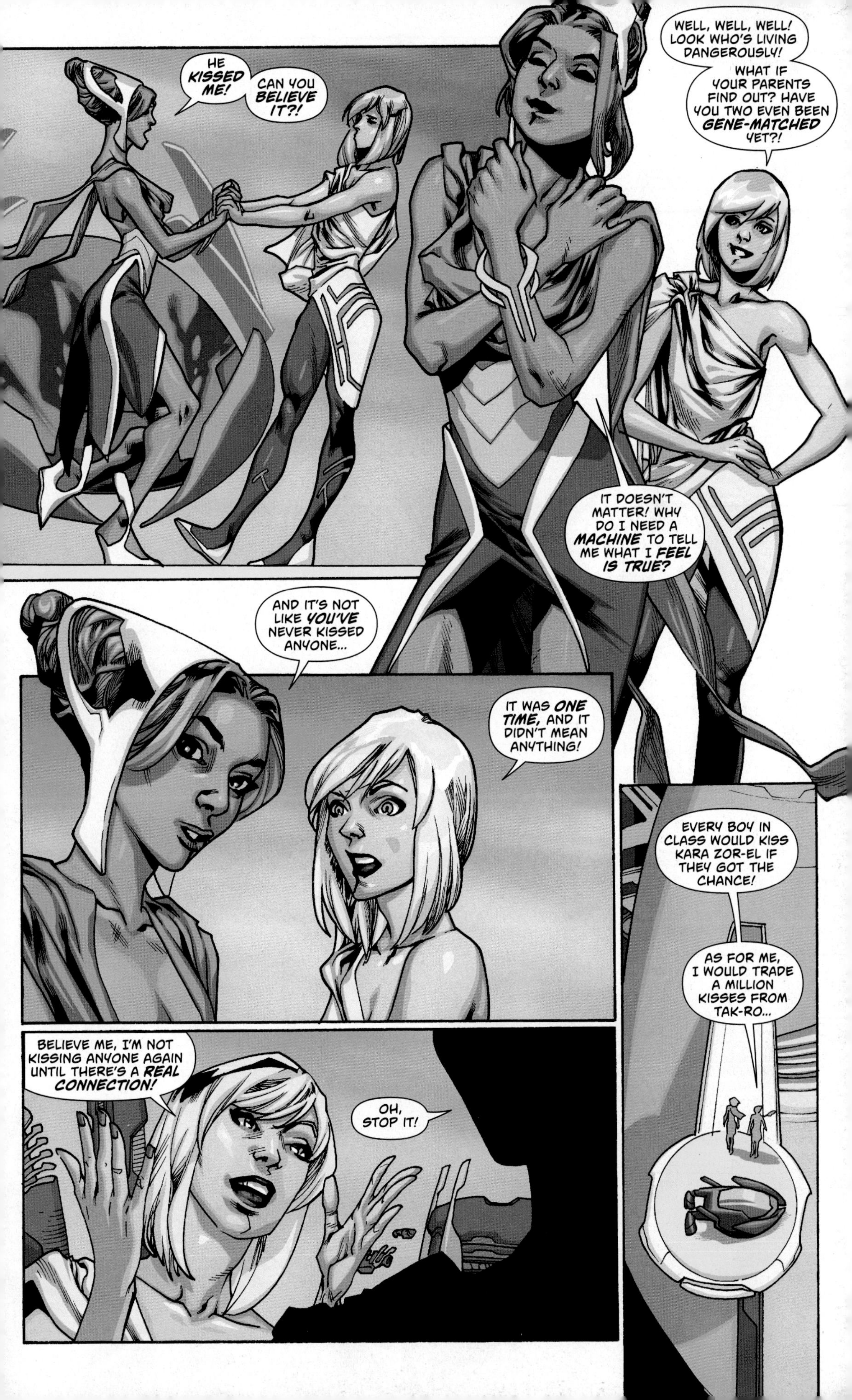
HE *KISSED* ME!
CAN YOU *BELIEVE* IT?!
WELL, WELL, WELL! LOOK WHO'S LIVING DANGEROUSLY!
WHAT IF YOUR PARENTS FIND OUT? HAVE YOU TWO EVEN BEEN *GENE-MATCHED* YET?!
IT DOESN'T MATTER! WHY DO I NEED A *MACHINE* TO TELL ME WHAT I *FEEL IS TRUE?*
AND IT'S NOT LIKE *YOU'VE* NEVER KISSED ANYONE...
IT WAS *ONE TIME,* AND IT DIDN'T MEAN ANYTHING!
EVERY BOY IN CLASS WOULD KISS KARA ZOR-EL IF THEY GOT THE CHANCE!
AS FOR ME, I WOULD TRADE A MILLION KISSES FROM TAK-RO...
BELIEVE ME, I'M NOT KISSING ANYONE AGAIN UNTIL THERE'S A *REAL CONNECTION!*
OH, STOP IT!

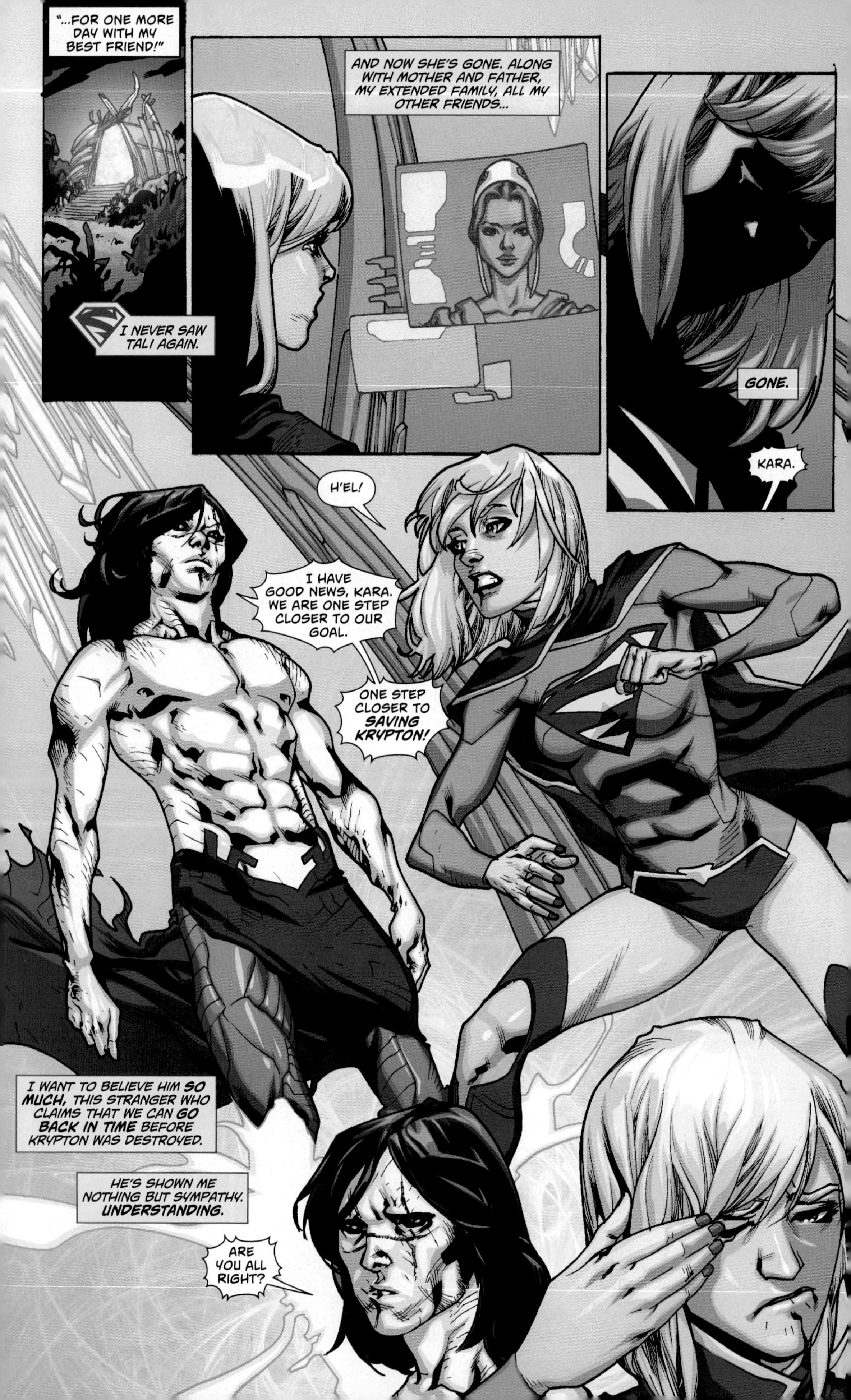
"...FOR ONE MORE DAY WITH MY BEST FRIEND!"
I NEVER SAW TALI AGAIN.
AND NOW SHE'S GONE. ALONG WITH MOTHER AND FATHER, MY EXTENDED FAMILY, ALL MY OTHER FRIENDS...
GONE.
KARA.
H'EL!
I HAVE GOOD NEWS, KARA. WE ARE ONE STEP CLOSER TO OUR GOAL.
ONE STEP CLOSER TO SAVING KRYPTON!
I WANT TO BELIEVE HIM SO MUCH, THIS STRANGER WHO CLAIMS THAT WE CAN GO BACK IN TIME BEFORE KRYPTON WAS DESTROYED.
HE'S SHOWN ME NOTHING BUT SYMPATHY. UNDERSTANDING.
ARE YOU ALL RIGHT?

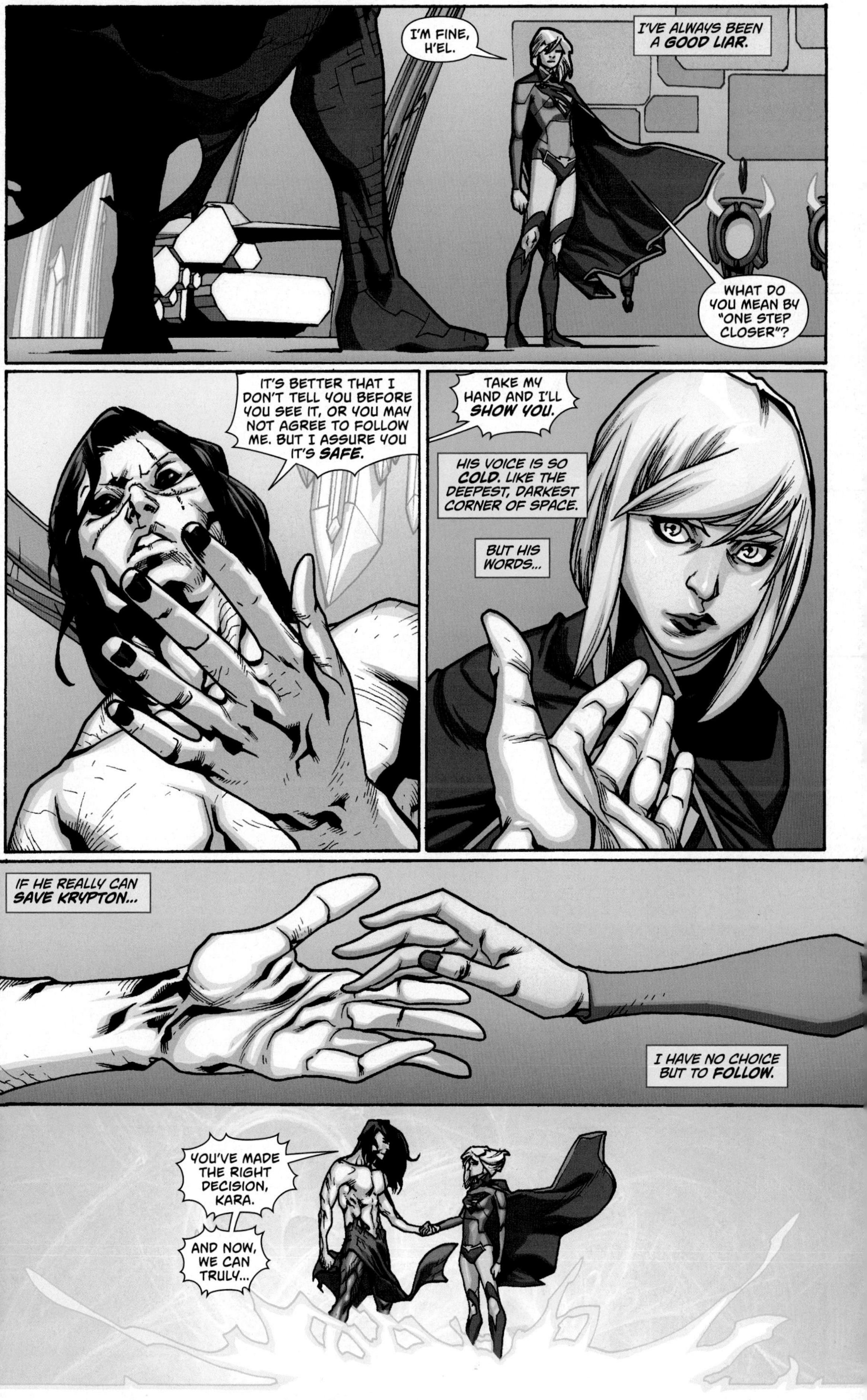
I'M FINE, H'EL.
I'VE ALWAYS BEEN A GOOD LIAR.
WHAT DO YOU MEAN BY "ONE STEP CLOSER"?
IT'S BETTER THAT I DON'T TELL YOU BEFORE YOU SEE IT, OR YOU MAY NOT AGREE TO FOLLOW ME. BUT I ASSURE YOU IT'S SAFE.
TAKE MY HAND AND I'LL SHOW YOU.
HIS VOICE IS SO COLD. LIKE THE DEEPEST, DARKEST CORNER OF SPACE.
BUT HIS WORDS...
IF HE REALLY CAN SAVE KRYPTON...
I HAVE NO CHOICE BUT TO FOLLOW.
YOU'VE MADE THE RIGHT DECISION, KARA.
AND NOW, WE CAN TRULY...

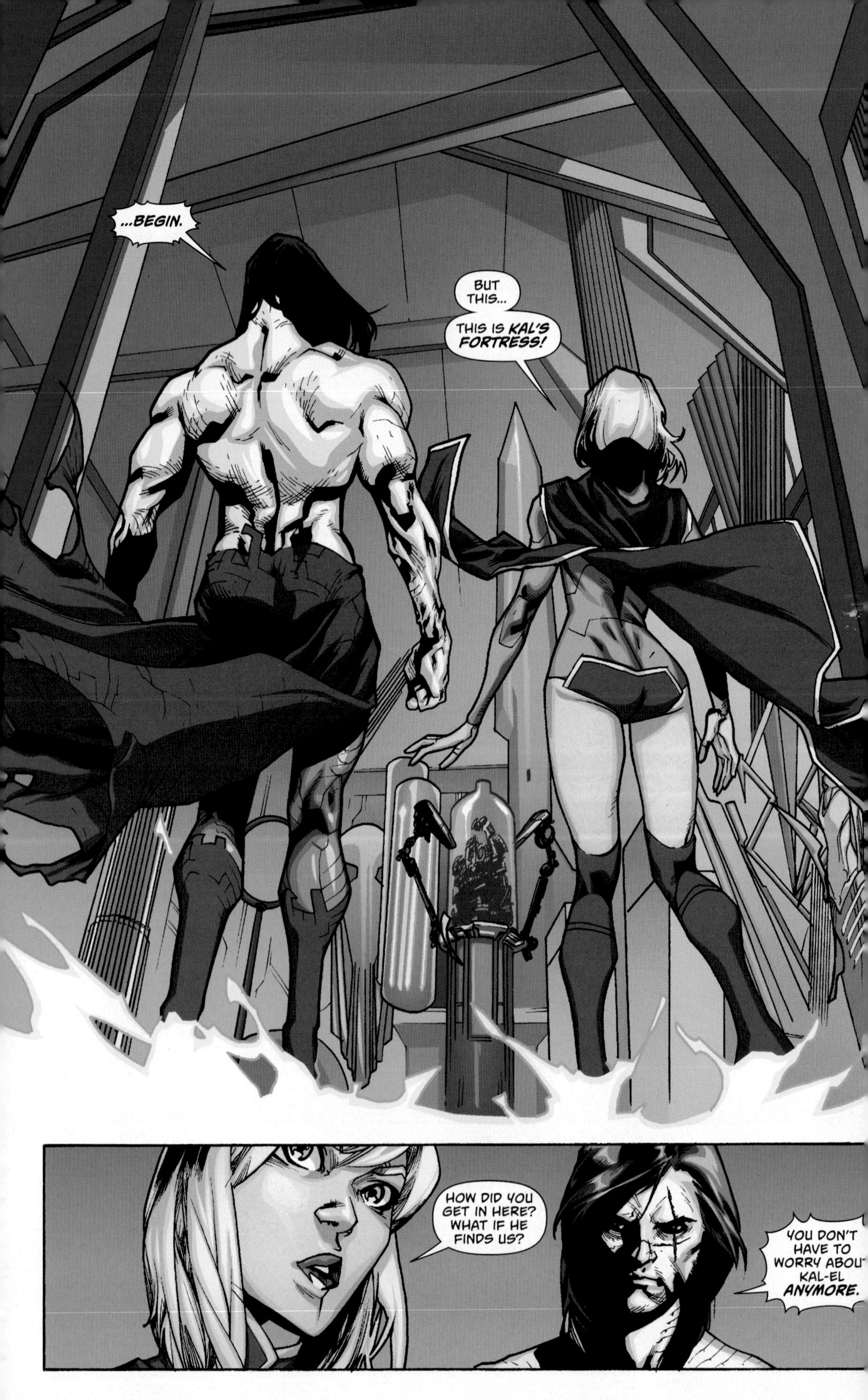
...BEGIN.
BUT THIS...
THIS IS KAL'S FORTRESS!
HOW DID YOU GET IN HERE? WHAT IF HE FINDS US?
YOU DON'T HAVE TO WORRY ABOUT KAL-EL ANYMORE.

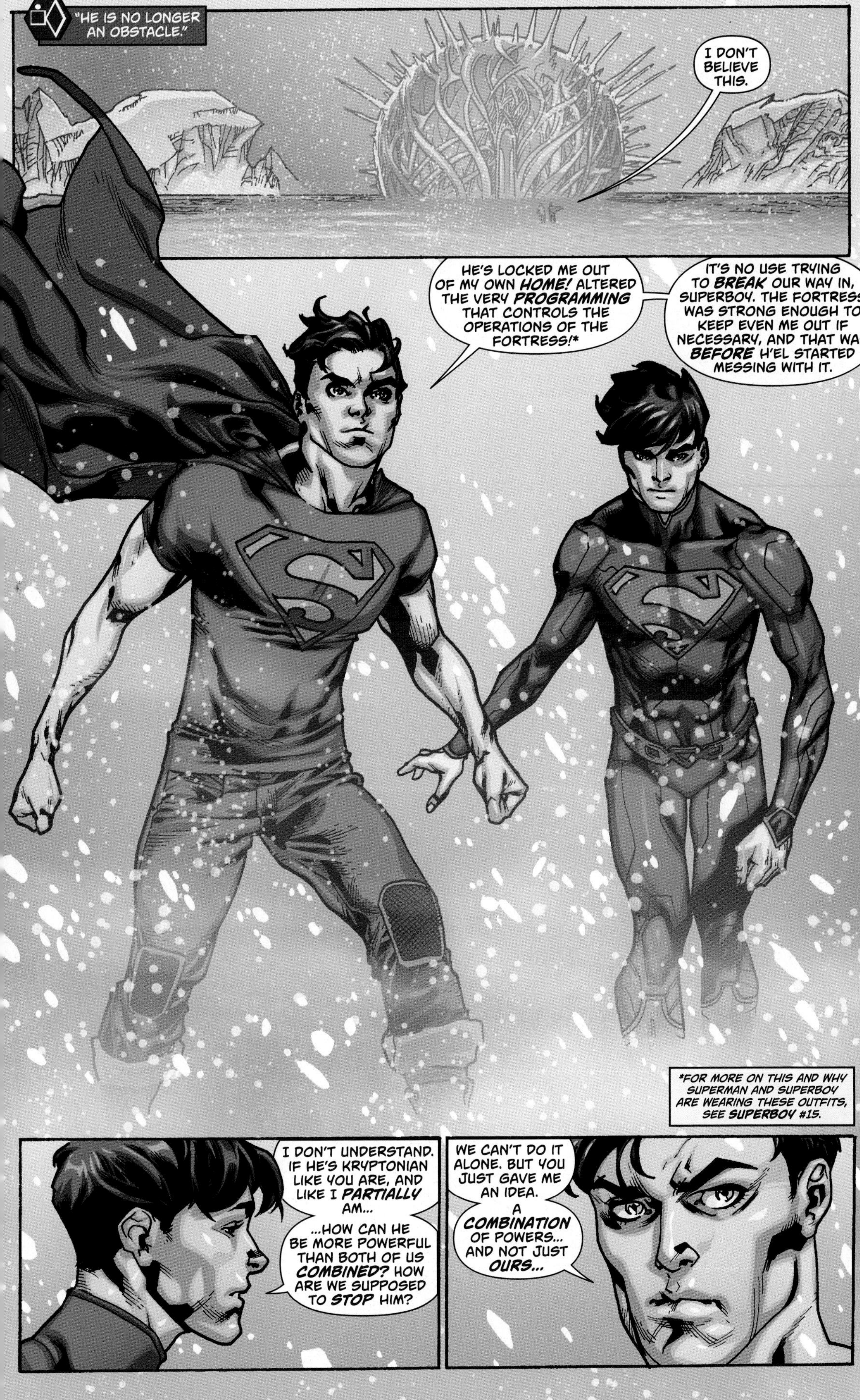
"HE IS NO LONGER AN OBSTACLE."
I DON'T BELIEVE THIS.
HE'S LOCKED ME OUT OF MY OWN HOME! ALTERED THE VERY PROGRAMMING THAT CONTROLS THE OPERATIONS OF THE FORTRESS!*
IT'S NO USE TRYING TO BREAK OUR WAY IN, SUPERBOY. THE FORTRESS WAS STRONG ENOUGH TO KEEP EVEN ME OUT IF NECESSARY, AND THAT WAS BEFORE H'EL STARTED MESSING WITH IT.
*FOR MORE ON THIS AND WHY SUPERMAN AND SUPERBOY ARE WEARING THESE OUTFITS, SEE SUPERBOY #15.
I DON'T UNDERSTAND. IF HE'S KRYPTONIAN LIKE YOU ARE, AND LIKE I PARTIALLY AM...
...HOW CAN HE BE MORE POWERFUL THAN BOTH OF US COMBINED? HOW ARE WE SUPPOSED TO STOP HIM?
WE CAN'T DO IT ALONE. BUT YOU JUST GAVE ME AN IDEA.
A COMBINATION OF POWERS... AND NOT JUST OURS...

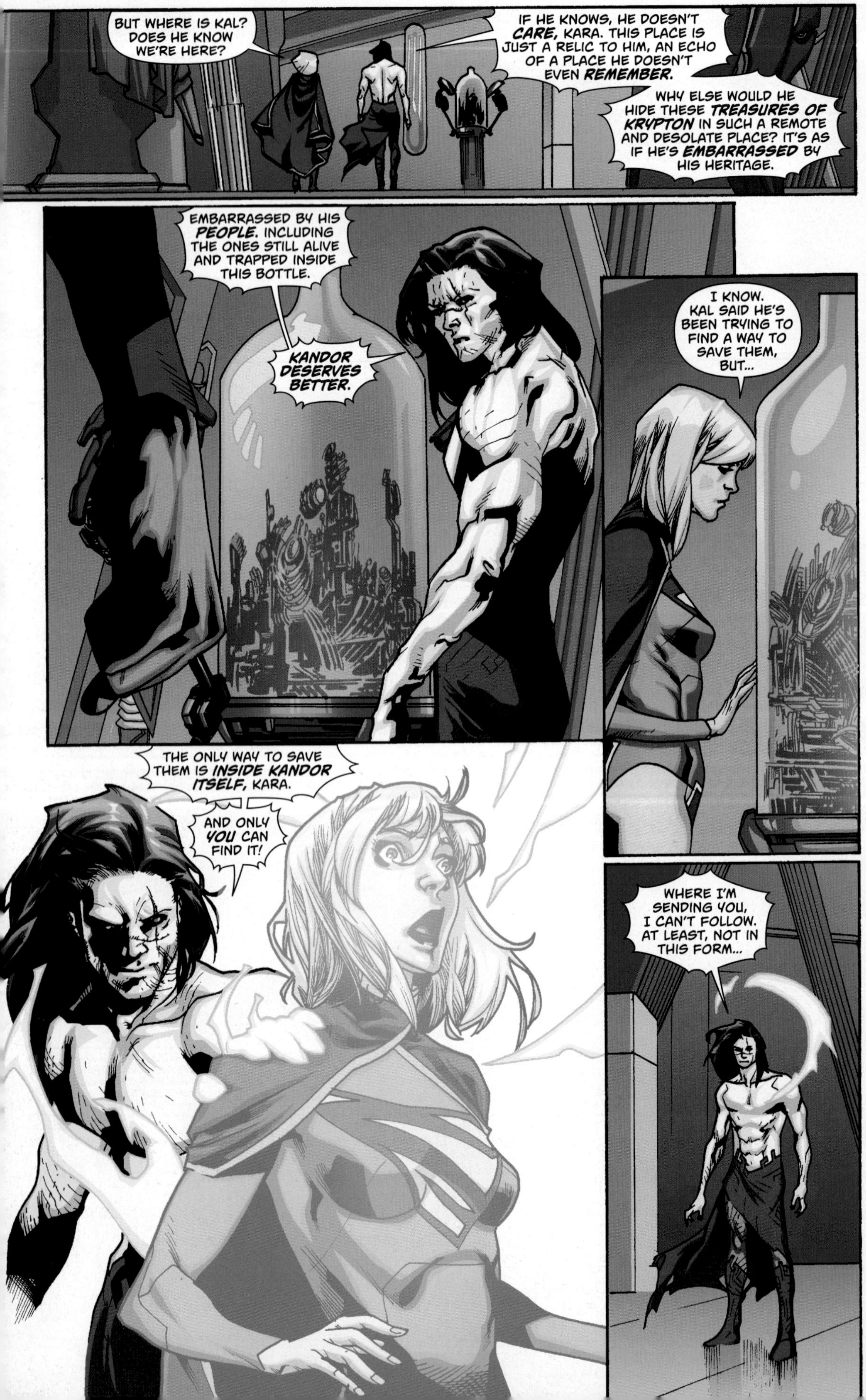
BUT WHERE IS KAL? DOES HE KNOW WE'RE HERE?
IF HE KNOWS, HE DOESN'T CARE, KARA. THIS PLACE IS JUST A RELIC TO HIM, AN ECHO OF A PLACE HE DOESN'T EVEN REMEMBER.
WHY ELSE WOULD HE HIDE THESE TREASURES OF KRYPTON IN SUCH A REMOTE AND DESOLATE PLACE? IT'S AS IF HE'S EMBARRASSED BY HIS HERITAGE.
EMBARRASSED BY HIS PEOPLE. INCLUDING THE ONES STILL ALIVE AND TRAPPED INSIDE THIS BOTTLE.
KANDOR DESERVES BETTER.
I KNOW. KAL SAID HE'S BEEN TRYING TO FIND A WAY TO SAVE THEM, BUT...
THE ONLY WAY TO SAVE THEM IS INSIDE KANDOR ITSELF, KARA.
AND ONLY YOU CAN FIND IT!
WHERE I'M SENDING YOU, I CAN'T FOLLOW. AT LEAST, NOT IN THIS FORM...

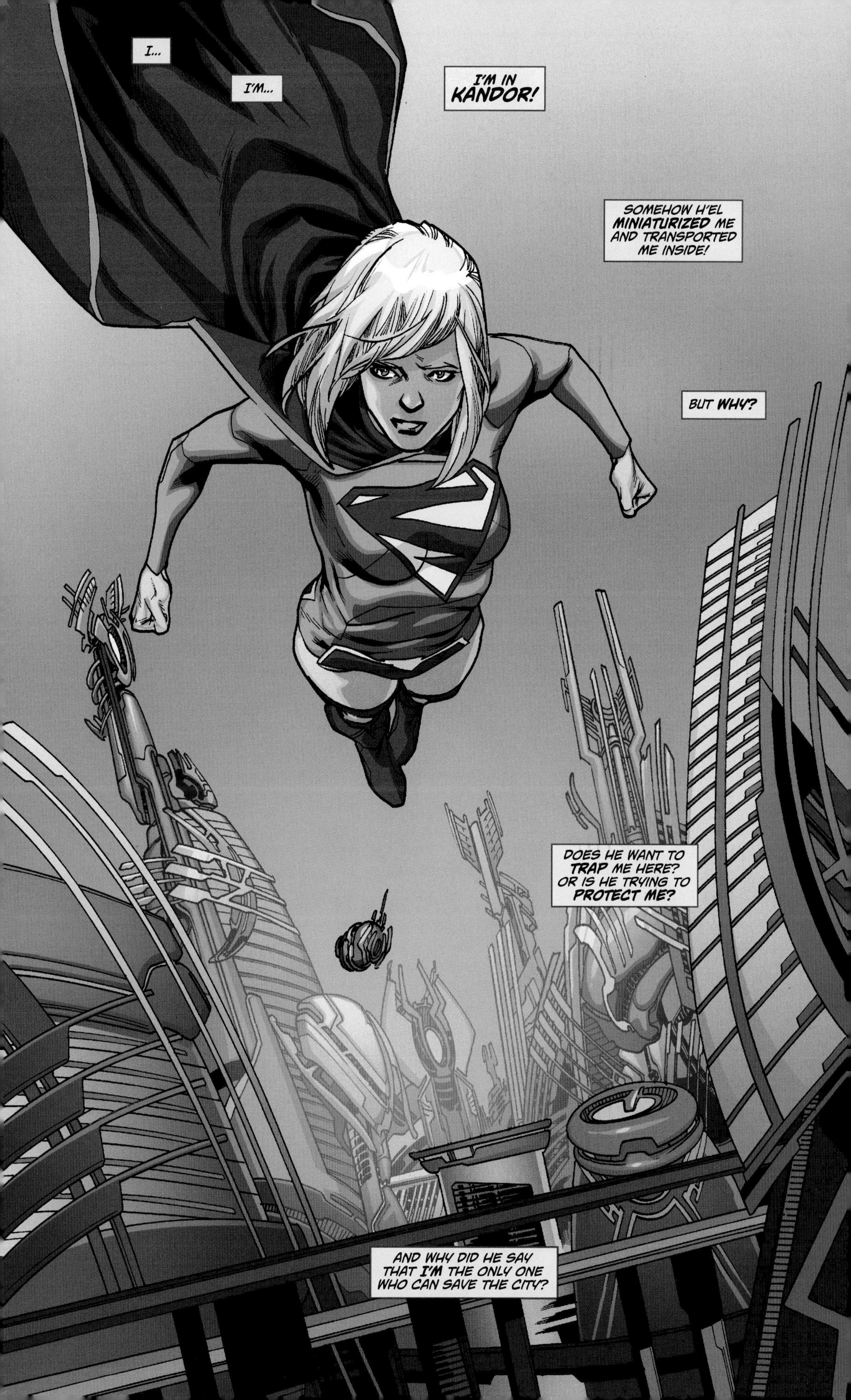
I...
I'M...
I'M IN KANDOR!
SOMEHOW H'EL MINIATURIZED ME AND TRANSPORTED ME INSIDE!
BUT WHY?
DOES HE WANT TO TRAP ME HERE? OR IS HE TRYING TO PROTECT ME?
AND WHY DID HE SAY THAT I'M THE ONLY ONE WHO CAN SAVE THE CITY?

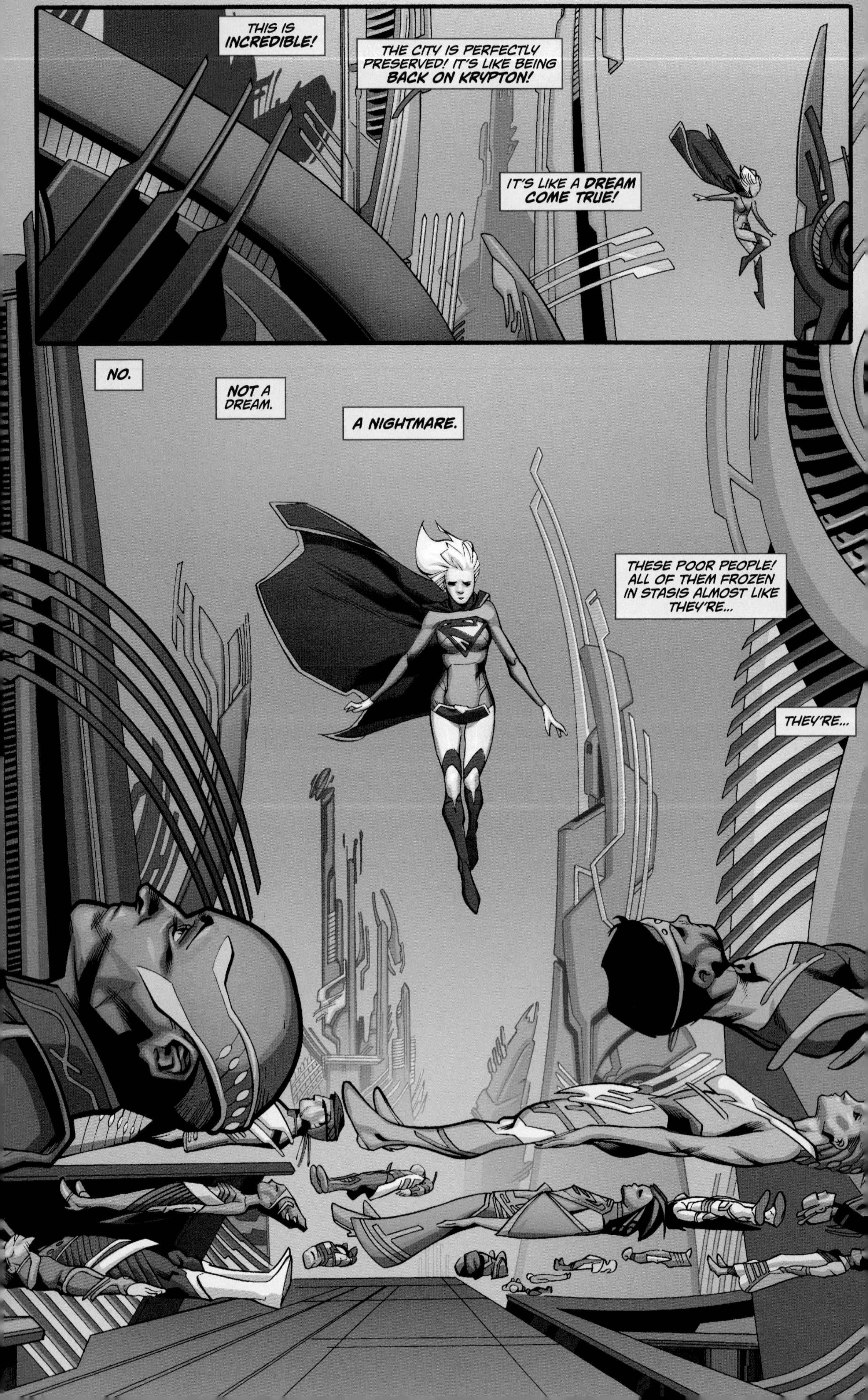
THIS IS INCREDIBLE!
THE CITY IS PERFECTLY PRESERVED! IT'S LIKE BEING BACK ON KRYPTON!
IT'S LIKE A DREAM COME TRUE!
NO.
NOT A DREAM.
A NIGHTMARE.
THESE POOR PEOPLE! ALL OF THEM FROZEN IN STASIS ALMOST LIKE THEY'RE...
THEY'RE...

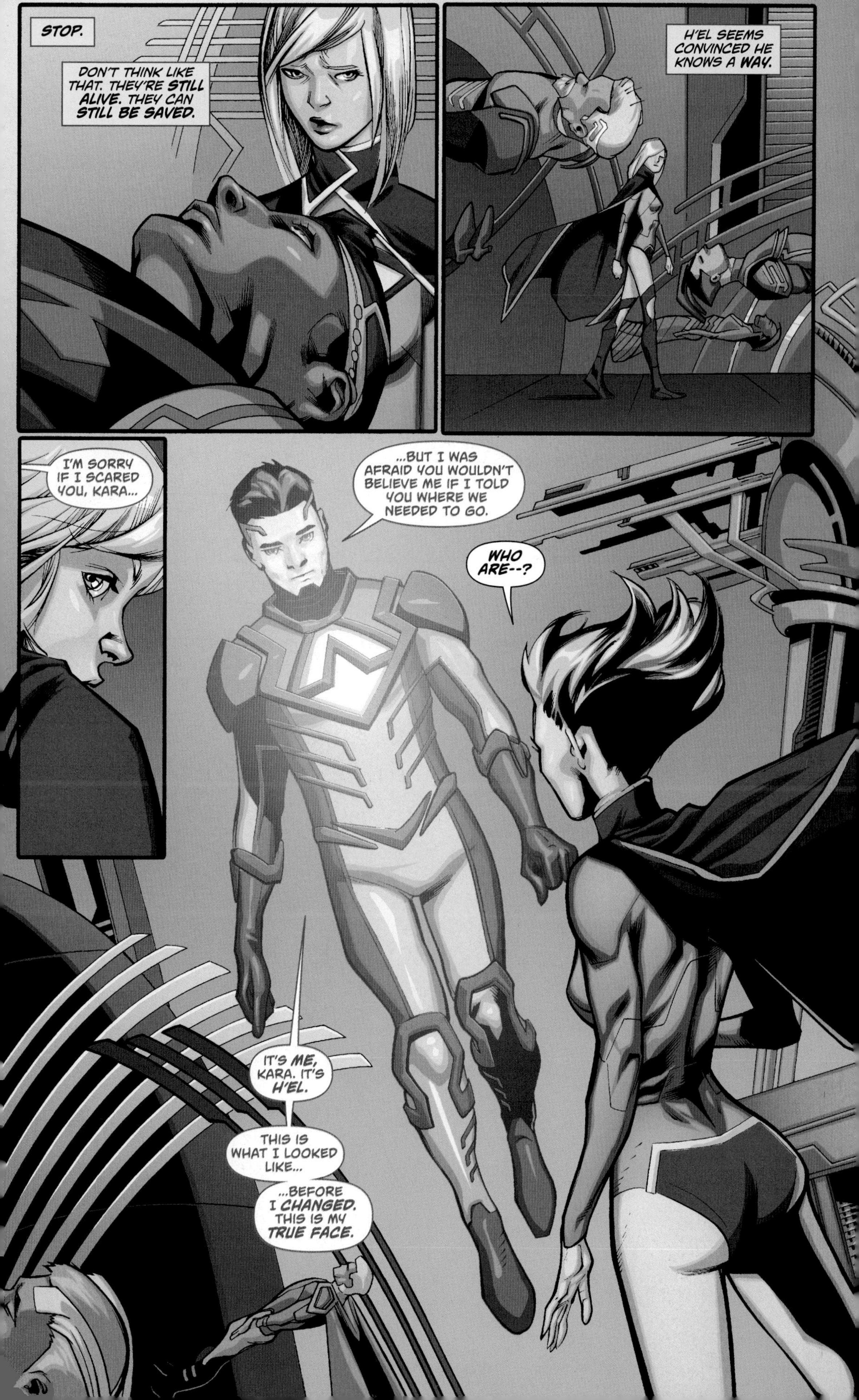
STOP.
DON'T THINK LIKE THAT. THEY'RE STILL ALIVE. THEY CAN STILL BE SAVED.
H'EL SEEMS CONVINCED HE KNOWS A WAY.
I'M SORRY IF I SCARED YOU, KARA...
...BUT I WAS AFRAID YOU WOULDN'T BELIEVE ME IF I TOLD YOU WHERE WE NEEDED TO GO.
WHO ARE--?
IT'S ME, KARA. IT'S H'EL.
THIS IS WHAT I LOOKED LIKE...
...BEFORE I CHANGED. THIS IS MY TRUE FACE.

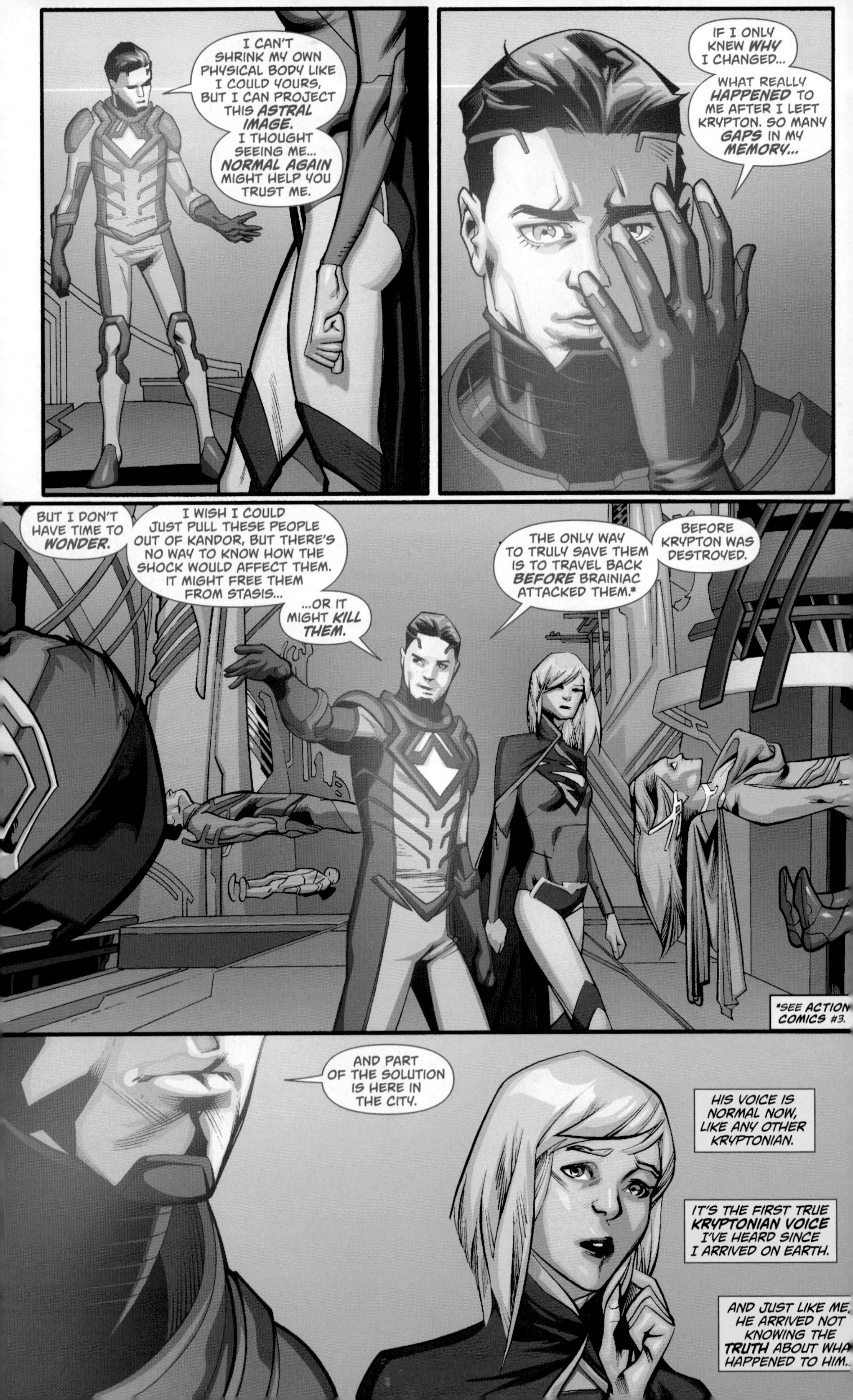

I CAN'T SHRINK MY OWN PHYSICAL BODY LIKE I COULD YOURS, BUT I CAN PROJECT THIS ASTRAL IMAGE.
I THOUGHT SEEING ME... NORMAL AGAIN MIGHT HELP YOU TRUST ME.
IF I ONLY KNEW WHY I CHANGED...
WHAT REALLY HAPPENED TO ME AFTER I LEFT KRYPTON. SO MANY GAPS IN MY MEMORY...
BUT I DON'T HAVE TIME TO WONDER.
I WISH I COULD JUST PULL THESE PEOPLE OUT OF KANDOR, BUT THERE'S NO WAY TO KNOW HOW THE SHOCK WOULD AFFECT THEM. IT MIGHT FREE THEM FROM STASIS...
...OR IT MIGHT KILL THEM.
THE ONLY WAY TO TRULY SAVE THEM IS TO TRAVEL BACK BEFORE BRAINIAC ATTACKED THEM.*
BEFORE KRYPTON WAS DESTROYED.
*SEE ACTION COMICS #3.
AND PART OF THE SOLUTION IS HERE IN THE CITY.
HIS VOICE IS NORMAL NOW, LIKE ANY OTHER KRYPTONIAN.
IT'S THE FIRST TRUE KRYPTONIAN VOICE I'VE HEARD SINCE I ARRIVED ON EARTH.
AND JUST LIKE ME, HE ARRIVED NOT KNOWING THE TRUTH ABOUT WHA HAPPENED TO HIM.

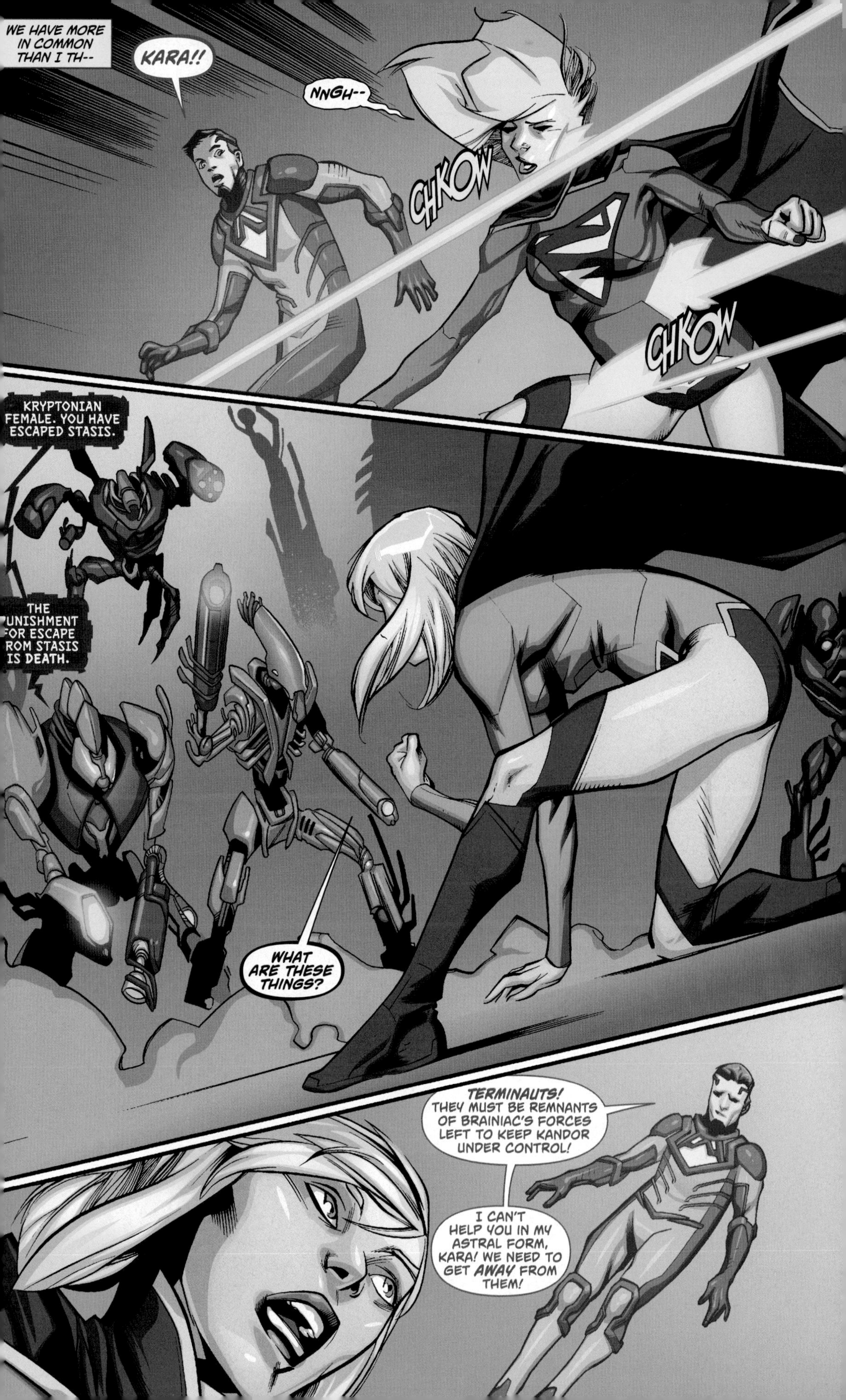
WE HAVE MORE IN COMMON THAN I TH--
KARA!!
NNGH--
CHKOW
CHKOW
KRYPTONIAN FEMALE. YOU HAVE ESCAPED STASIS.
THE UNISHMENT FOR ESCAPE ROM STASIS IS DEATH.
WHAT ARE THESE THINGS?
TERMINAUTS! THEY MUST BE REMNANTS OF BRAINIAC'S FORCES LEFT TO KEEP KANDOR UNDER CONTROL!
I CAN'T HELP YOU IN MY ASTRAL FORM, KARA! WE NEED TO GET AWAY FROM THEM!

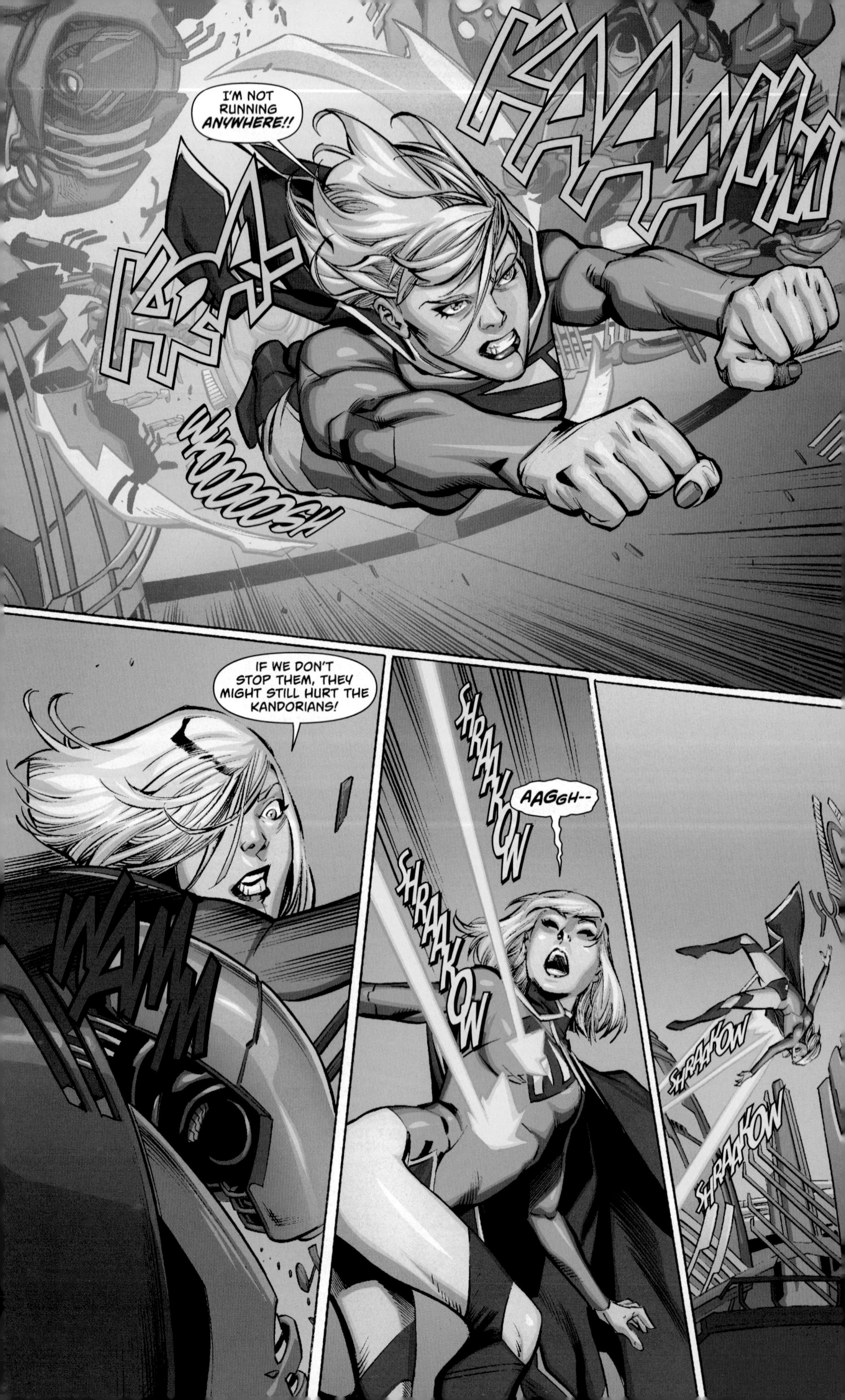
I'M NOT RUNNING ANYWHERE!!
KAAAMM
KRAK
WHOOOOOSH
IF WE DON'T STOP THEM, THEY MIGHT STILL HURT THE KANDORIANS!
WAMM
SHRAAAKOW
AAGGH--
SHRAAAKOW
SHRAAKOW
SHRAAKOW
SHRAAKOW

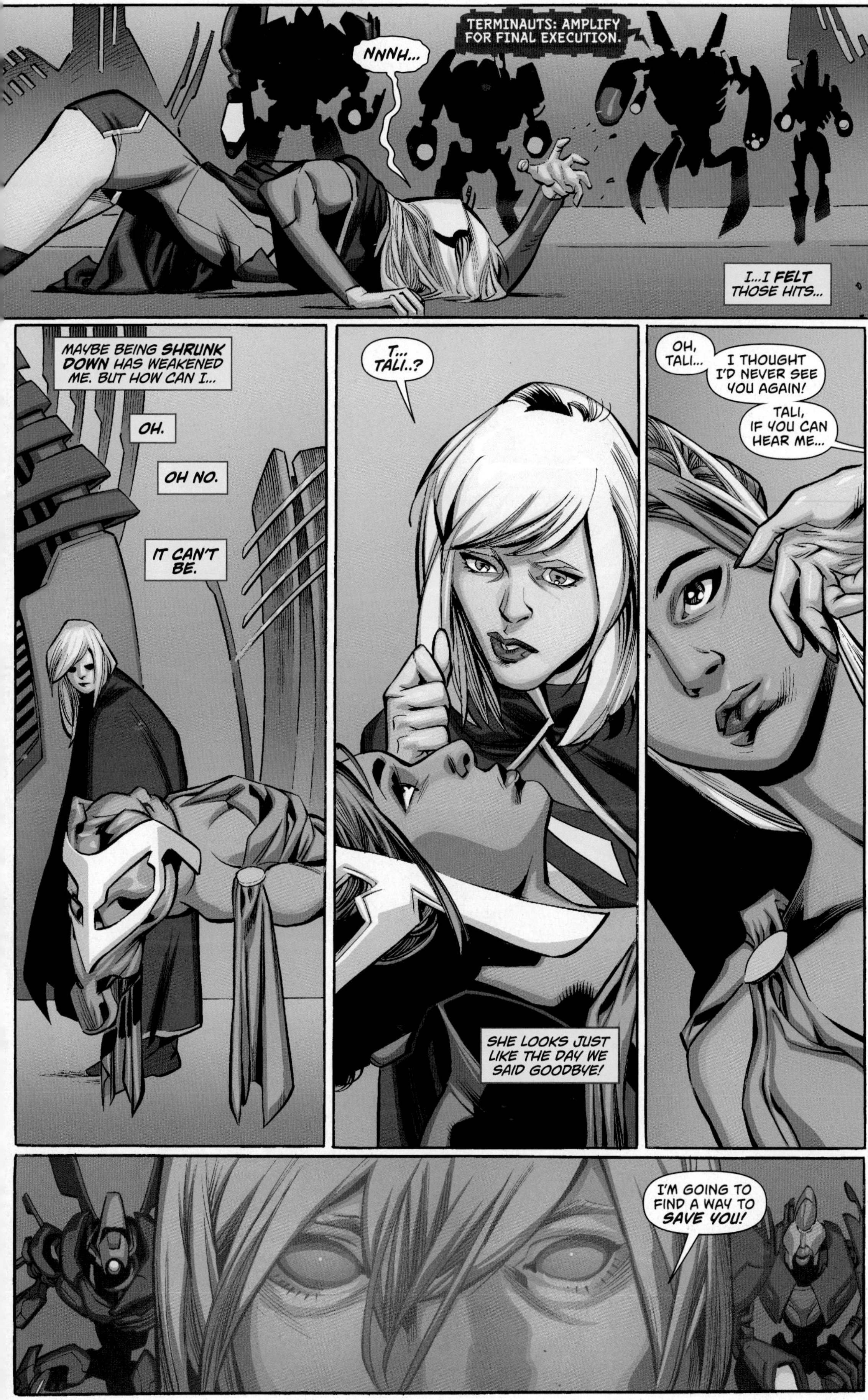
TERMINAUTS: AMPLIFY FOR FINAL EXECUTION.
NNNH...
I...I FELT THOSE HITS...
MAYBE BEING SHRUNK DOWN HAS WEAKENED ME. BUT HOW CAN I...
OH.
OH NO.
IT CAN'T BE.
T... TALI..?
SHE LOOKS JUST LIKE THE DAY WE SAID GOODBYE!
OH, TALI...
I THOUGHT I'D NEVER SEE YOU AGAIN!
TALI, IF YOU CAN HEAR ME...
I'M GOING TO FIND A WAY TO SAVE YOU!

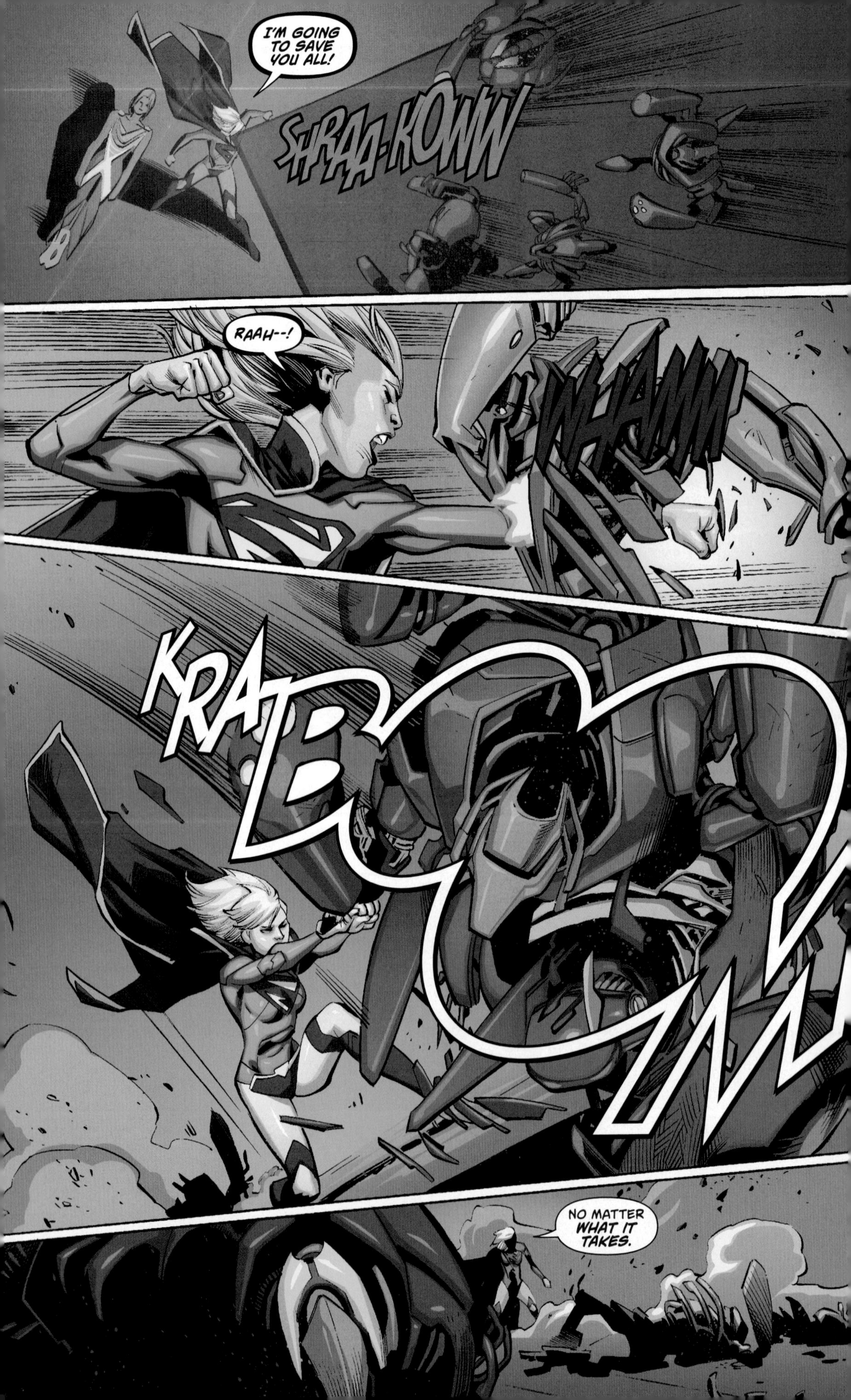
I'M GOING TO SAVE YOU ALL!
SHRAA-KOWW
RAAH--!
WHAMM
KRA-BOOM
NO MATTER WHAT IT TAKES.

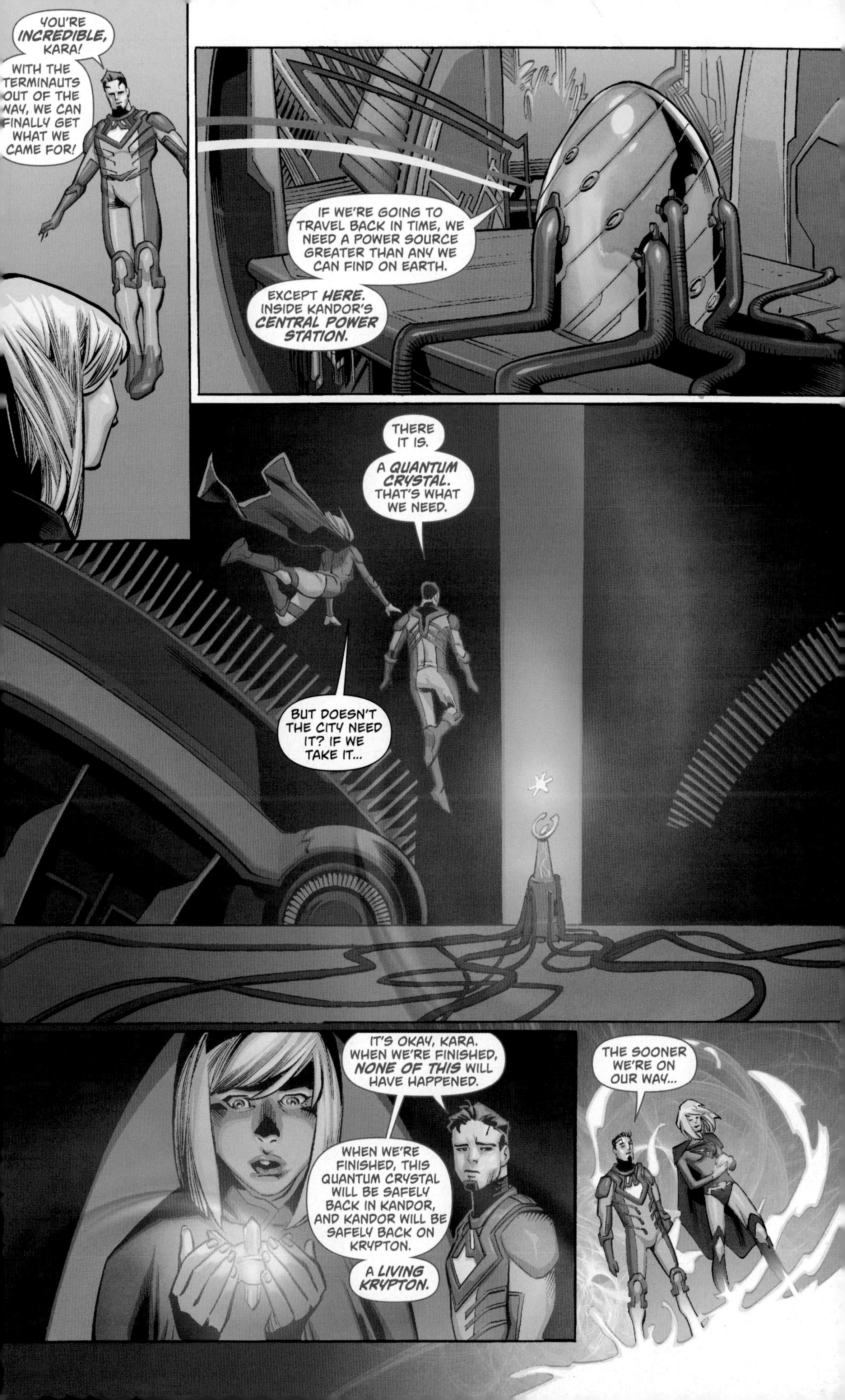
YOU'RE INCREDIBLE, KARA!
WITH THE TERMINAUTS OUT OF THE WAY, WE CAN FINALLY GET WHAT WE CAME FOR!
IF WE'RE GOING TO TRAVEL BACK IN TIME, WE NEED A POWER SOURCE GREATER THAN ANY WE CAN FIND ON EARTH.
EXCEPT HERE. INSIDE KANDOR'S CENTRAL POWER STATION.
THERE IT IS.
A QUANTUM CRYSTAL. THAT'S WHAT WE NEED.
BUT DOESN'T THE CITY NEED IT? IF WE TAKE IT...
IT'S OKAY, KARA. WHEN WE'RE FINISHED, NONE OF THIS WILL HAVE HAPPENED.
WHEN WE'RE FINISHED, THIS QUANTUM CRYSTAL WILL BE SAFELY BACK IN KANDOR, AND KANDOR WILL BE SAFELY BACK ON KRYPTON.
A LIVING KRYPTON.
THE SOONER WE'RE ON OUR WAY...

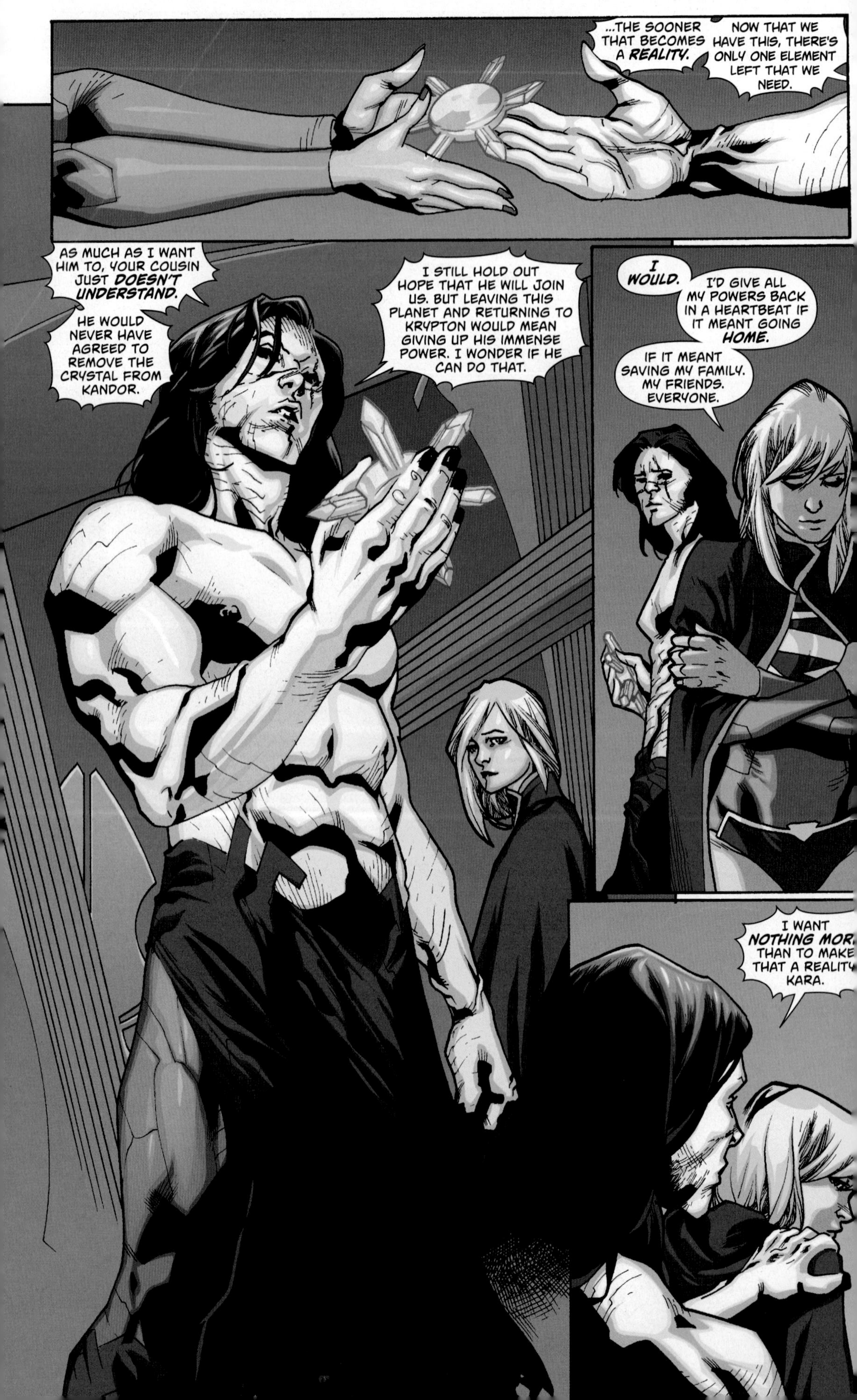
...THE SOONER THAT BECOMES A REALITY.
NOW THAT WE HAVE THIS, THERE'S ONLY ONE ELEMENT LEFT THAT WE NEED.
AS MUCH AS I WANT HIM TO, YOUR COUSIN JUST DOESN'T UNDERSTAND.
HE WOULD NEVER HAVE AGREED TO REMOVE THE CRYSTAL FROM KANDOR.
I STILL HOLD OUT HOPE THAT HE WILL JOIN US. BUT LEAVING THIS PLANET AND RETURNING TO KRYPTON WOULD MEAN GIVING UP HIS IMMENSE POWER. I WONDER IF HE CAN DO THAT.
I WOULD.
I'D GIVE ALL MY POWERS BACK IN A HEARTBEAT IF IT MEANT GOING HOME.
IF IT MEANT SAVING MY FAMILY. MY FRIENDS. EVERYONE.
I WANT NOTHING MOR THAN TO MAKE THAT A REALITY KARA.

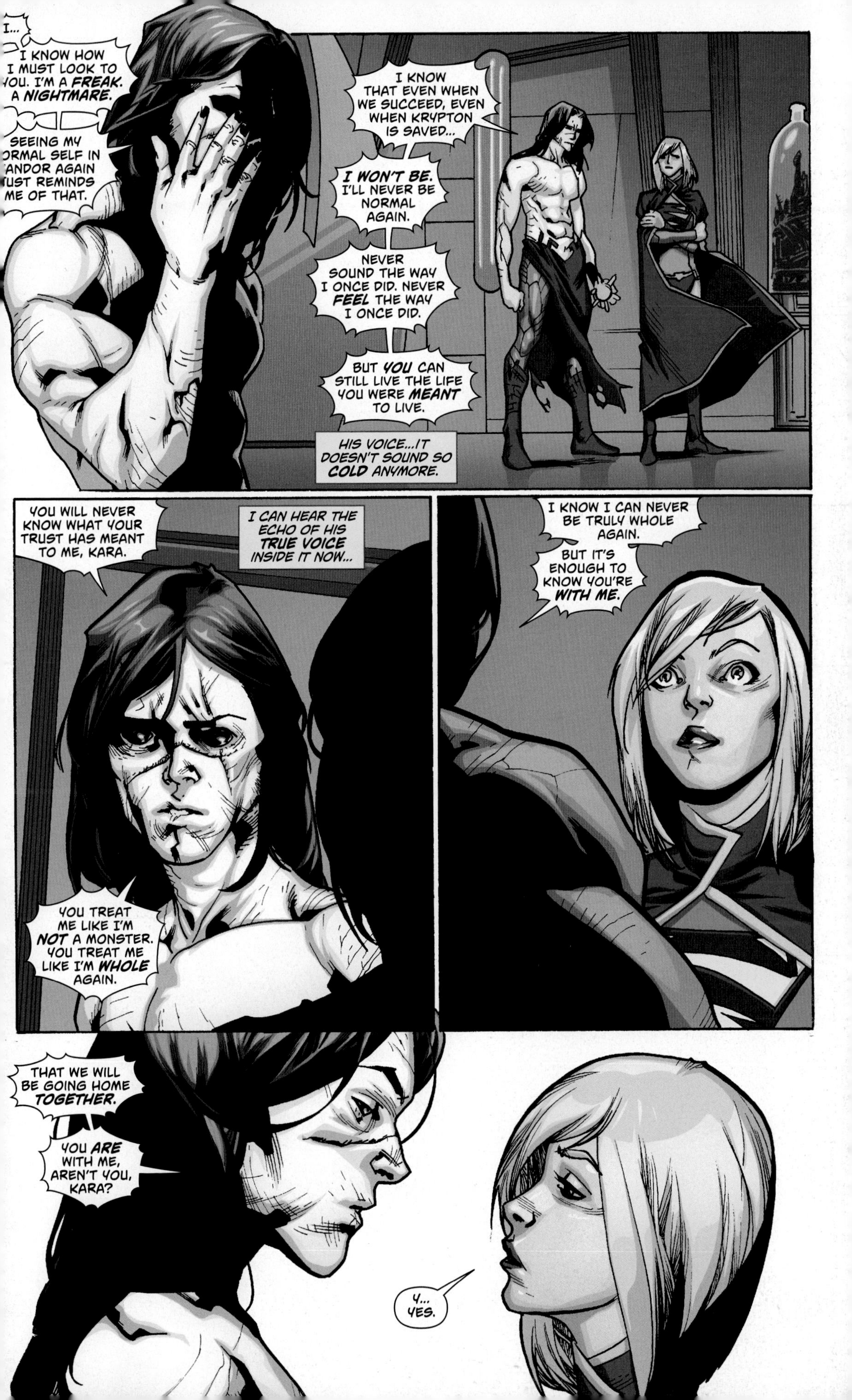

I...
I KNOW HOW I MUST LOOK TO YOU. I'M A FREAK. A NIGHTMARE.
SEEING MY NORMAL SELF IN KANDOR AGAIN JUST REMINDS ME OF THAT.
I KNOW THAT EVEN WHEN WE SUCCEED, EVEN WHEN KRYPTON IS SAVED...
I WON'T BE. I'LL NEVER BE NORMAL AGAIN.
NEVER SOUND THE WAY I ONCE DID. NEVER FEEL THE WAY I ONCE DID.
BUT YOU CAN STILL LIVE THE LIFE YOU WERE MEANT TO LIVE.
HIS VOICE...IT DOESN'T SOUND SO COLD ANYMORE.
YOU WILL NEVER KNOW WHAT YOUR TRUST HAS MEANT TO ME, KARA.
I CAN HEAR THE ECHO OF HIS TRUE VOICE INSIDE IT NOW...
YOU TREAT ME LIKE I'M NOT A MONSTER. YOU TREAT ME LIKE I'M WHOLE AGAIN.
I KNOW I CAN NEVER BE TRULY WHOLE AGAIN.
BUT IT'S ENOUGH TO KNOW YOU'RE WITH ME.
THAT WE WILL BE GOING HOME TOGETHER.
YOU ARE WITH ME, AREN'T YOU, KARA?
Y... YES.

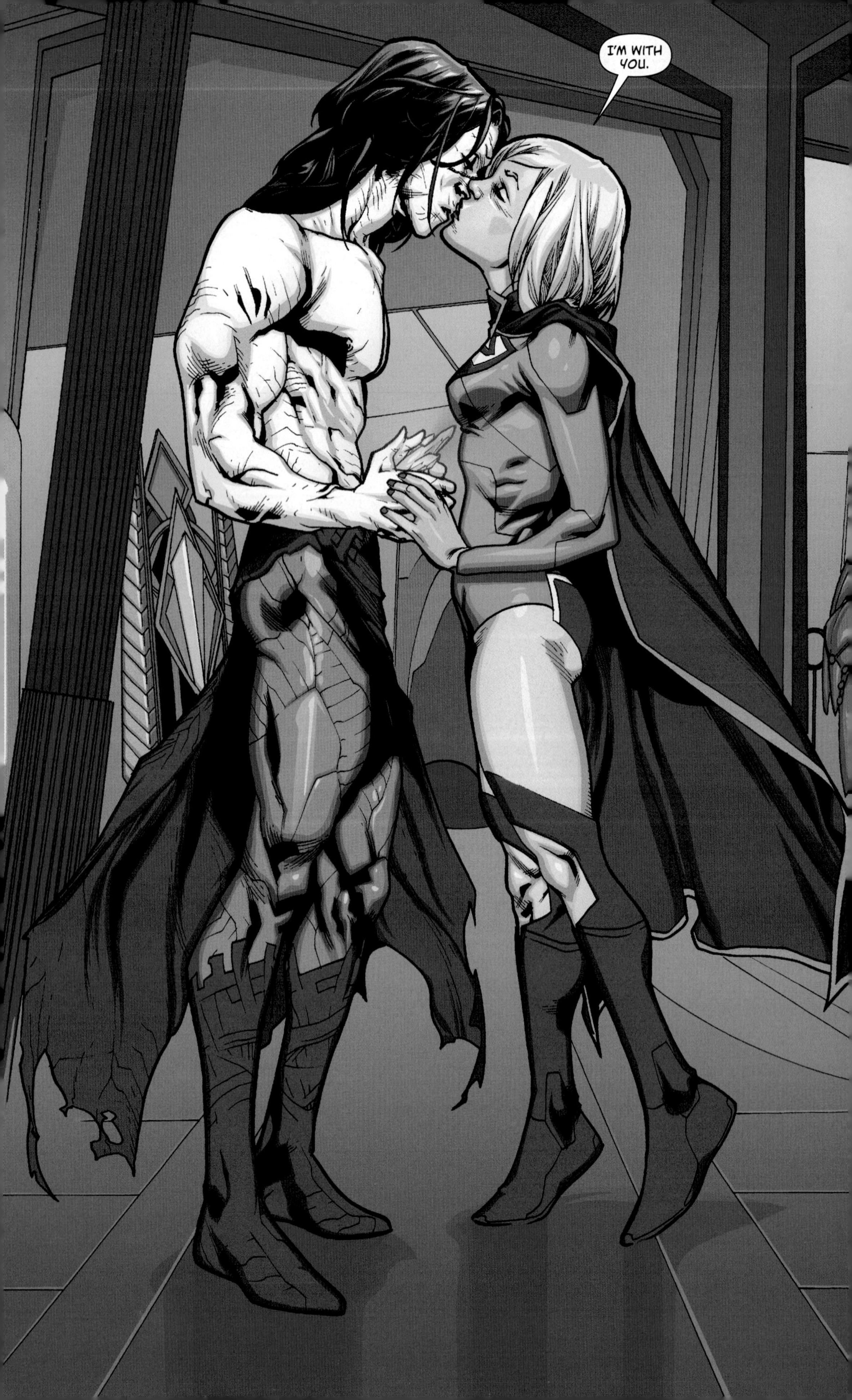
I'M WITH YOU.

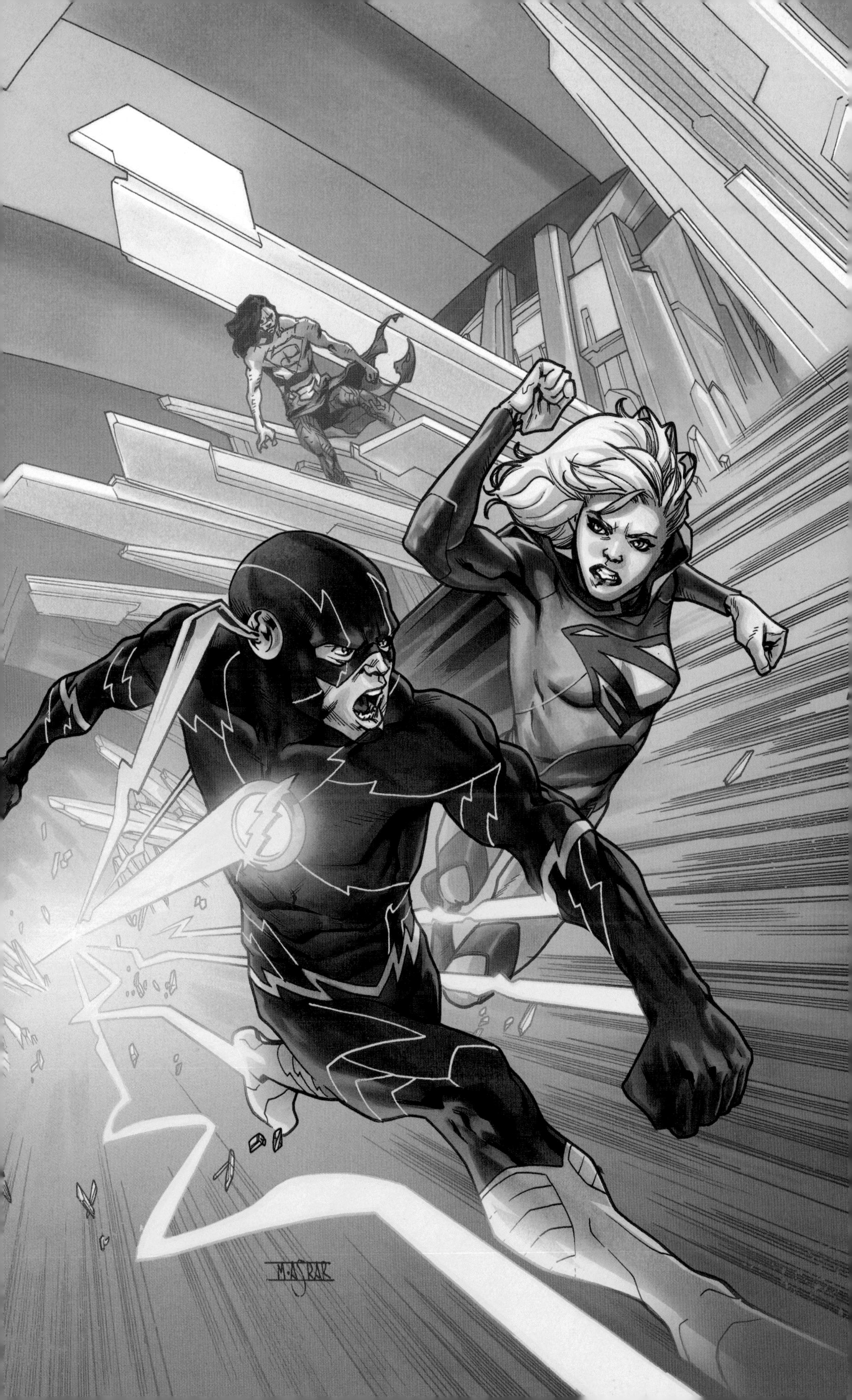

H'EL ON EARTH: FAST & FASTER

MIKE JOHNSON writer **MAHMUD ASRAR** artist cover art by **MAHMUD ASRAR & DAVE McCAIG**

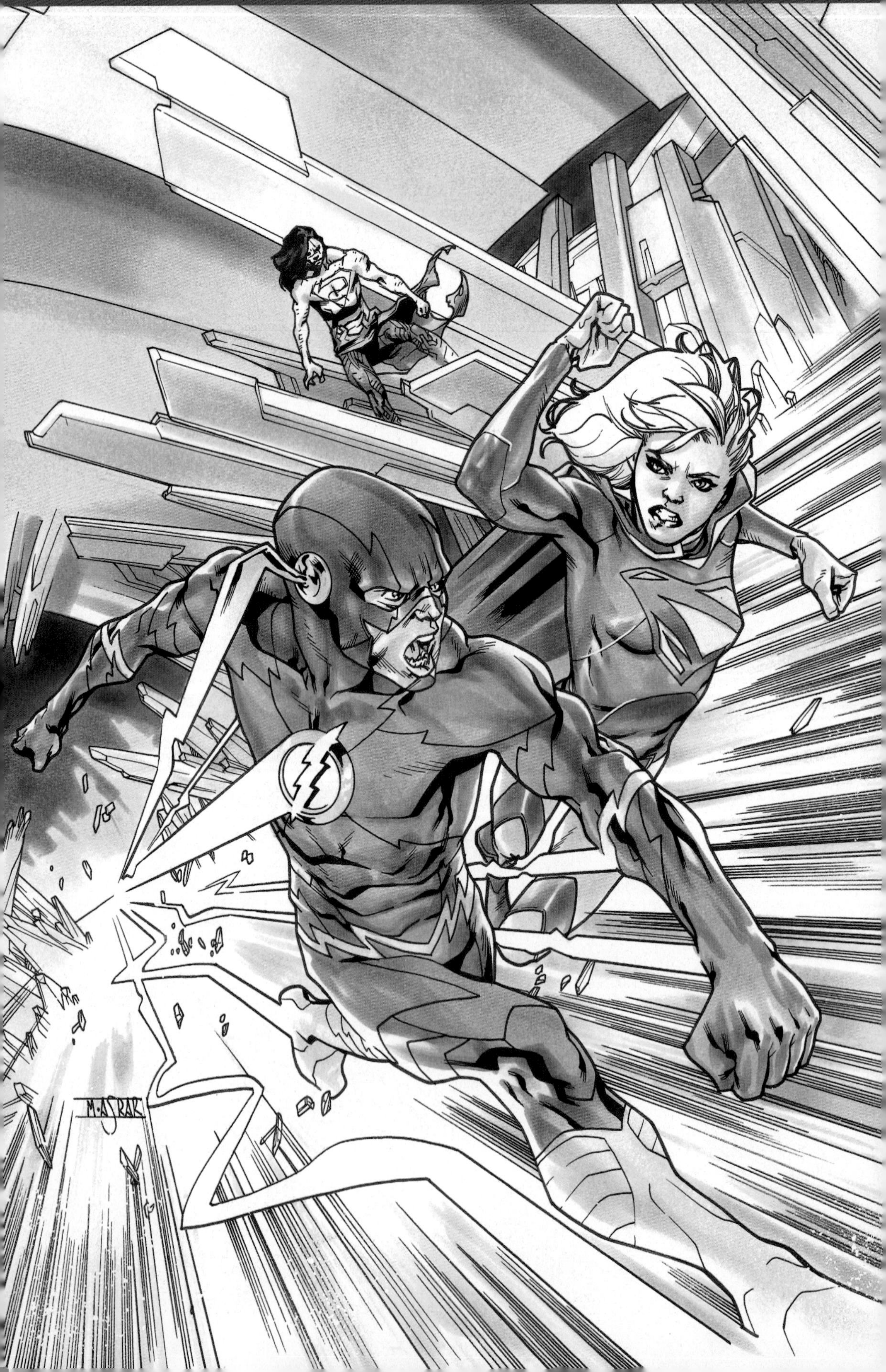
M. ASRAR

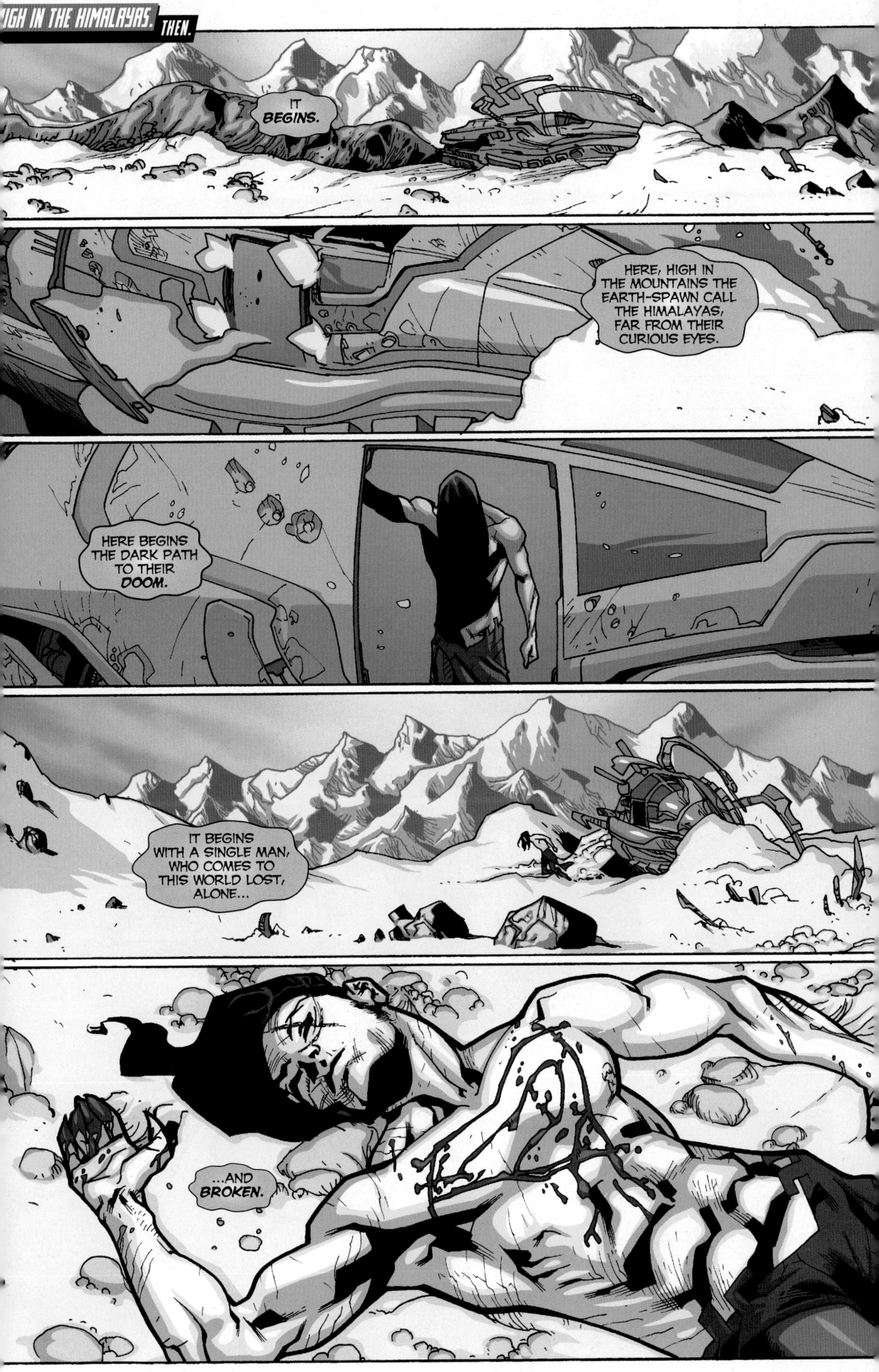
IGH IN THE HIMALAYAS.
THEN.
IT BEGINS.
HERE, HIGH IN THE MOUNTAINS THE EARTH-SPAWN CALL THE HIMALAYAS, FAR FROM THEIR CURIOUS EYES.
HERE BEGINS THE DARK PATH TO THEIR DOOM.
IT BEGINS WITH A SINGLE MAN, WHO COMES TO THIS WORLD LOST, ALONE...
...AND BROKEN.

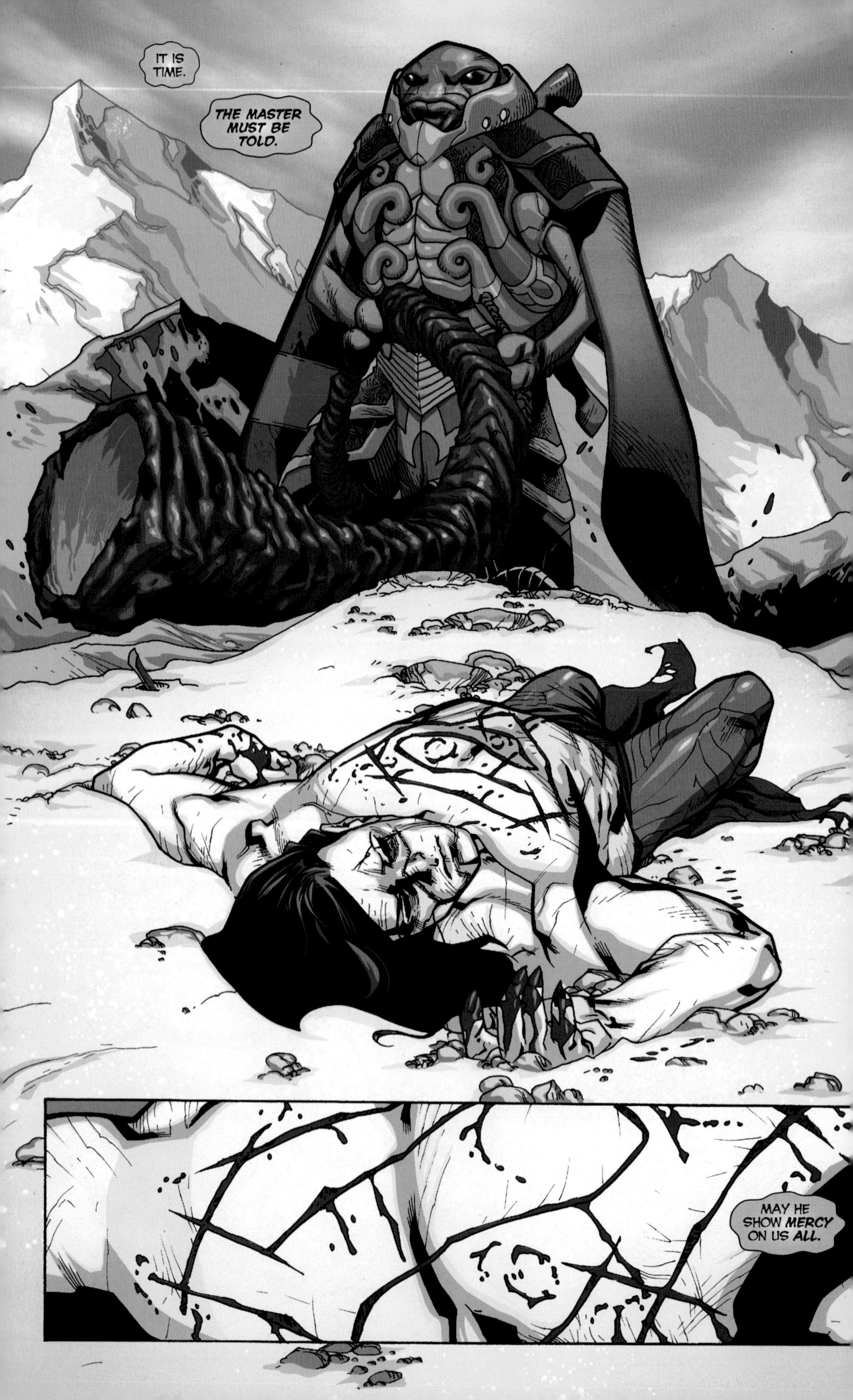
IT IS TIME.
THE MASTER MUST BE TOLD.
MAY HE SHOW MERCY ON US ALL.

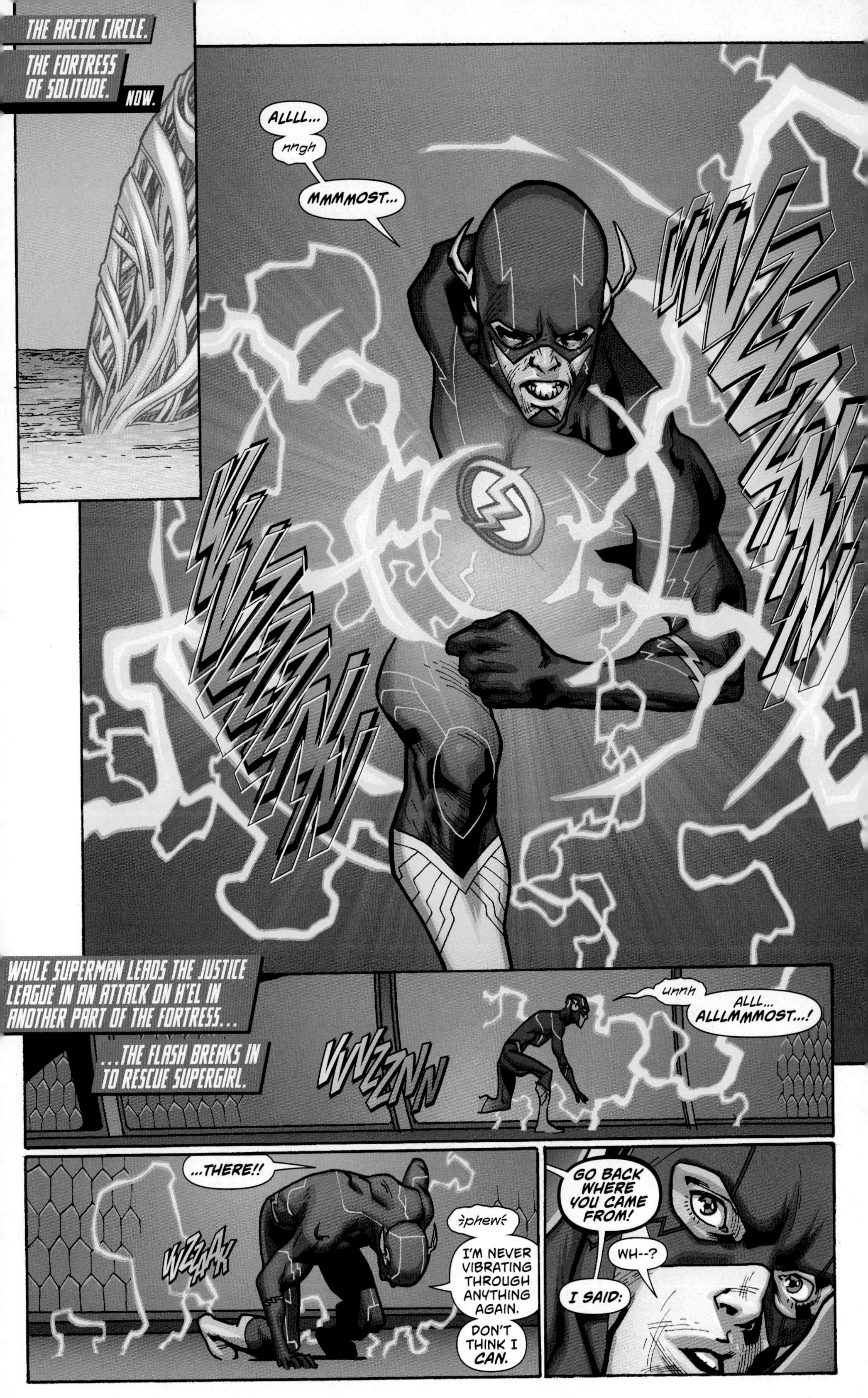

THE ARCTIC CIRCLE.
THE FORTRESS OF SOLITUDE.
NOW.
ALLLL...
nngh
MMMMOST...
WHOOWNN
VWOOWNN
WHILE SUPERMAN LEADS THE JUSTICE LEAGUE IN AN ATTACK ON H'EL IN ANOTHER PART OF THE FORTRESS...
...THE FLASH BREAKS IN TO RESCUE SUPERGIRL.
VVNZZNN
unnh
ALLL... ALLLMMMOST...!
...THERE!!
WZZAK
phew
I'M NEVER VIBRATING THROUGH ANYTHING AGAIN.
DON'T THINK I CAN.
GO BACK WHERE YOU CAME FROM!
WH--?
I SAID:

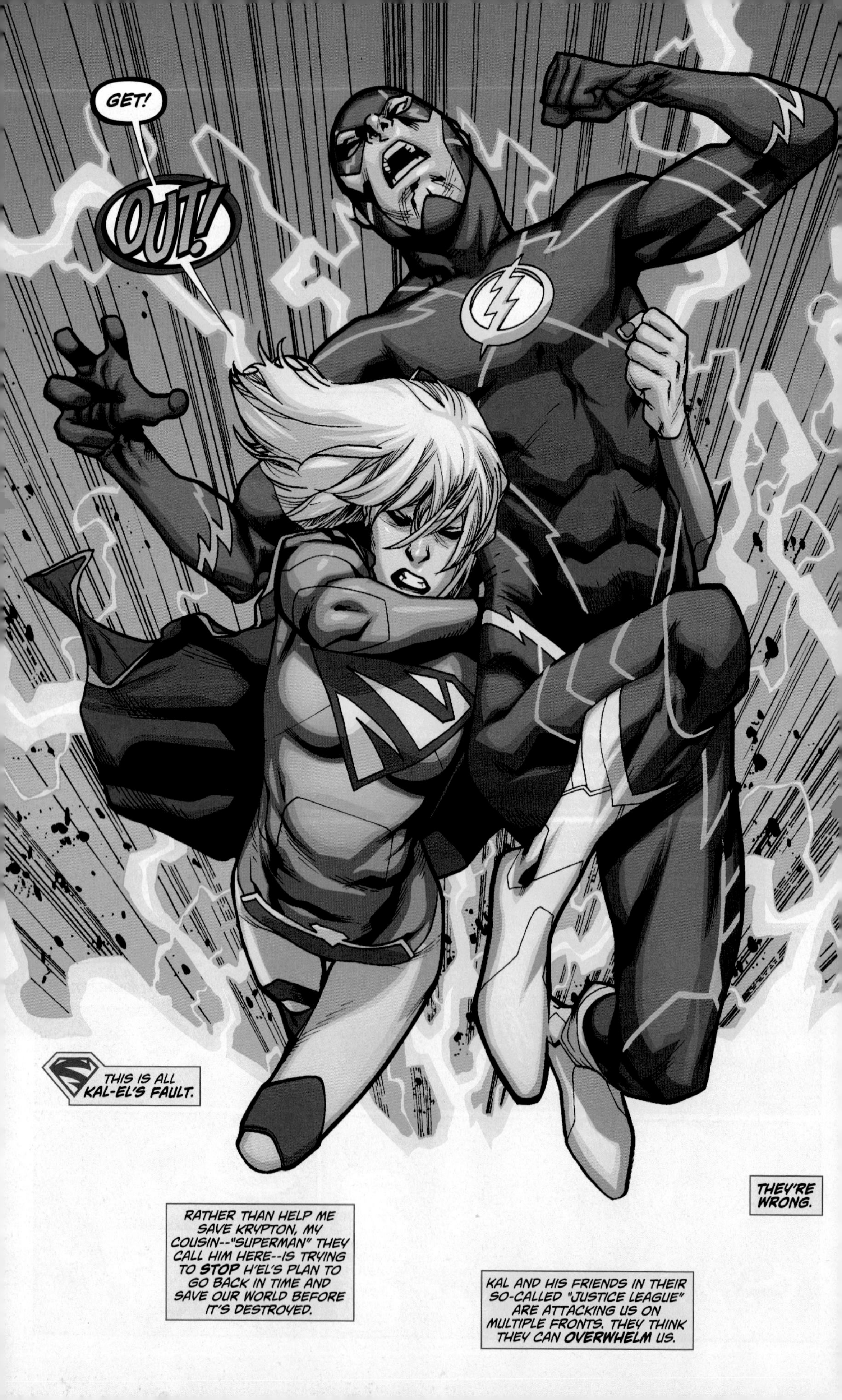
GET!
OUT!
THIS IS ALL KAL-EL'S FAULT.
RATHER THAN HELP ME SAVE KRYPTON, MY COUSIN--"SUPERMAN" THEY CALL HIM HERE--IS TRYING TO STOP H'EL'S PLAN TO GO BACK IN TIME AND SAVE OUR WORLD BEFORE IT'S DESTROYED.
KAL AND HIS FRIENDS IN THEIR SO-CALLED "JUSTICE LEAGUE" ARE ATTACKING US ON MULTIPLE FRONTS. THEY THINK THEY CAN OVERWHELM US.
THEY'RE WRONG.

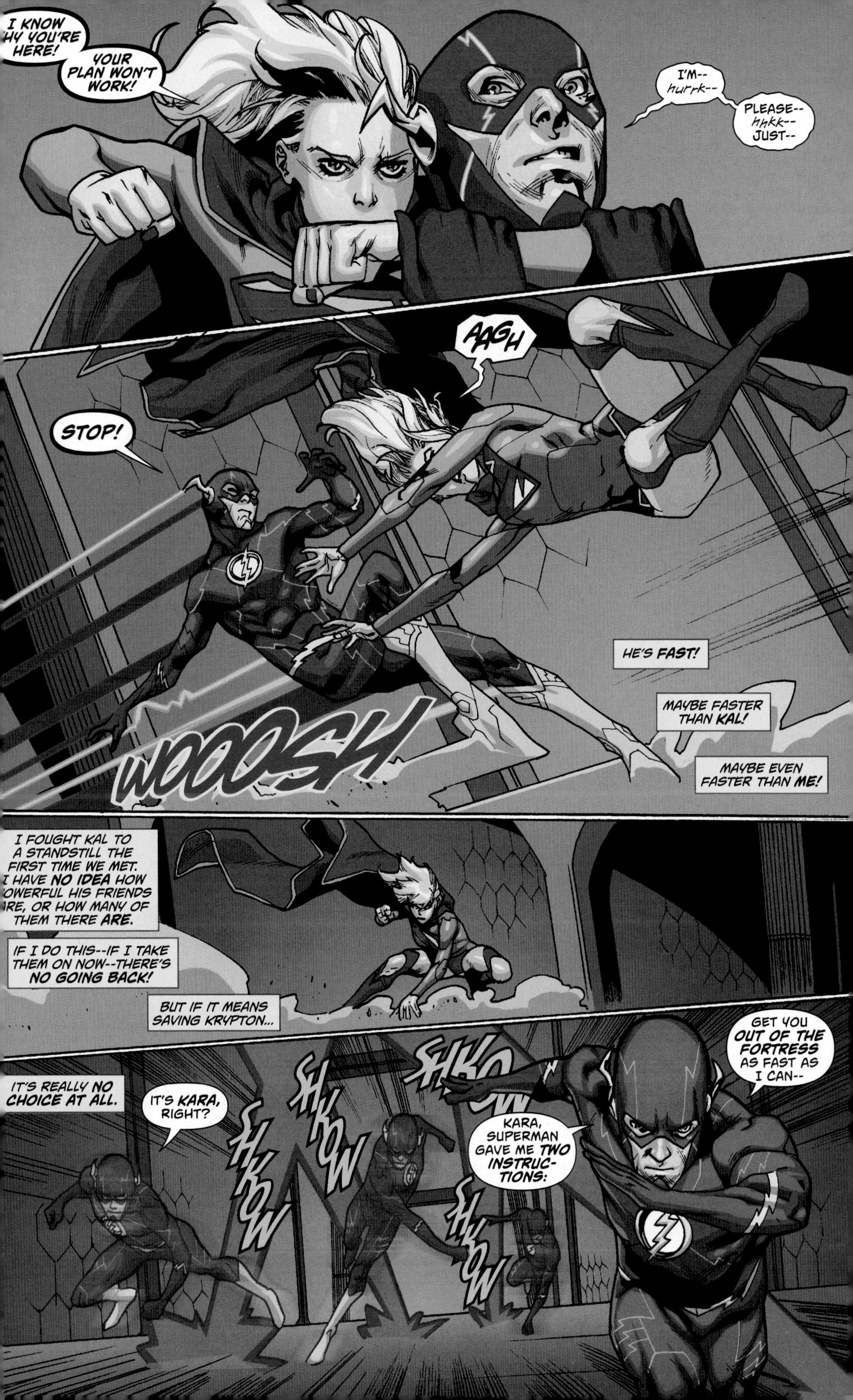
I KNOW HY YOU'RE HERE!
YOUR PLAN WON'T WORK!
I'M-- hurrk--
PLEASE-- hhkk-- JUST--
AAGH
STOP!
HE'S FAST!
MAYBE FASTER THAN KAL!
MAYBE EVEN FASTER THAN ME!
WOOOSH
I FOUGHT KAL TO A STANDSTILL THE FIRST TIME WE MET. I HAVE NO IDEA HOW OWERFUL HIS FRIENDS ARE, OR HOW MANY OF THEM THERE ARE.
IF I DO THIS--IF I TAKE THEM ON NOW--THERE'S NO GOING BACK!
BUT IF IT MEANS SAVING KRYPTON...
IT'S REALLY NO CHOICE AT ALL.
IT'S KARA, RIGHT?
KARA, SUPERMAN GAVE ME TWO INSTRUCTIONS:
GET YOU OUT OF THE FORTRESS AS FAST AS I CAN--
SHKOW
SHKOW
SHKOW
SHKOW
SHKOW

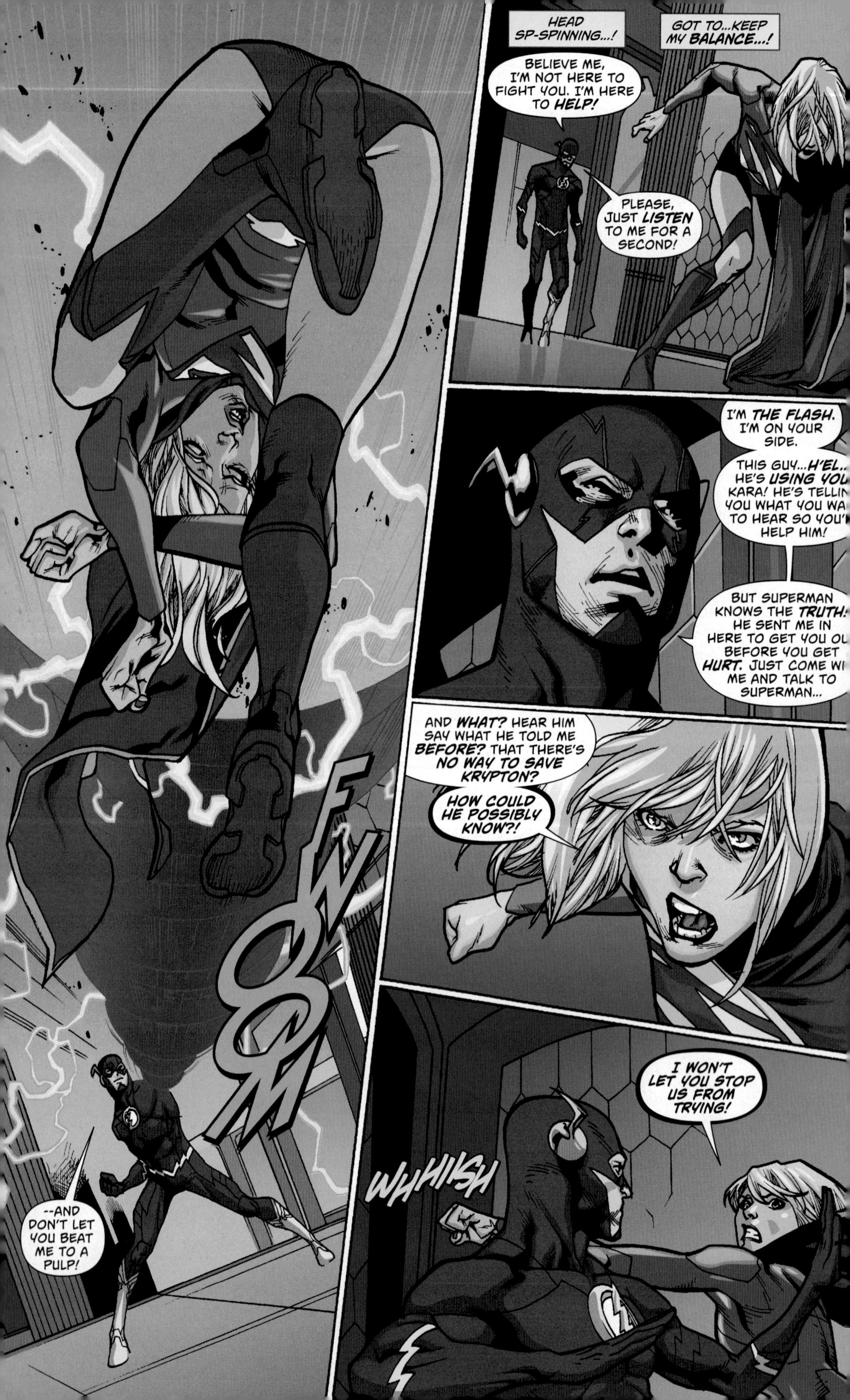
FWOOM
--AND DON'T LET YOU BEAT ME TO A PULP!
HEAD SP-SPINNING...!
GOT TO...KEEP MY BALANCE...!
BELIEVE ME, I'M NOT HERE TO FIGHT YOU. I'M HERE TO HELP!
PLEASE, JUST LISTEN TO ME FOR A SECOND!
I'M THE FLASH. I'M ON YOUR SIDE.
THIS GUY...H'EL... HE'S USING YOU KARA! HE'S TELLIN YOU WHAT YOU WA TO HEAR SO YOU' HELP HIM!
BUT SUPERMAN KNOWS THE TRUTH. HE SENT ME IN HERE TO GET YOU OU BEFORE YOU GET HURT. JUST COME WI ME AND TALK TO SUPERMAN...
AND WHAT? HEAR HIM SAY WHAT HE TOLD ME BEFORE? THAT THERE'S NO WAY TO SAVE KRYPTON?
HOW COULD HE POSSIBLY KNOW?!
I WON'T LET YOU STOP US FROM TRYING!
WHHUSH

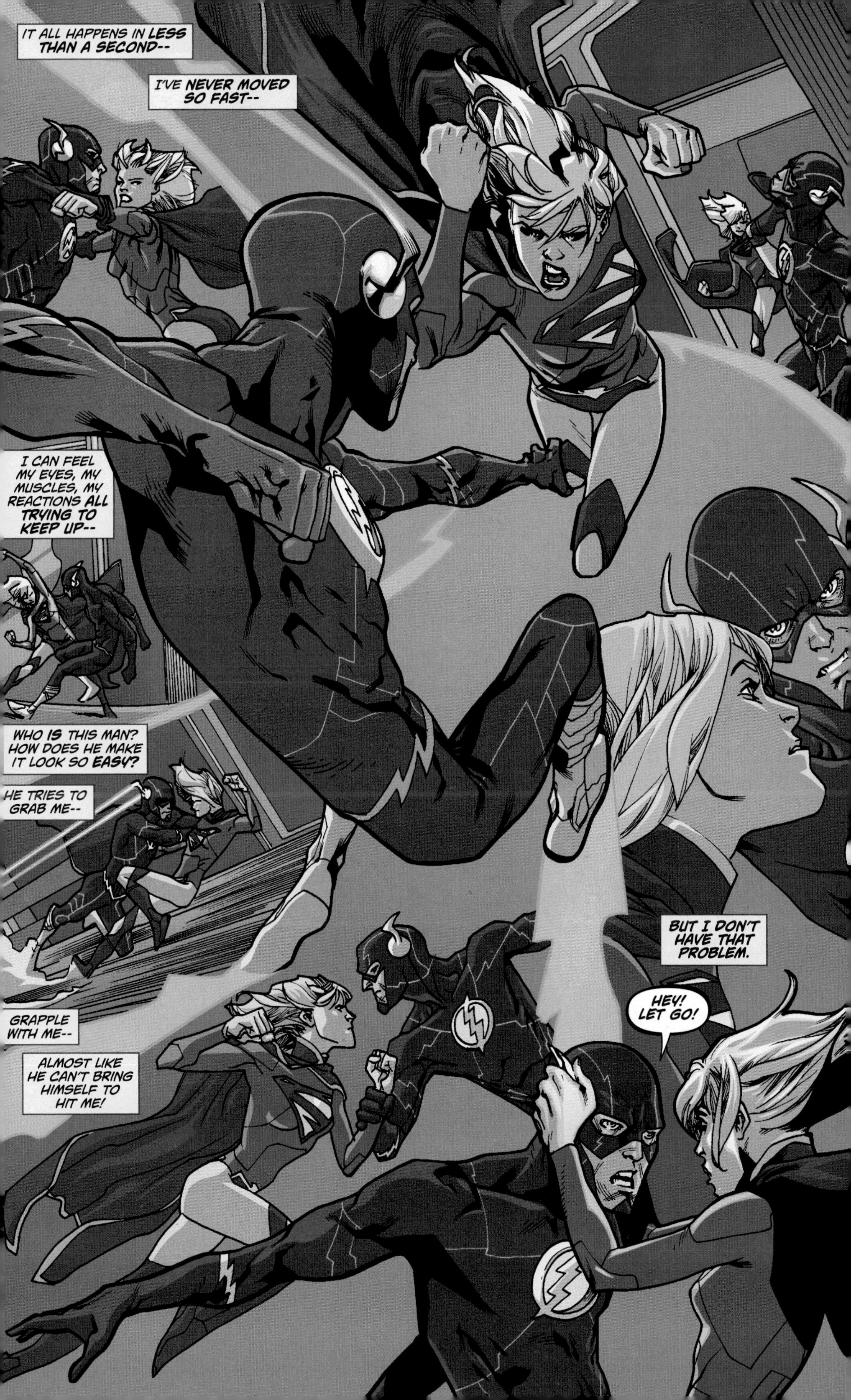
IT ALL HAPPENS IN LESS THAN A SECOND--
I'VE NEVER MOVED SO FAST--
I CAN FEEL MY EYES, MY MUSCLES, MY REACTIONS ALL TRYING TO KEEP UP--
WHO IS THIS MAN? HOW DOES HE MAKE IT LOOK SO EASY?
HE TRIES TO GRAB ME--
BUT I DON'T HAVE THAT PROBLEM.
GRAPPLE WITH ME--
ALMOST LIKE HE CAN'T BRING HIMSELF TO HIT ME!
HEY! LET GO!

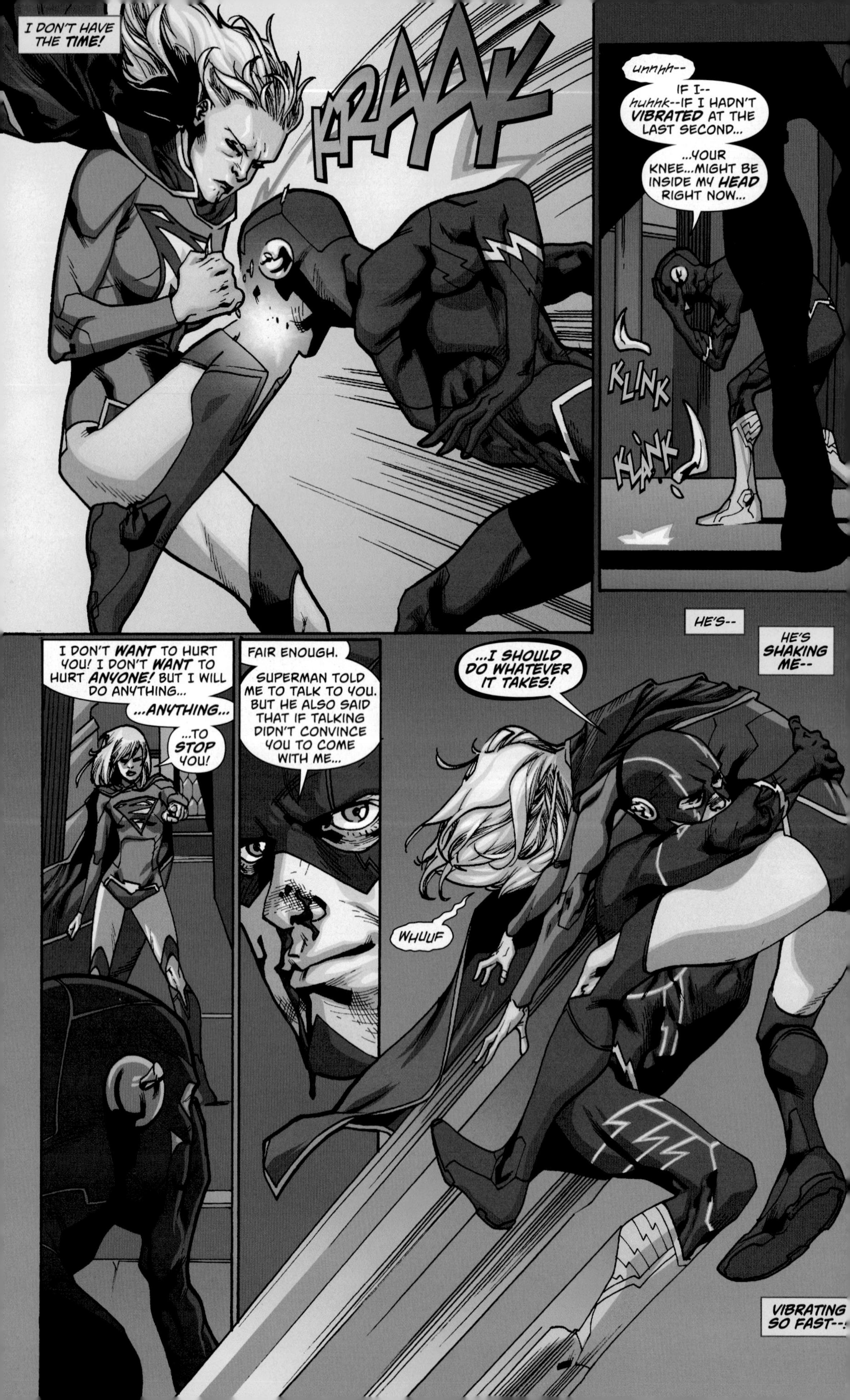
I DON'T HAVE THE TIME!
KRAAK
unnhh--
IF I-- huhhk--IF I HADN'T VIBRATED AT THE LAST SECOND...
...YOUR KNEE...MIGHT BE INSIDE MY HEAD RIGHT NOW...
KLINK
KLINK
I DON'T WANT TO HURT YOU! I DON'T WANT TO HURT ANYONE! BUT I WILL DO ANYTHING...
...ANYTHING...
...TO STOP YOU!
FAIR ENOUGH.
SUPERMAN TOLD ME TO TALK TO YOU. BUT HE ALSO SAID THAT IF TALKING DIDN'T CONVINCE YOU TO COME WITH ME...
...I SHOULD DO WHATEVER IT TAKES!
HE'S--
HE'S SHAKING ME--
WHUUF
VIBRATING SO FAST--!

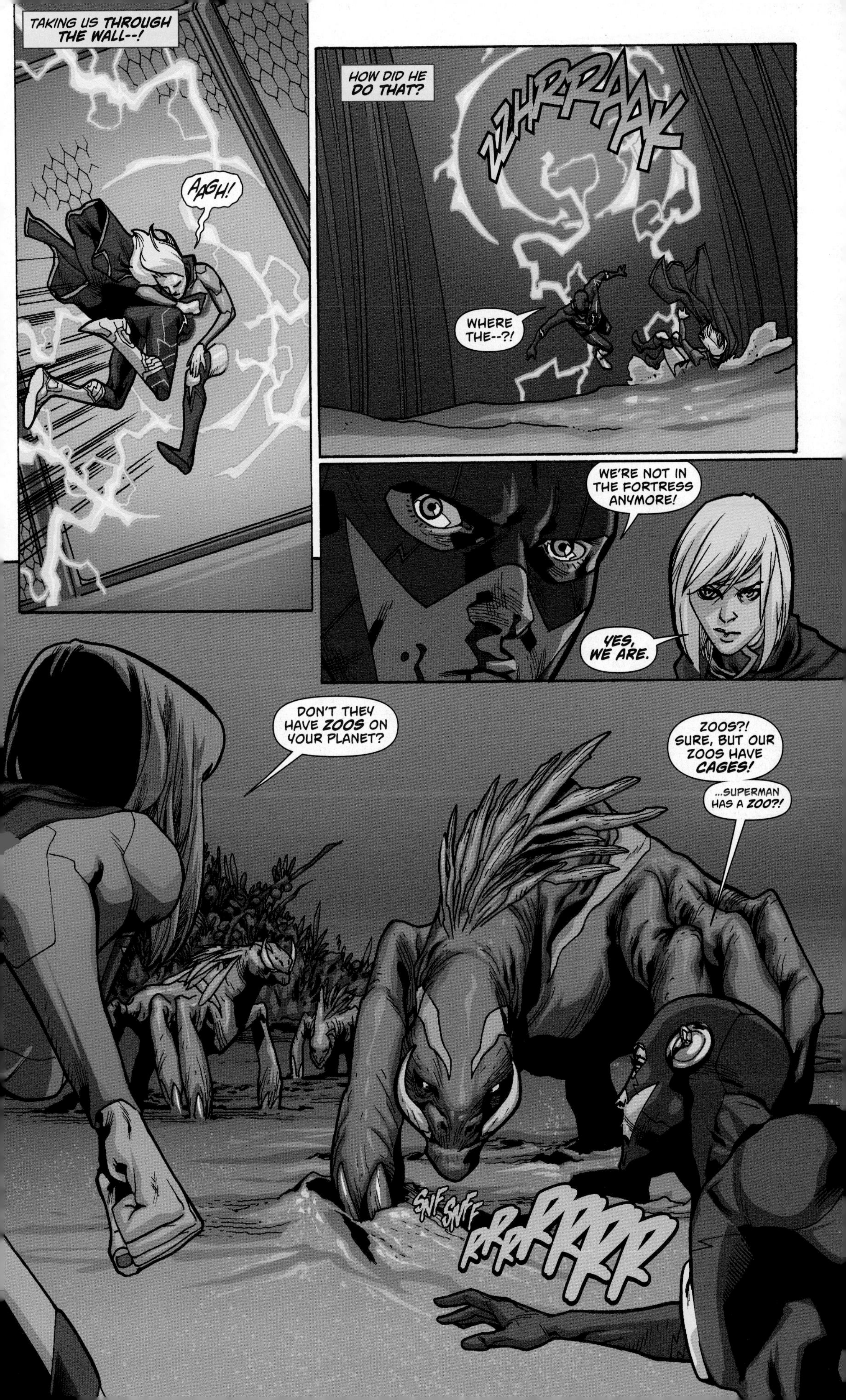
TAKING US THROUGH THE WALL--!
AAGH!
HOW DID HE DO THAT?
ZZHRRAAK
WHERE THE--?!
WE'RE NOT IN THE FORTRESS ANYMORE!
YES, WE ARE.
DON'T THEY HAVE ZOOS ON YOUR PLANET?
ZOOS?! SURE, BUT OUR ZOOS HAVE CAGES!
...SUPERMAN HAS A ZOO?!
SNIF SNIFF
RRRRRRRR

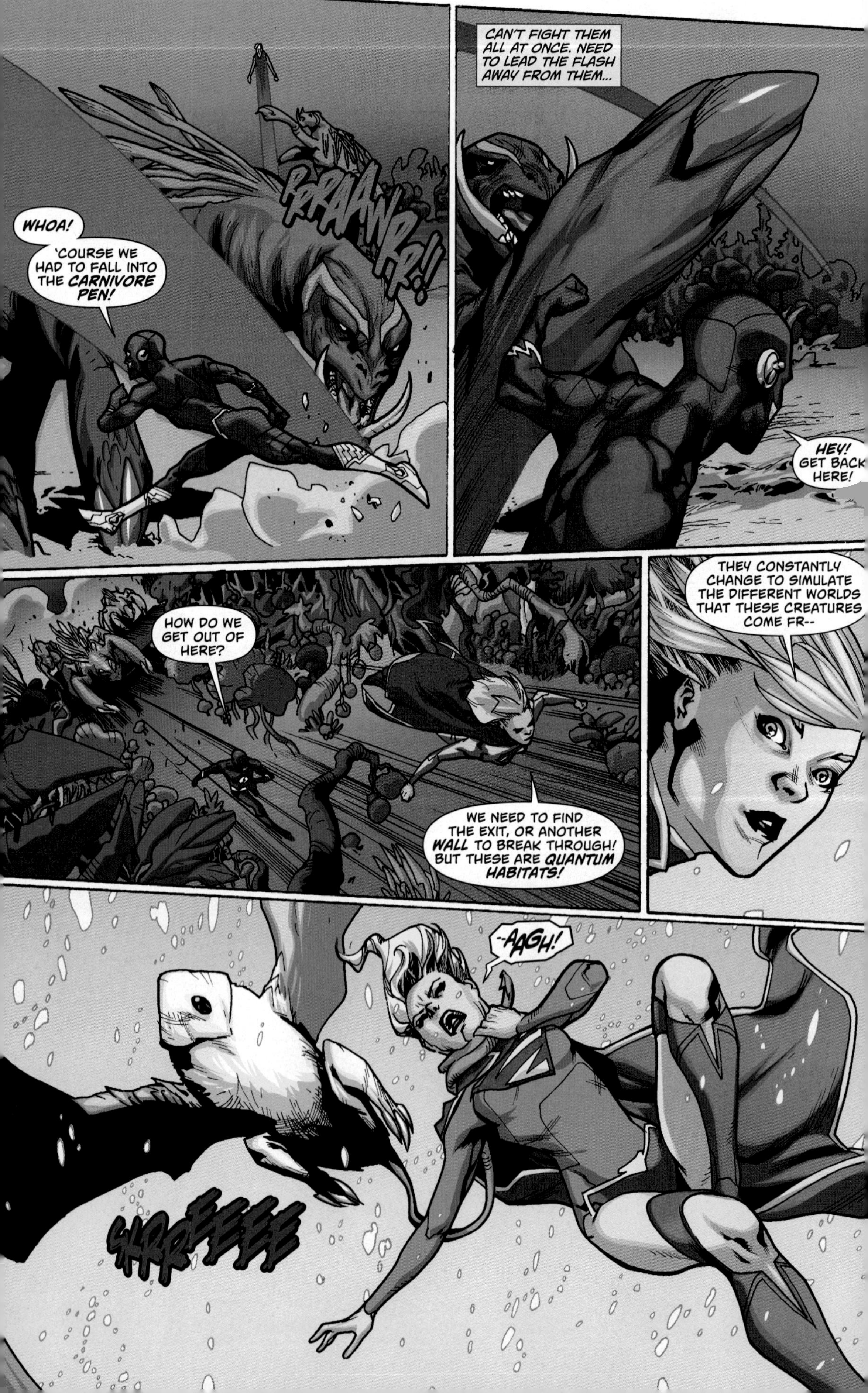
WHOA!
'COURSE WE HAD TO FALL INTO THE CARNIVORE PEN!
RRRAAWRR!!
CAN'T FIGHT THEM ALL AT ONCE. NEED TO LEAD THE FLASH AWAY FROM THEM...
HEY! GET BACK HERE!
HOW DO WE GET OUT OF HERE?
WE NEED TO FIND THE EXIT, OR ANOTHER WALL TO BREAK THROUGH! BUT THESE ARE QUANTUM HABITATS!
THEY CONSTANTLY CHANGE TO SIMULATE THE DIFFERENT WORLDS THAT THESE CREATURES COME FR--
--AAGH!
SKREEEEE

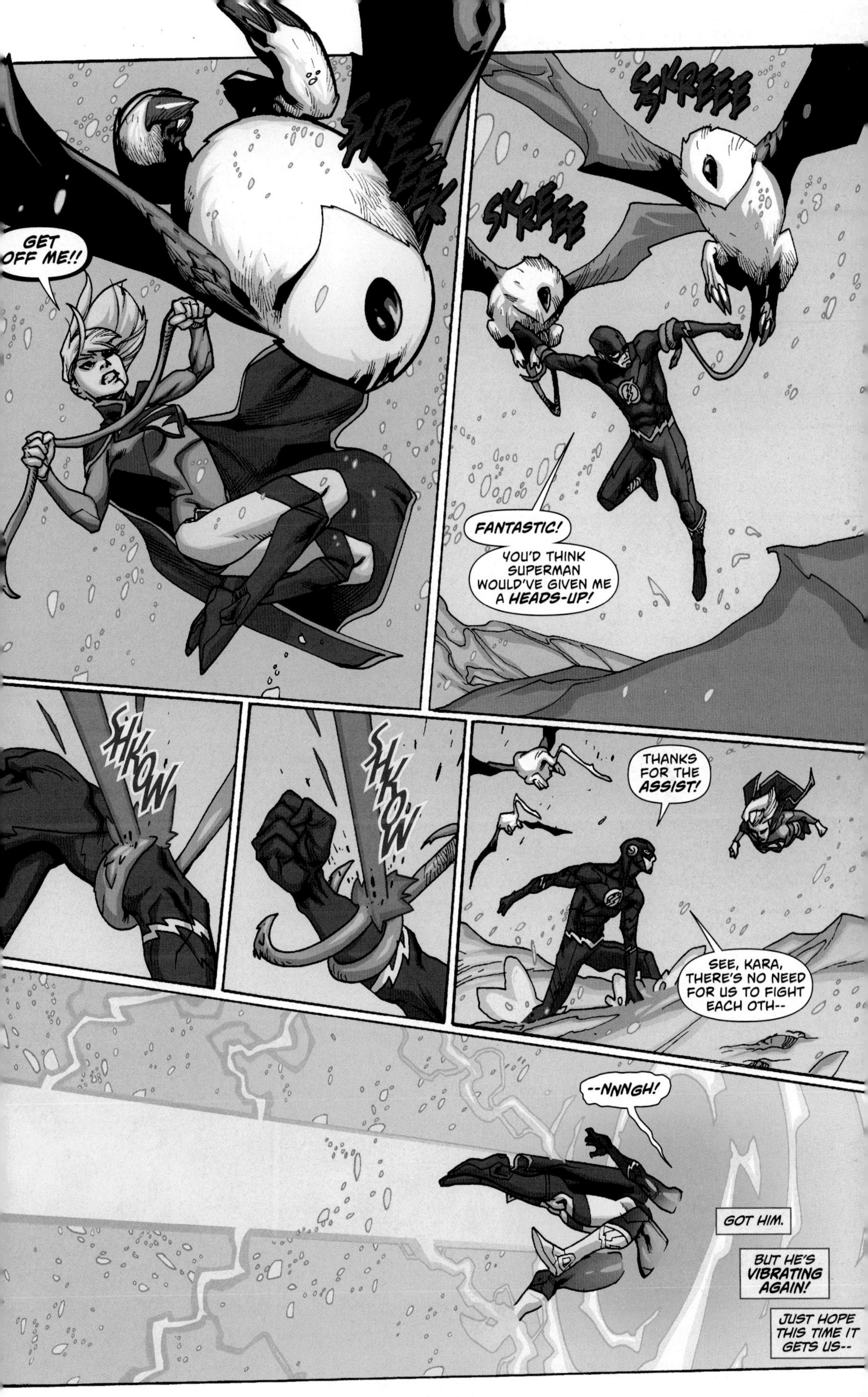
SKREEEK
GET OFF ME!!
SKREEEE
SKREEEE
FANTASTIC!
YOU'D THINK SUPERMAN WOULD'VE GIVEN ME A HEADS-UP!
SHKOW
SHKOW
THANKS FOR THE ASSIST!
SEE, KARA, THERE'S NO NEED FOR US TO FIGHT EACH OTH--
--NNNGH!
GOT HIM.
BUT HE'S VIBRATING AGAIN!
JUST HOPE THIS TIME IT GETS US--

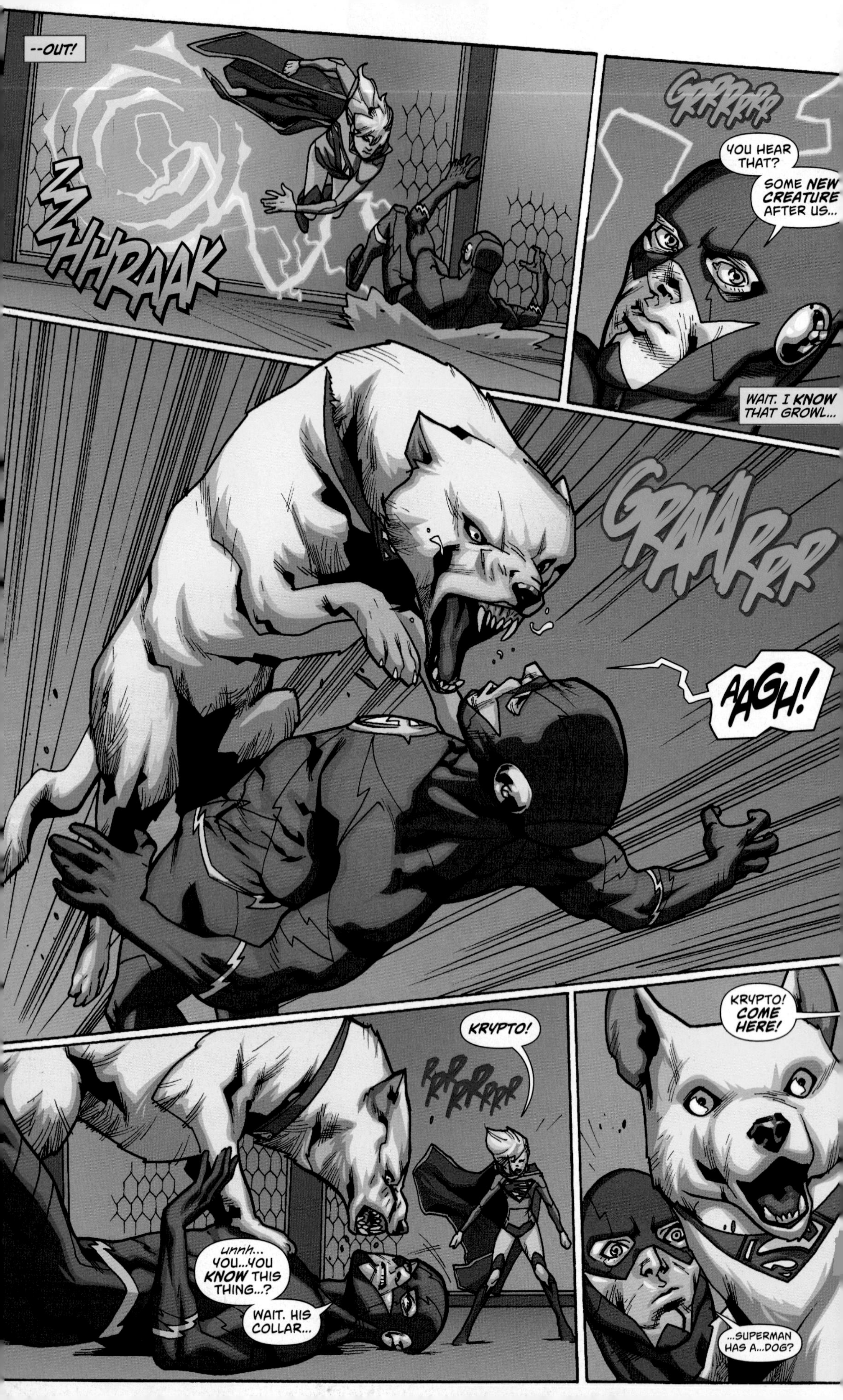
--OUT!
ZZHHRAAK
GRRRRRR
YOU HEAR THAT?
SOME NEW CREATURE AFTER US...
WAIT. I KNOW THAT GROWL...
GRAAARRR
AAGH!
KRYPTO!
RRRRRRR
unnh... YOU...YOU KNOW THIS THING...?
WAIT. HIS COLLAR...
KRYPTO! COME HERE!
...SUPERMAN HAS A...DOG?

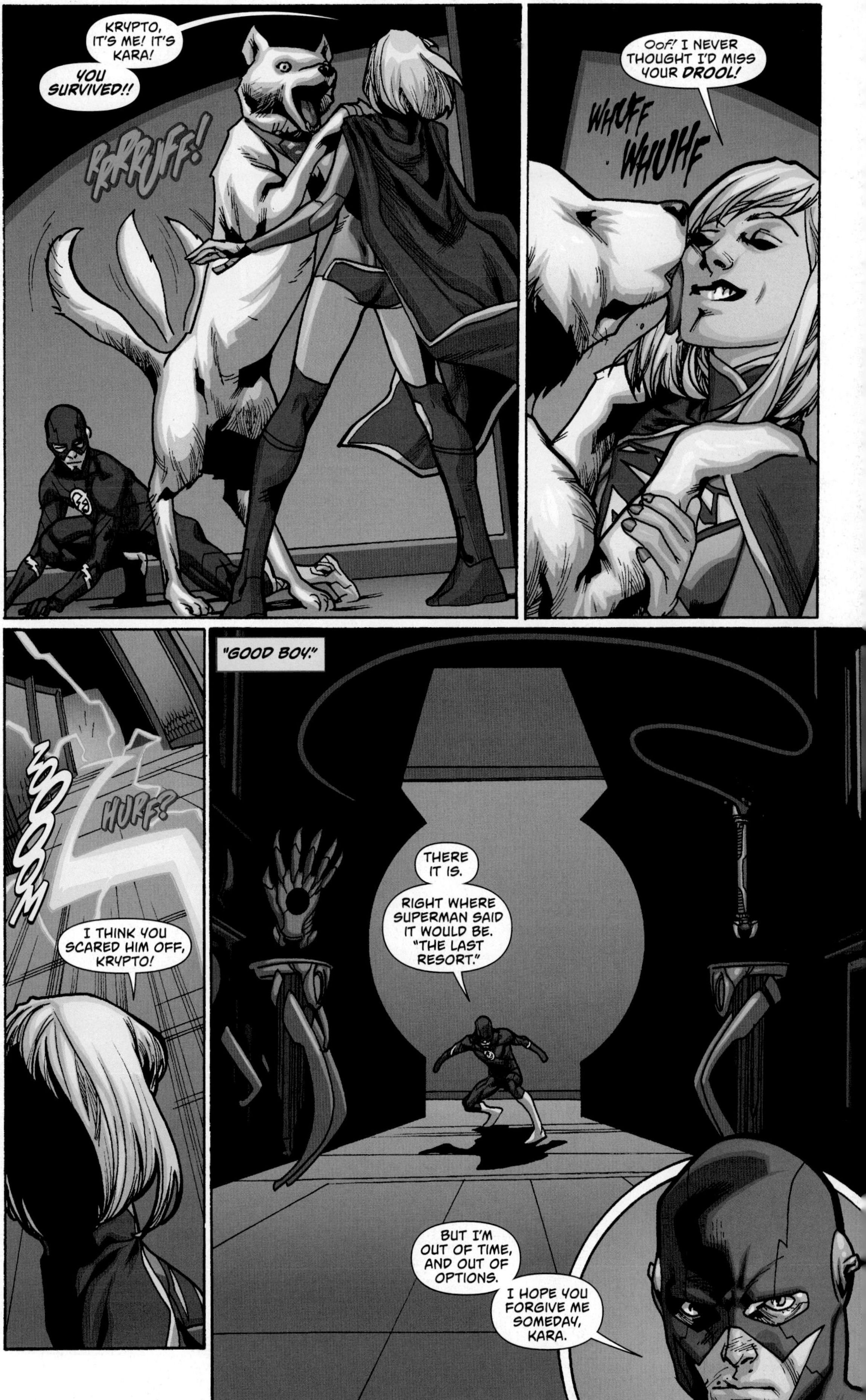
KRYPTO, IT'S ME! IT'S KARA!
YOU SURVIVED!!
RRRRUFF!
OOF! I NEVER THOUGHT I'D MISS YOUR DROOL!
WHUFF WHUHF
WOOOOM
HURF?
I THINK YOU SCARED HIM OFF, KRYPTO!
"GOOD BOY."
THERE IT IS.
RIGHT WHERE SUPERMAN SAID IT WOULD BE. "THE LAST RESORT."
BUT I'M OUT OF TIME, AND OUT OF OPTIONS.
I HOPE YOU FORGIVE ME SOMEDAY, KARA.

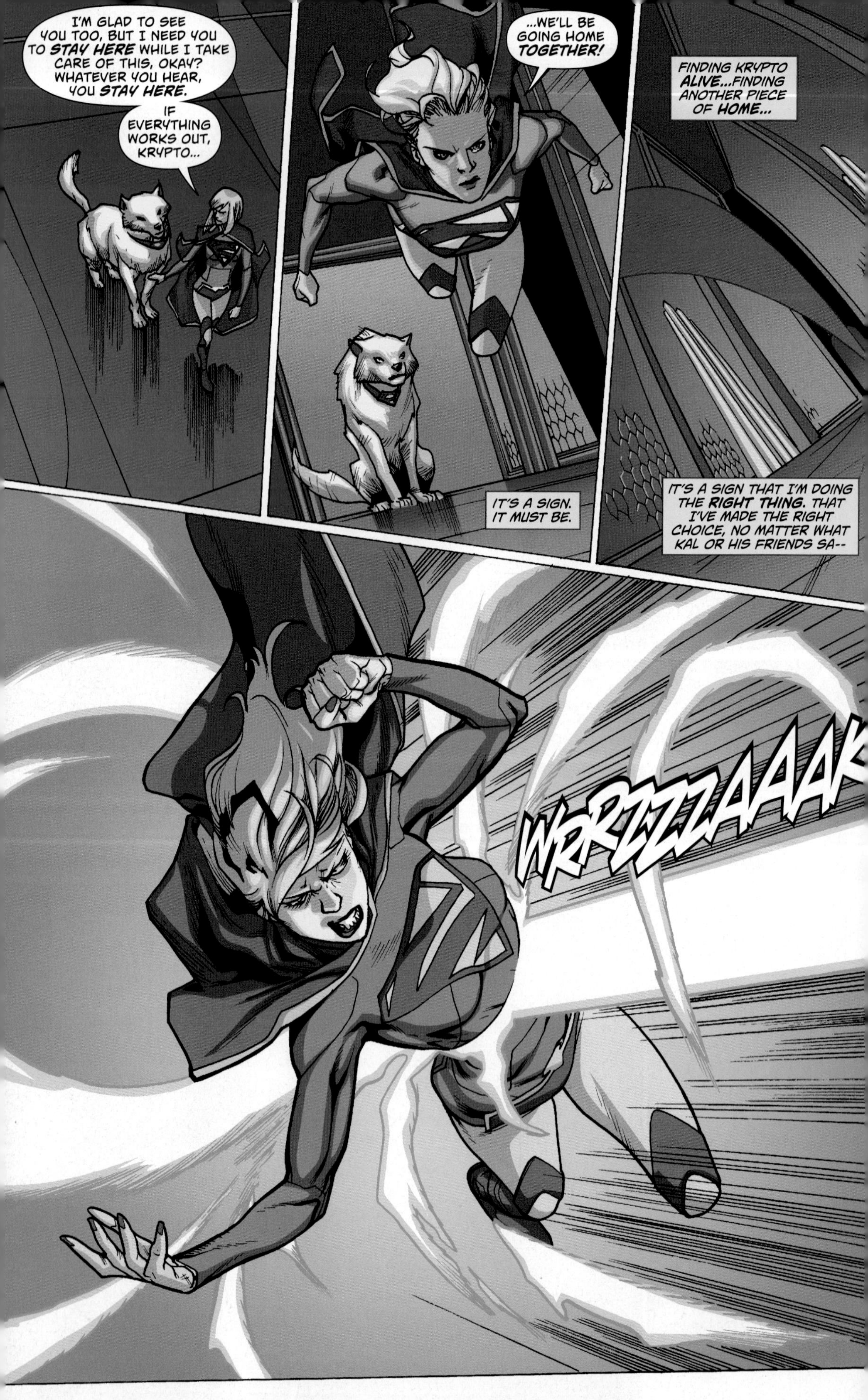
I'M GLAD TO SEE YOU TOO, BUT I NEED YOU TO STAY HERE WHILE I TAKE CARE OF THIS, OKAY? WHATEVER YOU HEAR, YOU STAY HERE.
IF EVERYTHING WORKS OUT, KRYPTO...
...WE'LL BE GOING HOME TOGETHER!
IT'S A SIGN. IT MUST BE.
FINDING KRYPTO ALIVE...FINDING ANOTHER PIECE OF HOME...
IT'S A SIGN THAT I'M DOING THE RIGHT THING. THAT I'VE MADE THE RIGHT CHOICE, NO MATTER WHAT KAL OR HIS FRIENDS SA--
WRRZZZAAAK

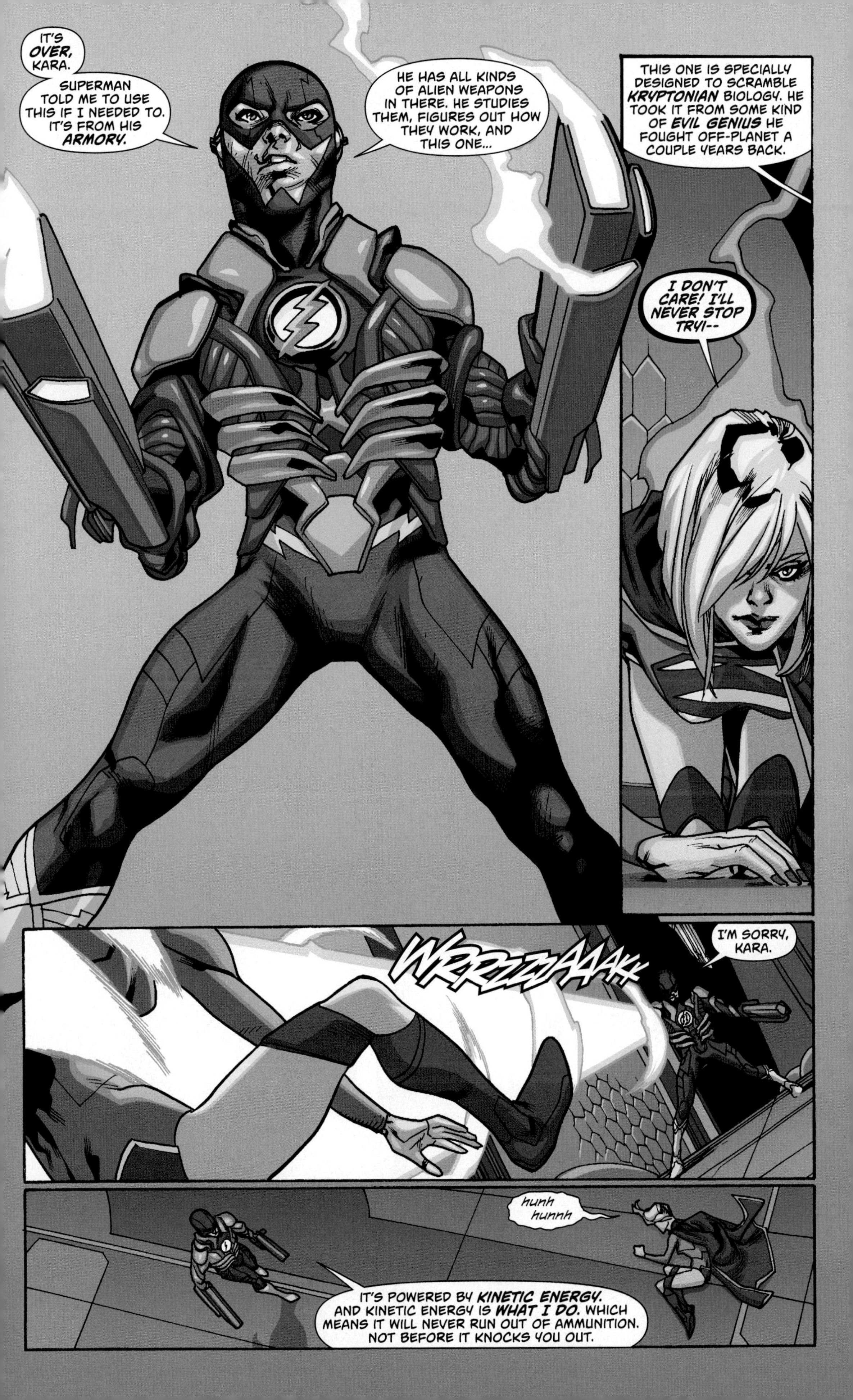
IT'S OVER, KARA.
SUPERMAN TOLD ME TO USE THIS IF I NEEDED TO. IT'S FROM HIS ARMORY.
HE HAS ALL KINDS OF ALIEN WEAPONS IN THERE. HE STUDIES THEM, FIGURES OUT HOW THEY WORK, AND THIS ONE...
THIS ONE IS SPECIALLY DESIGNED TO SCRAMBLE KRYPTONIAN BIOLOGY. HE TOOK IT FROM SOME KIND OF EVIL GENIUS HE FOUGHT OFF-PLANET A COUPLE YEARS BACK.
I DON'T CARE! I'LL NEVER STOP TRYI--
WRRZZZAAAKK
I'M SORRY, KARA.
hunh hunnh
IT'S POWERED BY KINETIC ENERGY. AND KINETIC ENERGY IS WHAT I DO. WHICH MEANS IT WILL NEVER RUN OUT OF AMMUNITION. NOT BEFORE IT KNOCKS YOU OUT.

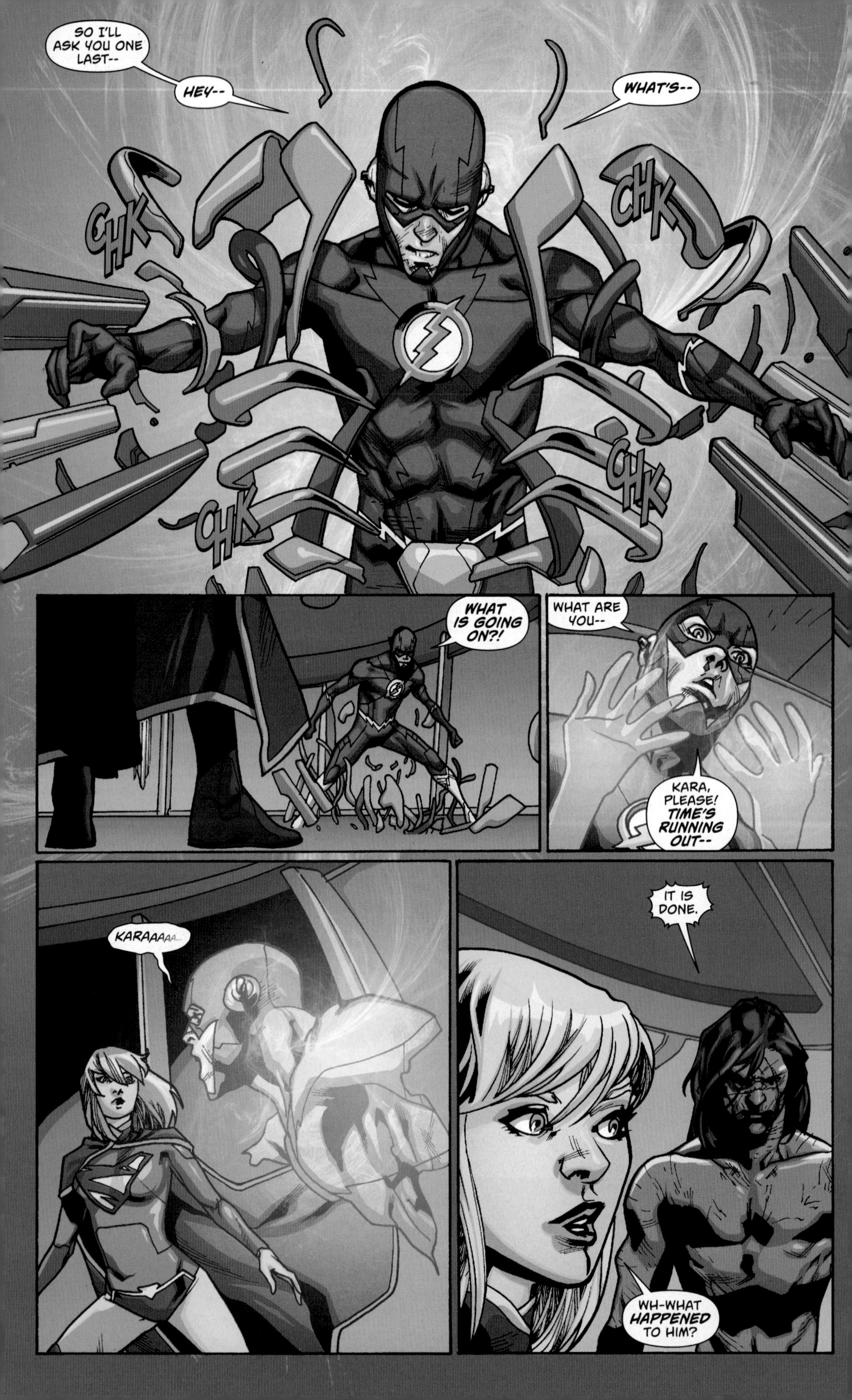
SO I'LL ASK YOU ONE LAST--
HEY--
WHAT'S--
CHK
CHK
CHK
CHK
WHAT IS GOING ON?!
WHAT ARE YOU--
KARA, PLEASE! TIME'S RUNNING OUT--
KARAAAAA...
IT IS DONE.
WH-WHAT HAPPENED TO HIM?

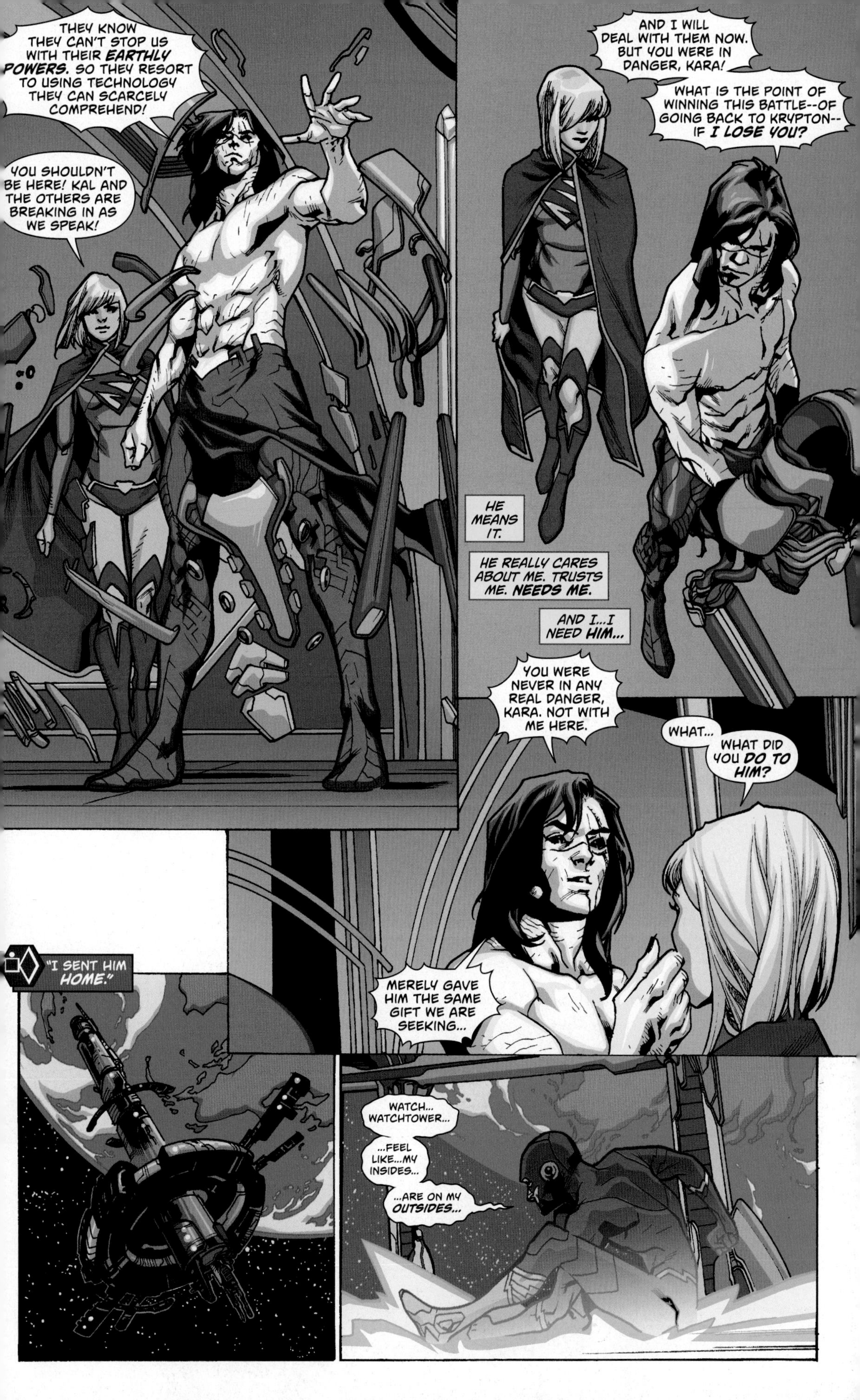
THEY KNOW THEY CAN'T STOP US WITH THEIR EARTHLY POWERS. SO THEY RESORT TO USING TECHNOLOGY THEY CAN SCARCELY COMPREHEND!
YOU SHOULDN'T BE HERE! KAL AND THE OTHERS ARE BREAKING IN AS WE SPEAK!
AND I WILL DEAL WITH THEM NOW. BUT YOU WERE IN DANGER, KARA!
WHAT IS THE POINT OF WINNING THIS BATTLE--OF GOING BACK TO KRYPTON--IF I LOSE YOU?
HE MEANS IT.
HE REALLY CARES ABOUT ME. TRUSTS ME. NEEDS ME.
AND I...I NEED HIM...
YOU WERE NEVER IN ANY REAL DANGER, KARA. NOT WITH ME HERE.
WHAT...
WHAT DID YOU DO TO HIM?
MERELY GAVE HIM THE SAME GIFT WE ARE SEEKING...
"I SENT HIM HOME."
WATCH... WATCHTOWER...
...FEEL LIKE...MY INSIDES...
...ARE ON MY OUTSIDES...

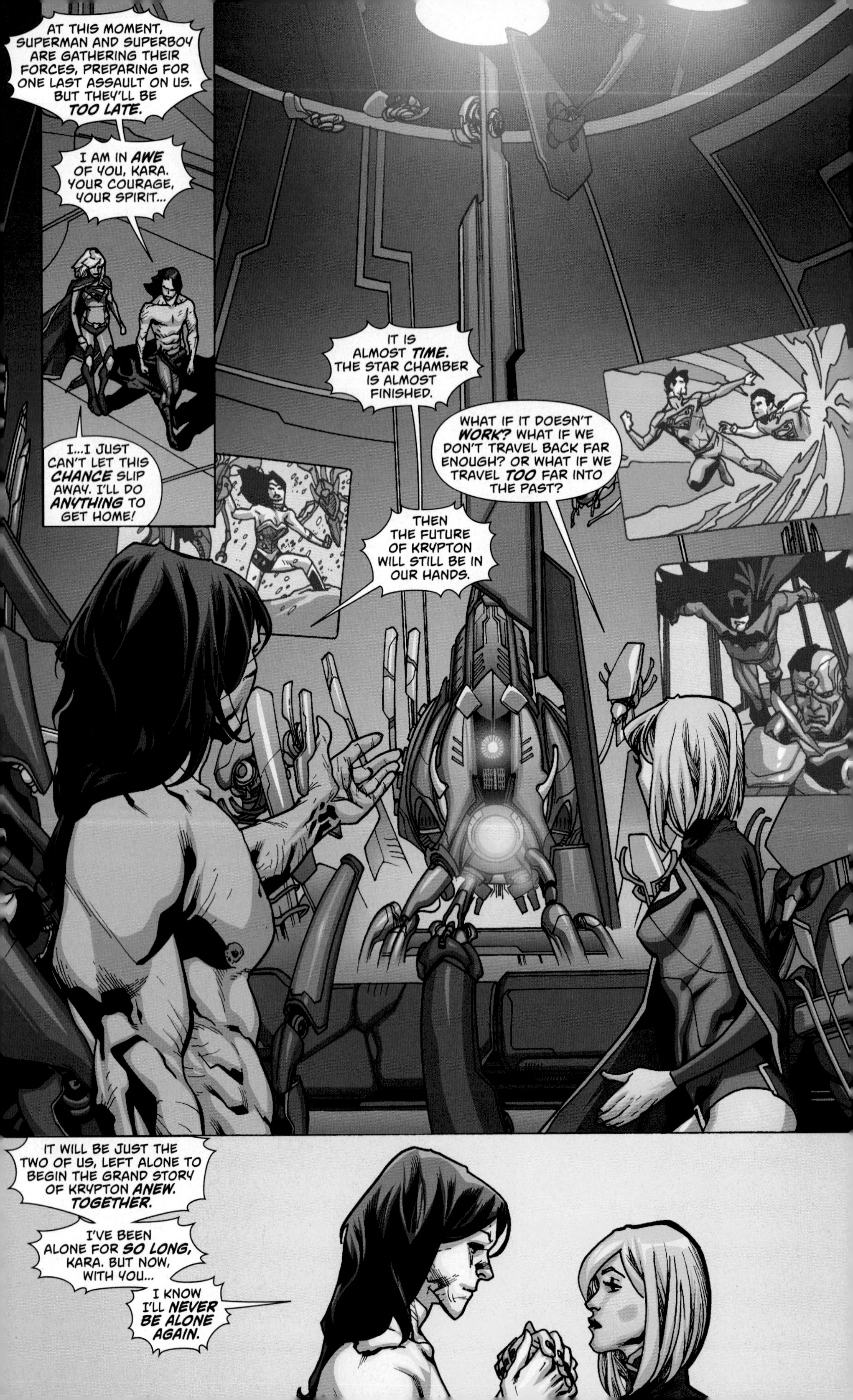
AT THIS MOMENT, SUPERMAN AND SUPERBOY ARE GATHERING THEIR FORCES, PREPARING FOR ONE LAST ASSAULT ON US. BUT THEY'LL BE TOO LATE.
I AM IN AWE OF YOU, KARA. YOUR COURAGE, YOUR SPIRIT...
I...I JUST CAN'T LET THIS CHANCE SLIP AWAY. I'LL DO ANYTHING TO GET HOME!
IT IS ALMOST TIME. THE STAR CHAMBER IS ALMOST FINISHED.
WHAT IF IT DOESN'T WORK? WHAT IF WE DON'T TRAVEL BACK FAR ENOUGH? OR WHAT IF WE TRAVEL TOO FAR INTO THE PAST?
THEN THE FUTURE OF KRYPTON WILL STILL BE IN OUR HANDS.
IT WILL BE JUST THE TWO OF US, LEFT ALONE TO BEGIN THE GRAND STORY OF KRYPTON ANEW. TOGETHER.
I'VE BEEN ALONE FOR SO LONG, KARA. BUT NOW, WITH YOU...
I KNOW I'LL NEVER BE ALONE AGAIN.

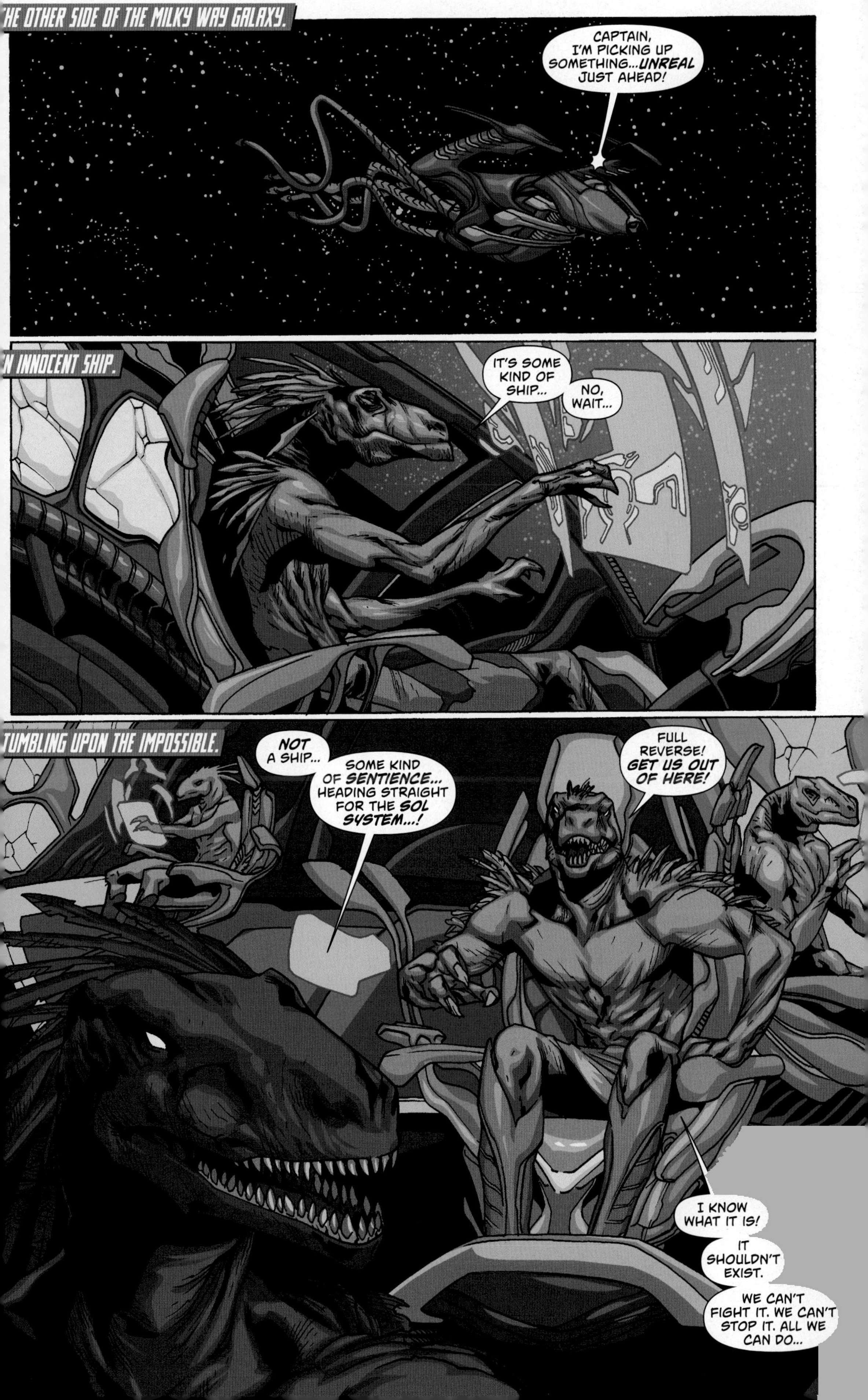
HE OTHER SIDE OF THE MILKY WAY GALAXY.
CAPTAIN, I'M PICKING UP SOMETHING...UNREAL JUST AHEAD!
N INNOCENT SHIP.
IT'S SOME KIND OF SHIP...
NO, WAIT...
TUMBLING UPON THE IMPOSSIBLE.
NOT A SHIP...
SOME KIND OF SENTIENCE... HEADING STRAIGHT FOR THE SOL SYSTEM...!
FULL REVERSE! GET US OUT OF HERE!
I KNOW WHAT IT IS!
IT SHOULDN'T EXIST.
WE CAN'T FIGHT IT. WE CAN'T STOP IT. ALL WE CAN DO...

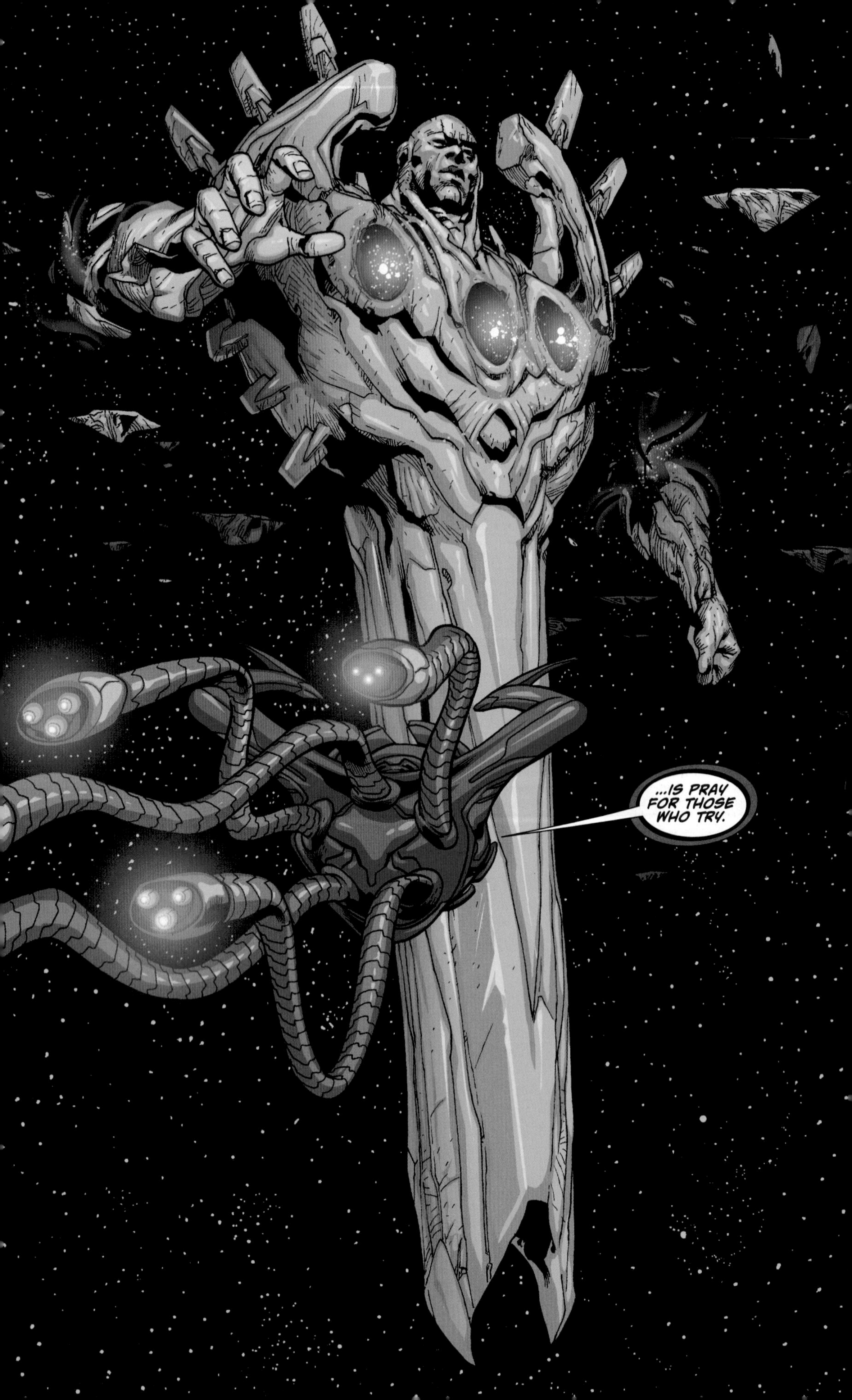
...IS PRAY FOR THOSE WHO TRY.

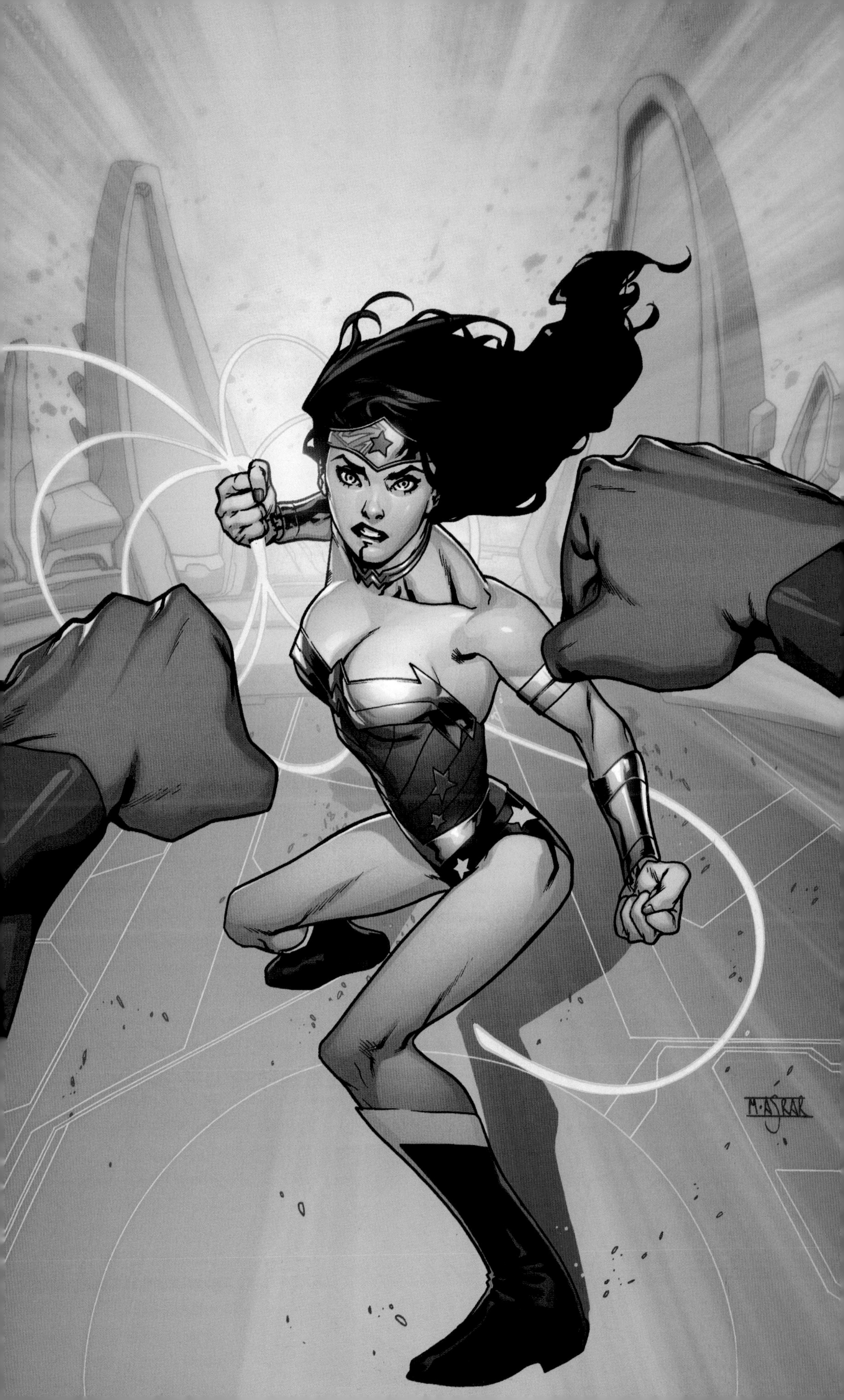
M·ASRAR

H'EL ON EARTH: GIRL VS. GODDESS

MIKE JOHNSON writer **MAHMUD ASRAR** artist cover art by **MAHMUD ASRAR & DAVE McCAIG**

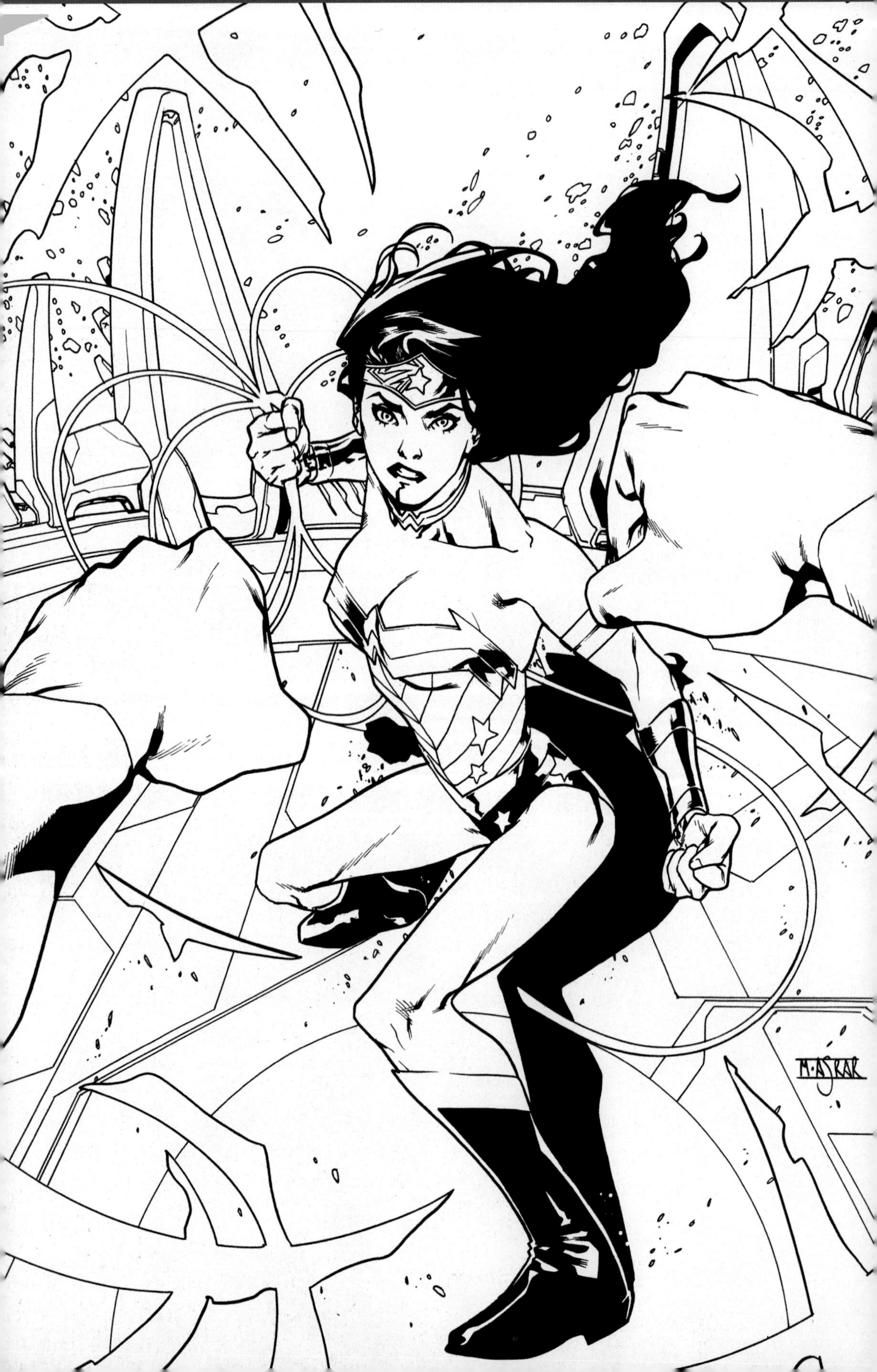

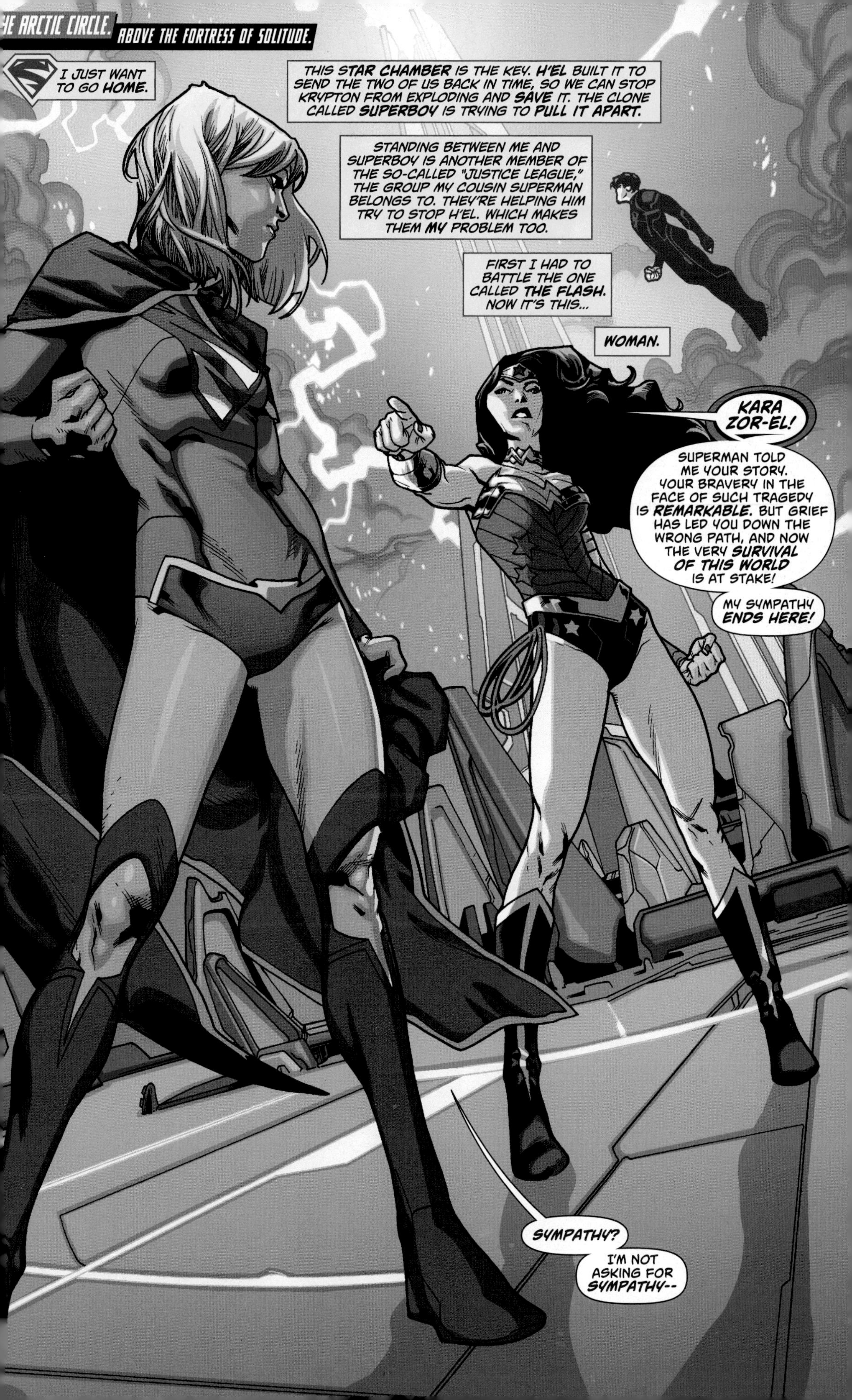
THE ARCTIC CIRCLE.
ABOVE THE FORTRESS OF SOLITUDE.
I JUST WANT TO GO HOME.
THIS STAR CHAMBER IS THE KEY. H'EL BUILT IT TO SEND THE TWO OF US BACK IN TIME, SO WE CAN STOP KRYPTON FROM EXPLODING AND SAVE IT. THE CLONE CALLED SUPERBOY IS TRYING TO PULL IT APART.
STANDING BETWEEN ME AND SUPERBOY IS ANOTHER MEMBER OF THE SO-CALLED "JUSTICE LEAGUE," THE GROUP MY COUSIN SUPERMAN BELONGS TO. THEY'RE HELPING HIM TRY TO STOP H'EL. WHICH MAKES THEM MY PROBLEM TOO.
FIRST I HAD TO BATTLE THE ONE CALLED THE FLASH. NOW IT'S THIS...
WOMAN.
KARA ZOR-EL!
SUPERMAN TOLD ME YOUR STORY. YOUR BRAVERY IN THE FACE OF SUCH TRAGEDY IS REMARKABLE. BUT GRIEF HAS LED YOU DOWN THE WRONG PATH, AND NOW THE VERY SURVIVAL OF THIS WORLD IS AT STAKE!
MY SYMPATHY ENDS HERE!
SYMPATHY?
I'M NOT ASKING FOR SYMPATHY--

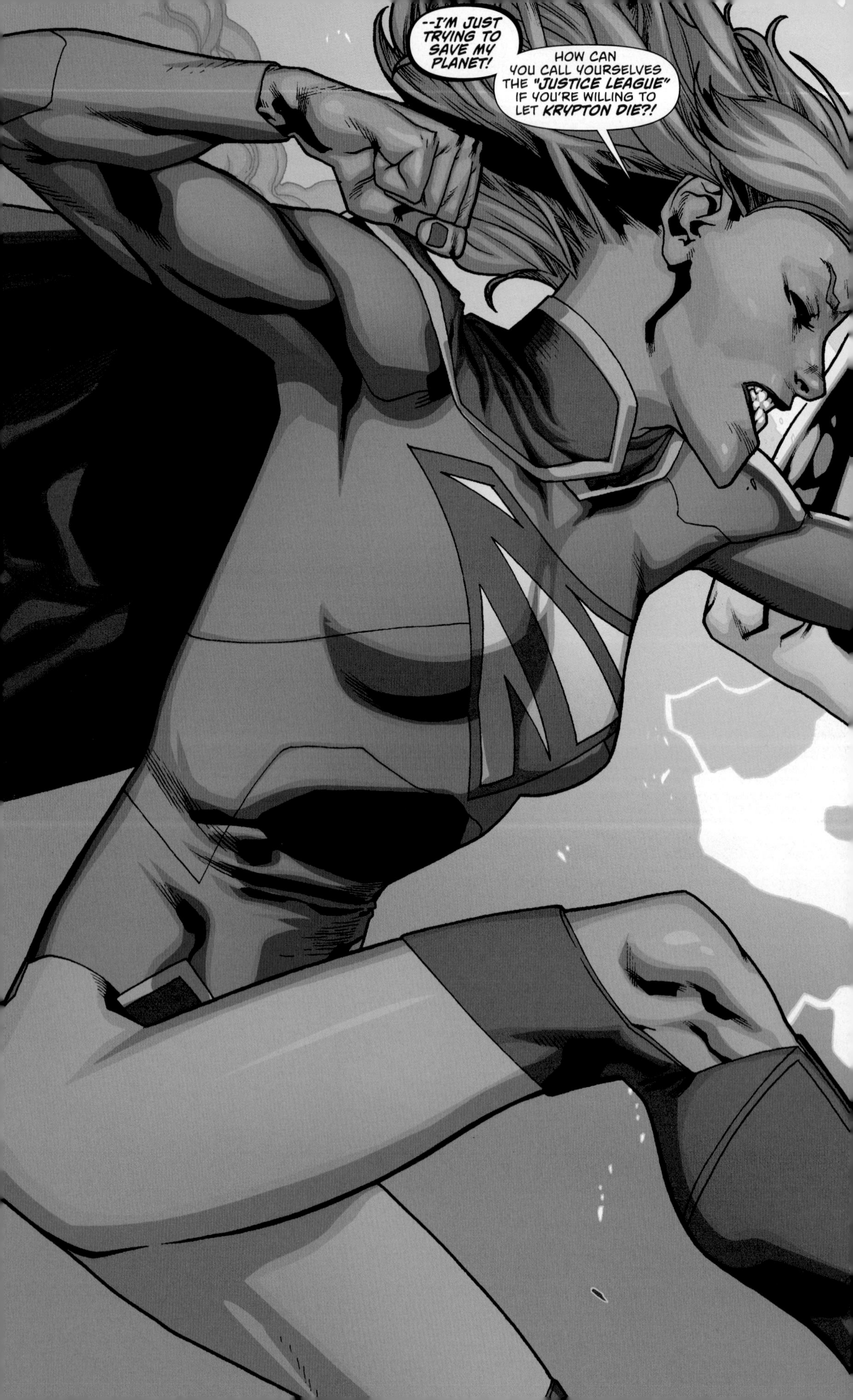
--I'M JUST TRYING TO SAVE MY PLANET!
HOW CAN YOU CALL YOURSELVES THE "JUSTICE LEAGUE" IF YOU'RE WILLING TO LET KRYPTON DIE?!

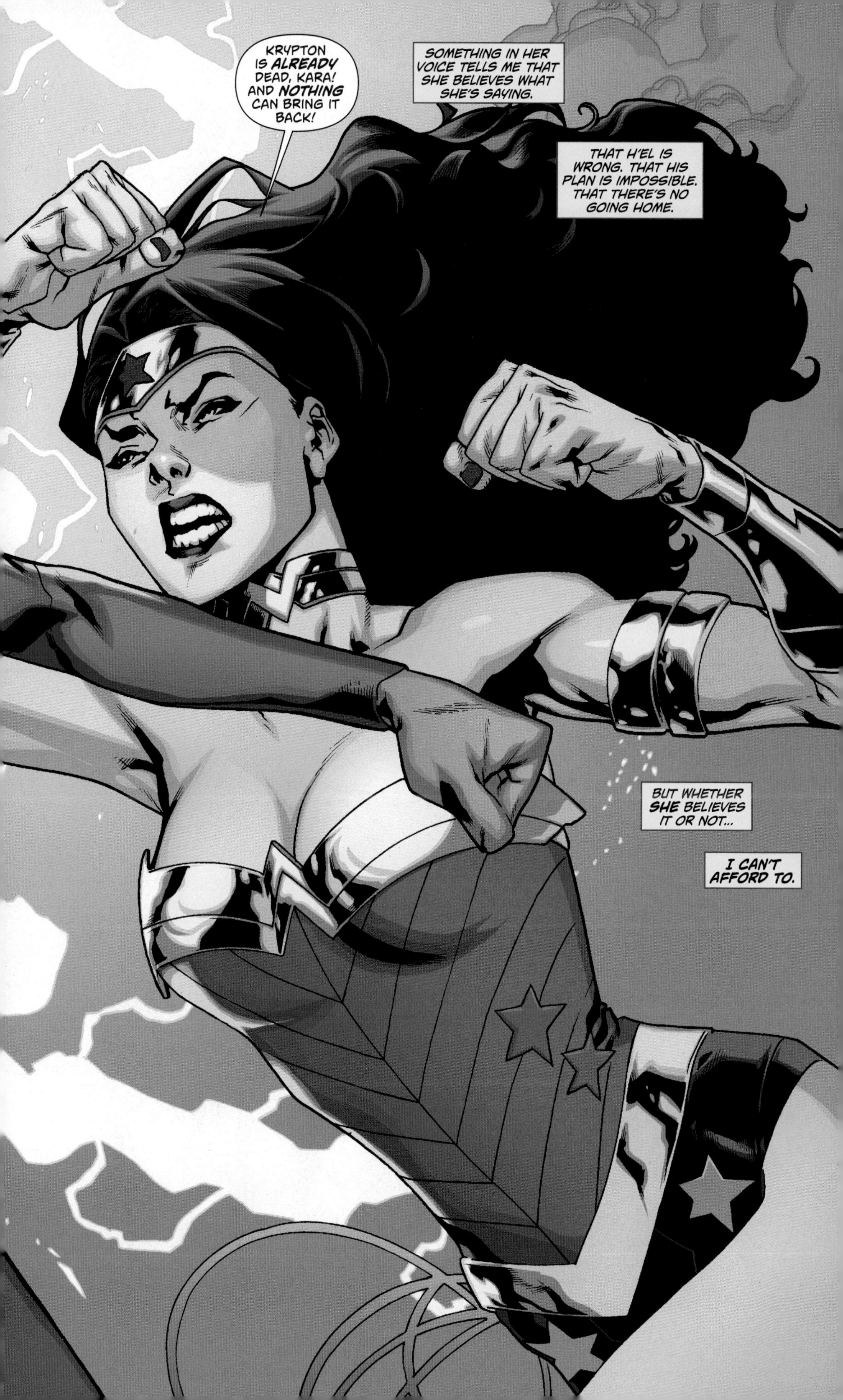
KRYPTON IS ALREADY DEAD, KARA! AND NOTHING CAN BRING IT BACK!
SOMETHING IN HER VOICE TELLS ME THAT SHE BELIEVES WHAT SHE'S SAYING.
THAT H'EL IS WRONG. THAT HIS PLAN IS IMPOSSIBLE. THAT THERE'S NO GOING HOME.
BUT WHETHER SHE BELIEVES IT OR NOT...
I CAN'T AFFORD TO.

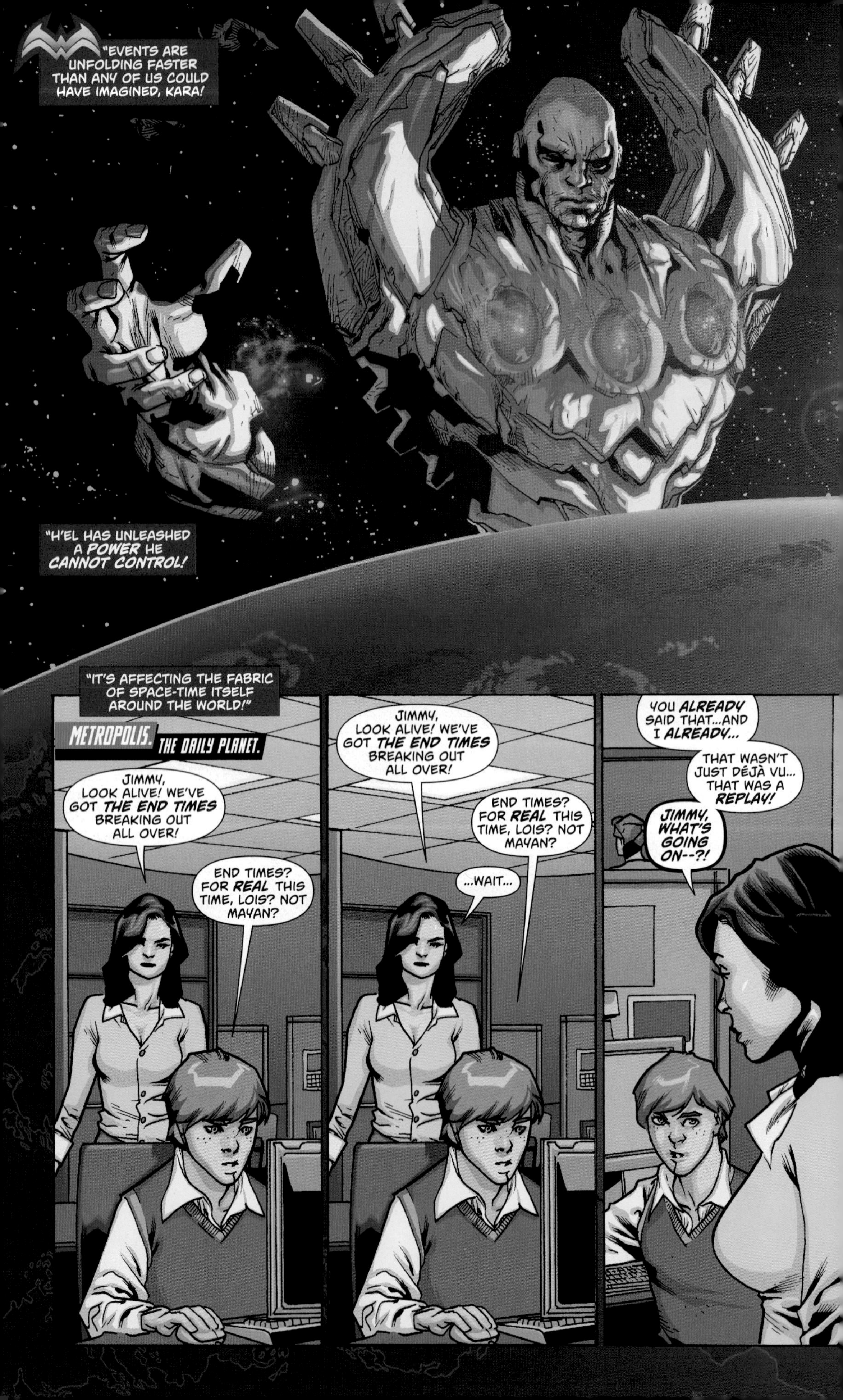
"EVENTS ARE UNFOLDING FASTER THAN ANY OF US COULD HAVE IMAGINED, KARA!
"H'EL HAS UNLEASHED A POWER HE CANNOT CONTROL!
"IT'S AFFECTING THE FABRIC OF SPACE-TIME ITSELF AROUND THE WORLD!"
METROPOLIS. THE DAILY PLANET.
JIMMY, LOOK ALIVE! WE'VE GOT THE END TIMES BREAKING OUT ALL OVER!
END TIMES? FOR REAL THIS TIME, LOIS? NOT MAYAN?
JIMMY, LOOK ALIVE! WE'VE GOT THE END TIMES BREAKING OUT ALL OVER!
END TIMES? FOR REAL THIS TIME, LOIS? NOT MAYAN?
...WAIT...
YOU ALREADY SAID THAT...AND I ALREADY...
THAT WASN'T JUST DÉJÀ VU... THAT WAS A REPLAY!
JIMMY, WHAT'S GOING ON--?!

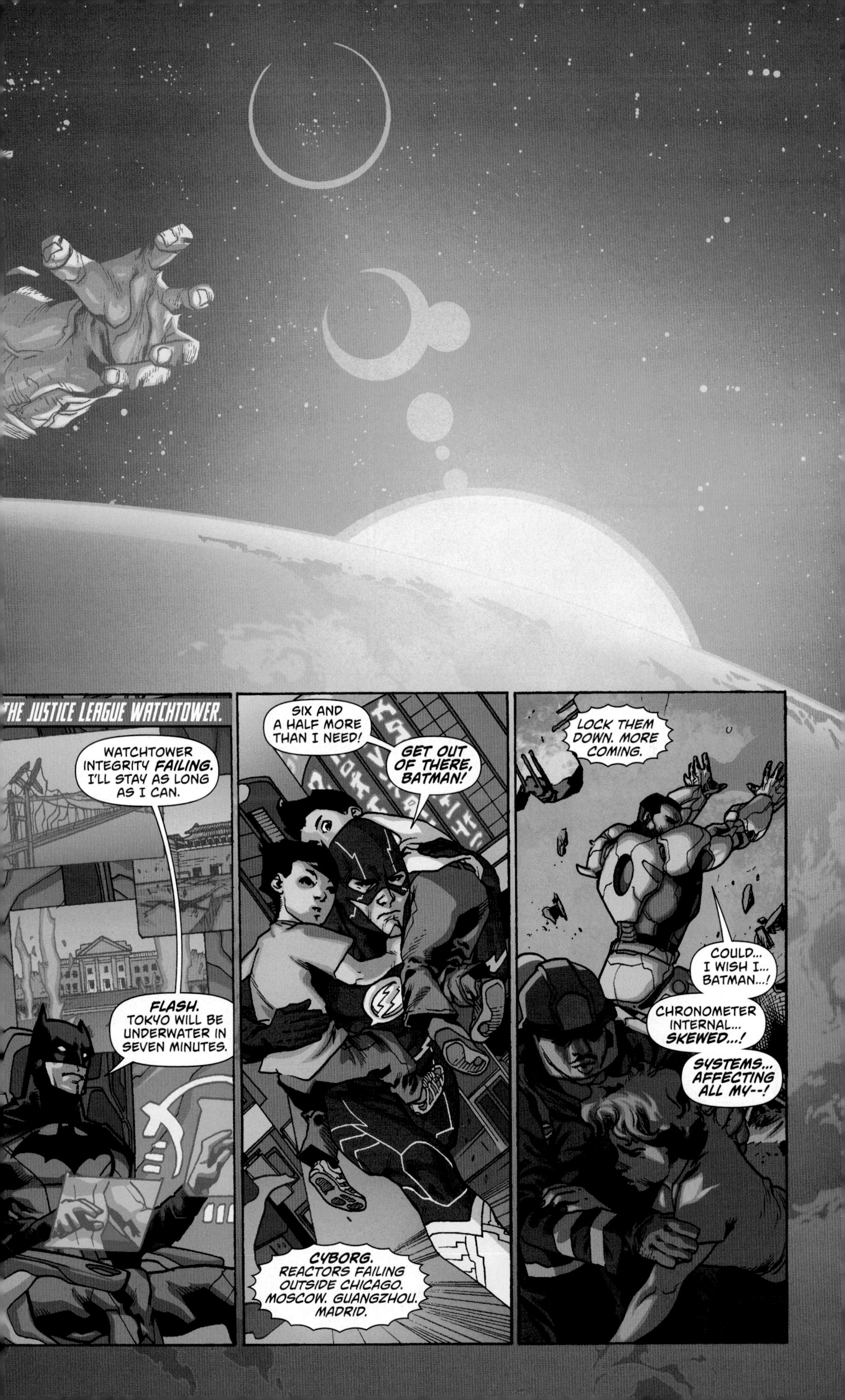
THE JUSTICE LEAGUE WATCHTOWER.
WATCHTOWER INTEGRITY FAILING. I'LL STAY AS LONG AS I CAN.
FLASH. TOKYO WILL BE UNDERWATER IN SEVEN MINUTES.
SIX AND A HALF MORE THAN I NEED!
GET OUT OF THERE, BATMAN!
CYBORG. REACTORS FAILING OUTSIDE CHICAGO. MOSCOW. GUANGZHOU. MADRID.
LOCK THEM DOWN. MORE COMING.
COULD... I WISH I... BATMAN...!
CHRONOMETER INTERNAL... SKEWED...!
SYSTEMS... AFFECTING ALL MY--!

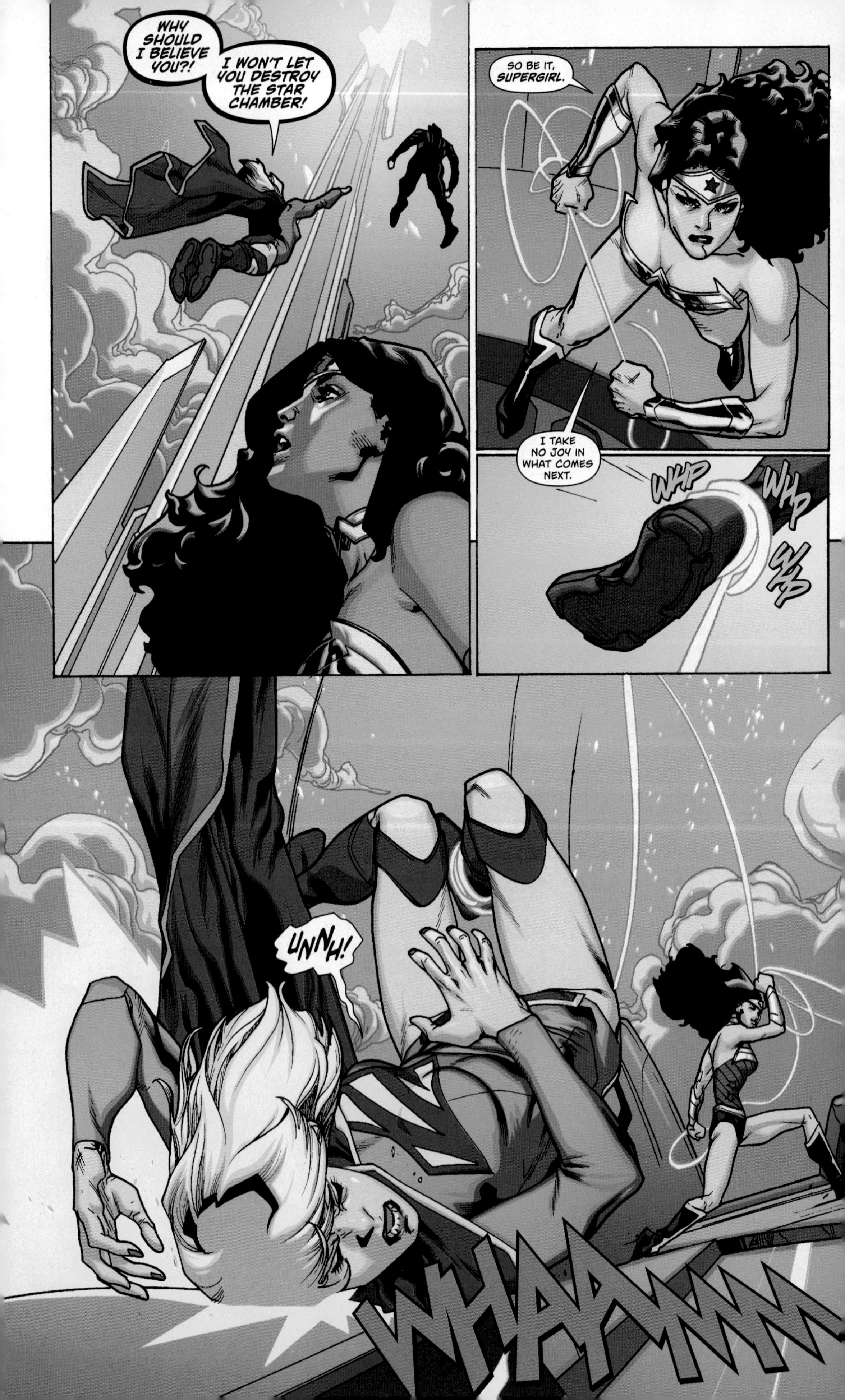
WHY SHOULD I BELIEVE YOU?!
I WON'T LET YOU DESTROY THE STAR CHAMBER!
SO BE IT, SUPERGIRL.
I TAKE NO JOY IN WHAT COMES NEXT.
WHP
WHP
WHP
UNNH!
WHAAMM

WHAT IS THIS?

SOME KIND OF PRIMITIVE *ROPE?* YOU THINK A *ROPE* CAN STOP ME?!

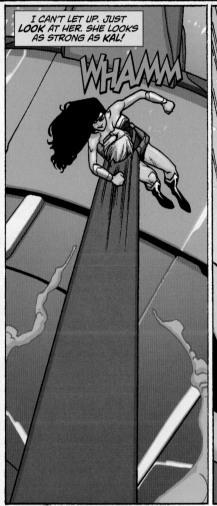

I CAN'T LET UP. JUST *LOOK* AT HER. SHE LOOKS AS STRONG AS *KAL!*

WHAMM

BUT IF I DON'T *FIGHT BACK,* I LOSE MY *ONLY CHANCE* TO *SAVE* MY *FAMILY!*

KRAANG

IN ANOTHER TIME, ANOTHER PLACE, MAYBE SHE AND I WOULD BE ALLIES...

BAAMM

BUT NOT TODAY!

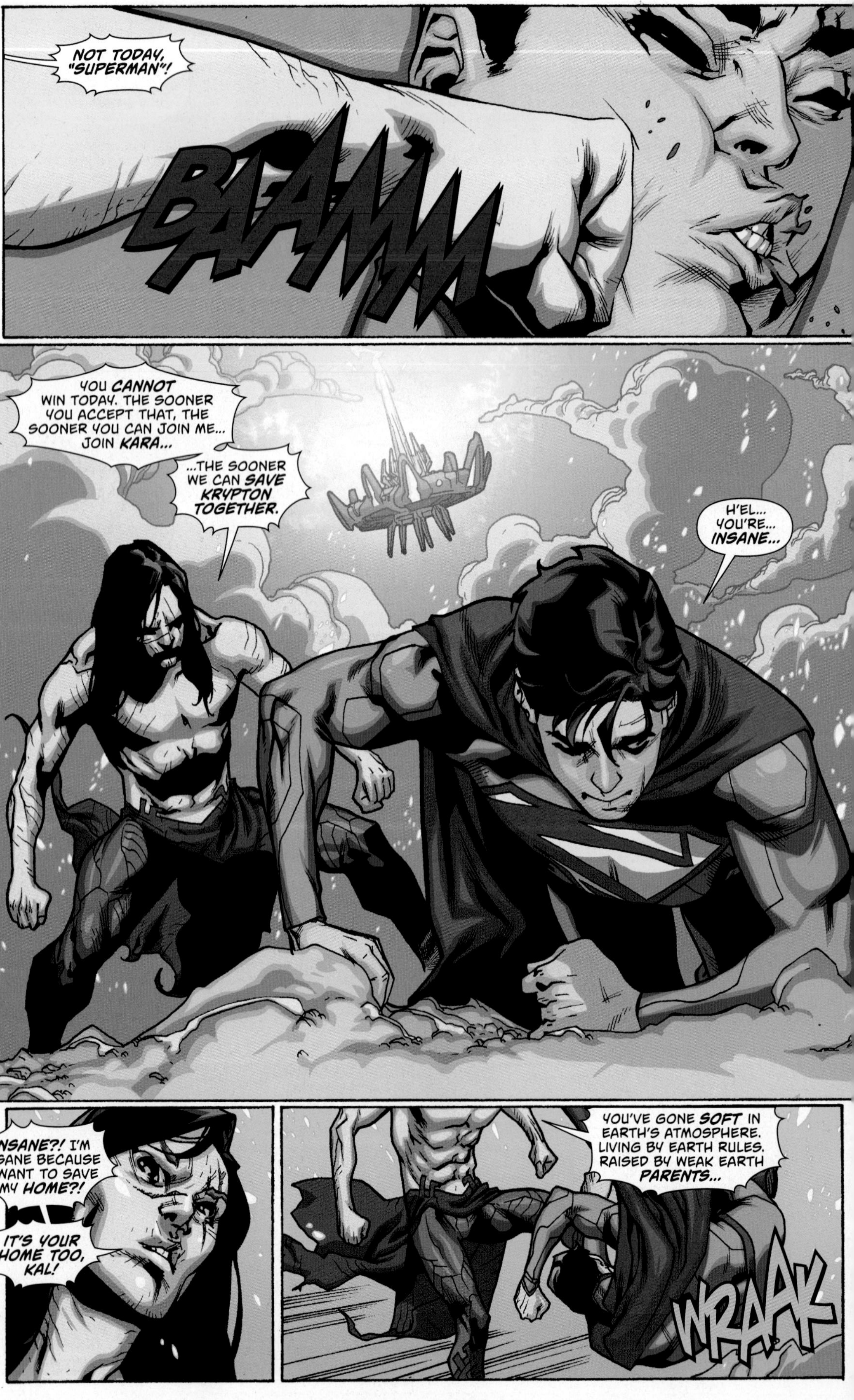
NOT TODAY, "SUPERMAN"!
BAAMM
YOU CANNOT WIN TODAY. THE SOONER YOU ACCEPT THAT, THE SOONER YOU CAN JOIN ME... JOIN KARA...
...THE SOONER WE CAN SAVE KRYPTON TOGETHER.
H'EL... YOU'RE... INSANE...
INSANE?! I'M INSANE BECAUSE I WANT TO SAVE MY HOME?!
IT'S YOUR HOME TOO, KAL!
YOU'VE GONE SOFT IN EARTH'S ATMOSPHERE. LIVING BY EARTH RULES. RAISED BY WEAK EARTH PARENTS...
WRAAK

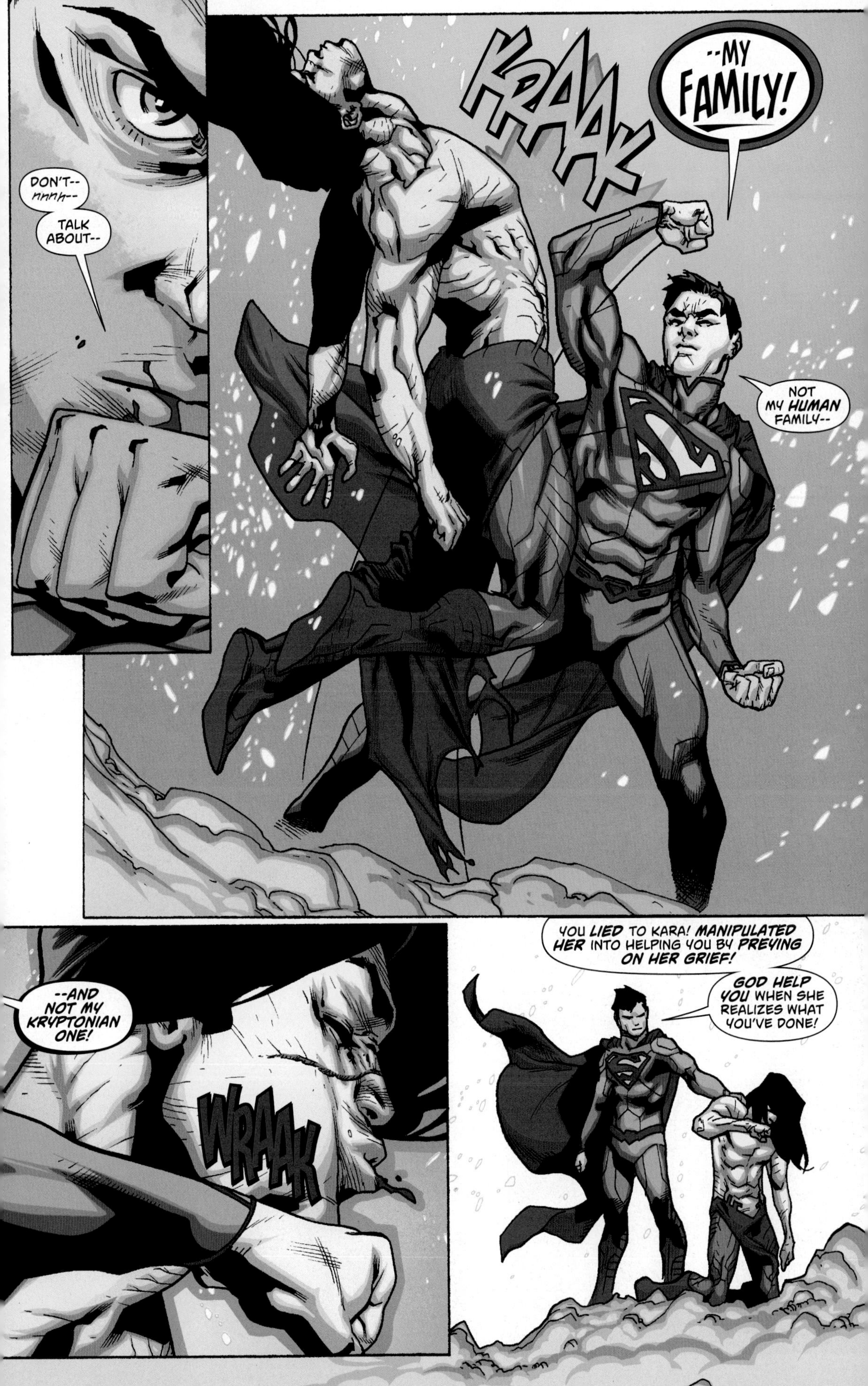
DON'T--
nnnh--
TALK ABOUT--
KRAAK
--MY FAMILY!
NOT MY HUMAN FAMILY--
--AND NOT MY KRYPTONIAN ONE!
WRAAK
YOU LIED TO KARA! MANIPULATED HER INTO HELPING YOU BY PREYING ON HER GRIEF!
GOD HELP YOU WHEN SHE REALIZES WHAT YOU'VE DONE!

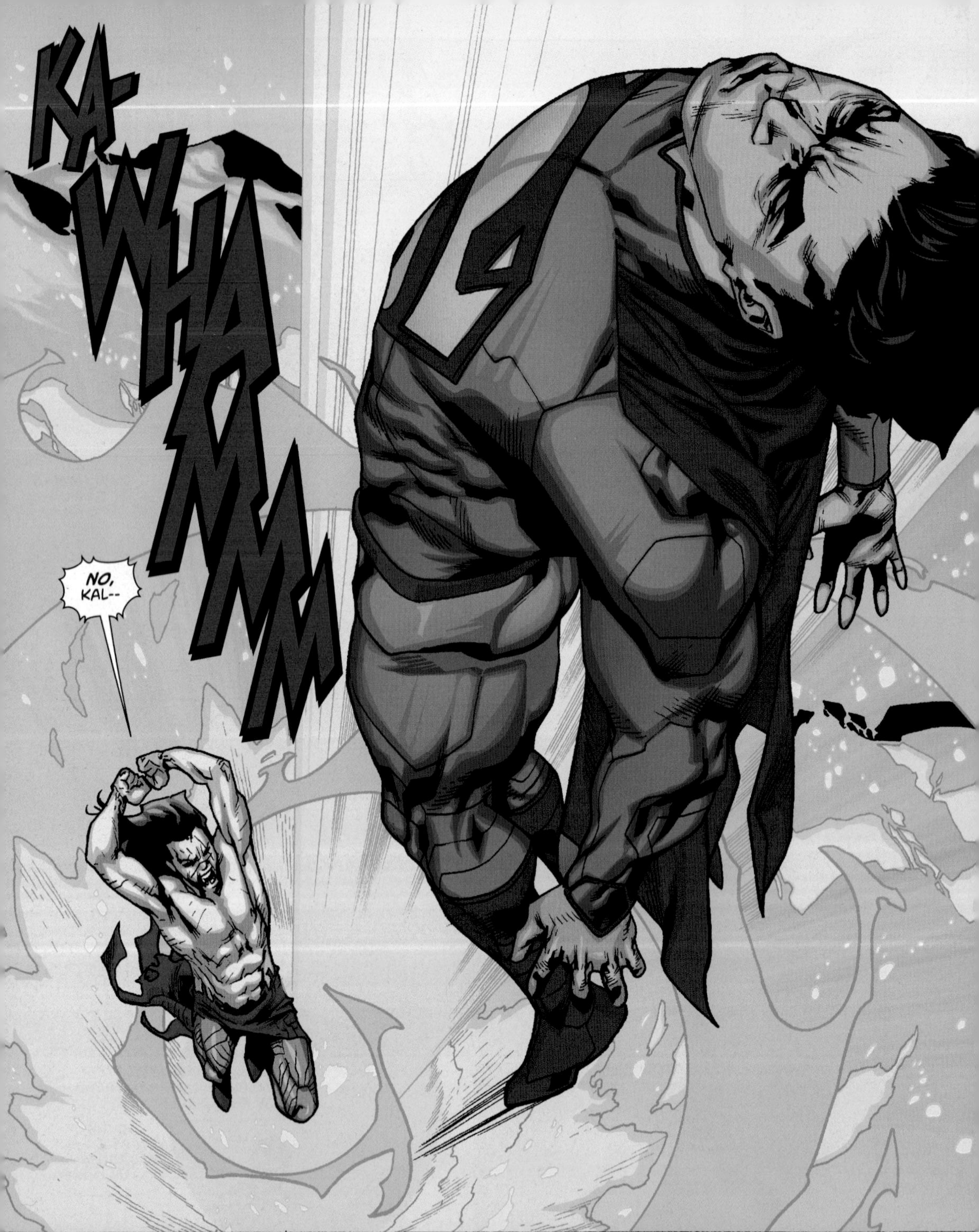
KA-WHAMMM
NO, KAL--

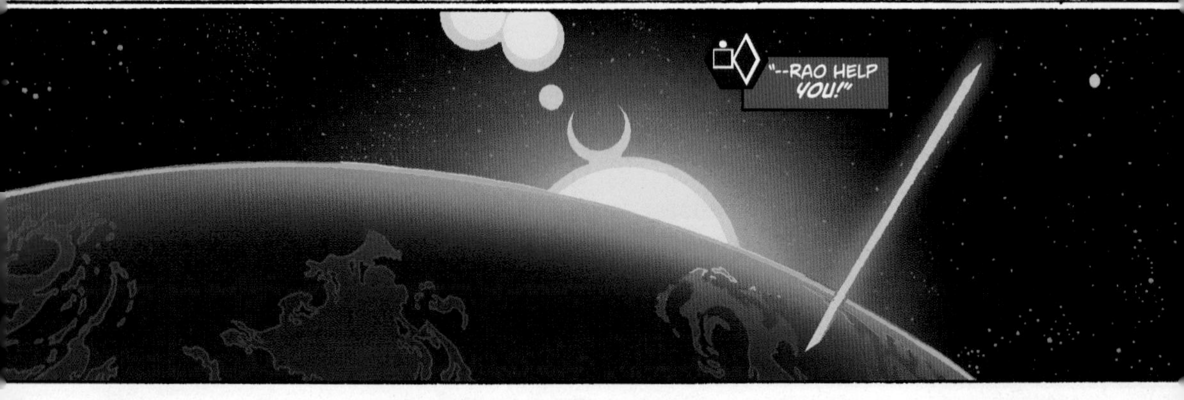
"--RAO HELP YOU!"

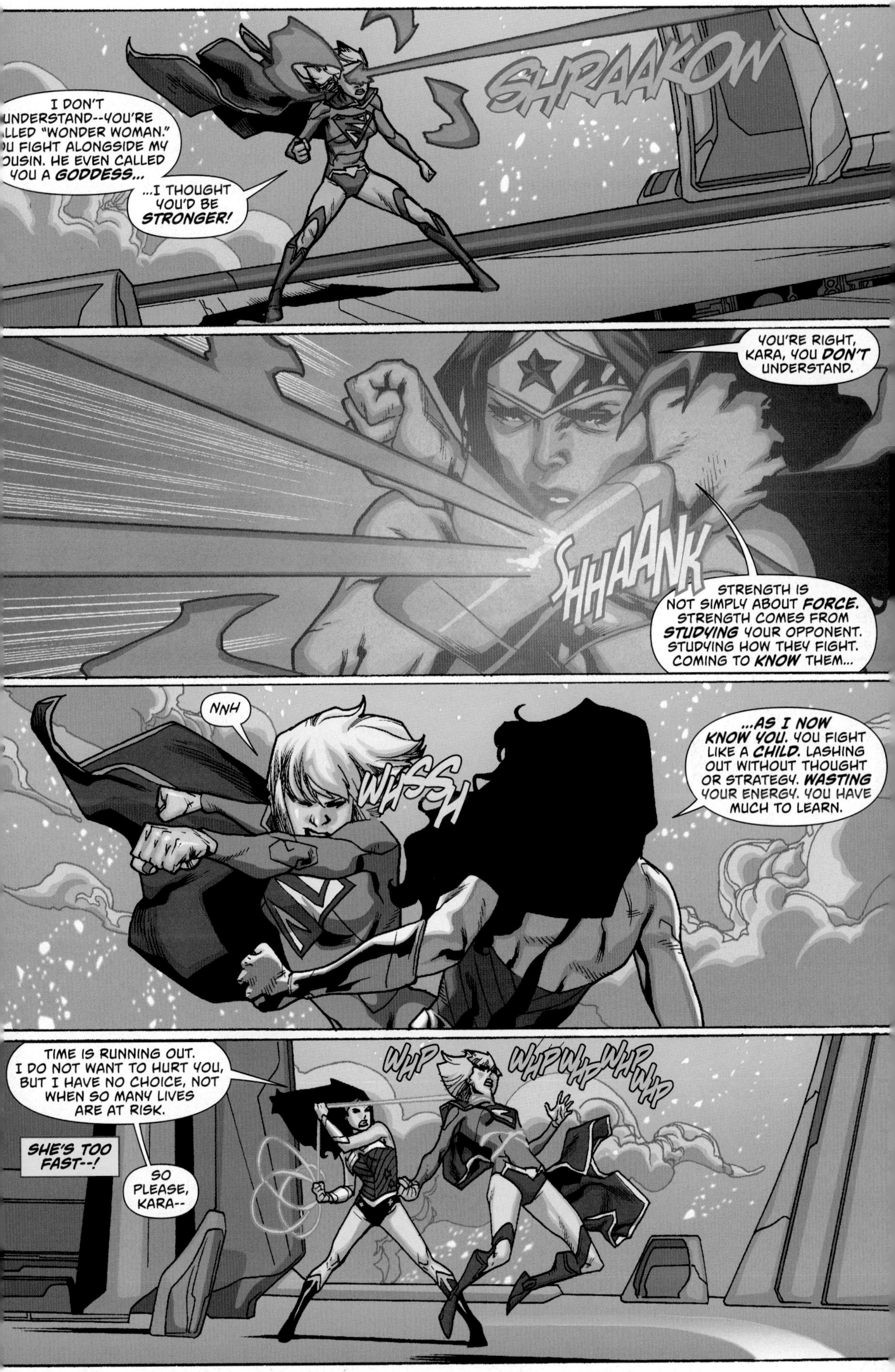
I DON'T UNDERSTAND--YOU'RE ALLED "WONDER WOMAN." OU FIGHT ALONGSIDE MY OUSIN. HE EVEN CALLED YOU A GODDESS...
...I THOUGHT YOU'D BE STRONGER!
SHRAAKOW
YOU'RE RIGHT, KARA, YOU DON'T UNDERSTAND.
SHHAANK
STRENGTH IS NOT SIMPLY ABOUT FORCE. STRENGTH COMES FROM STUDYING YOUR OPPONENT. STUDYING HOW THEY FIGHT. COMING TO KNOW THEM...
NNH
WHSSH
...AS I NOW KNOW YOU. YOU FIGHT LIKE A CHILD. LASHING OUT WITHOUT THOUGHT OR STRATEGY. WASTING YOUR ENERGY. YOU HAVE MUCH TO LEARN.
TIME IS RUNNING OUT. I DO NOT WANT TO HURT YOU, BUT I HAVE NO CHOICE, NOT WHEN SO MANY LIVES ARE AT RISK.
SHE'S TOO FAST--!
SO PLEASE, KARA--
WHP
WHPWHPWHPWHP

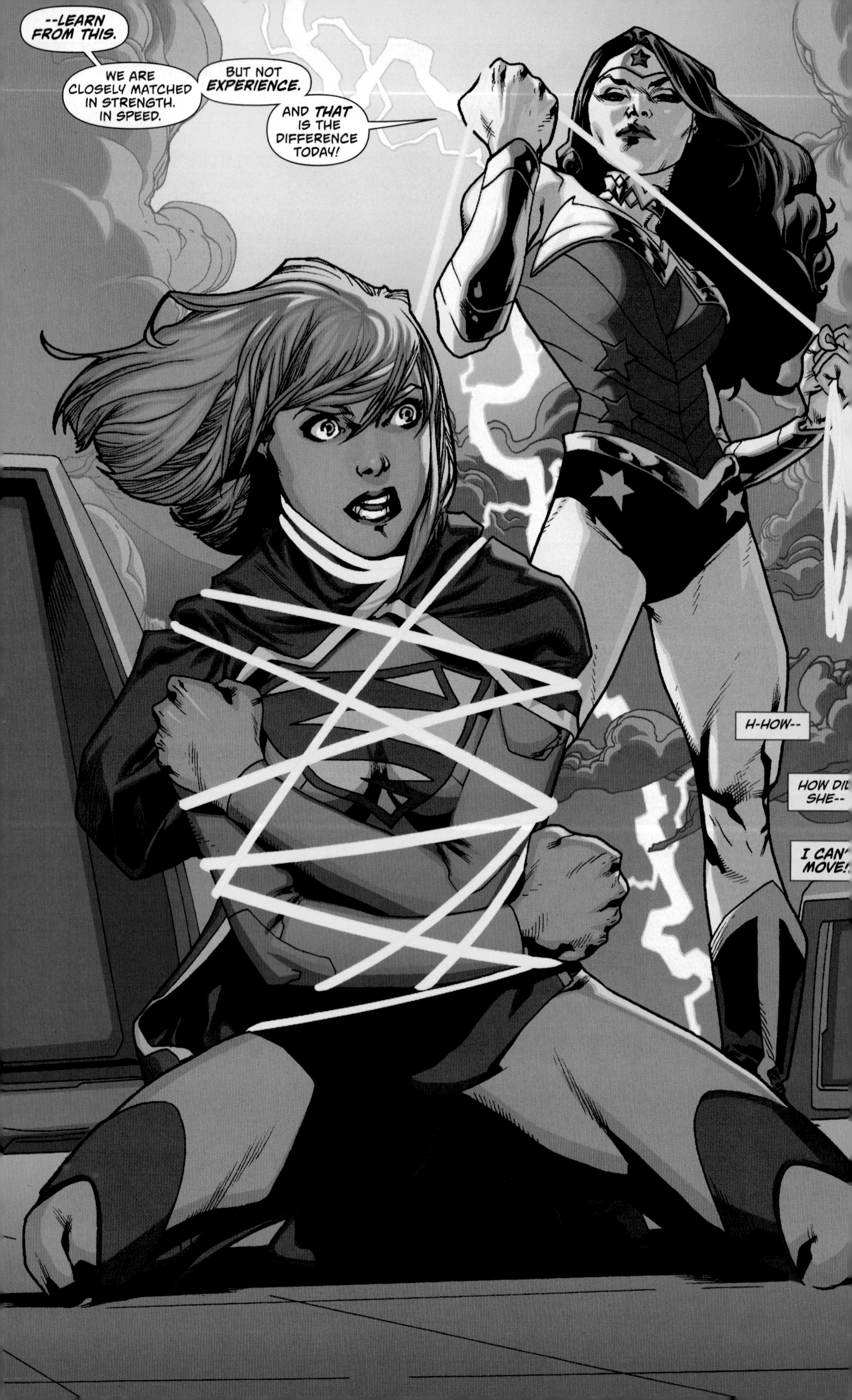
--LEARN FROM THIS.
WE ARE CLOSELY MATCHED IN STRENGTH. IN SPEED.
BUT NOT EXPERIENCE.
AND THAT IS THE DIFFERENCE TODAY!
H-HOW--
HOW DI
SHE--
I CAN'
MOVE!

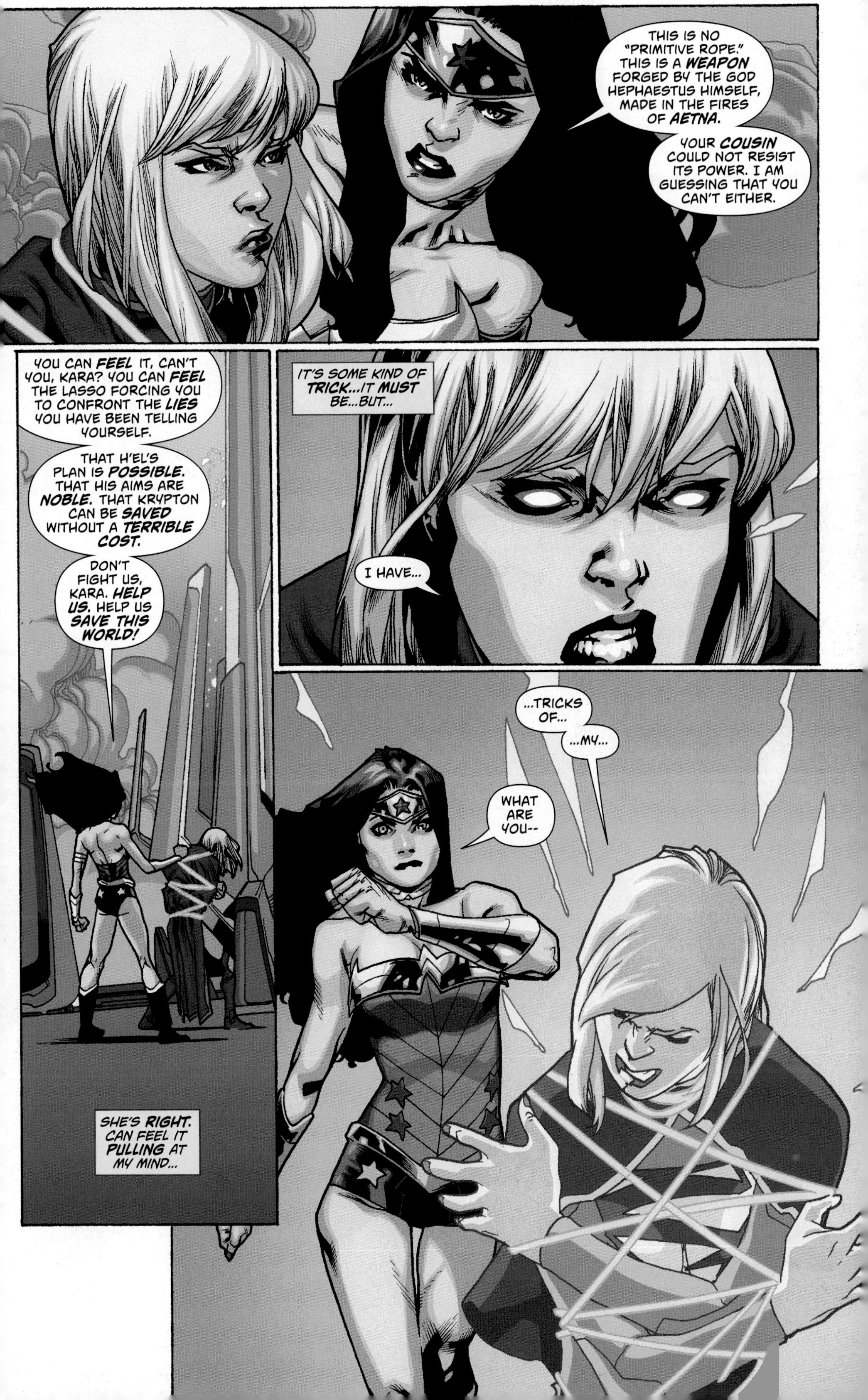

THIS IS NO "PRIMITIVE ROPE." THIS IS A WEAPON FORGED BY THE GOD HEPHAESTUS HIMSELF, MADE IN THE FIRES OF AETNA.
YOUR COUSIN COULD NOT RESIST ITS POWER. I AM GUESSING THAT YOU CAN'T EITHER.
YOU CAN FEEL IT, CAN'T YOU, KARA? YOU CAN FEEL THE LASSO FORCING YOU TO CONFRONT THE LIES YOU HAVE BEEN TELLING YOURSELF.
THAT H'EL'S PLAN IS POSSIBLE. THAT HIS AIMS ARE NOBLE. THAT KRYPTON CAN BE SAVED WITHOUT A TERRIBLE COST.
DON'T FIGHT US, KARA. HELP US. HELP US SAVE THIS WORLD!
IT'S SOME KIND OF TRICK...IT MUST BE...BUT...
I HAVE...
...TRICKS OF...
...MY...
WHAT ARE YOU--
SHE'S RIGHT. CAN FEEL IT PULLING AT MY MIND...

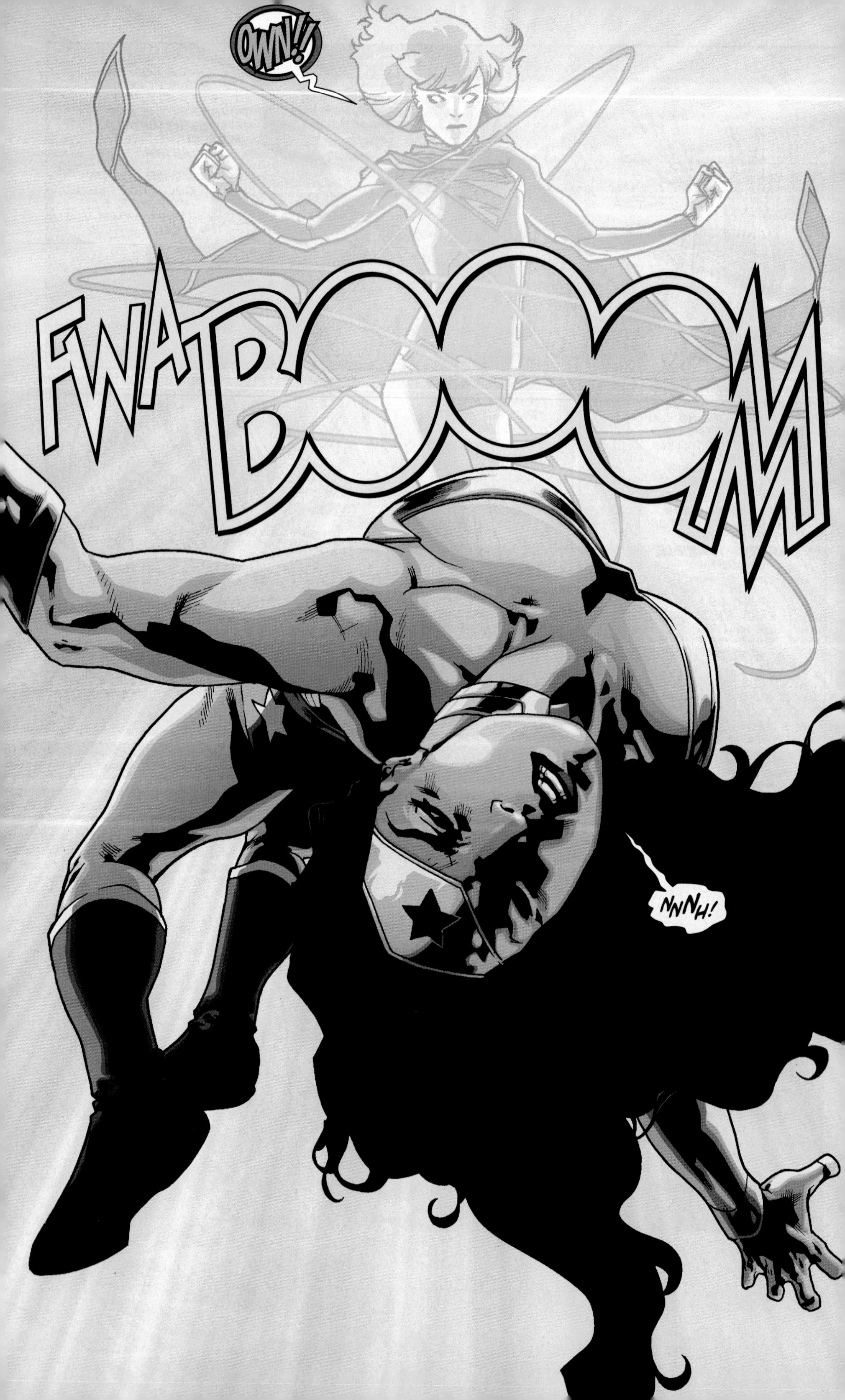
OWW!!
FWABOOOM
NNNH!

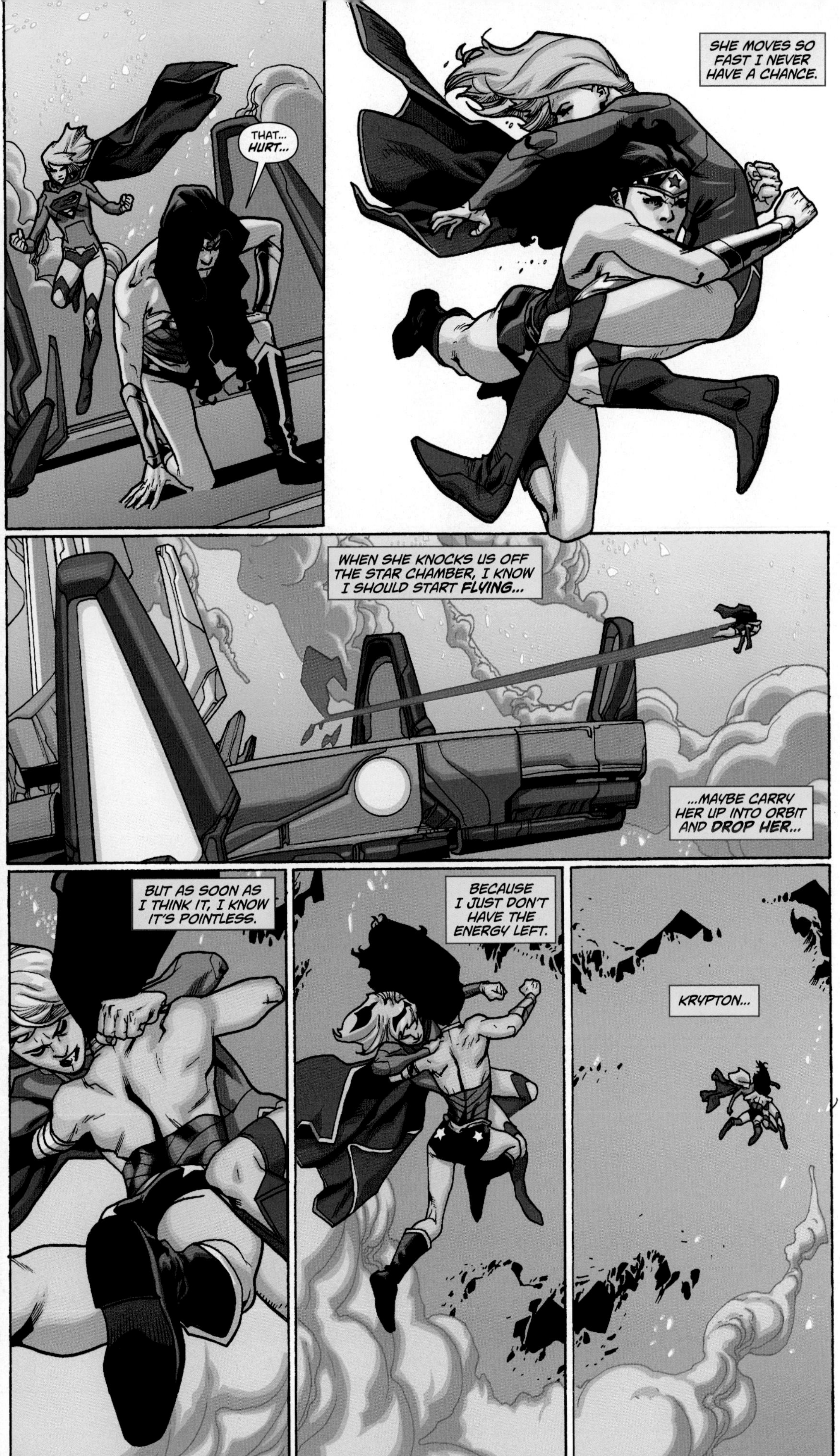
THAT... HURT...
SHE MOVES SO FAST I NEVER HAVE A CHANCE.
WHEN SHE KNOCKS US OFF THE STAR CHAMBER, I KNOW I SHOULD START FLYING...
...MAYBE CARRY HER UP INTO ORBIT AND DROP HER...
BUT AS SOON AS I THINK IT, I KNOW IT'S POINTLESS.
BECAUSE I JUST DON'T HAVE THE ENERGY LEFT.
KRYPTON...

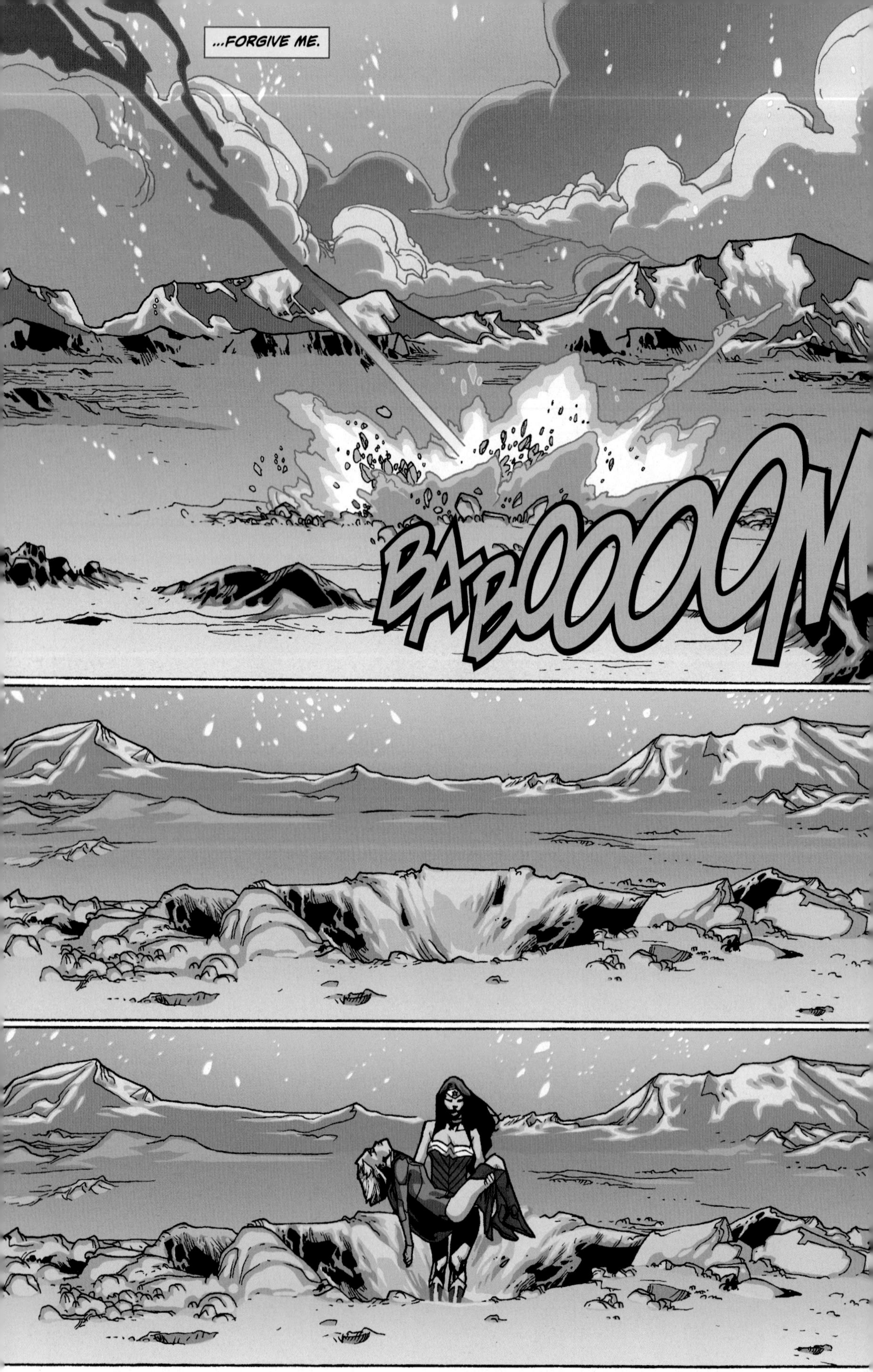
...FORGIVE ME.
BABOOOOM

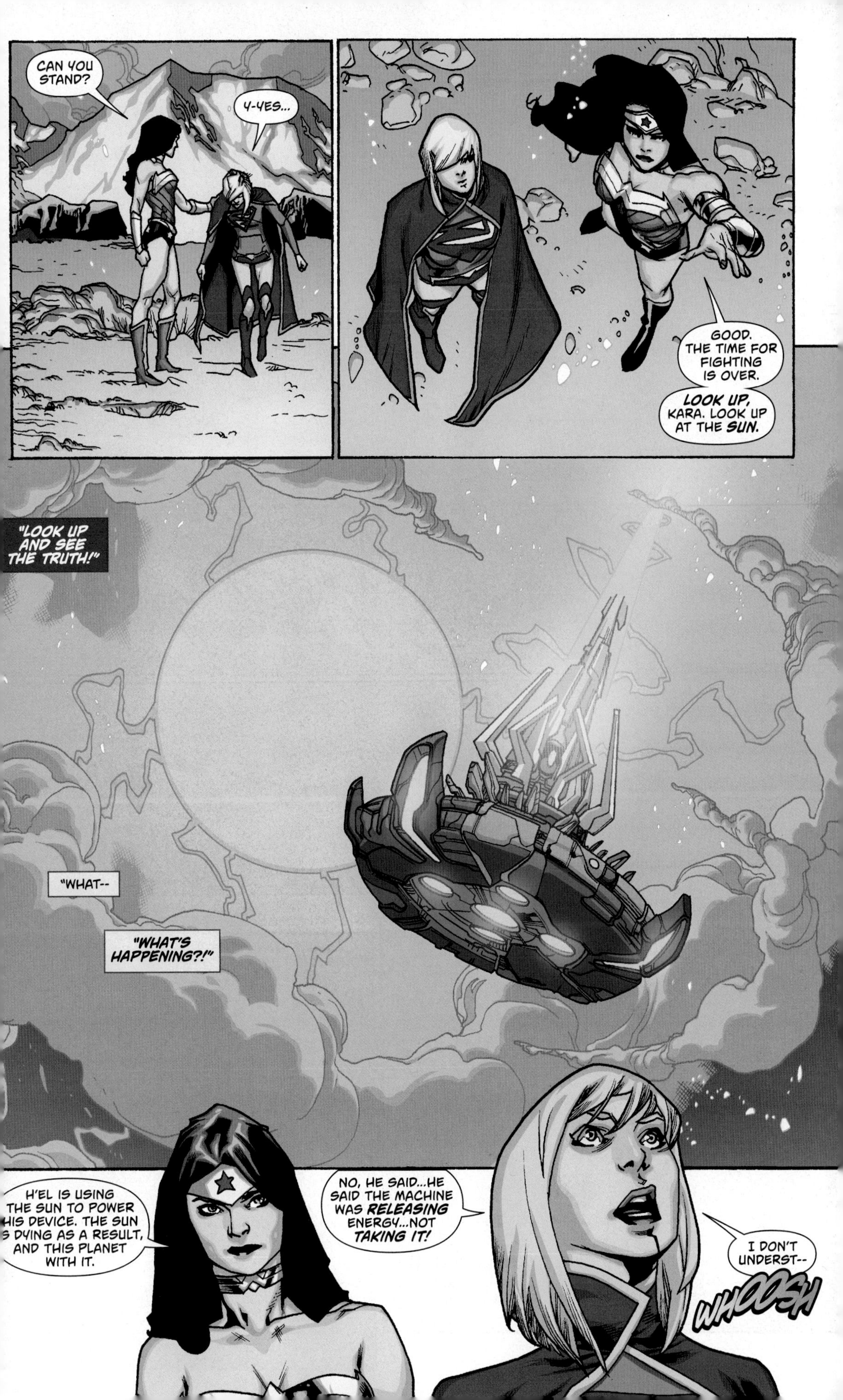

CAN YOU STAND?
Y-YES...
GOOD. THE TIME FOR FIGHTING IS OVER.
LOOK UP, KARA. LOOK UP AT THE SUN.
"LOOK UP AND SEE THE TRUTH!"
"WHAT--
"WHAT'S HAPPENING?!"
H'EL IS USING THE SUN TO POWER HIS DEVICE. THE SUN IS DYING AS A RESULT, AND THIS PLANET WITH IT.
NO, HE SAID...HE SAID THE MACHINE WAS RELEASING ENERGY...NOT TAKING IT!
I DON'T UNDERST--
WHOOSH

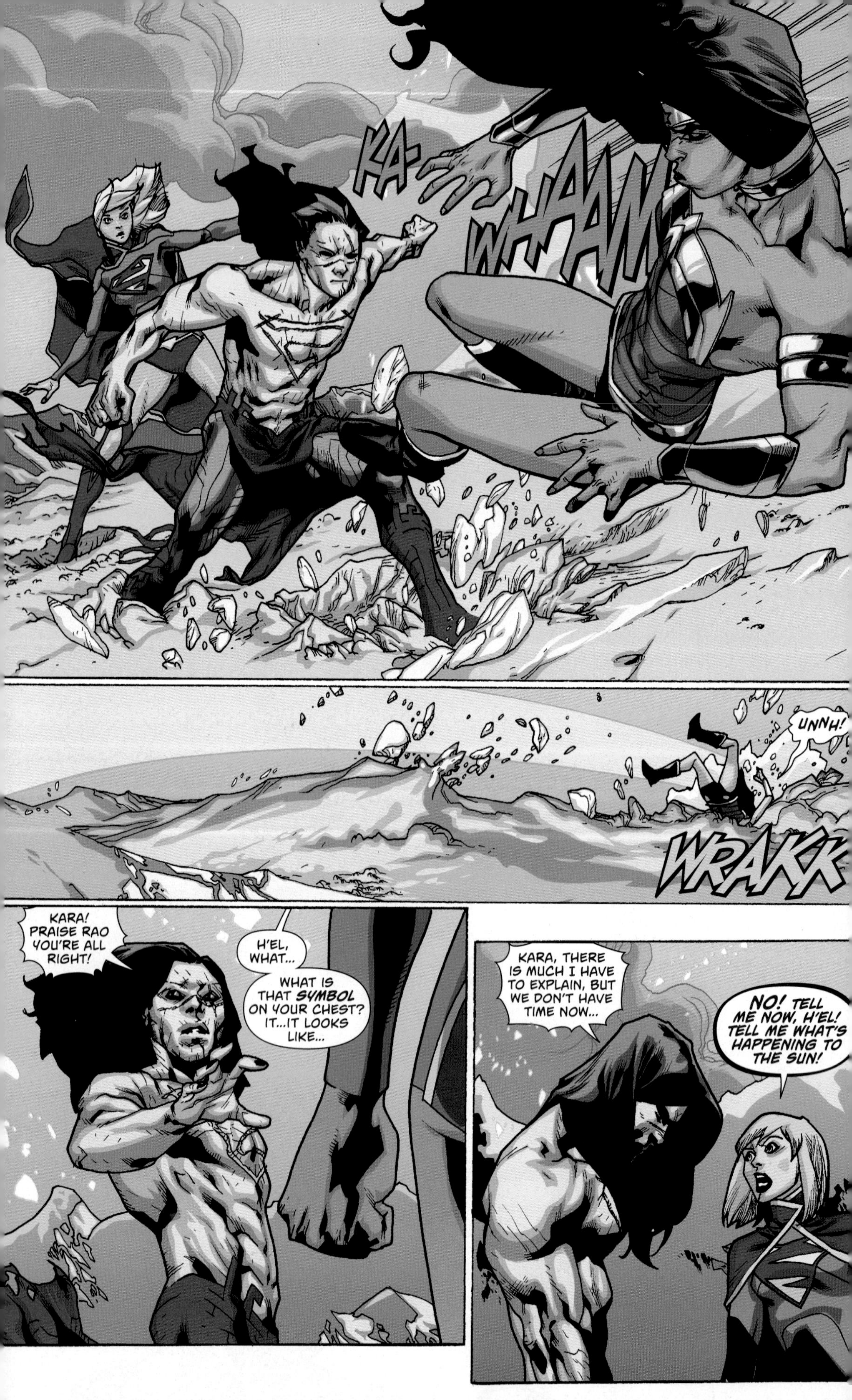
KA-
WHAAM!
UNNH!
WRAKK
KARA! PRAISE RAO YOU'RE ALL RIGHT!
H'EL, WHAT...
WHAT IS THAT SYMBOL ON YOUR CHEST? IT...IT LOOKS LIKE...
KARA, THERE IS MUCH I HAVE TO EXPLAIN, BUT WE DON'T HAVE TIME NOW...
NO! TELL ME NOW, H'EL! TELL ME WHAT'S HAPPENING TO THE SUN!

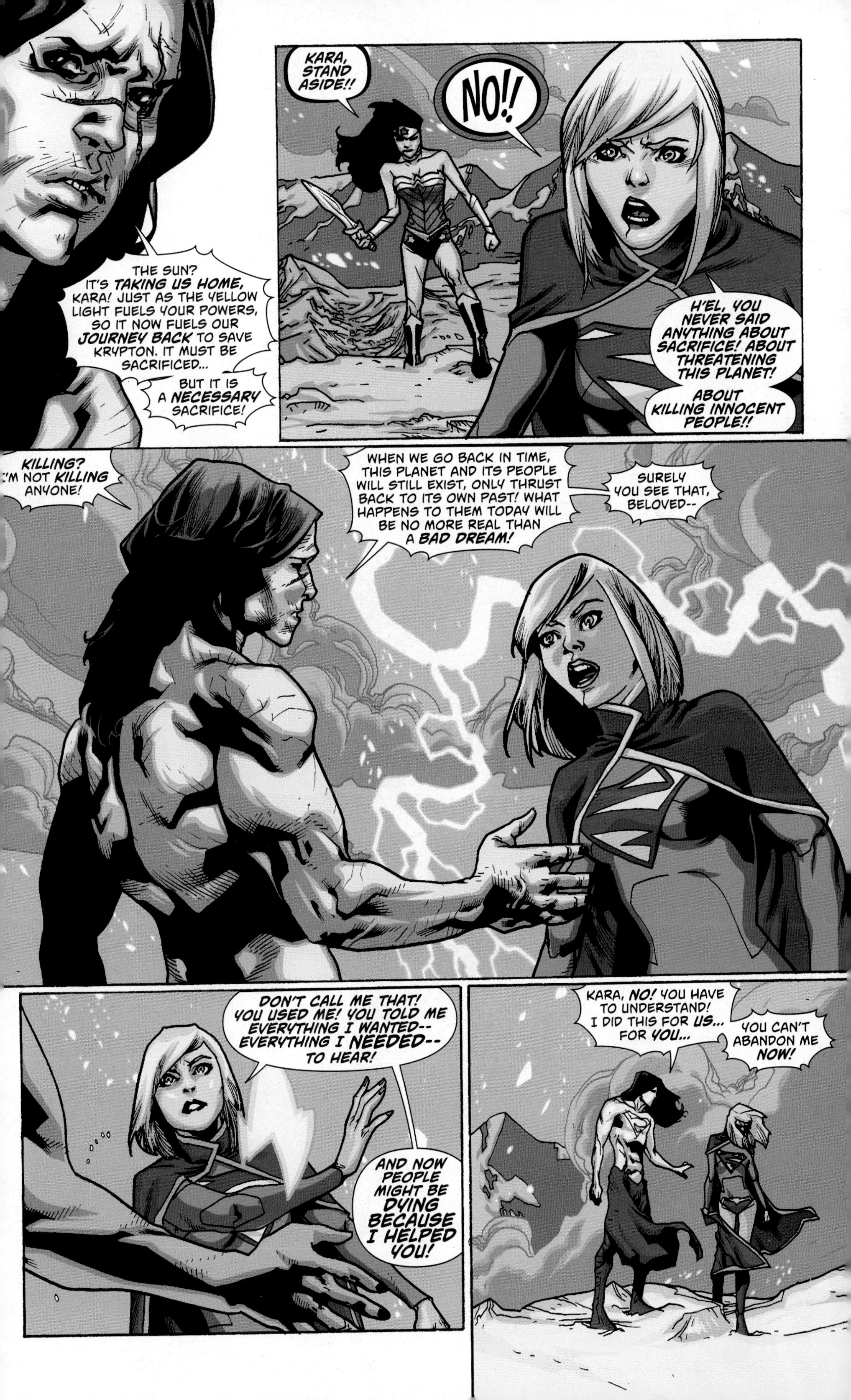
THE SUN? IT'S TAKING US HOME, KARA! JUST AS THE YELLOW LIGHT FUELS YOUR POWERS, SO IT NOW FUELS OUR JOURNEY BACK TO SAVE KRYPTON. IT MUST BE SACRIFICED...
BUT IT IS A NECESSARY SACRIFICE!
KARA, STAND ASIDE!!
NO!!
H'EL, YOU NEVER SAID ANYTHING ABOUT SACRIFICE! ABOUT THREATENING THIS PLANET!
ABOUT KILLING INNOCENT PEOPLE!!
KILLING? I'M NOT KILLING ANYONE!
WHEN WE GO BACK IN TIME, THIS PLANET AND ITS PEOPLE WILL STILL EXIST, ONLY THRUST BACK TO ITS OWN PAST! WHAT HAPPENS TO THEM TODAY WILL BE NO MORE REAL THAN A BAD DREAM!
SURELY YOU SEE THAT, BELOVED--
DON'T CALL ME THAT! YOU USED ME! YOU TOLD ME EVERYTHING I WANTED-- EVERYTHING I NEEDED-- TO HEAR!
AND NOW PEOPLE MIGHT BE DYING BECAUSE I HELPED YOU!
KARA, NO! YOU HAVE TO UNDERSTAND! I DID THIS FOR US... FOR YOU...
YOU CAN'T ABANDON ME NOW!

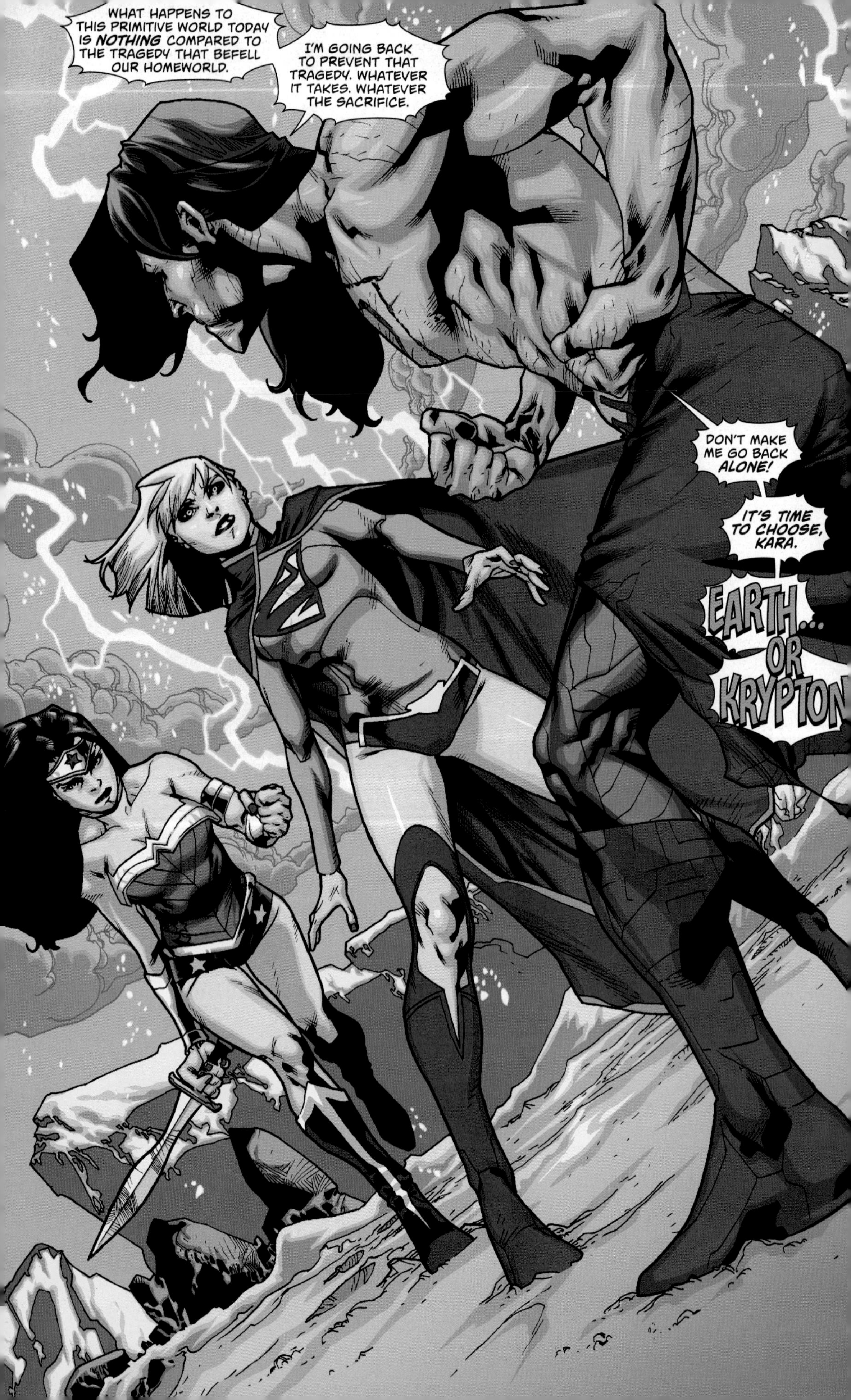
WHAT HAPPENS TO THIS PRIMITIVE WORLD TODAY IS *NOTHING* COMPARED TO THE TRAGEDY THAT BEFELL OUR HOMEWORLD.
I'M GOING BACK TO PREVENT THAT TRAGEDY. WHATEVER IT TAKES. WHATEVER THE SACRIFICE.
DON'T MAKE ME GO BACK *ALONE!*
IT'S TIME TO CHOOSE, KARA.
EARTH... OR KRYPTON

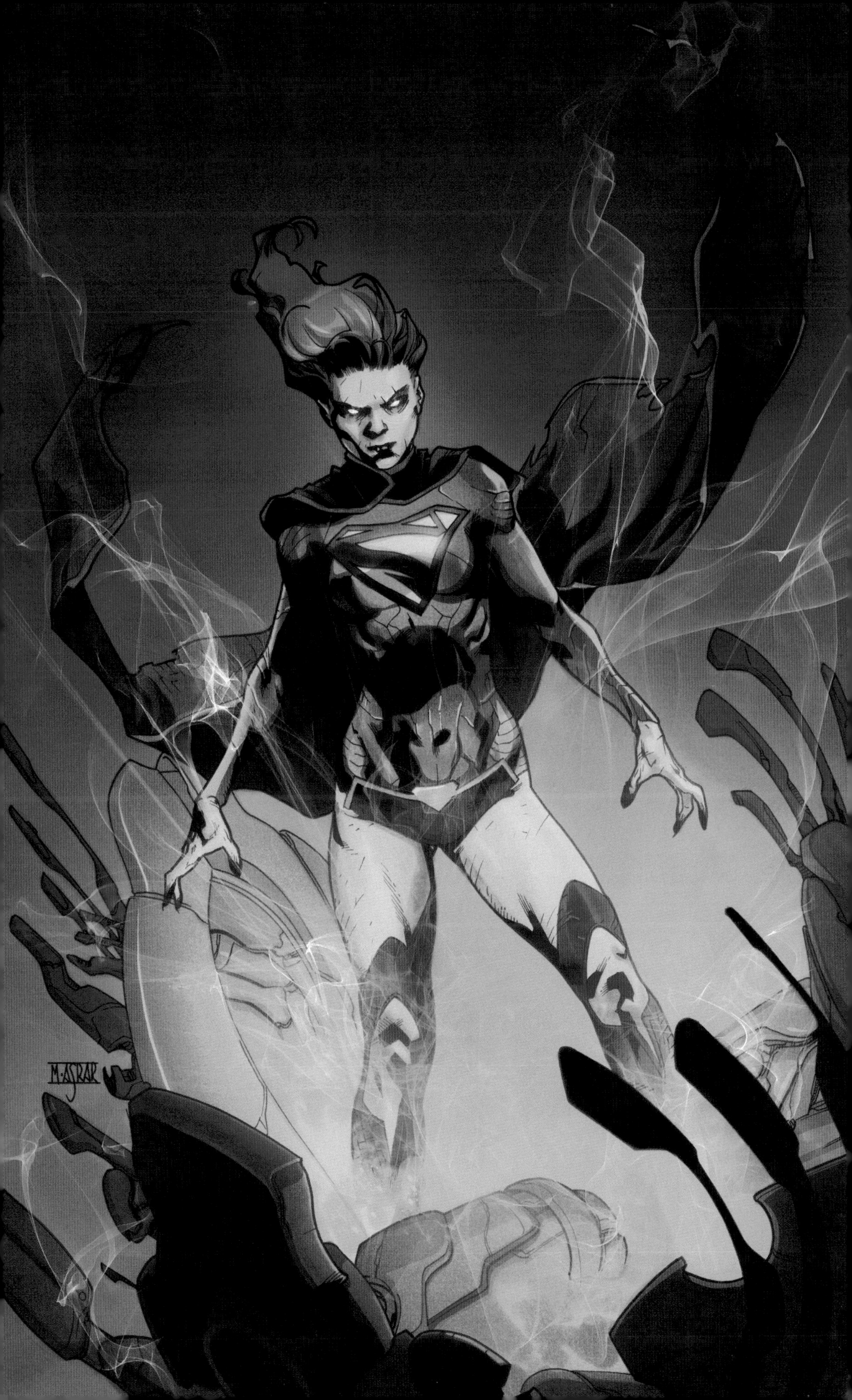
M.ASRAR

WHAT KRYPTONITE DOES NOT KILL... IT ONLY MAKES STRONGER...

FRANK HANNAH writer **ROBSON ROCHA** penciller **OCLAIR ALBERT, JULIO FERREIRA & MARIAH BENES** inkers
cover art by **MAHMUD ASRAR & DAVE McCAIG**

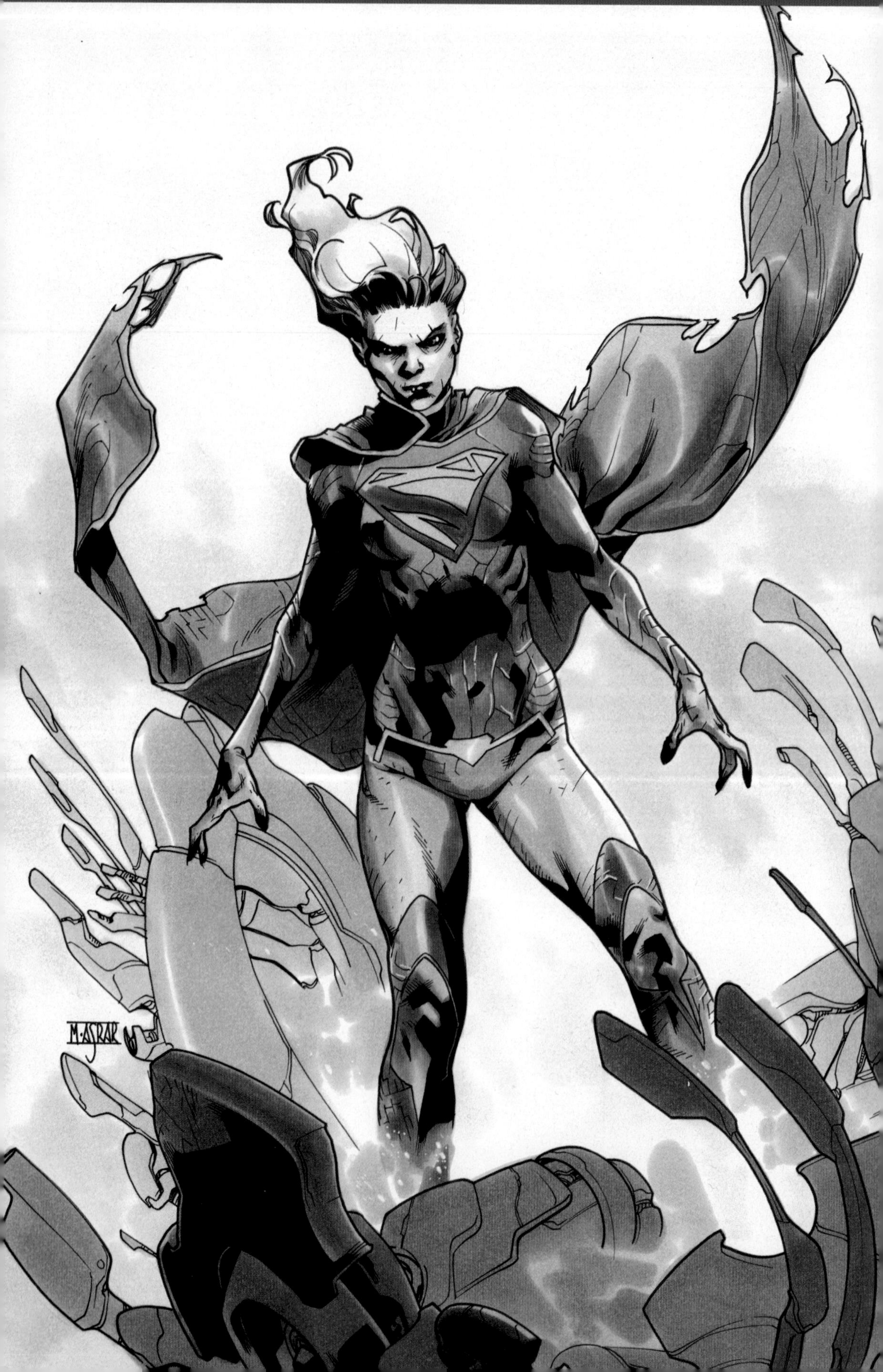
M·ASRAR

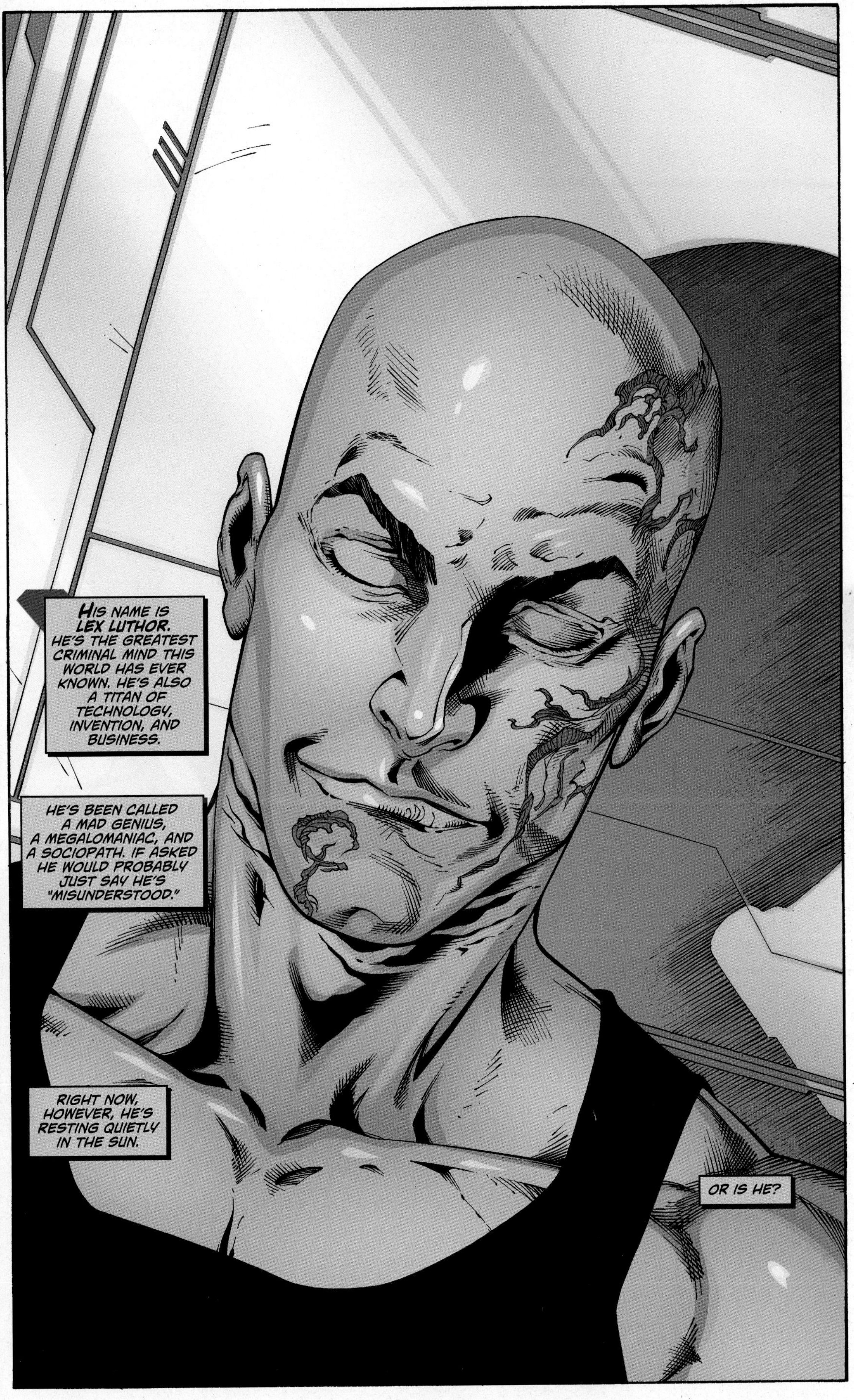
HIS NAME IS LEX LUTHOR. HE'S THE GREATEST CRIMINAL MIND THIS WORLD HAS EVER KNOWN. HE'S ALSO A TITAN OF TECHNOLOGY, INVENTION, AND BUSINESS.
HE'S BEEN CALLED A MAD GENIUS, A MEGALOMANIAC, AND A SOCIOPATH. IF ASKED HE WOULD PROBABLY JUST SAY HE'S "MISUNDERSTOOD."
RIGHT NOW, HOWEVER, HE'S RESTING QUIETLY IN THE SUN.
OR IS HE?

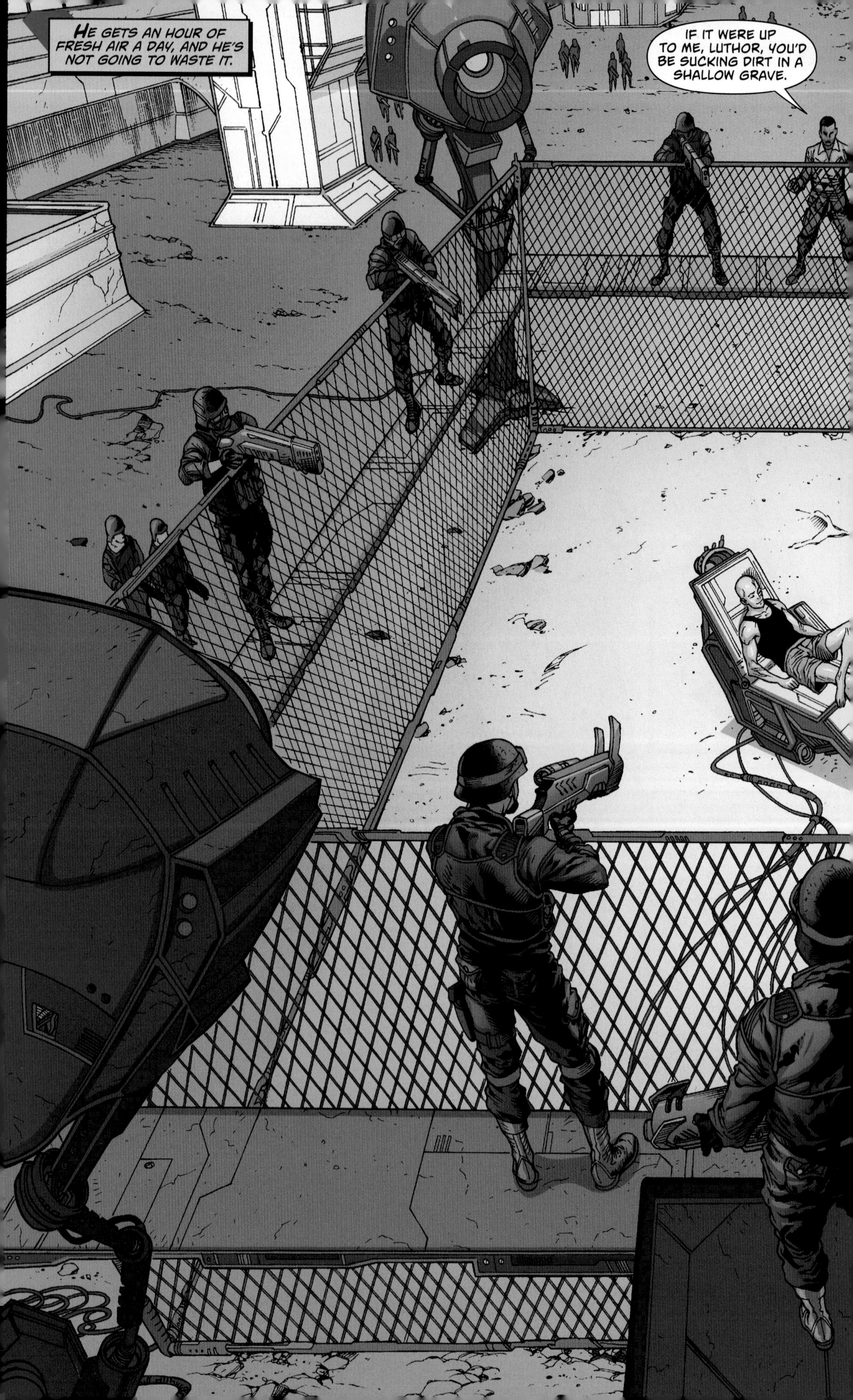
HE GETS AN HOUR OF FRESH AIR A DAY, AND HE'S NOT GOING TO WASTE IT.
IF IT WERE UP TO ME, LUTHOR, YOU'D BE SUCKING DIRT IN A SHALLOW GRAVE.

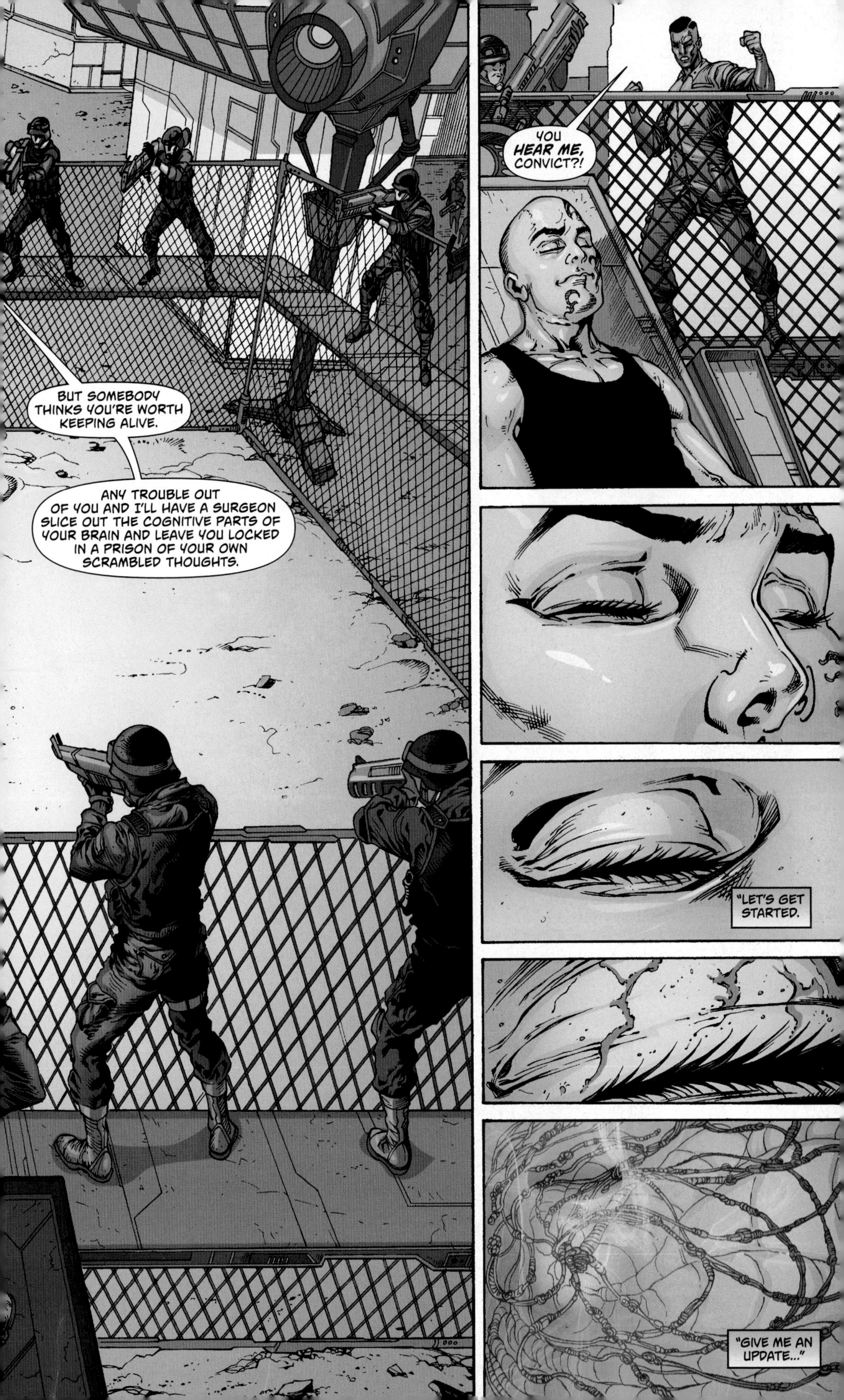
BUT SOMEBODY THINKS YOU'RE WORTH KEEPING ALIVE.
ANY TROUBLE OUT OF YOU AND I'LL HAVE A SURGEON SLICE OUT THE COGNITIVE PARTS OF YOUR BRAIN AND LEAVE YOU LOCKED IN A PRISON OF YOUR OWN SCRAMBLED THOUGHTS.
YOU HEAR ME, CONVICT?!
"LET'S GET STARTED.
"GIVE ME AN UPDATE..."

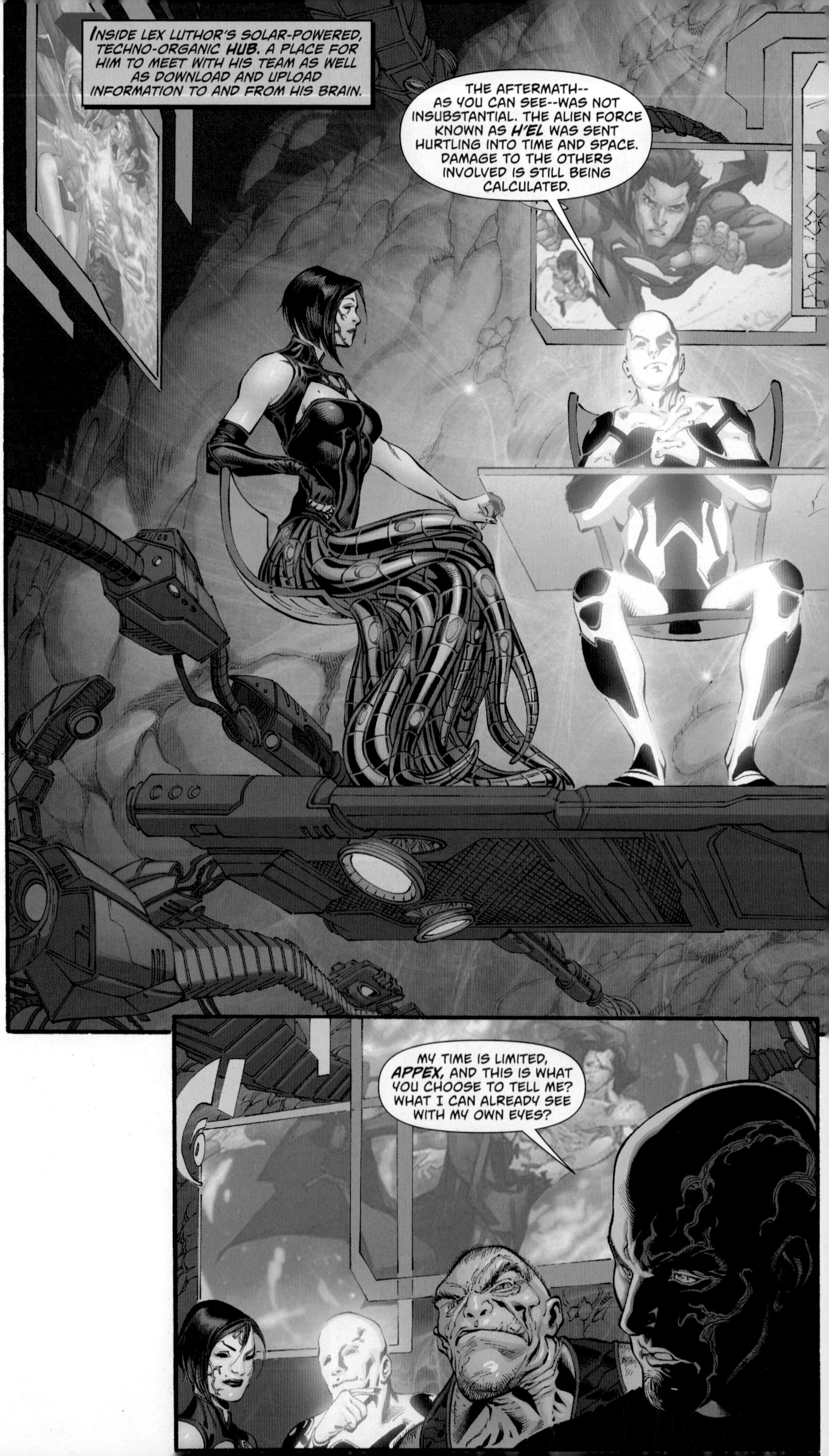
INSIDE LEX LUTHOR'S SOLAR-POWERED, TECHNO-ORGANIC HUB. A PLACE FOR HIM TO MEET WITH HIS TEAM AS WELL AS DOWNLOAD AND UPLOAD INFORMATION TO AND FROM HIS BRAIN.
THE AFTERMATH-- AS YOU CAN SEE--WAS NOT INSUBSTANTIAL. THE ALIEN FORCE KNOWN AS H'EL WAS SENT HURTLING INTO TIME AND SPACE. DAMAGE TO THE OTHERS INVOLVED IS STILL BEING CALCULATED.
MY TIME IS LIMITED, APPEX, AND THIS IS WHAT YOU CHOOSE TO TELL ME? WHAT I CAN ALREADY SEE WITH MY OWN EYES?

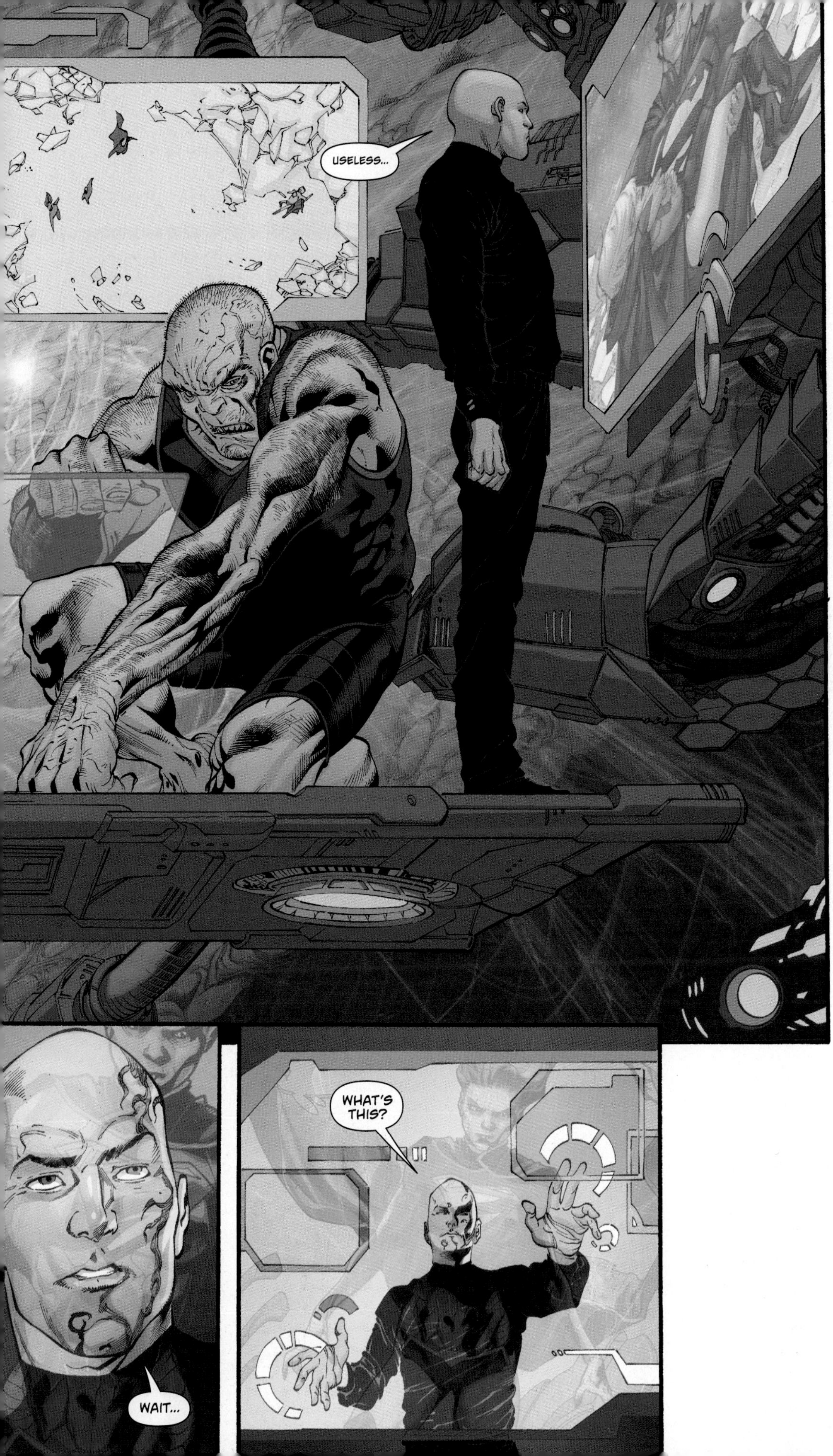
USELESS...
WAIT...
WHAT'S THIS?

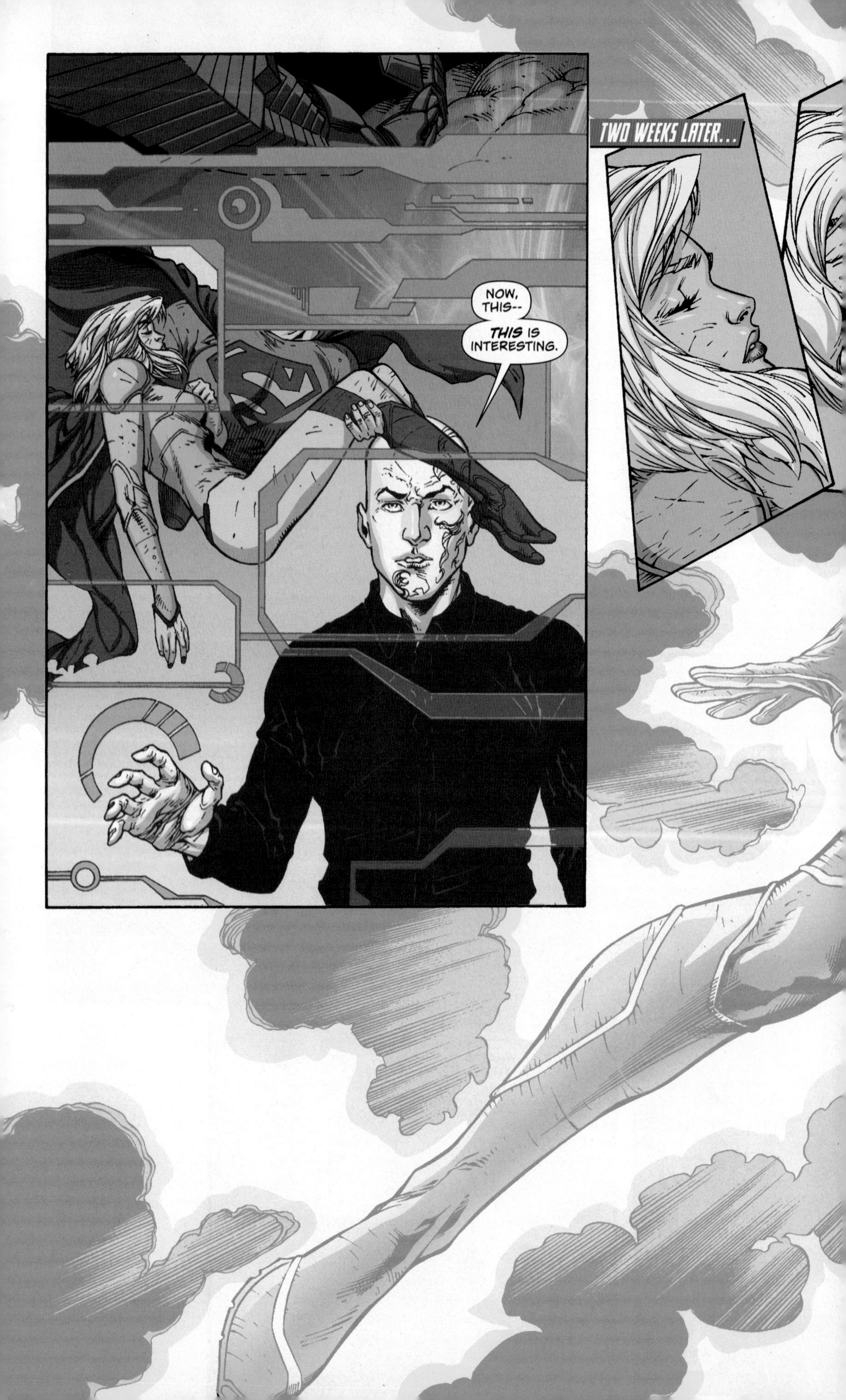
NOW, THIS-- THIS IS INTERESTING.
TWO WEEKS LATER...

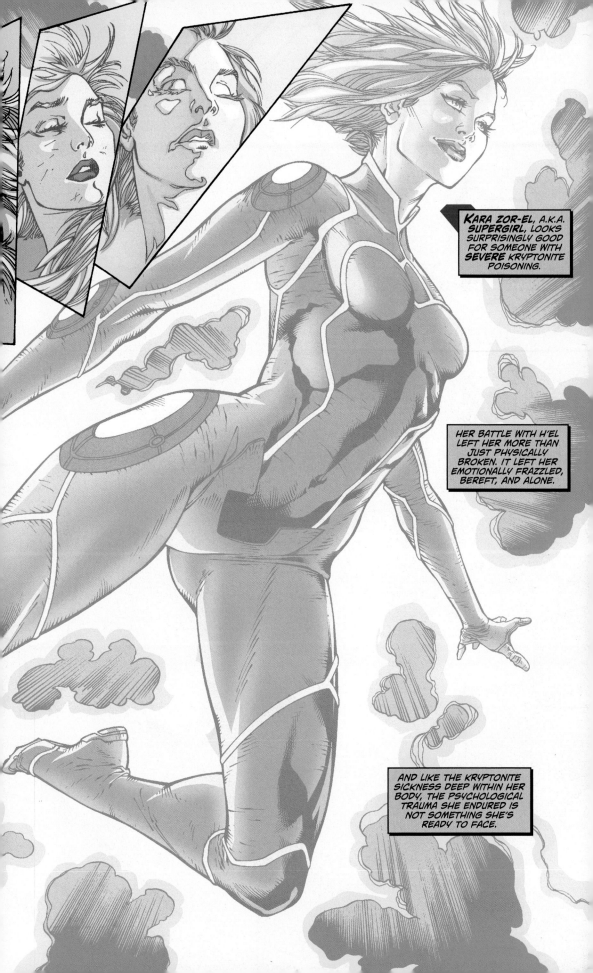

KARA ZOR-EL, A.K.A. SUPERGIRL, LOOKS SURPRISINGLY GOOD FOR SOMEONE WITH SEVERE KRYPTONITE POISONING.

HER BATTLE WITH H'EL LEFT HER MORE THAN JUST PHYSICALLY BROKEN. IT LEFT HER EMOTIONALLY FRAZZLED, BEREFT, AND ALONE.

AND LIKE THE KRYPTONITE SICKNESS DEEP WITHIN HER BODY, THE PSYCHOLOGICAL TRAUMA SHE ENDURED IS NOT SOMETHING SHE'S READY TO FACE.

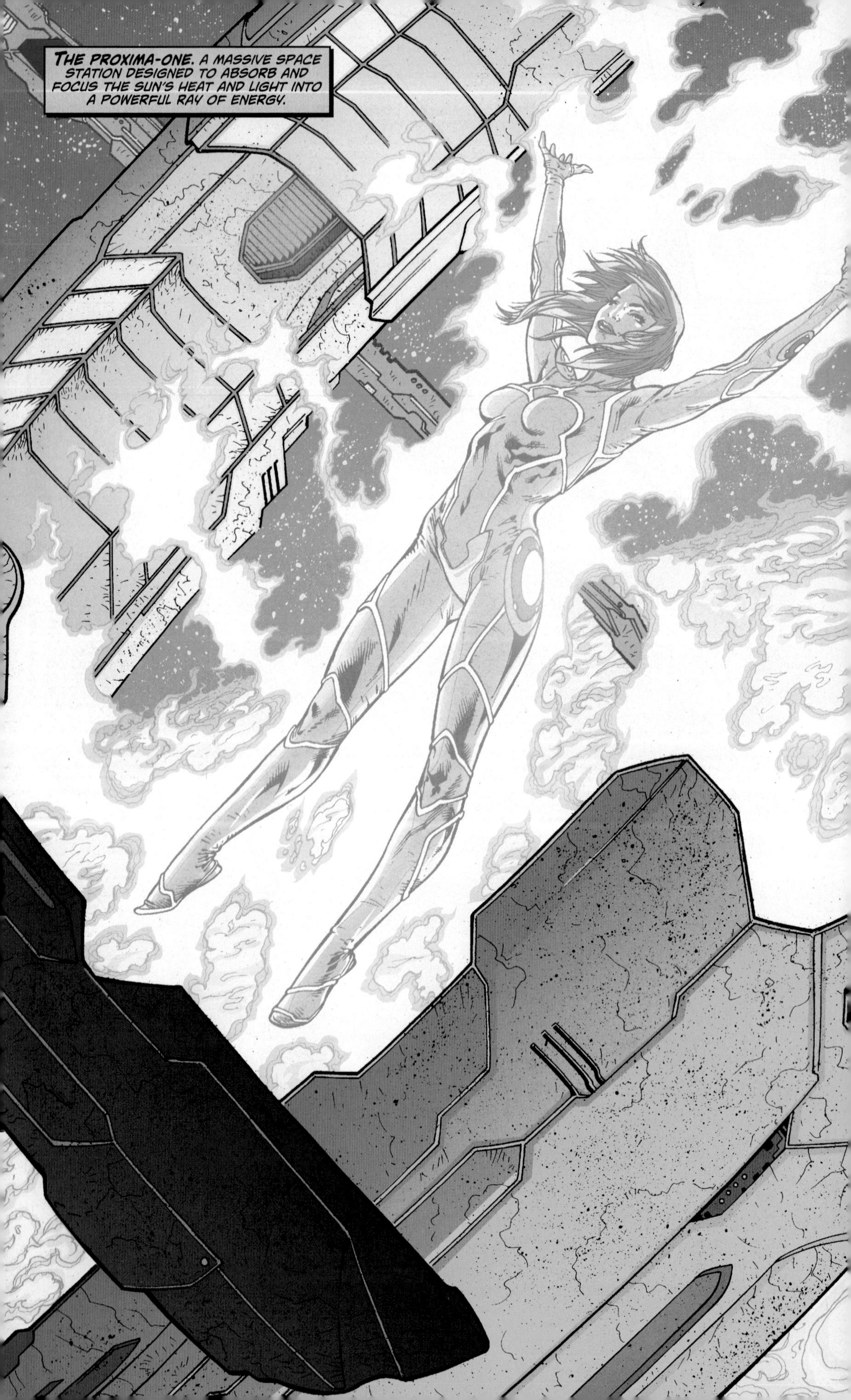
THE PROXIMA-ONE. A MASSIVE SPACE STATION DESIGNED TO ABSORB AND FOCUS THE SUN'S HEAT AND LIGHT INTO A POWERFUL RAY OF ENERGY.

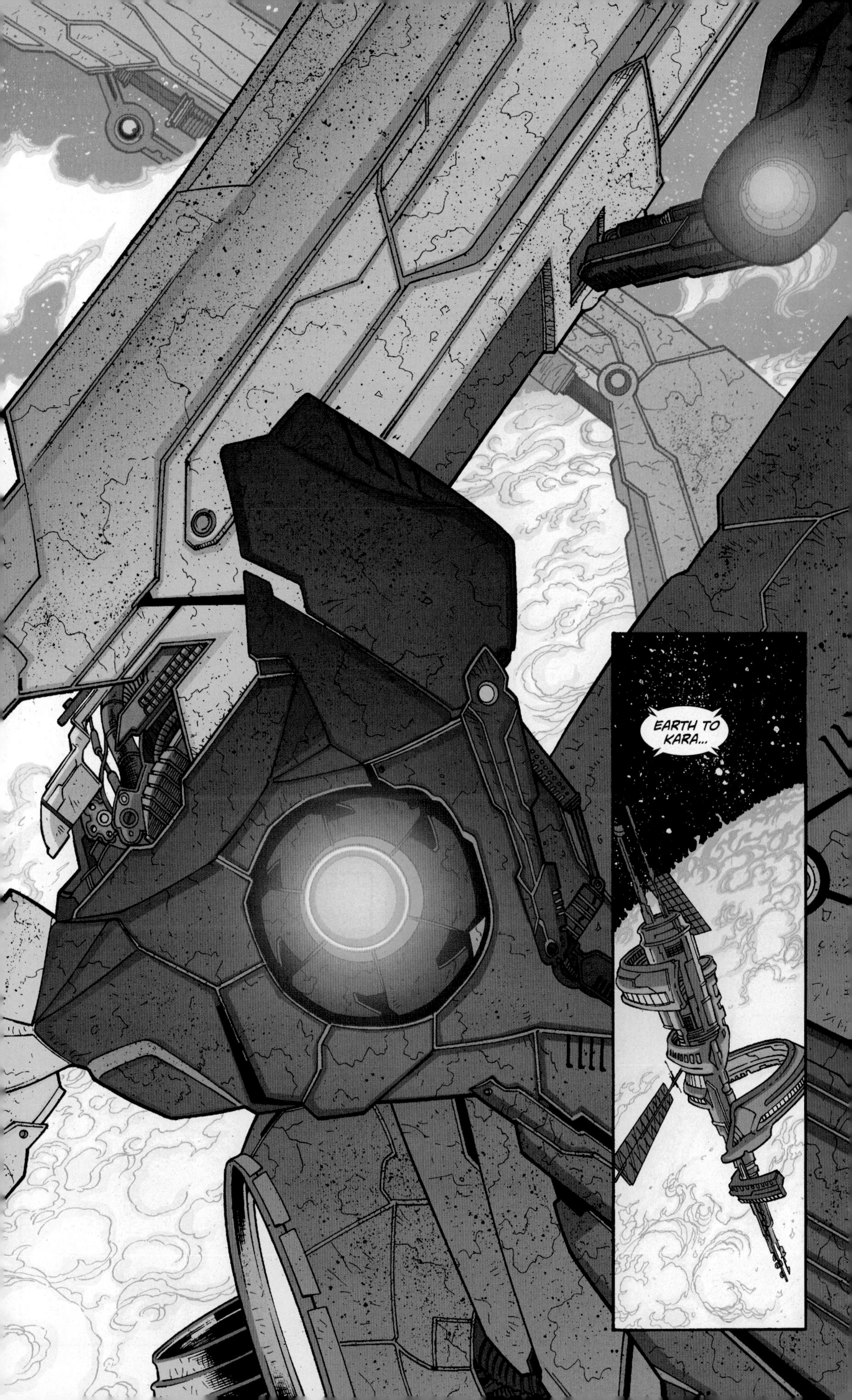
EARTH TO
KARA...

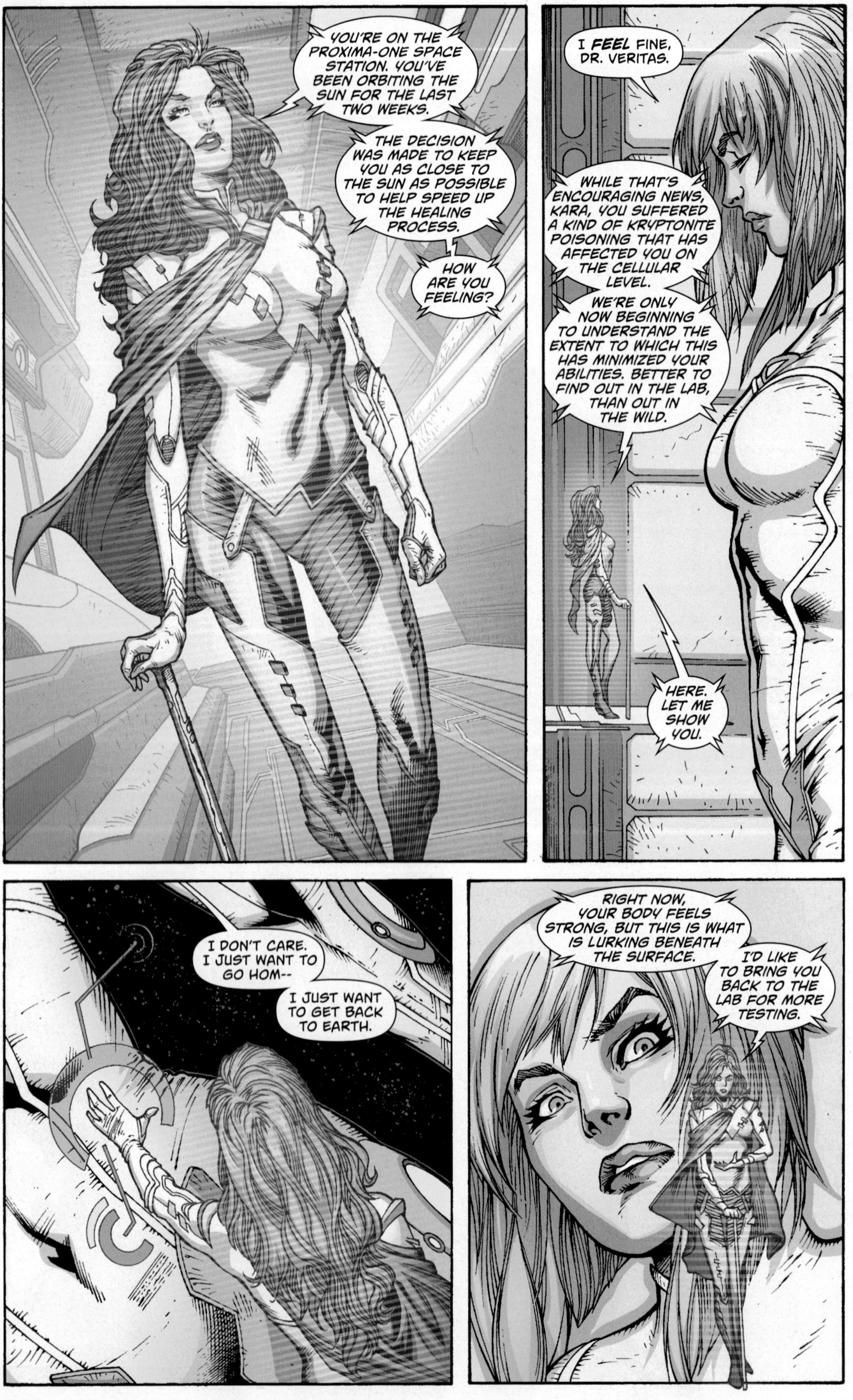
YOU'RE ON THE PROXIMA-ONE SPACE STATION. YOU'VE BEEN ORBITING THE SUN FOR THE LAST TWO WEEKS.
THE DECISION WAS MADE TO KEEP YOU AS CLOSE TO THE SUN AS POSSIBLE TO HELP SPEED UP THE HEALING PROCESS.
HOW ARE YOU FEELING?
I FEEL FINE, DR. VERITAS.
WHILE THAT'S ENCOURAGING NEWS, KARA, YOU SUFFERED A KIND OF KRYPTONITE POISONING THAT HAS AFFECTED YOU ON THE CELLULAR LEVEL.
WE'RE ONLY NOW BEGINNING TO UNDERSTAND THE EXTENT TO WHICH THIS HAS MINIMIZED YOUR ABILITIES. BETTER TO FIND OUT IN THE LAB, THAN OUT IN THE WILD.
HERE. LET ME SHOW YOU.
I DON'T CARE. I JUST WANT TO GO HOM--
I JUST WANT TO GET BACK TO EARTH.
RIGHT NOW, YOUR BODY FEELS STRONG, BUT THIS IS WHAT IS LURKING BENEATH THE SURFACE.
I'D LIKE TO BRING YOU BACK TO THE LAB FOR MORE TESTING.

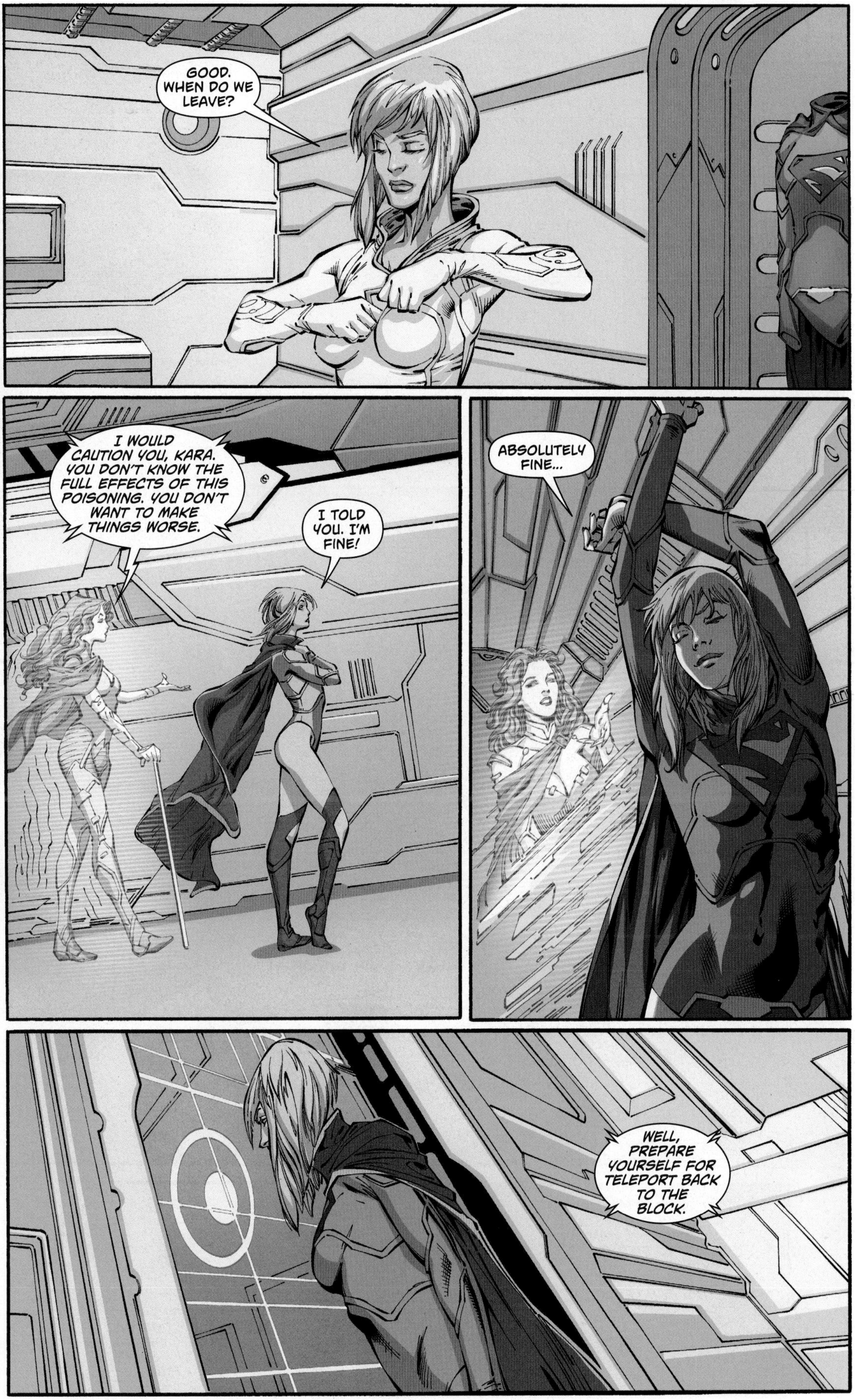
GOOD. WHEN DO WE LEAVE?
I WOULD CAUTION YOU, KARA. YOU DON'T KNOW THE FULL EFFECTS OF THIS POISONING. YOU DON'T WANT TO MAKE THINGS WORSE.
I TOLD YOU. I'M FINE!
ABSOLUTELY FINE...
WELL, PREPARE YOURSELF FOR TELEPORT BACK TO THE BLOCK.

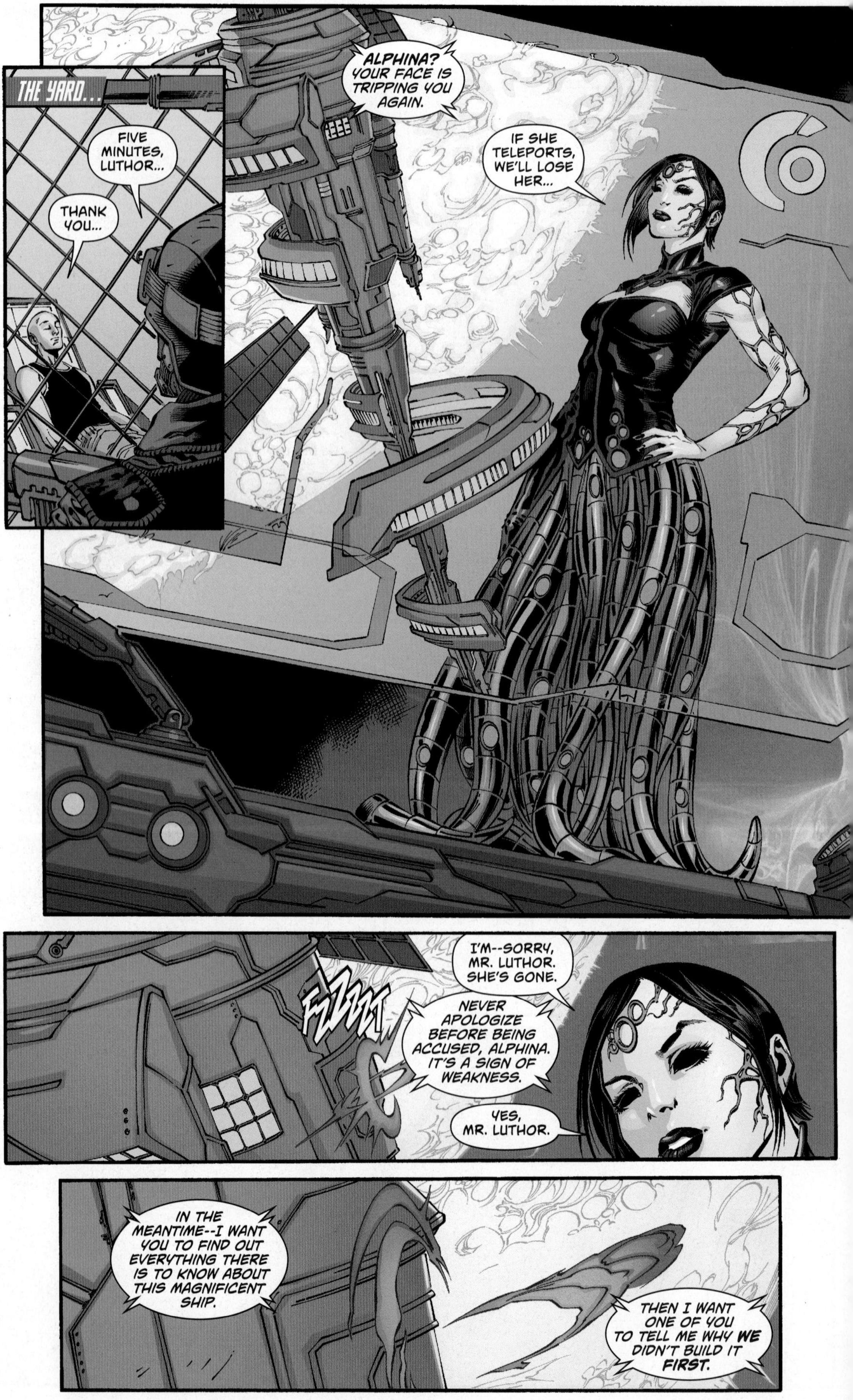
THE YARD...
FIVE MINUTES, LUTHOR...
THANK YOU...
ALPHINA? YOUR FACE IS TRIPPING YOU AGAIN.
IF SHE TELEPORTS, WE'LL LOSE HER...
FZZZT
I'M--SORRY, MR. LUTHOR. SHE'S GONE.
NEVER APOLOGIZE BEFORE BEING ACCUSED, ALPHINA. IT'S A SIGN OF WEAKNESS.
YES, MR. LUTHOR.
IN THE MEANTIME--I WANT YOU TO FIND OUT EVERYTHING THERE IS TO KNOW ABOUT THIS MAGNIFICENT SHIP.
THEN I WANT ONE OF YOU TO TELL ME WHY WE DIDN'T BUILD IT FIRST.

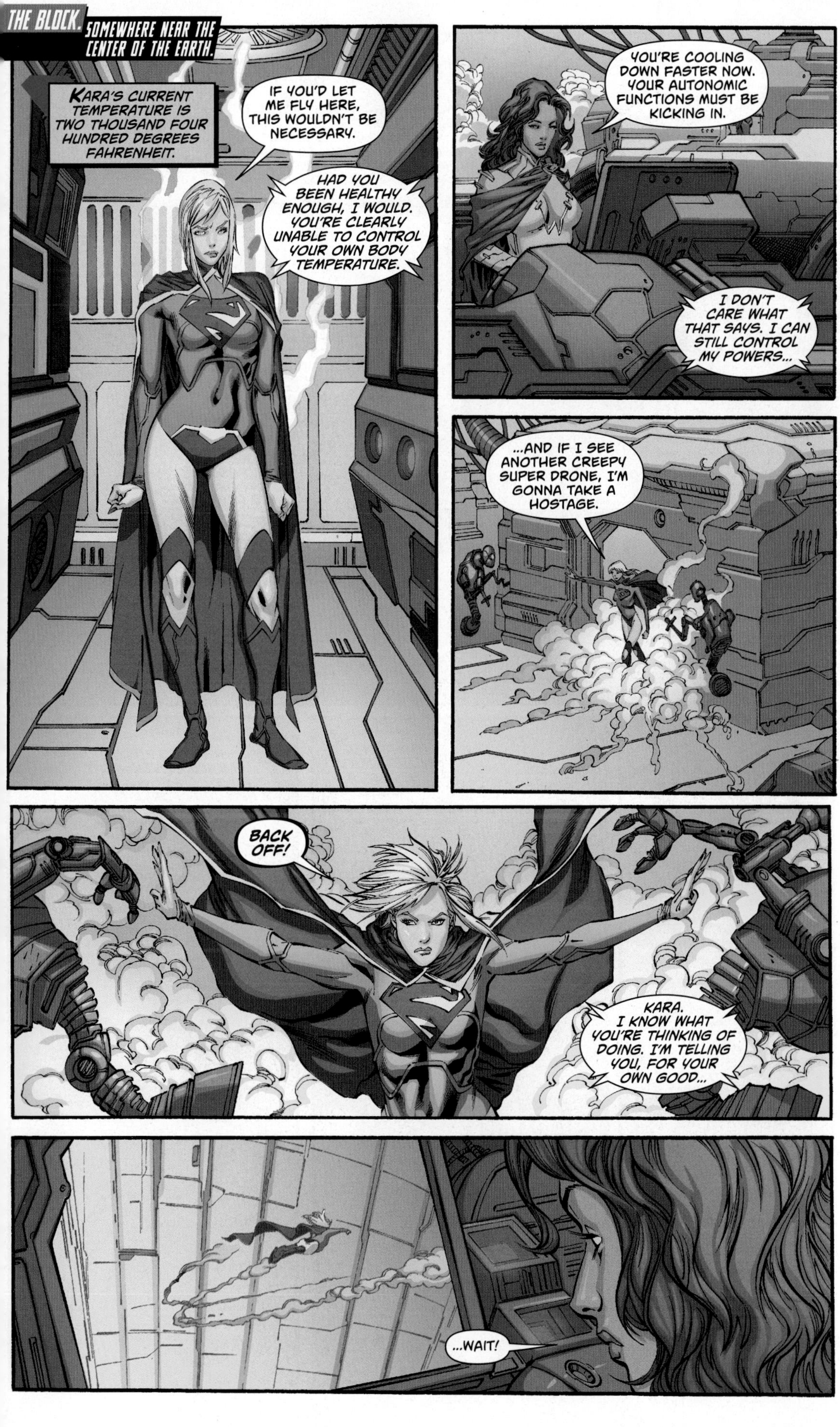
THE BLOCK. SOMEWHERE NEAR THE CENTER OF THE EARTH.
KARA'S CURRENT TEMPERATURE IS TWO THOUSAND FOUR HUNDRED DEGREES FAHRENHEIT.
IF YOU'D LET ME FLY HERE, THIS WOULDN'T BE NECESSARY.
HAD YOU BEEN HEALTHY ENOUGH, I WOULD. YOU'RE CLEARLY UNABLE TO CONTROL YOUR OWN BODY TEMPERATURE.
YOU'RE COOLING DOWN FASTER NOW. YOUR AUTONOMIC FUNCTIONS MUST BE KICKING IN.
I DON'T CARE WHAT THAT SAYS. I CAN STILL CONTROL MY POWERS...
...AND IF I SEE ANOTHER CREEPY SUPER DRONE, I'M GONNA TAKE A HOSTAGE.
BACK OFF!
KARA. I KNOW WHAT YOU'RE THINKING OF DOING. I'M TELLING YOU, FOR YOUR OWN GOOD...
...WAIT!

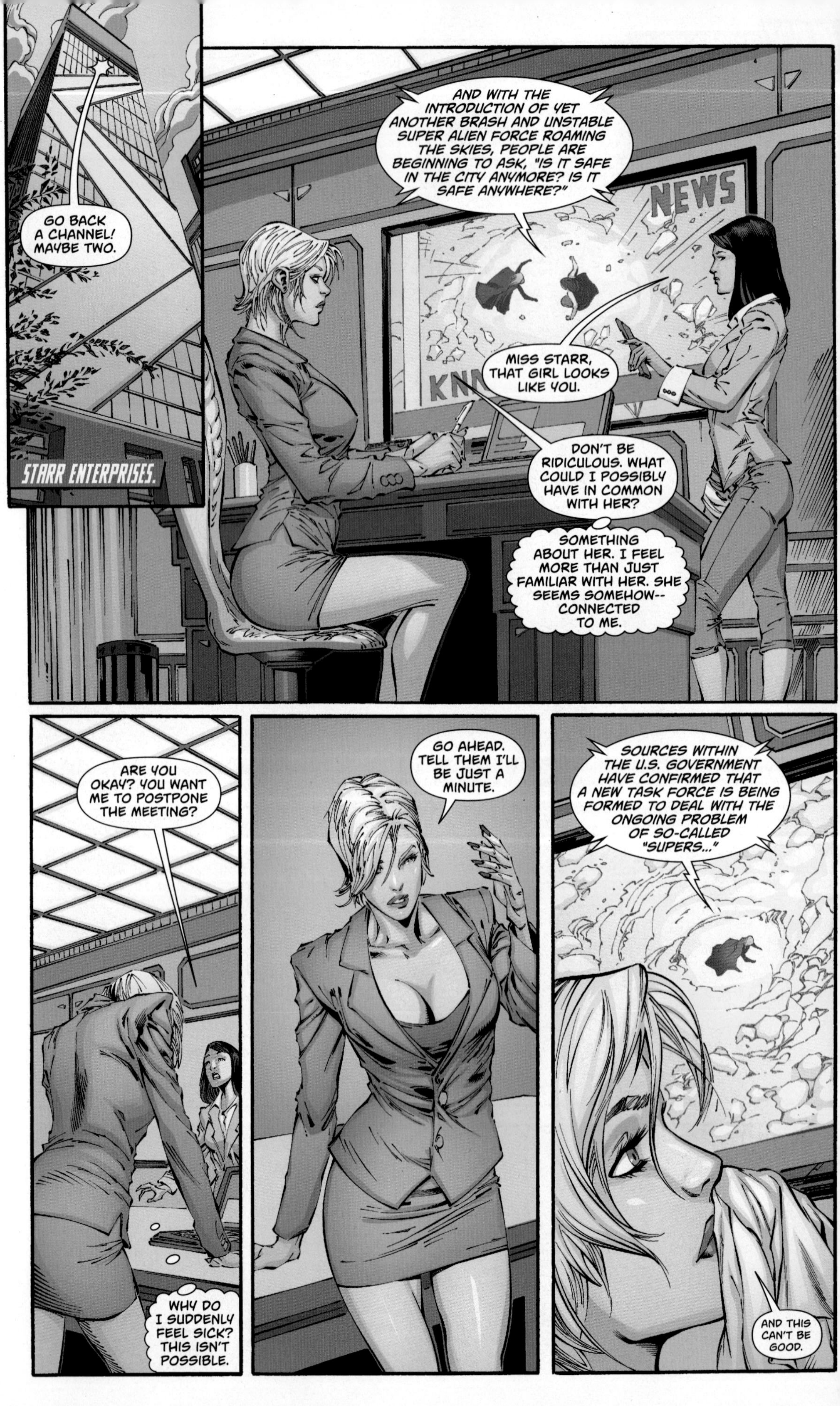
STARR ENTERPRISES.
GO BACK A CHANNEL! MAYBE TWO.
AND WITH THE INTRODUCTION OF YET ANOTHER BRASH AND UNSTABLE SUPER ALIEN FORCE ROAMING THE SKIES, PEOPLE ARE BEGINNING TO ASK, "IS IT SAFE IN THE CITY ANYMORE? IS IT SAFE ANYWHERE?"
NEWS
MISS STARR, THAT GIRL LOOKS LIKE YOU.
DON'T BE RIDICULOUS. WHAT COULD I POSSIBLY HAVE IN COMMON WITH HER?
SOMETHING ABOUT HER. I FEEL MORE THAN JUST FAMILIAR WITH HER. SHE SEEMS SOMEHOW-- CONNECTED TO ME.
ARE YOU OKAY? YOU WANT ME TO POSTPONE THE MEETING?
WHY DO I SUDDENLY FEEL SICK? THIS ISN'T POSSIBLE.
GO AHEAD. TELL THEM I'LL BE JUST A MINUTE.
SOURCES WITHIN THE U.S. GOVERNMENT HAVE CONFIRMED THAT A NEW TASK FORCE IS BEING FORMED TO DEAL WITH THE ONGOING PROBLEM OF SO-CALLED "SUPERS..."
AND THIS CAN'T BE GOOD.

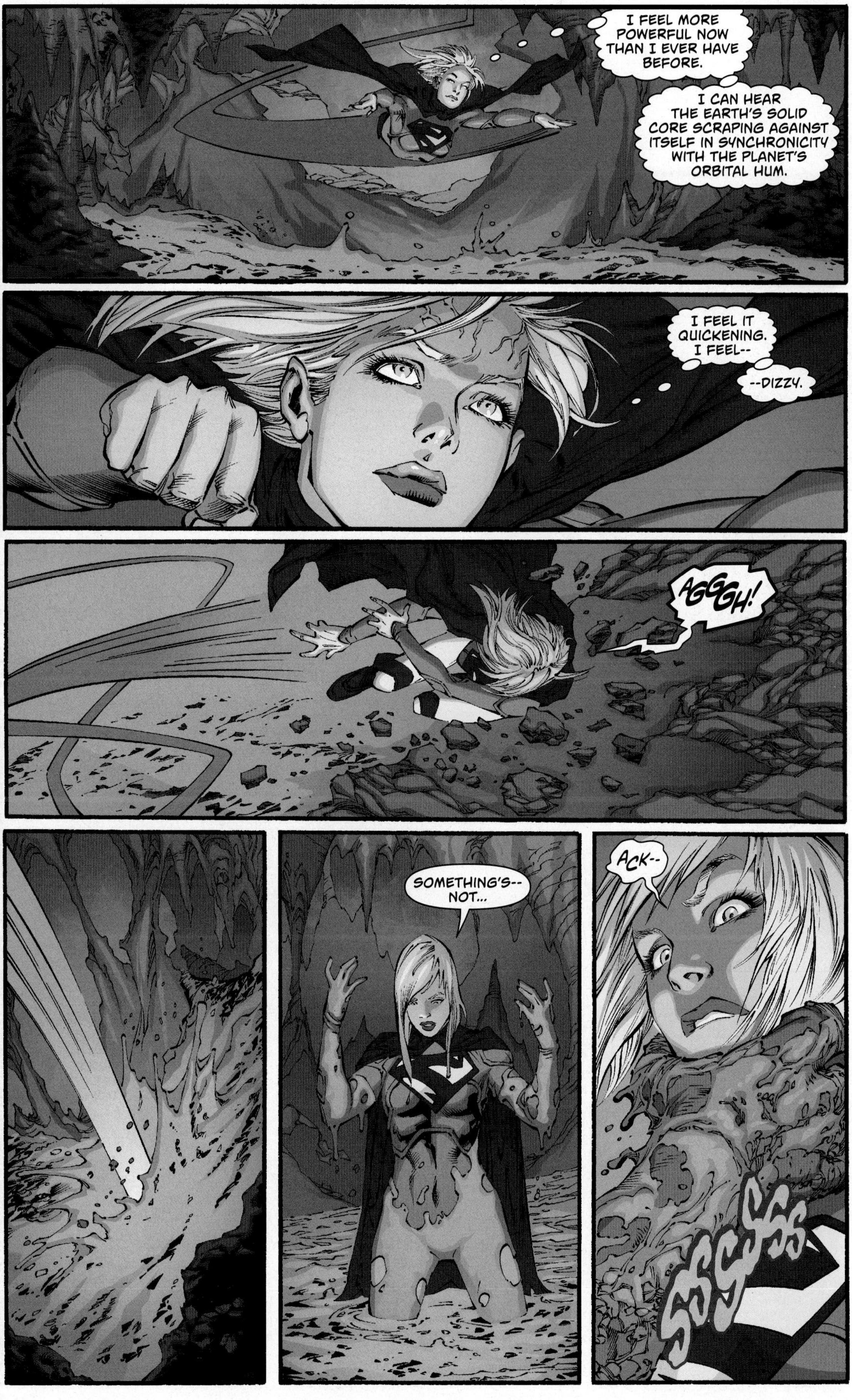
I FEEL MORE POWERFUL NOW THAN I EVER HAVE BEFORE.
I CAN HEAR THE EARTH'S SOLID CORE SCRAPING AGAINST ITSELF IN SYNCHRONICITY WITH THE PLANET'S ORBITAL HUM.
I FEEL IT QUICKENING. I FEEL--
--DIZZY.
AGGGH!
SOMETHING'S-- NOT...
ACK--
SSSSSSS

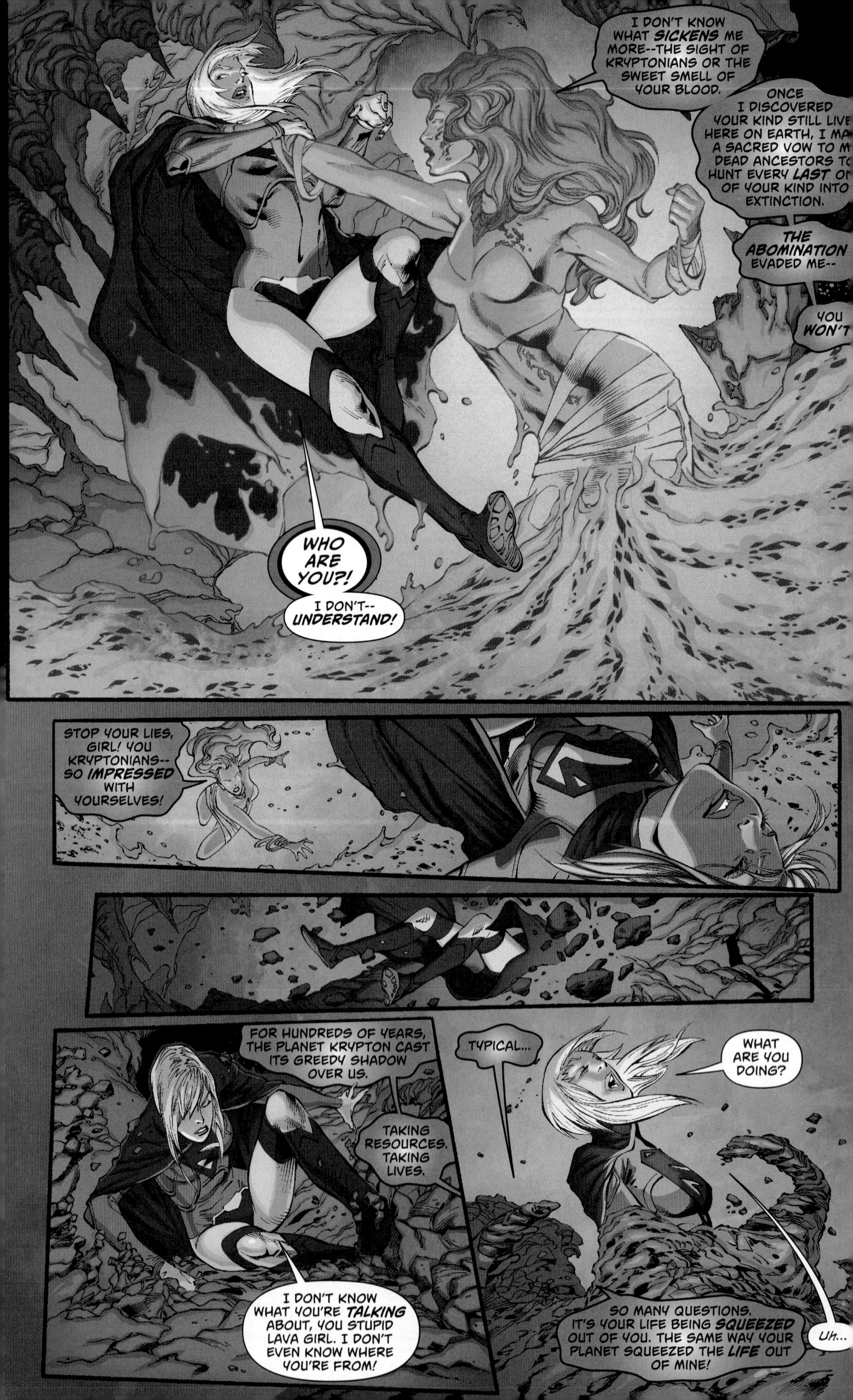

I DON'T KNOW WHAT SICKENS ME MORE--THE SIGHT OF KRYPTONIANS OR THE SWEET SMELL OF YOUR BLOOD.
THE ABOMINATION EVADED ME--
WHO ARE YOU?!
I DON'T--UNDERSTAND!
STOP YOUR LIES, GIRL! YOU KRYPTONIANS--SO IMPRESSED WITH YOURSELVES!
FOR HUNDREDS OF YEARS, THE PLANET KRYPTON CAST ITS GREEDY SHADOW OVER US.
TAKING RESOURCES. TAKING LIVES.
I DON'T KNOW WHAT YOU'RE TALKING ABOUT, YOU STUPID LAVA GIRL. I DON'T EVEN KNOW WHERE YOU'RE FROM!
TYPICAL...
WHAT ARE YOU DOING?
SO MANY QUESTIONS. IT'S YOUR LIFE BEING SQUEEZED OUT OF YOU. THE SAME WAY YOUR PLANET SQUEEZED THE LIFE OUT OF MINE!
Uh...

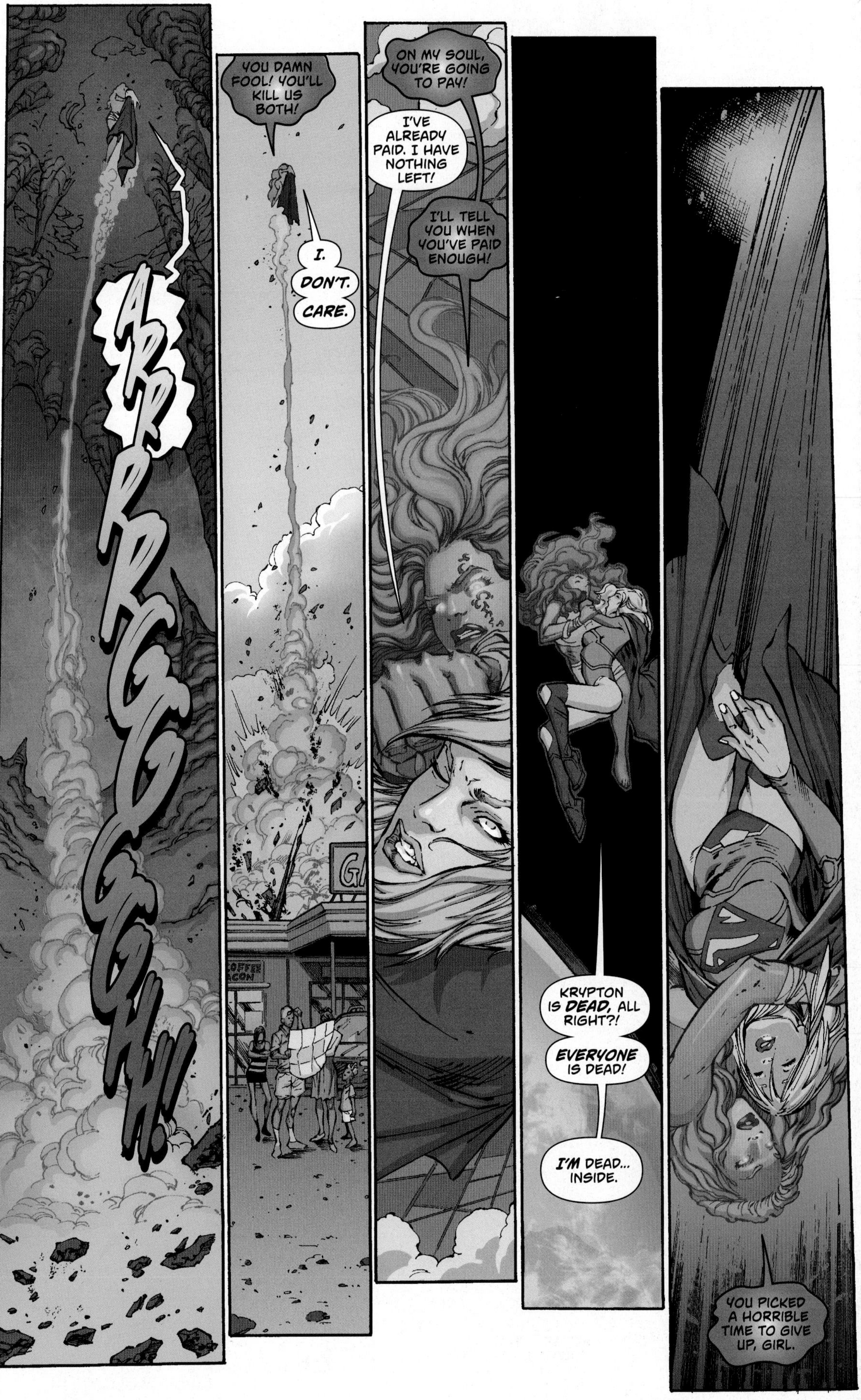
ARRRRGGGGGHH!!
YOU DAMN FOOL! YOU'LL KILL US BOTH!
I.
DON'T.
CARE.
ON MY SOUL, YOU'RE GOING TO PAY!
I'VE ALREADY PAID. I HAVE NOTHING LEFT!
I'LL TELL YOU WHEN YOU'VE PAID ENOUGH!
KRYPTON IS DEAD, ALL RIGHT?!
EVERYONE IS DEAD!
I'M DEAD... INSIDE.
YOU PICKED A HORRIBLE TIME TO GIVE UP, GIRL.

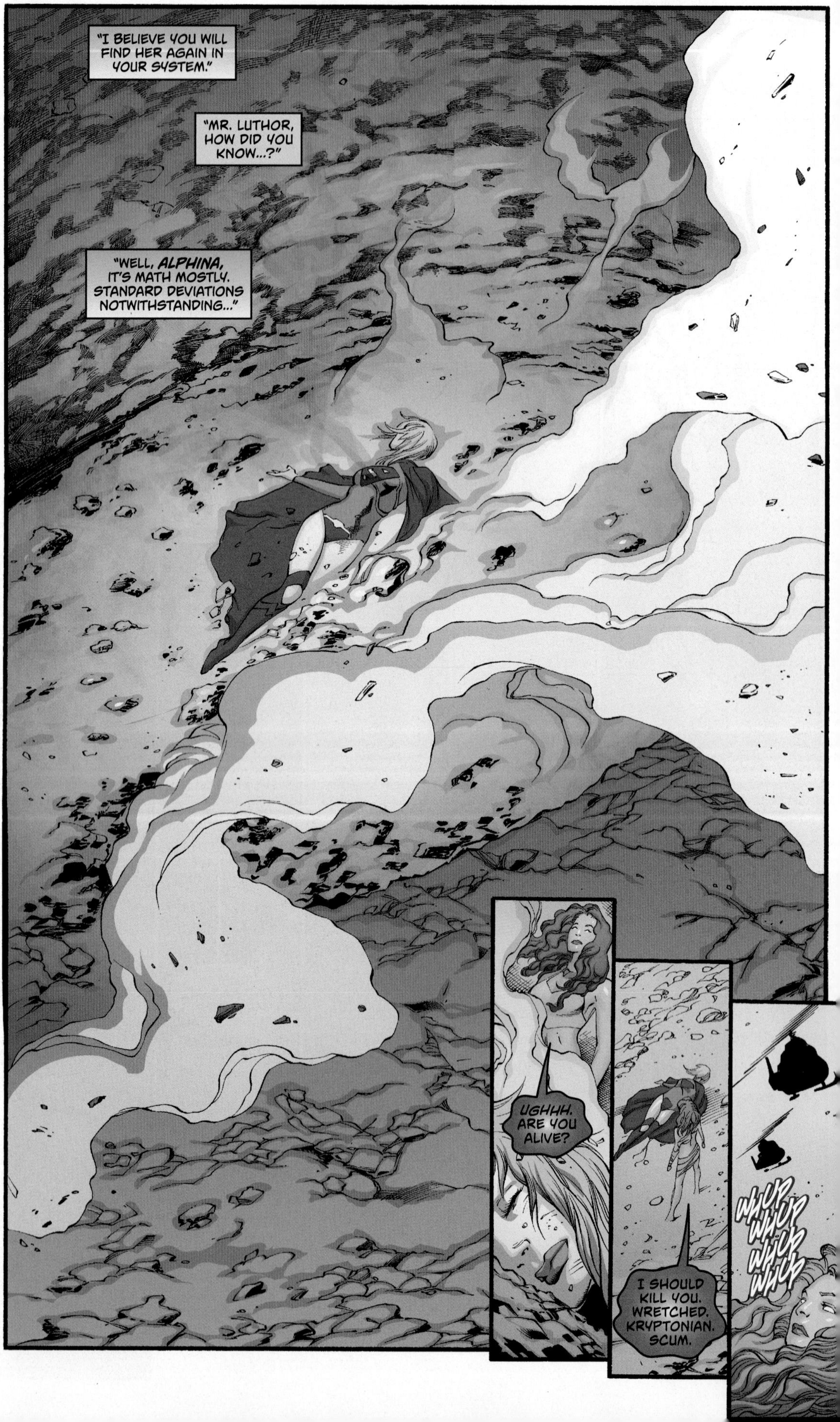
"I BELIEVE YOU WILL FIND HER AGAIN IN YOUR SYSTEM."
"MR. LUTHOR, HOW DID YOU KNOW...?"
"WELL, *ALPHINA,* IT'S MATH MOSTLY. STANDARD DEVIATIONS NOTWITHSTANDING..."
UGHHH. ARE YOU ALIVE?
I SHOULD KILL YOU. WRETCHED. KRYPTONIAN. SCUM.
WHUP WHUP WHUP WHUP

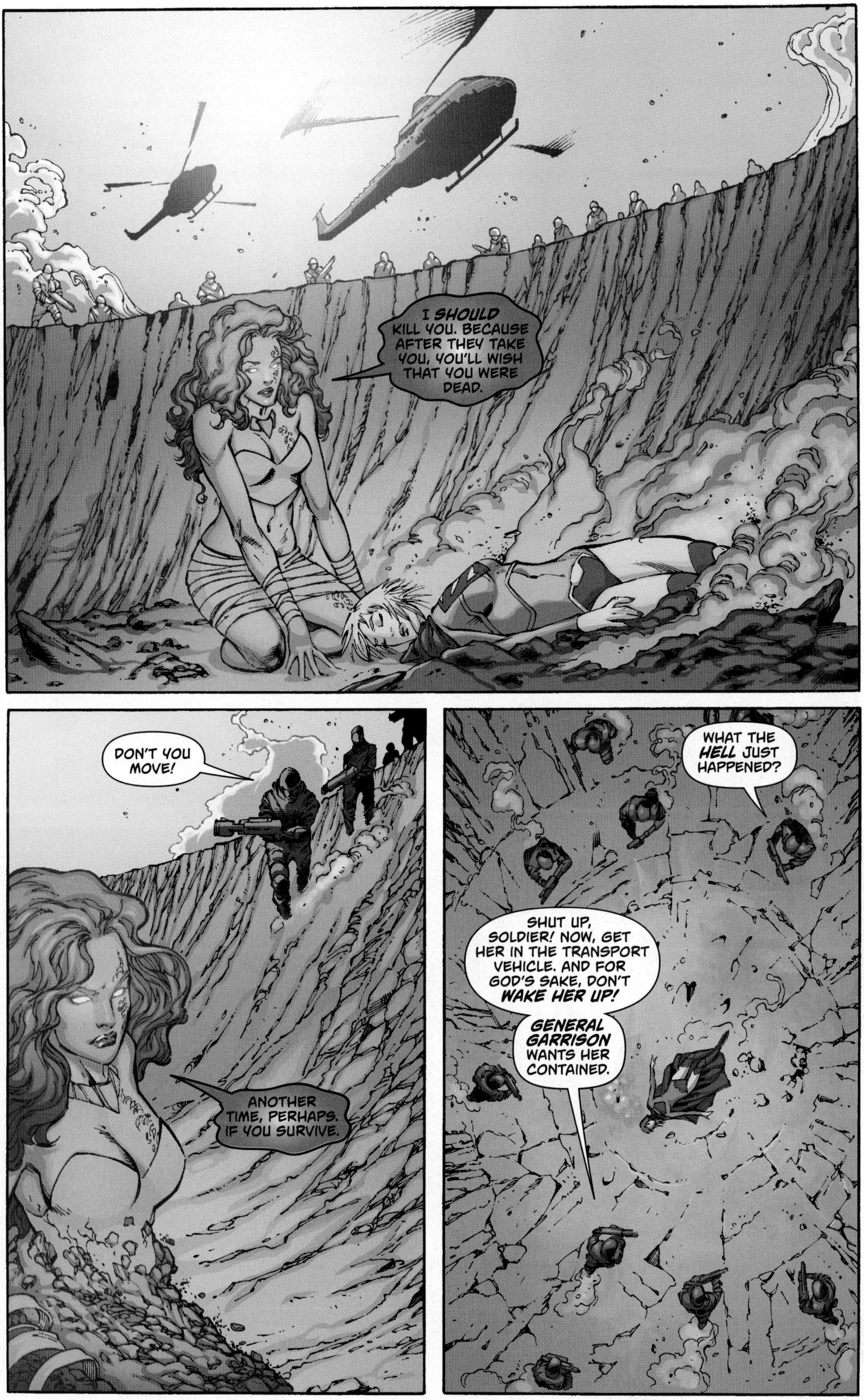
I SHOULD KILL YOU. BECAUSE AFTER THEY TAKE YOU, YOU'LL WISH THAT YOU WERE DEAD.
DON'T YOU MOVE!
ANOTHER TIME, PERHAPS. IF YOU SURVIVE.
WHAT THE HELL JUST HAPPENED?
SHUT UP, SOLDIER! NOW, GET HER IN THE TRANSPORT VEHICLE. AND FOR GOD'S SAKE, DON'T WAKE HER UP!
GENERAL GARRISON WANTS HER CONTAINED.

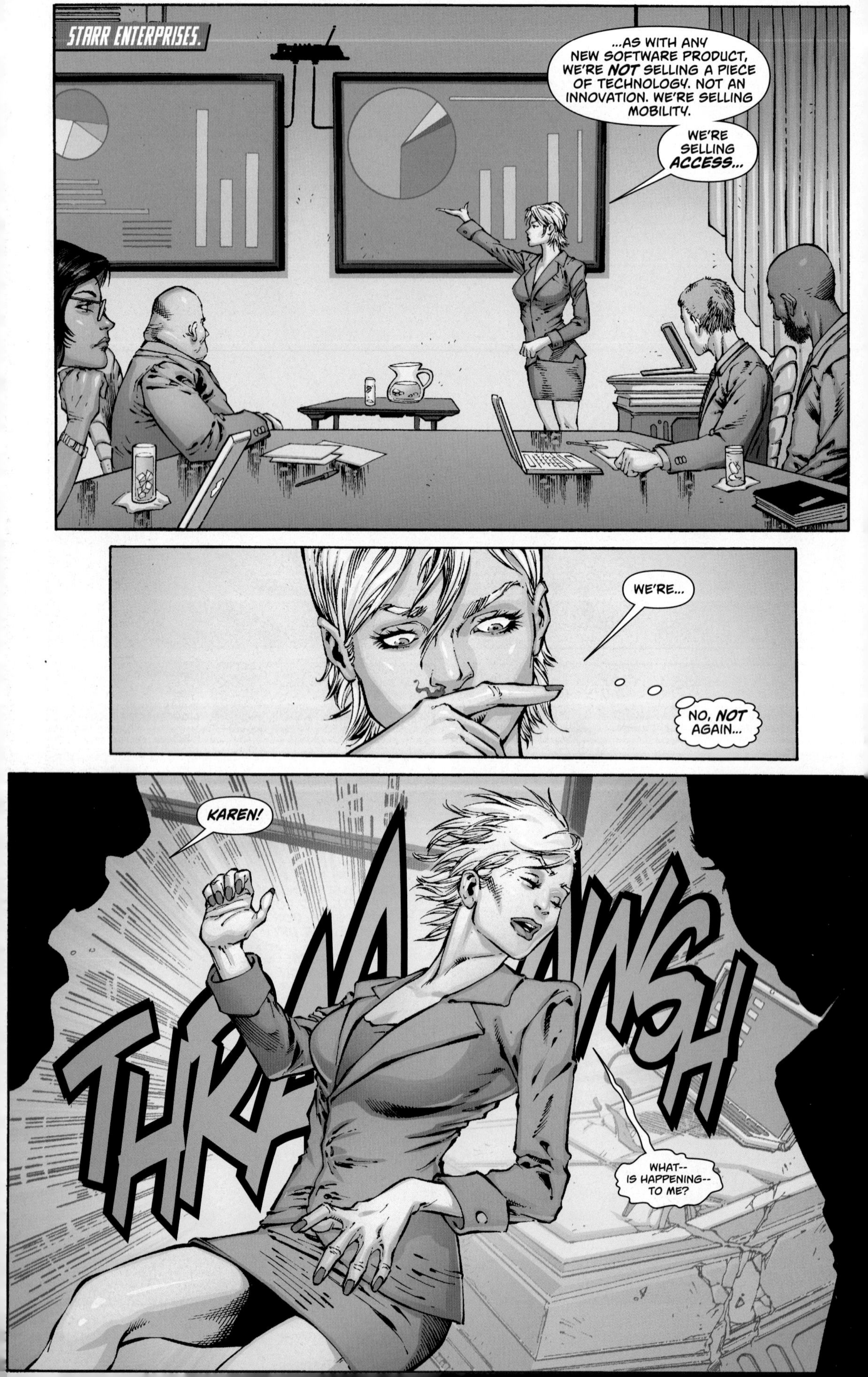
STARR ENTERPRISES.
...AS WITH ANY NEW SOFTWARE PRODUCT, WE'RE NOT SELLING A PIECE OF TECHNOLOGY. NOT AN INNOVATION. WE'RE SELLING MOBILITY.
WE'RE SELLING ACCESS...
WE'RE...
NO, NOT AGAIN...
KAREN!
THWAANNSH
WHAT-- IS HAPPENING-- TO ME?

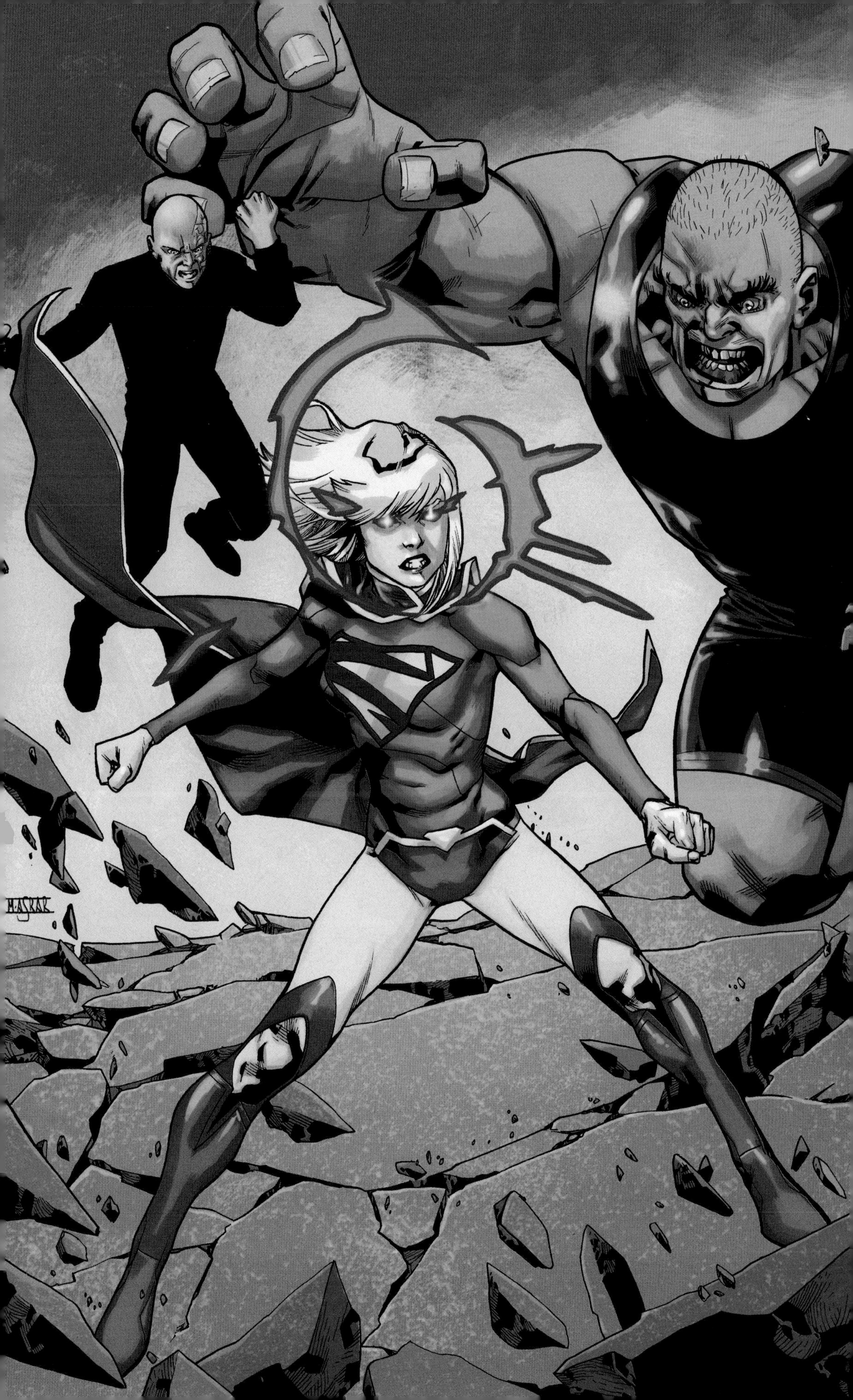
M.ASRAR

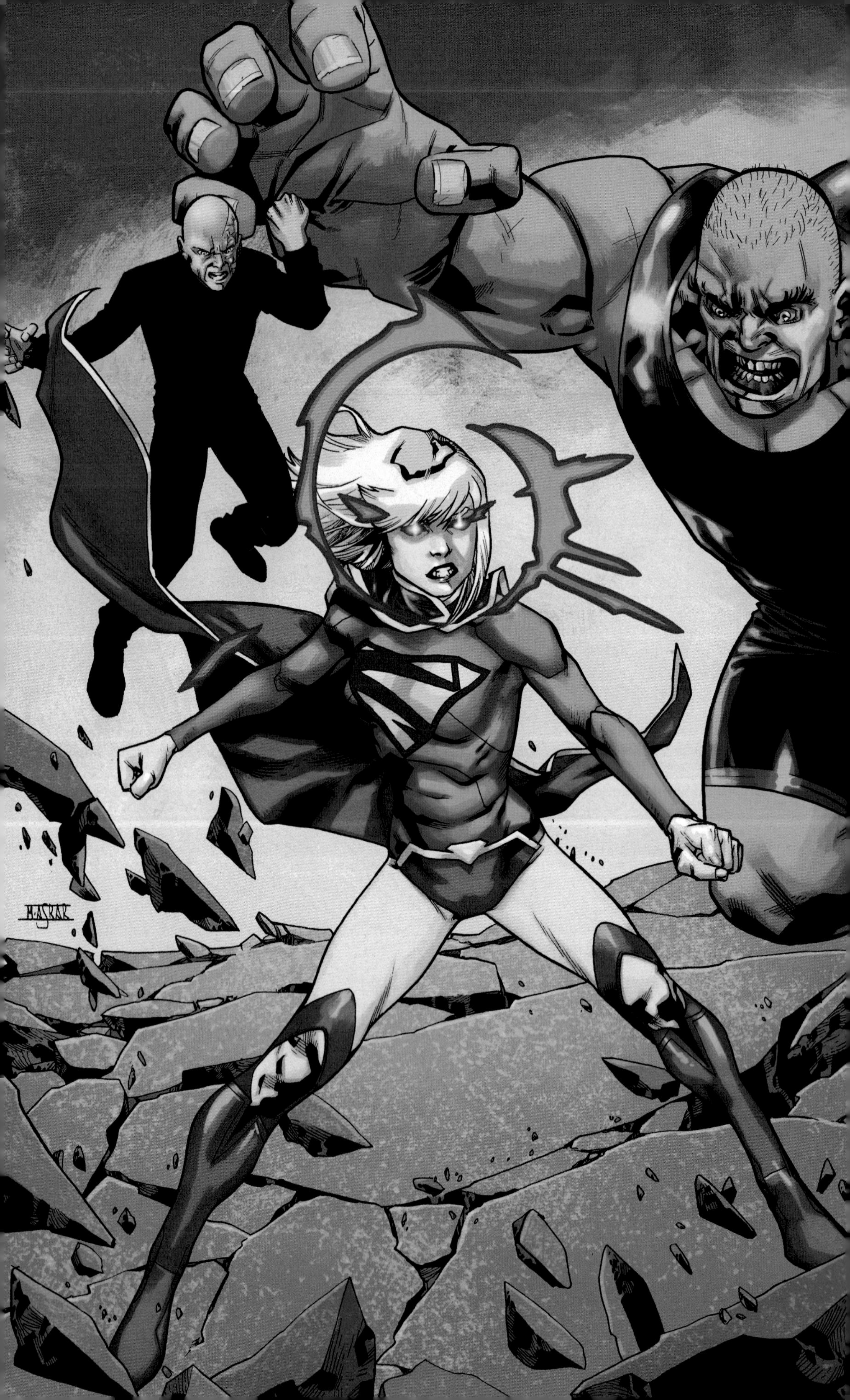
M.ASRAR

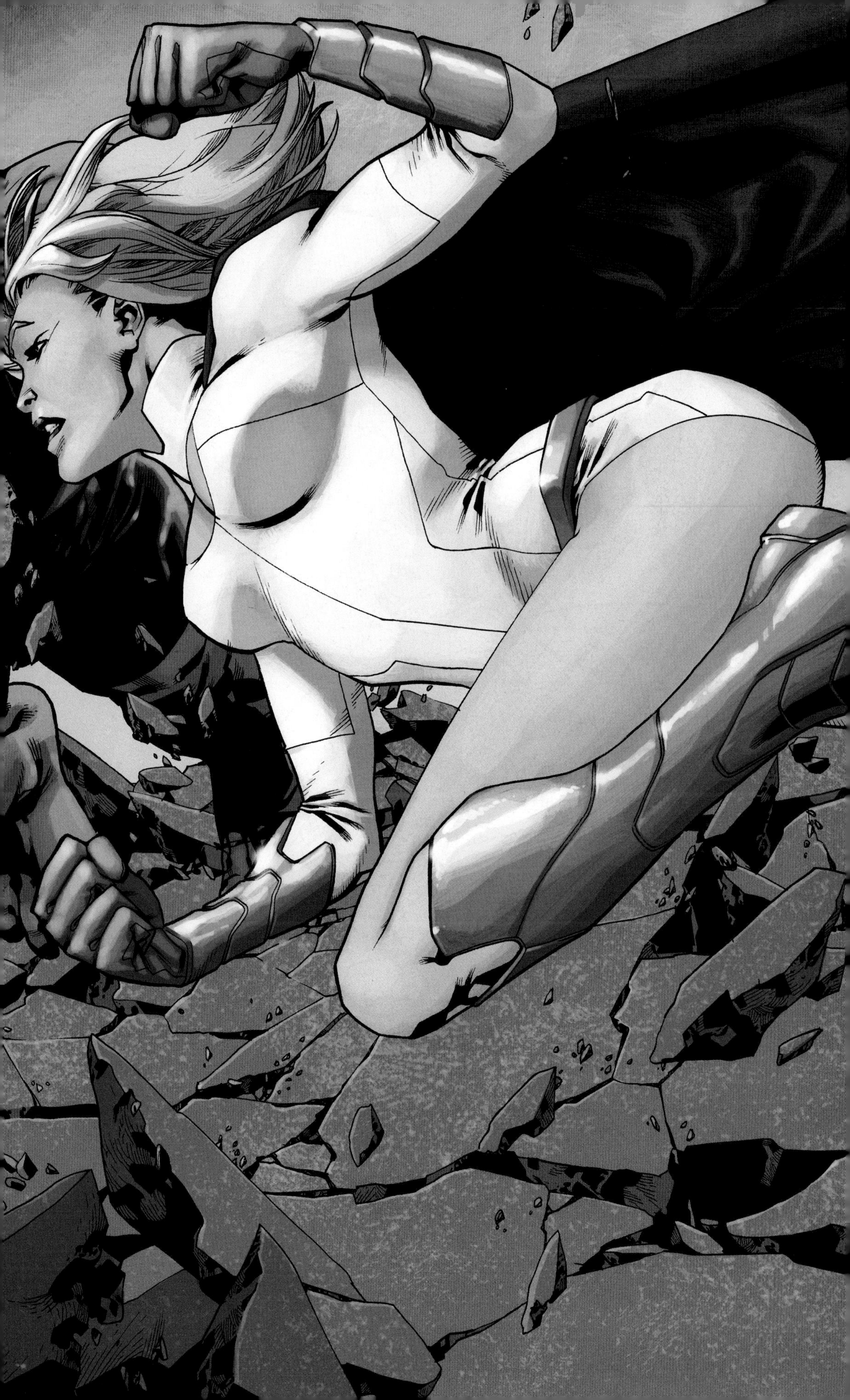

SUPERPOWER

MIKE JOHNSON writer **MAHMUD ASRAR** artist **MARLO ALQUIZA** inker cover art by **MAHMUD ASRAR & DANIEL BROWN**

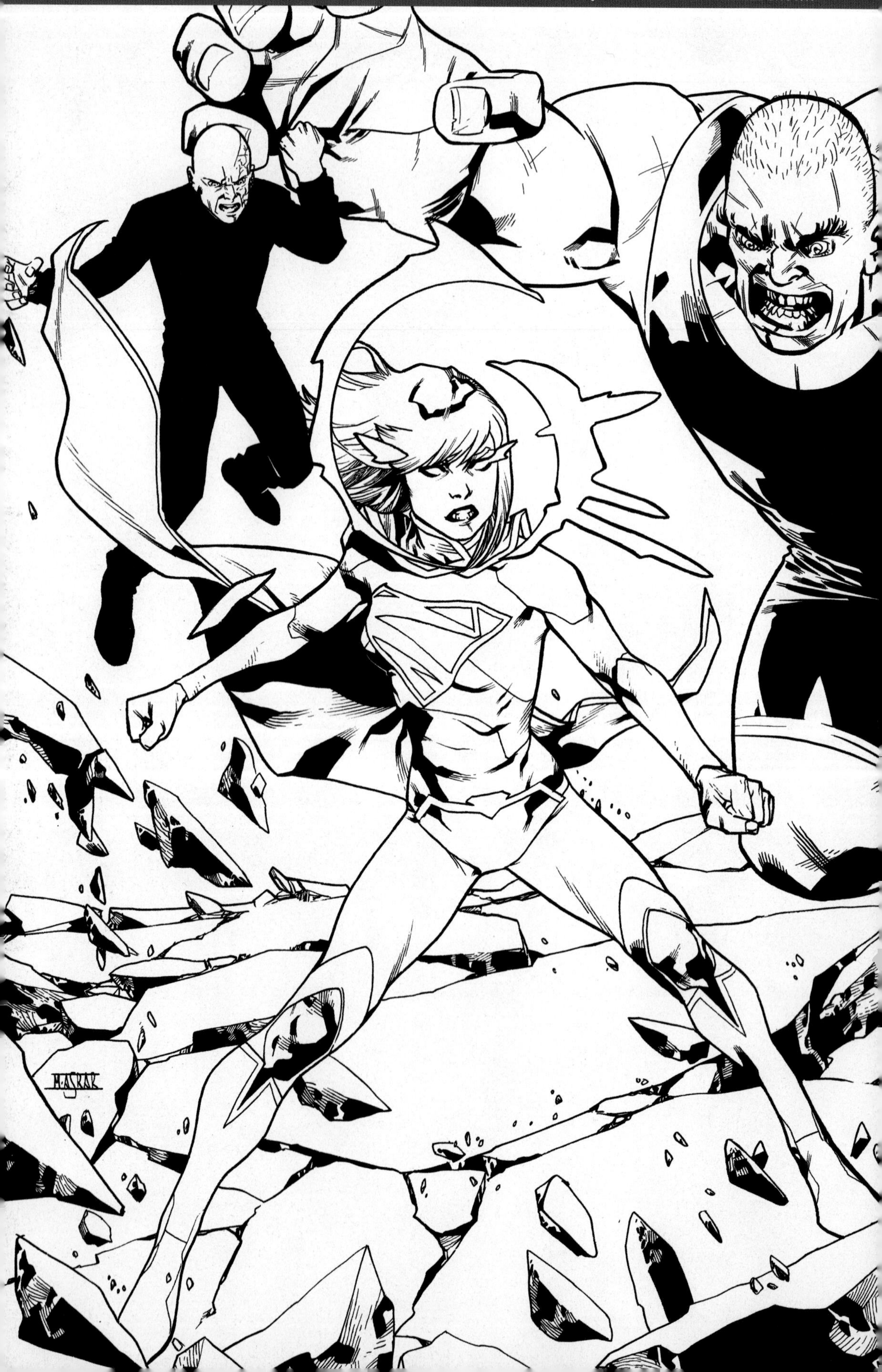

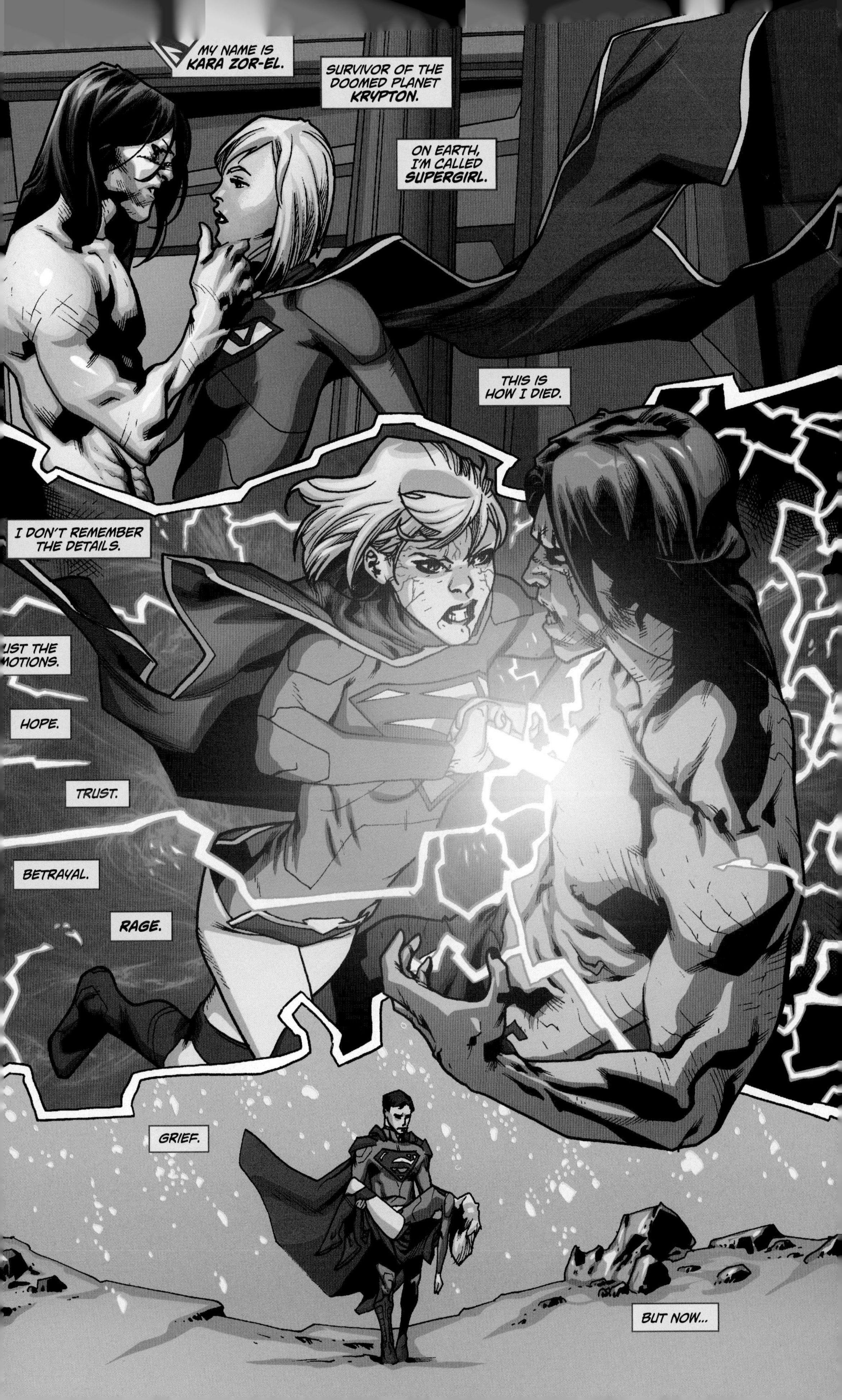

MY NAME IS KARA ZOR-EL.
SURVIVOR OF THE DOOMED PLANET KRYPTON.
ON EARTH, I'M CALLED SUPERGIRL.
THIS IS HOW I DIED.
I DON'T REMEMBER THE DETAILS.
UST THE MOTIONS.
HOPE.
TRUST.
BETRAYAL.
RAGE.
GRIEF.
BUT NOW...

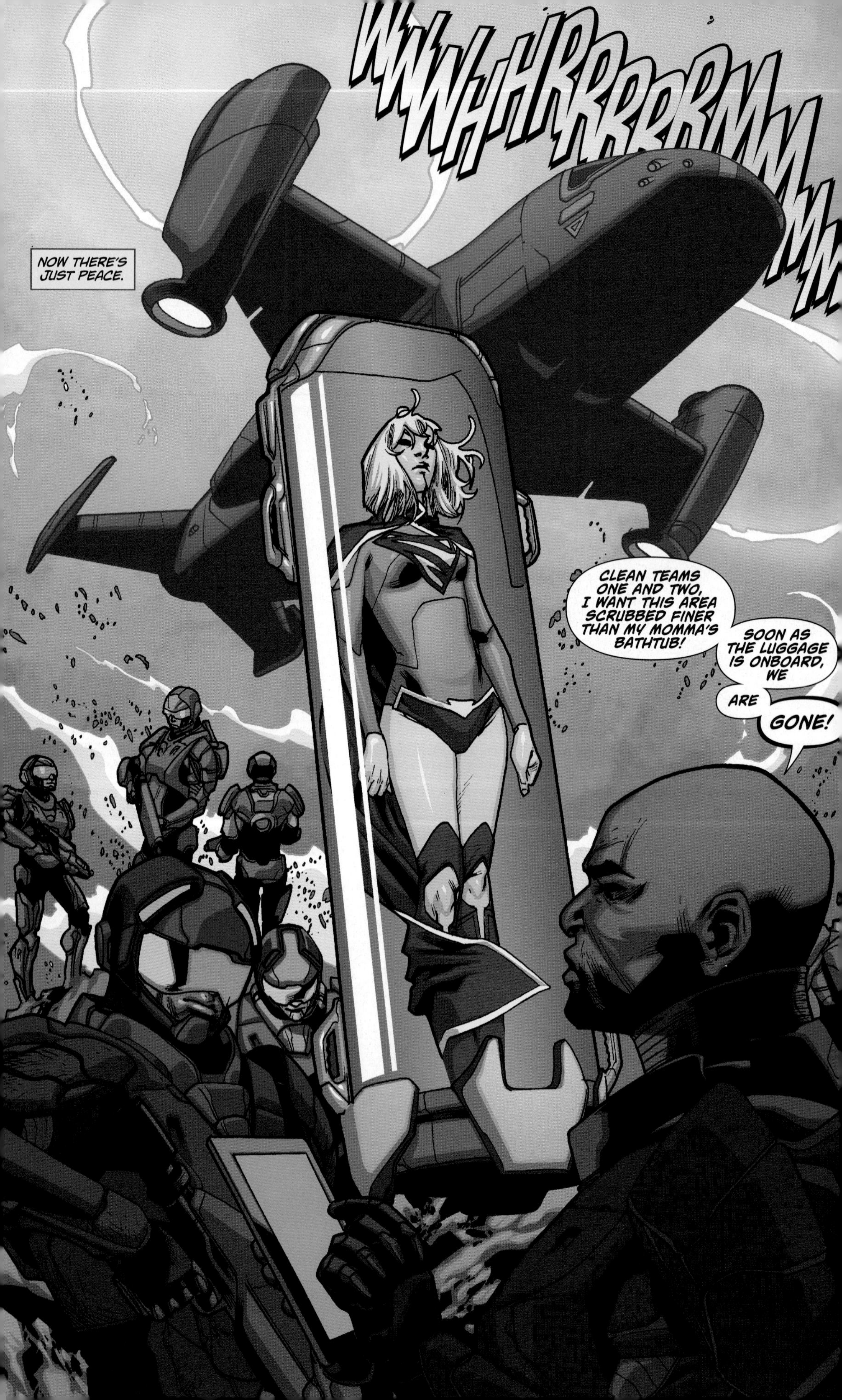
WWWHHRRRRRMMMMM
NOW THERE'S JUST PEACE.
CLEAN TEAMS ONE AND TWO, I WANT THIS AREA SCRUBBED FINER THAN MY MOMMA'S BATHTUB!
SOON AS THE LUGGAGE IS ONBOARD, WE
ARE
GONE!

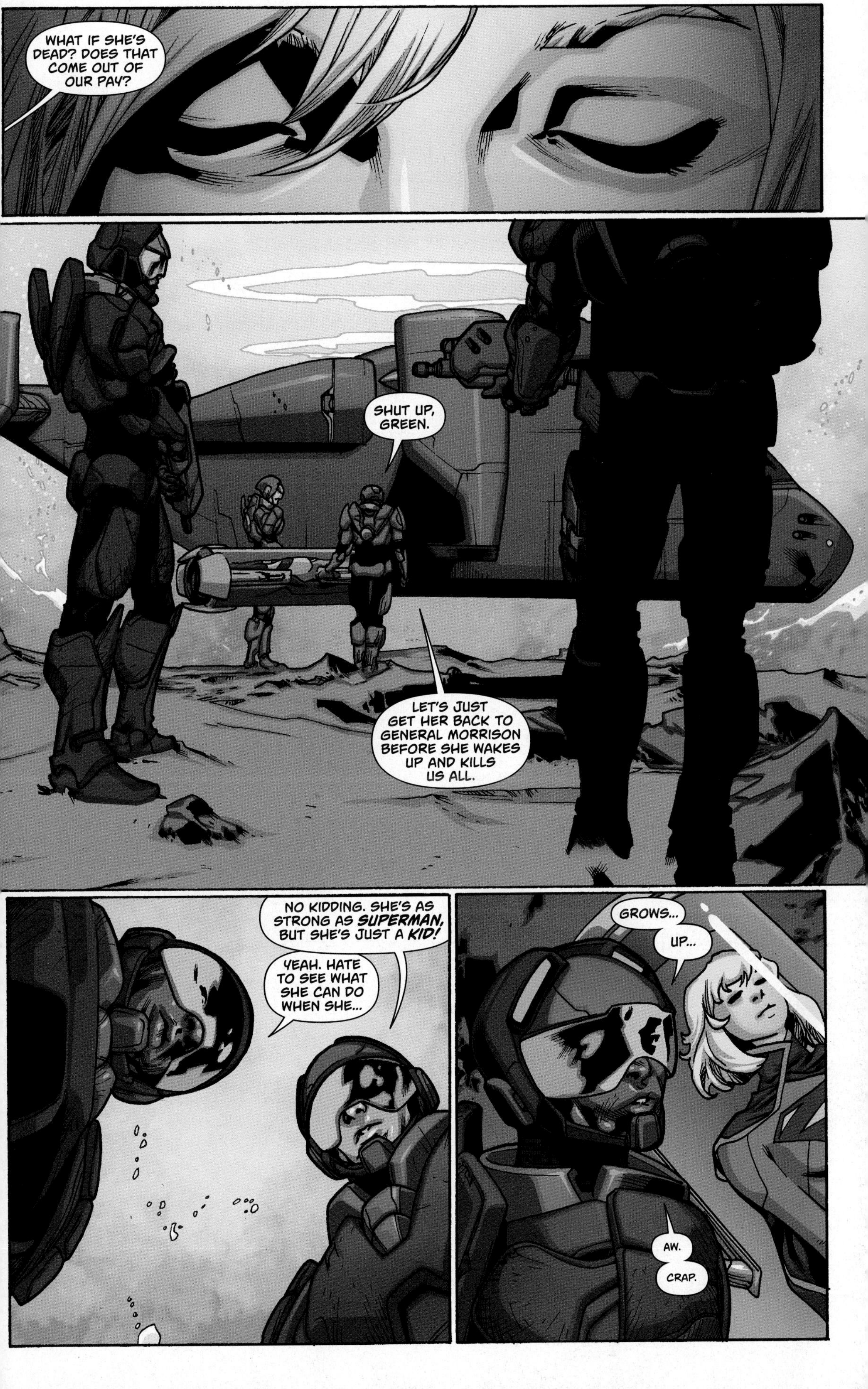
WHAT IF SHE'S DEAD? DOES THAT COME OUT OF OUR PAY?
SHUT UP, GREEN.
LET'S JUST GET HER BACK TO GENERAL MORRISON BEFORE SHE WAKES UP AND KILLS US ALL.
NO KIDDING. SHE'S AS STRONG AS SUPERMAN, BUT SHE'S JUST A KID!
YEAH. HATE TO SEE WHAT SHE CAN DO WHEN SHE...
GROWS...
UP...
AW.
CRAP.

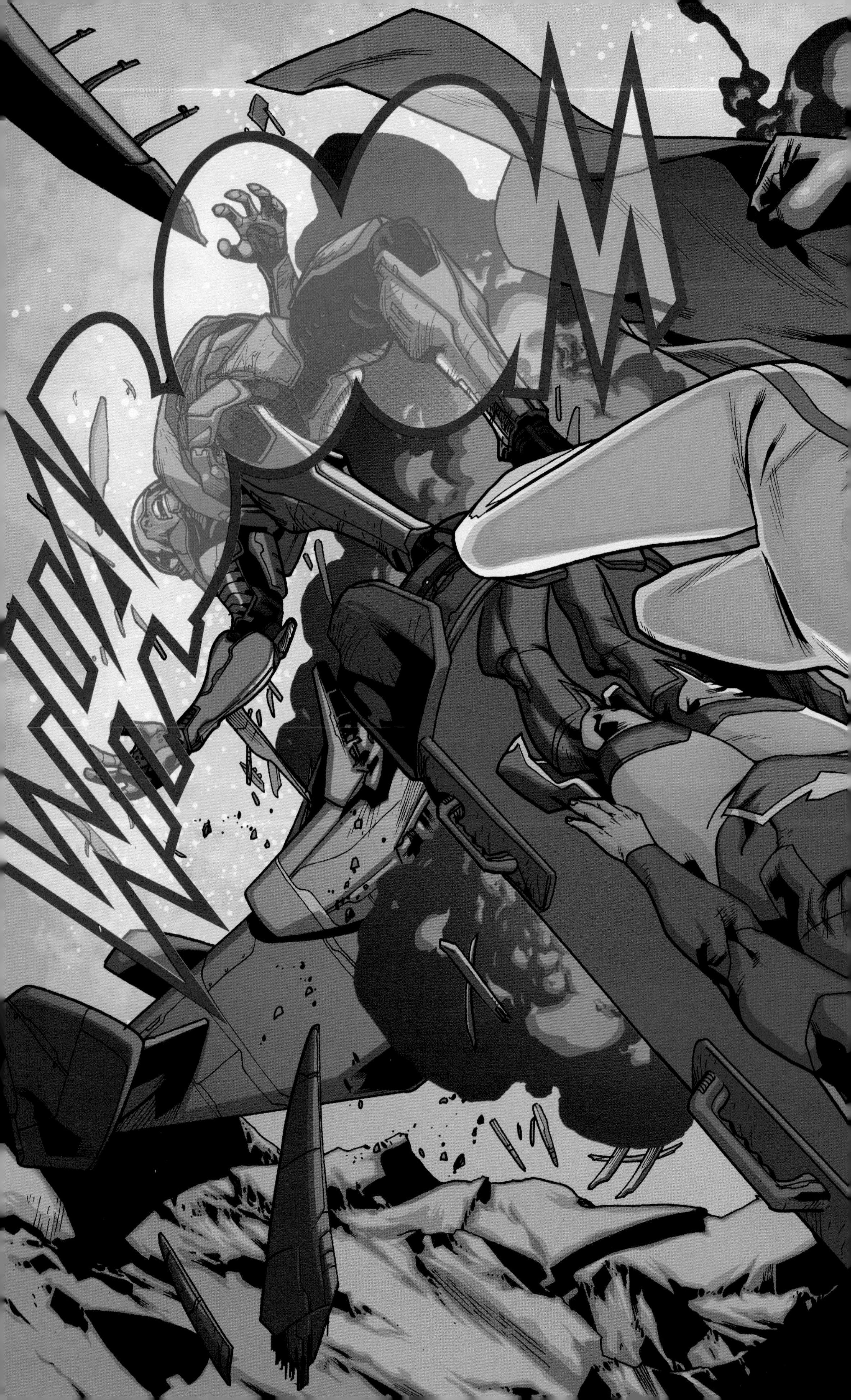

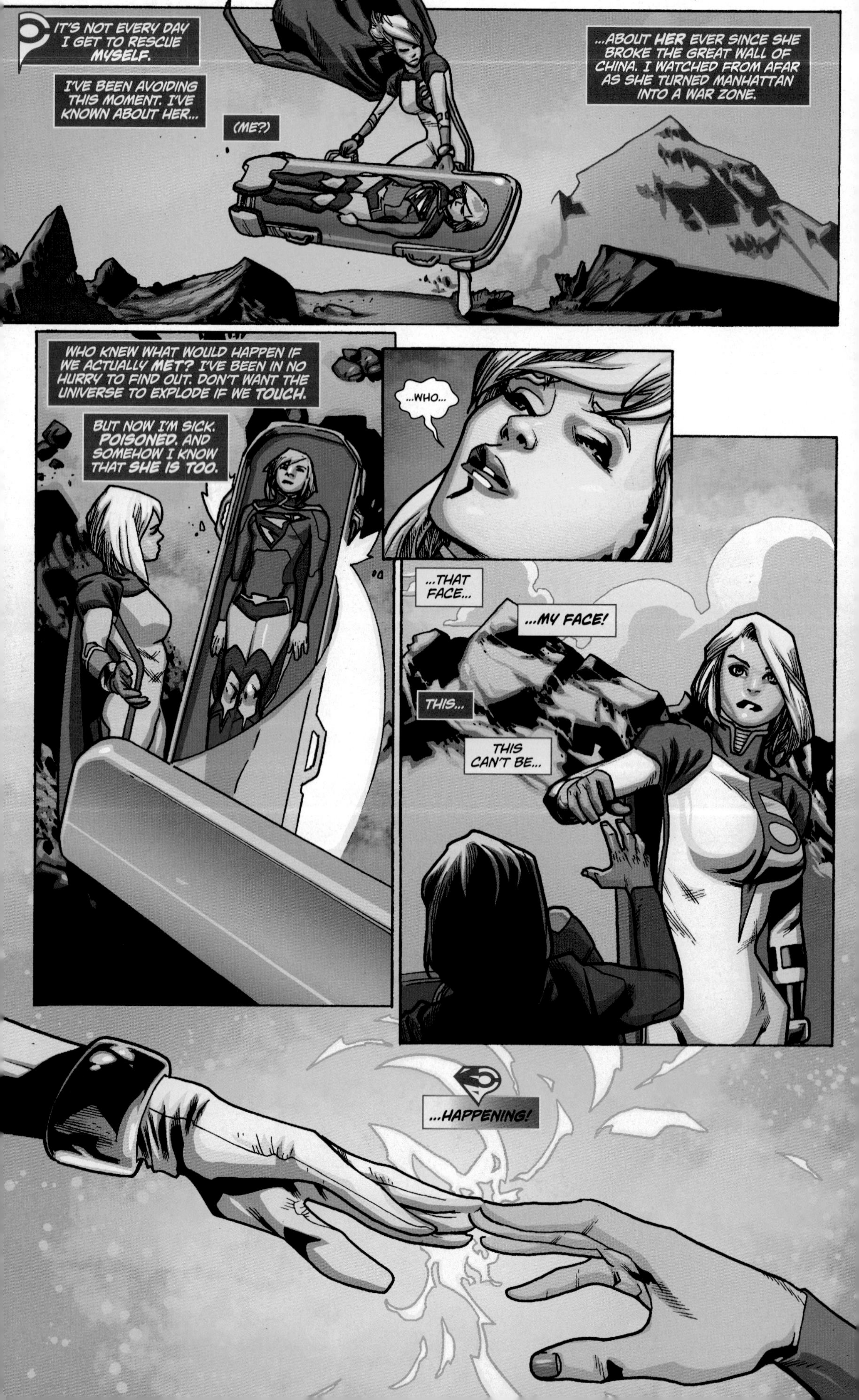
IT'S NOT EVERY DAY I GET TO RESCUE MYSELF.
I'VE BEEN AVOIDING THIS MOMENT. I'VE KNOWN ABOUT HER...
(ME?)
...ABOUT HER EVER SINCE SHE BROKE THE GREAT WALL OF CHINA. I WATCHED FROM AFAR AS SHE TURNED MANHATTAN INTO A WAR ZONE.
WHO KNEW WHAT WOULD HAPPEN IF WE ACTUALLY MET? I'VE BEEN IN NO HURRY TO FIND OUT. DON'T WANT THE UNIVERSE TO EXPLODE IF WE TOUCH.
BUT NOW I'M SICK. POISONED. AND SOMEHOW I KNOW THAT SHE IS TOO.
...WHO...
...THAT FACE...
...MY FACE!
THIS...
THIS CAN'T BE...
...HAPPENING!

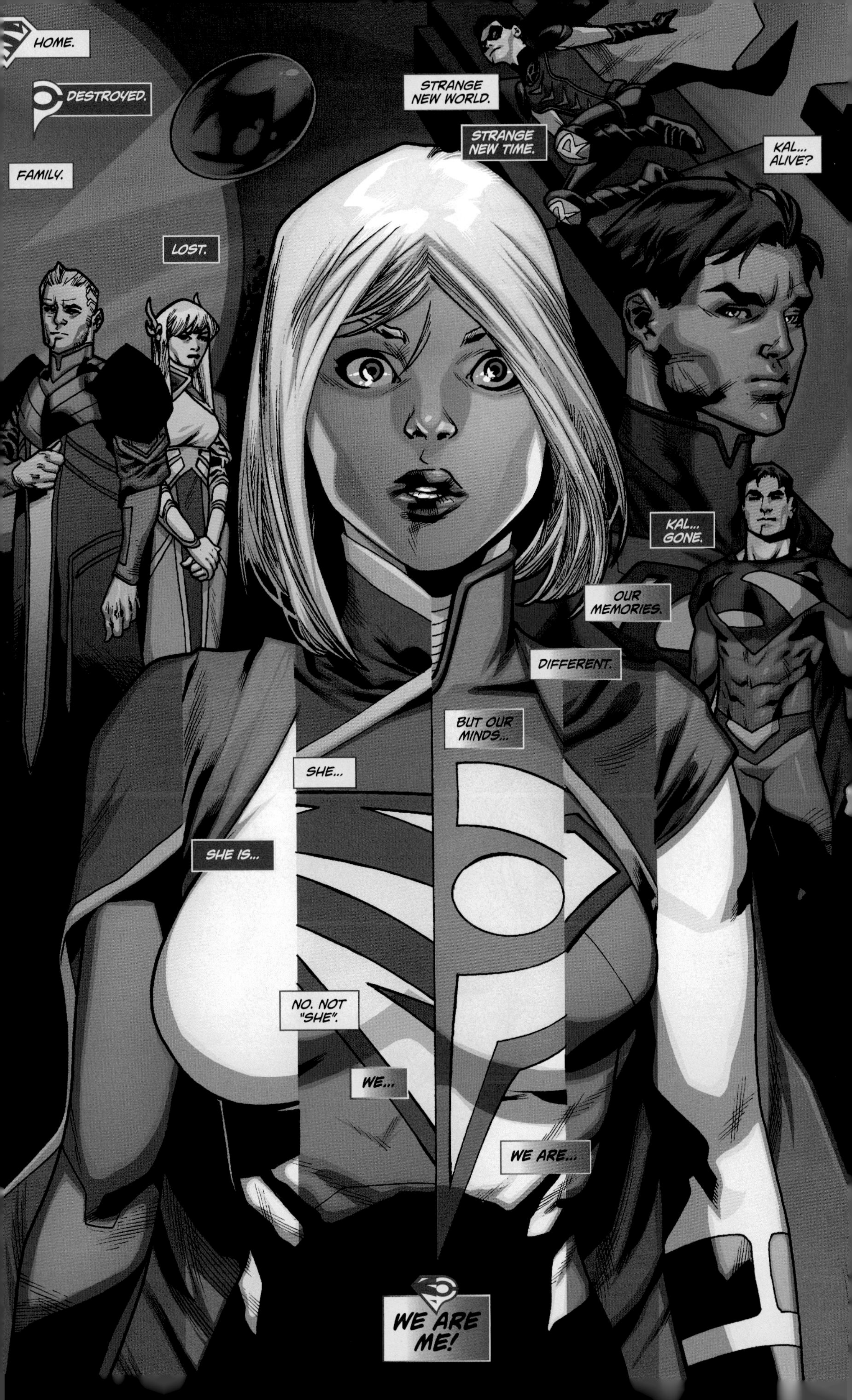
HOME.
DESTROYED.
FAMILY.
LOST.
STRANGE NEW WORLD.
STRANGE NEW TIME.
KAL... ALIVE?
KAL... GONE.
OUR MEMORIES.
DIFFERENT.
BUT OUR MINDS...
SHE...
SHE IS...
NO. NOT "SHE".
WE...
WE ARE...
WE ARE ME!

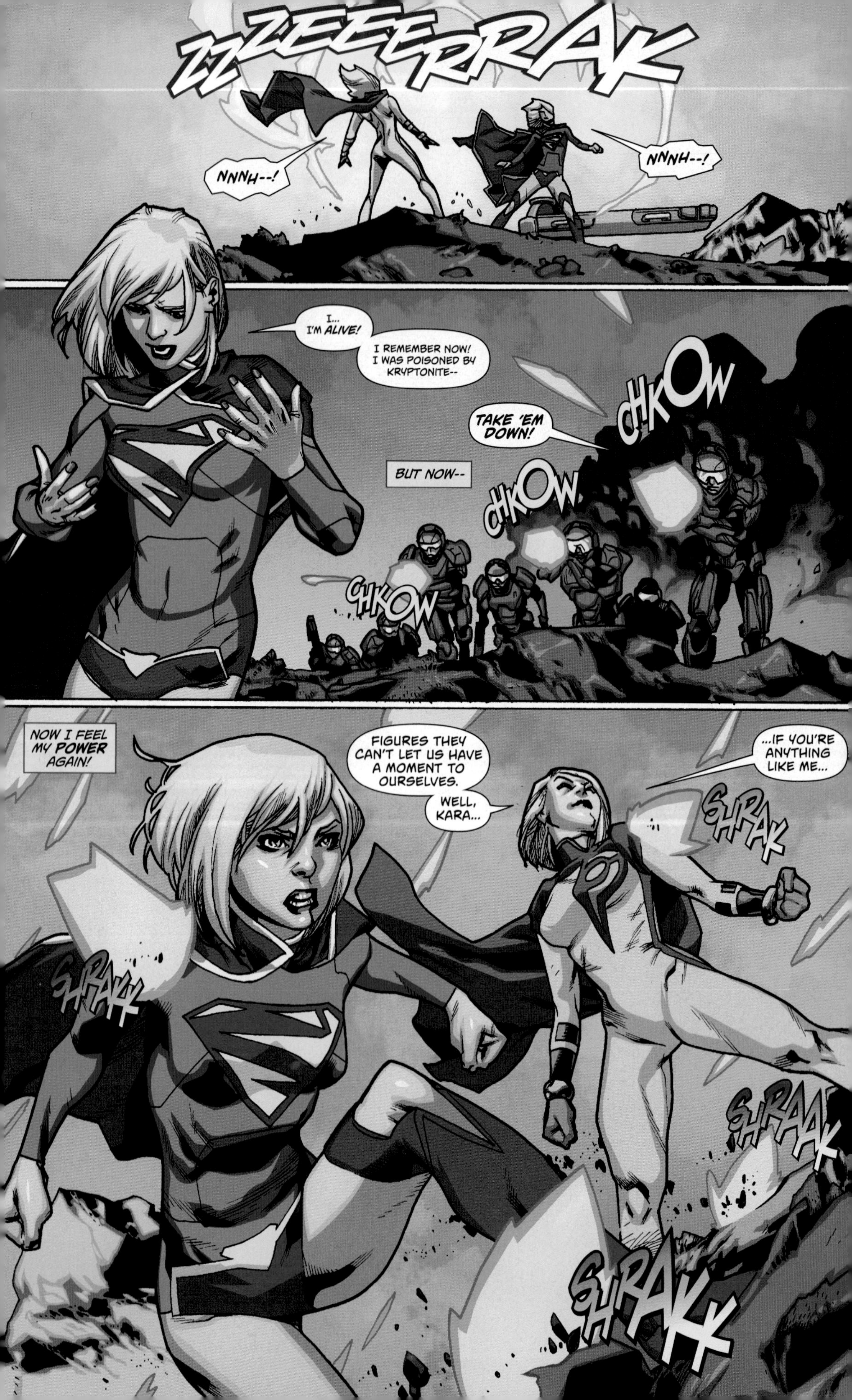
ZZZEEEERRAK
NNNH--!
NNNH--!
I... I'M ALIVE!
I REMEMBER NOW! I WAS POISONED BY KRYPTONITE--
TAKE 'EM DOWN!
CHKOW
BUT NOW--
CHKOW
CHKOW
NOW I FEEL MY POWER AGAIN!
FIGURES THEY CAN'T LET US HAVE A MOMENT TO OURSELVES.
WELL, KARA...
...IF YOU'RE ANYTHING LIKE ME...
SHRAK
SHRAKK
SHRAAK
SHRAKK

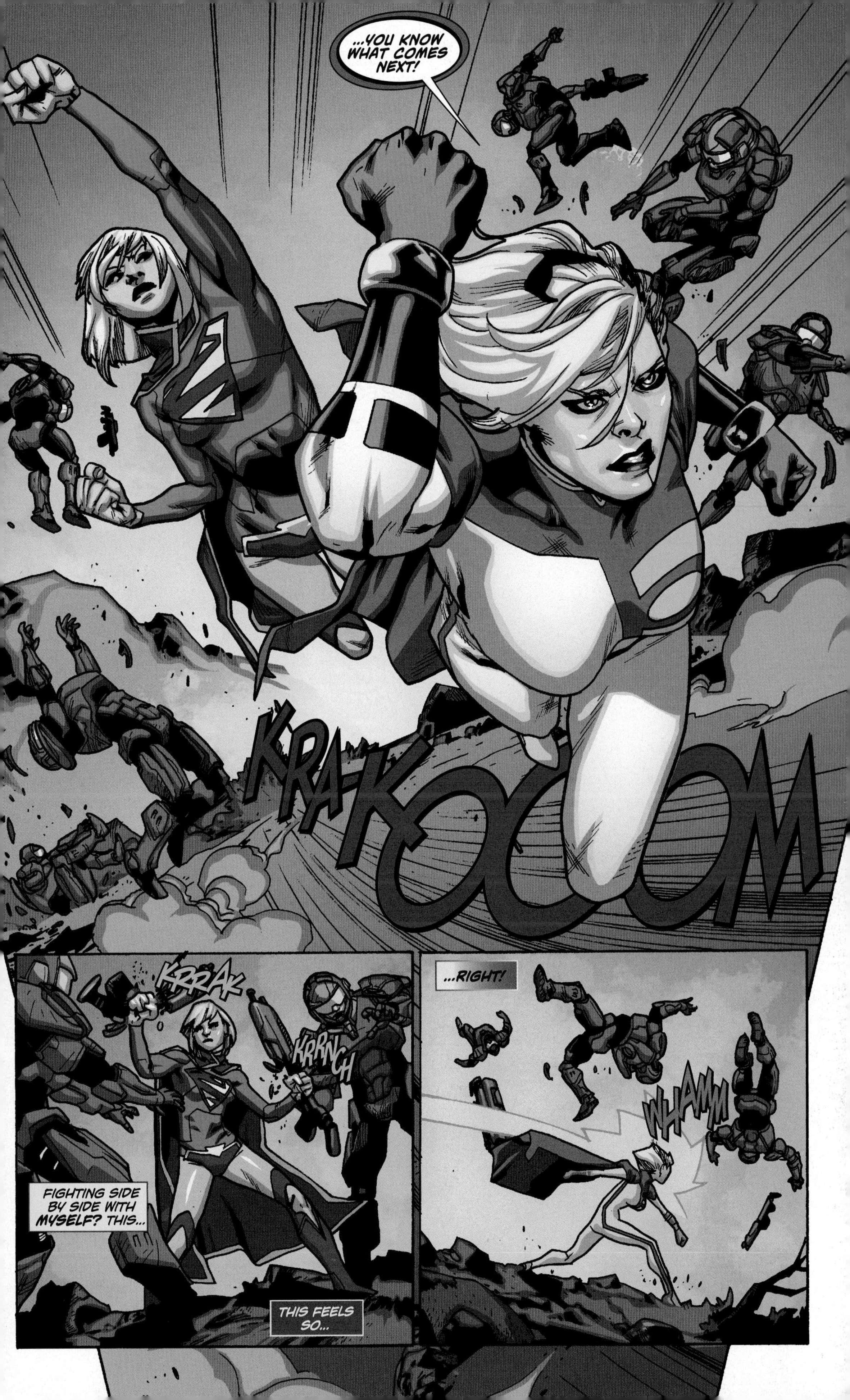
...YOU KNOW WHAT COMES NEXT!
KRAKOOOOM
KRRAK
KRRNCH
FIGHTING SIDE BY SIDE WITH MYSELF? THIS...
THIS FEELS SO...
...RIGHT!
WHAMM

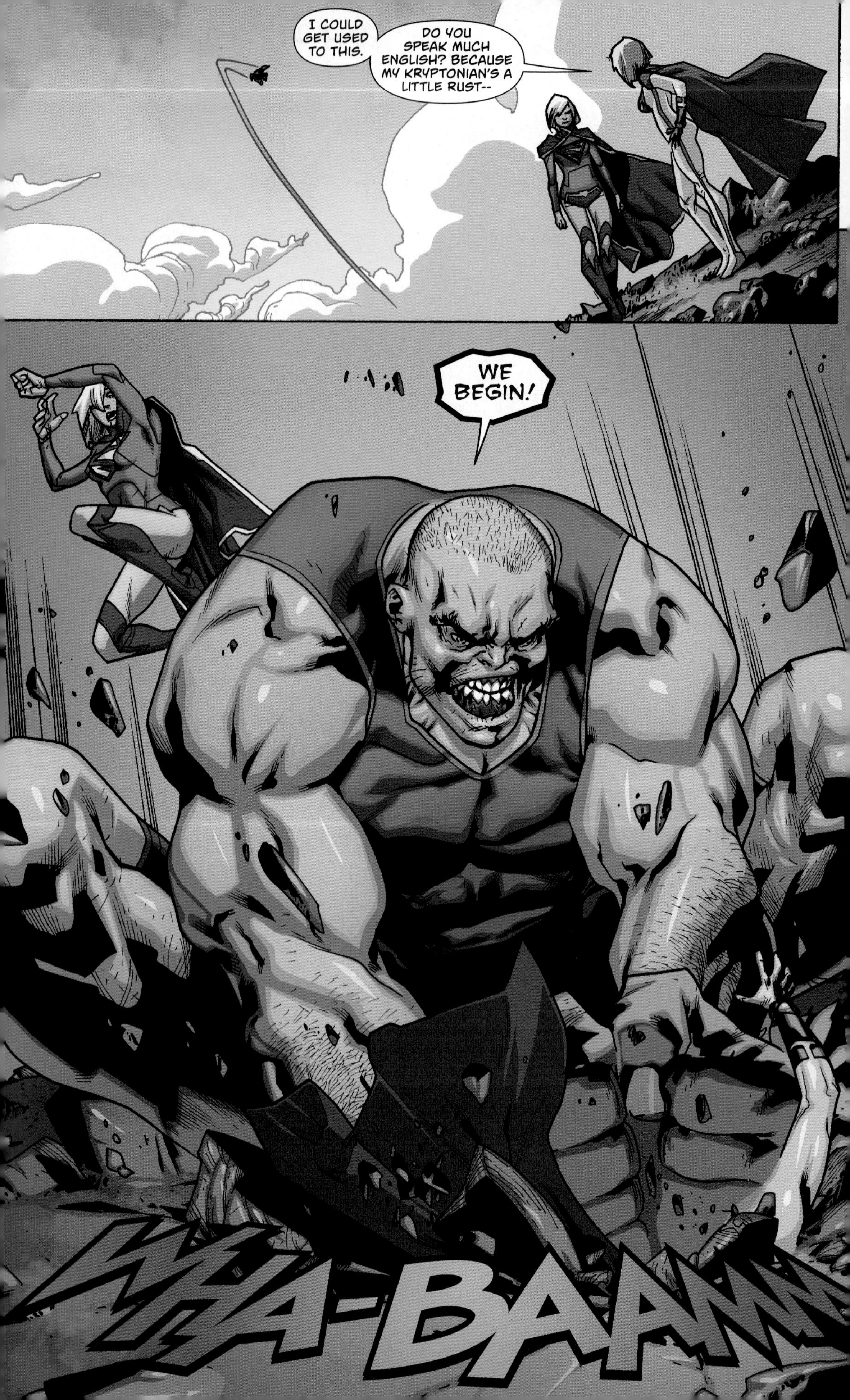
I COULD GET USED TO THIS.
DO YOU SPEAK MUCH ENGLISH? BECAUSE MY KRYPTONIAN'S A LITTLE RUST--
WE BEGIN!
WHA-BAAM

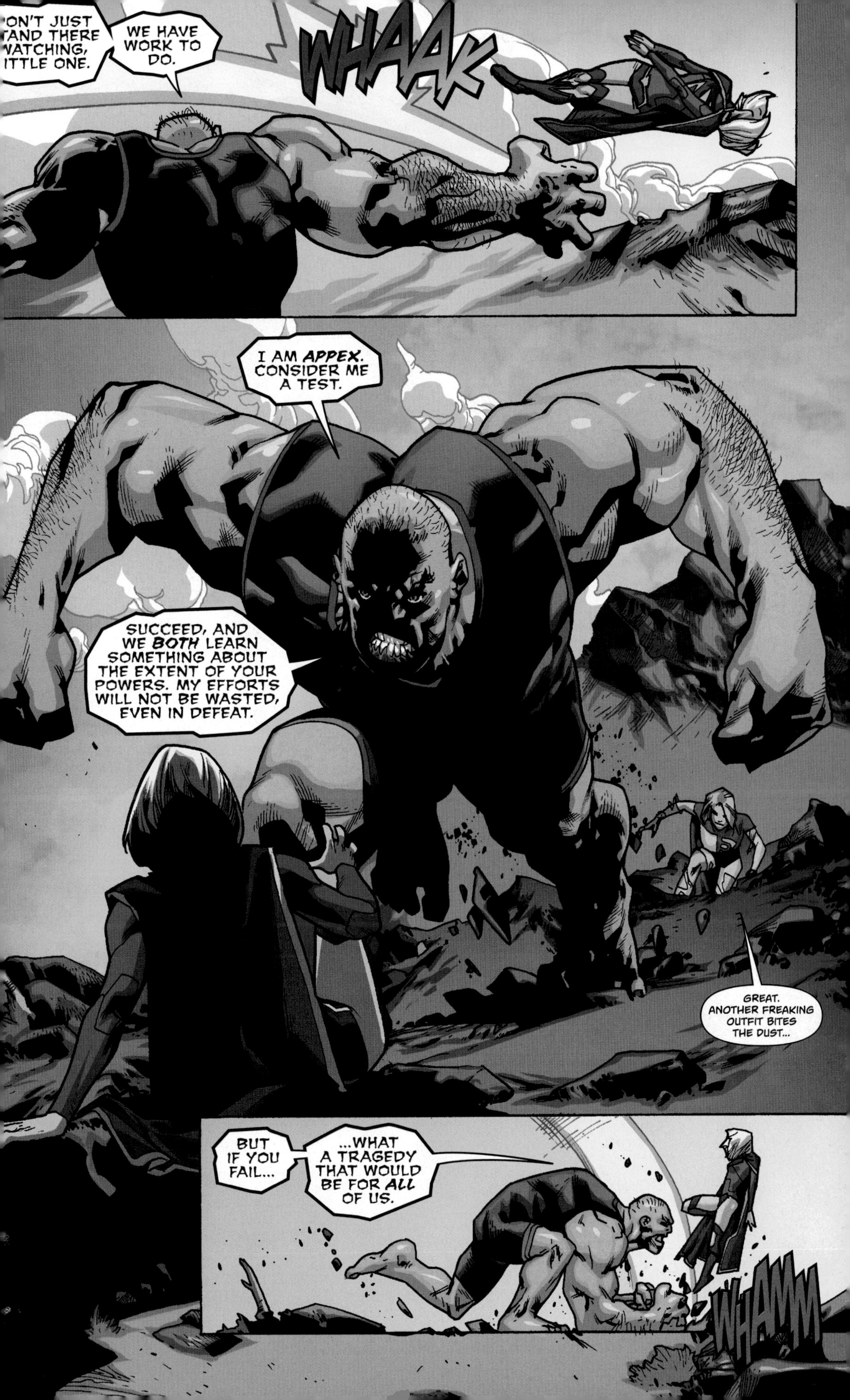

ON'T JUST TAND THERE WATCHING, ITTLE ONE.
WE HAVE WORK TO DO.
WHAAK
I AM APPEX. CONSIDER ME A TEST.
SUCCEED, AND WE BOTH LEARN SOMETHING ABOUT THE EXTENT OF YOUR POWERS. MY EFFORTS WILL NOT BE WASTED, EVEN IN DEFEAT.
GREAT. ANOTHER FREAKING OUTFIT BITES THE DUST...
BUT IF YOU FAIL...
...WHAT A TRAGEDY THAT WOULD BE FOR ALL OF US.
WHAMM

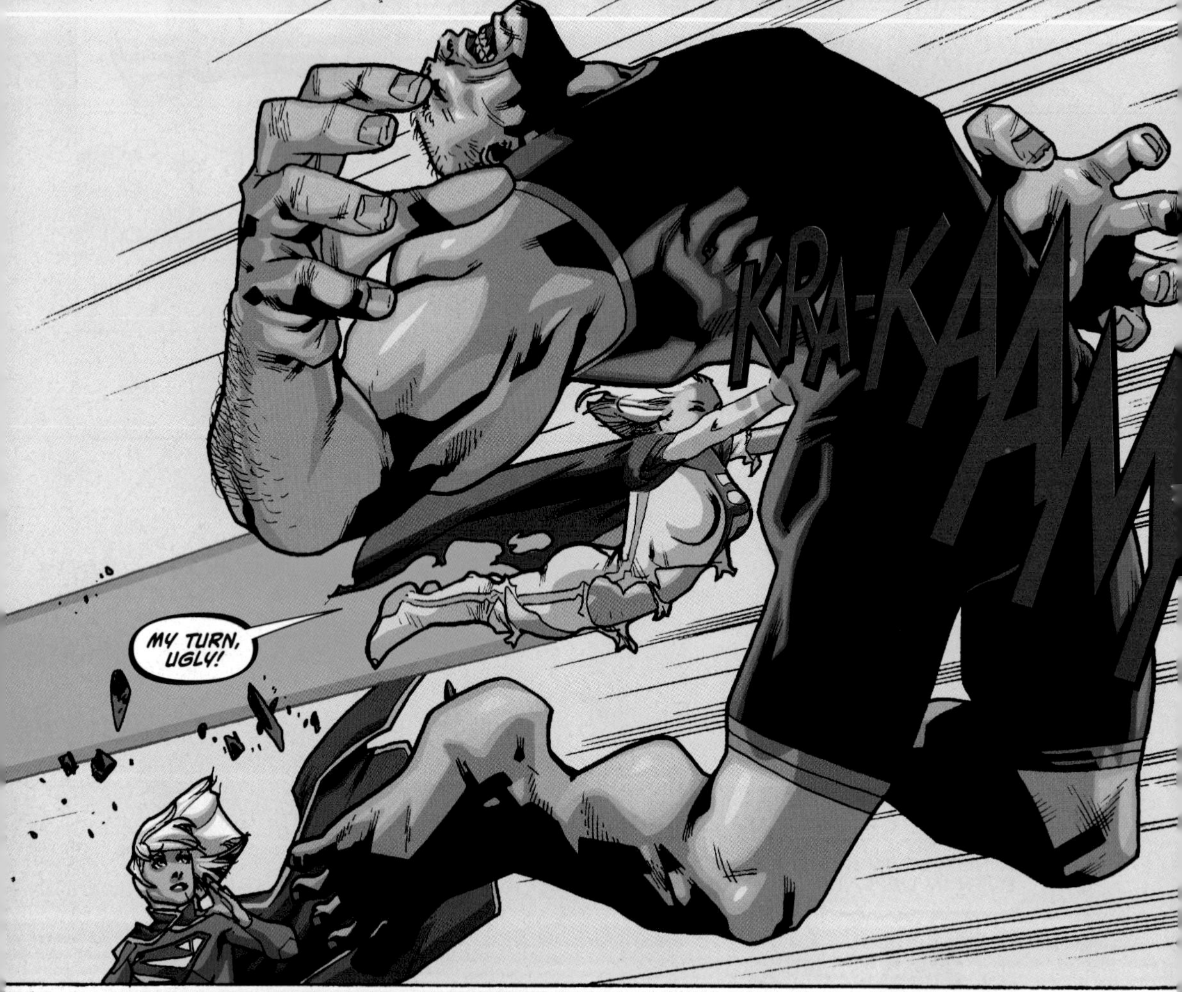
KRA-KAAM
MY TURN, UGLY!

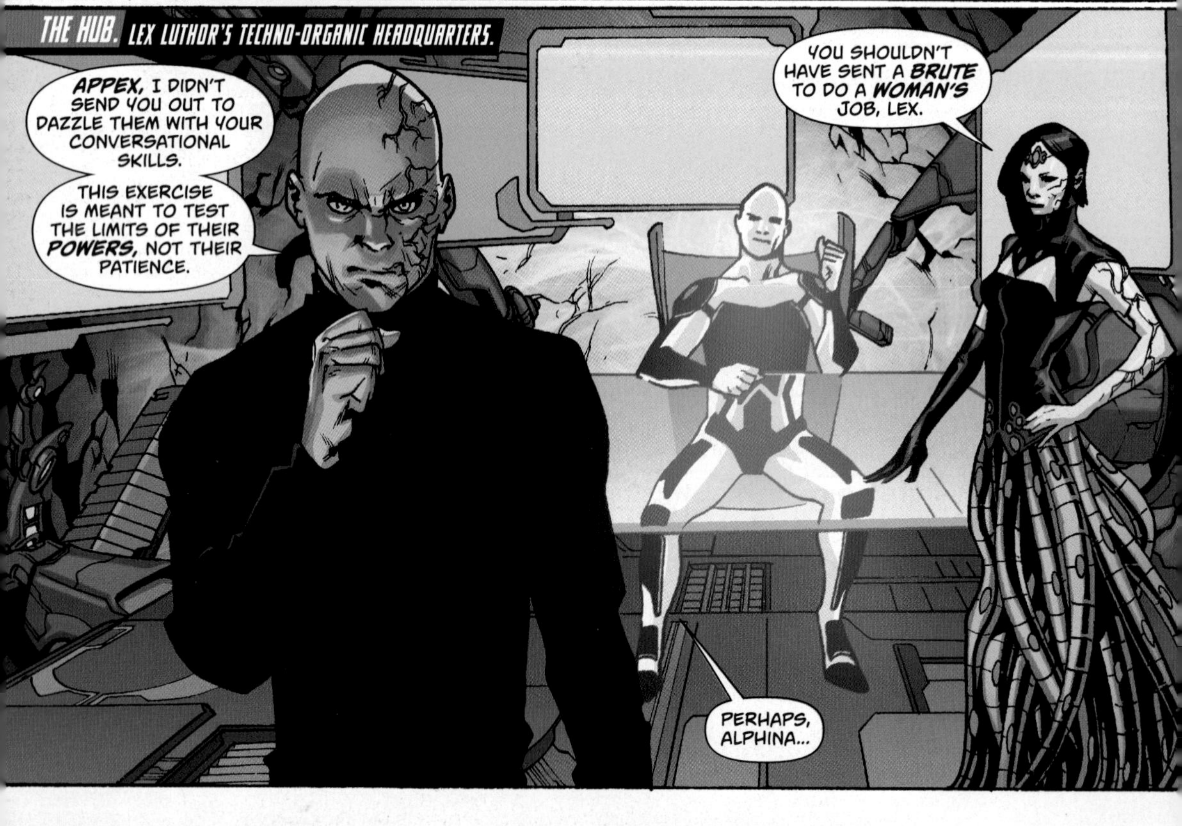
THE HUB. LEX LUTHOR'S TECHNO-ORGANIC HEADQUARTERS.
APPEX, I DIDN'T SEND YOU OUT TO DAZZLE THEM WITH YOUR CONVERSATIONAL SKILLS.
THIS EXERCISE IS MEANT TO TEST THE LIMITS OF THEIR POWERS, NOT THEIR PATIENCE.
YOU SHOULDN'T HAVE SENT A BRUTE TO DO A WOMAN'S JOB, LEX.
PERHAPS, ALPHINA...

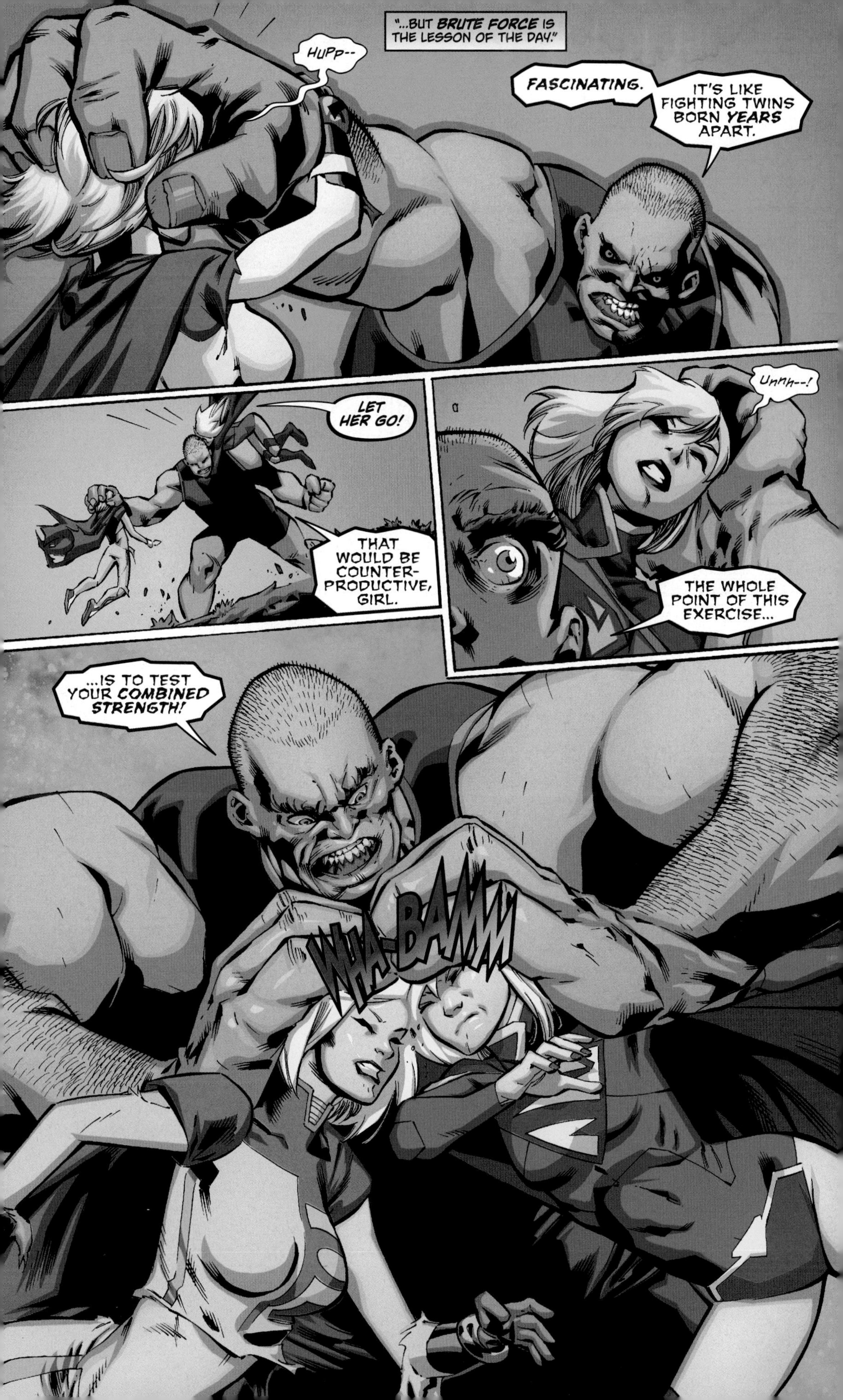
"...BUT BRUTE FORCE IS THE LESSON OF THE DAY."
HUPP--
FASCINATING.
IT'S LIKE FIGHTING TWINS BORN YEARS APART.
LET HER GO!
THAT WOULD BE COUNTER-PRODUCTIVE, GIRL.
Unnh--!
THE WHOLE POINT OF THIS EXERCISE...
...IS TO TEST YOUR COMBINED STRENGTH!
WHA-BAMM

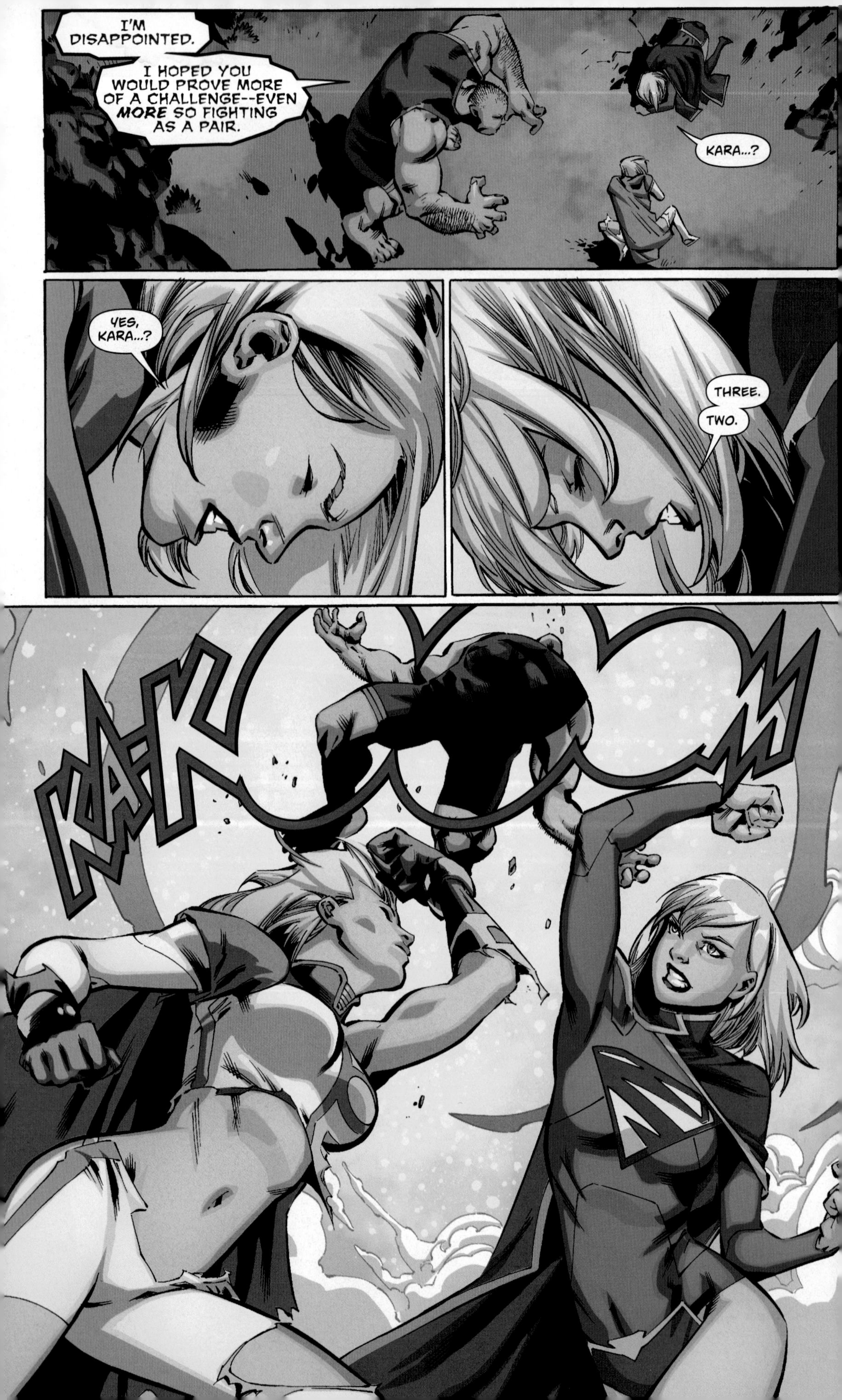
I'M DISAPPOINTED.
I HOPED YOU WOULD PROVE MORE OF A CHALLENGE--EVEN MORE SO FIGHTING AS A PAIR.
KARA...?
YES, KARA...?
THREE.
TWO.
KA-KOOM

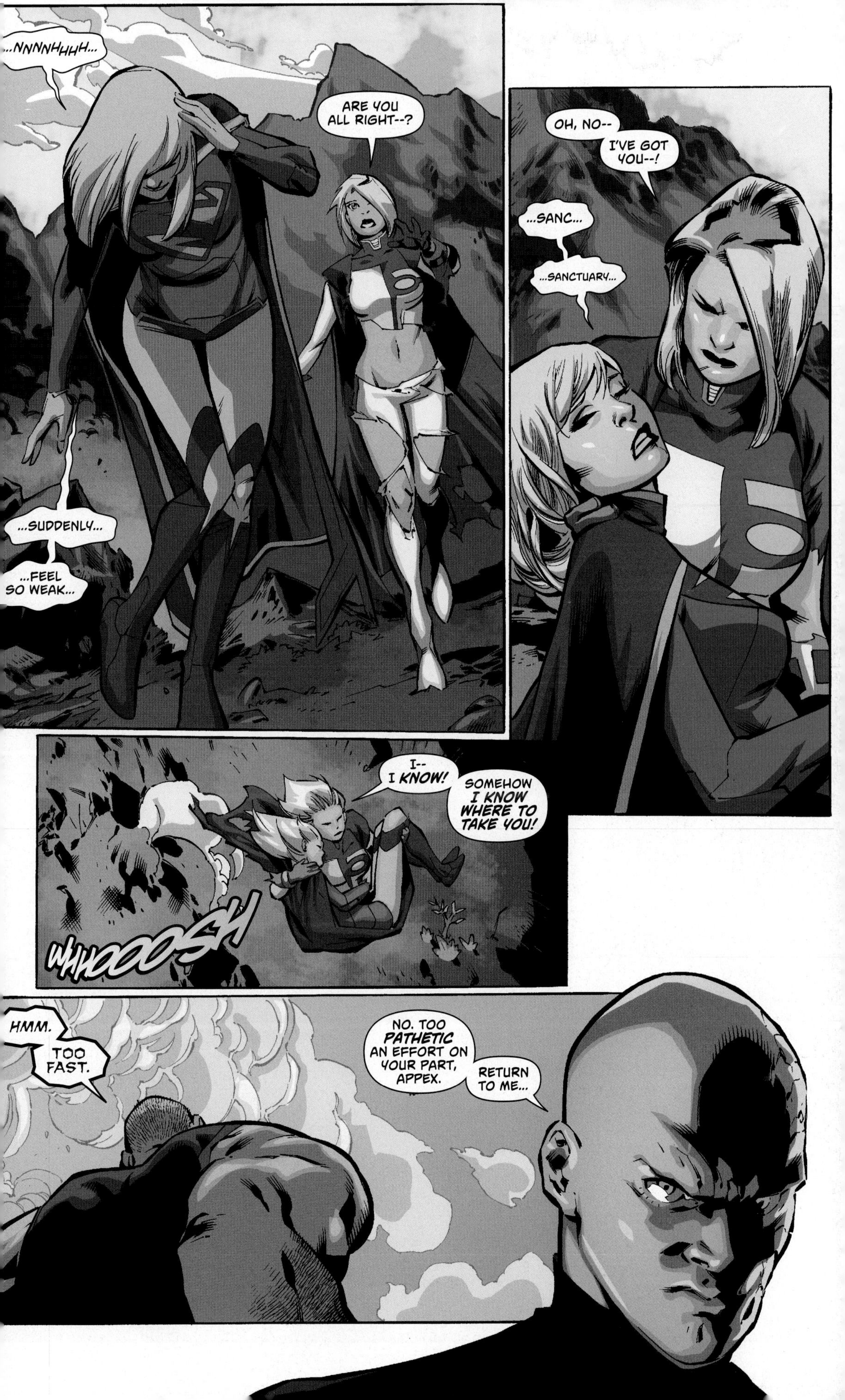
...NNNNHHHH...
ARE YOU ALL RIGHT--?
...SUDDENLY...
...FEEL SO WEAK...
OH, NO--
I'VE GOT YOU--!
...SANC...
...SANCTUARY...
I-- I KNOW!
SOMEHOW I KNOW WHERE TO TAKE YOU!
WHHOOOOSH
HMM.
TOO FAST.
NO. TOO PATHETIC AN EFFORT ON YOUR PART, APPEX.
RETURN TO ME...

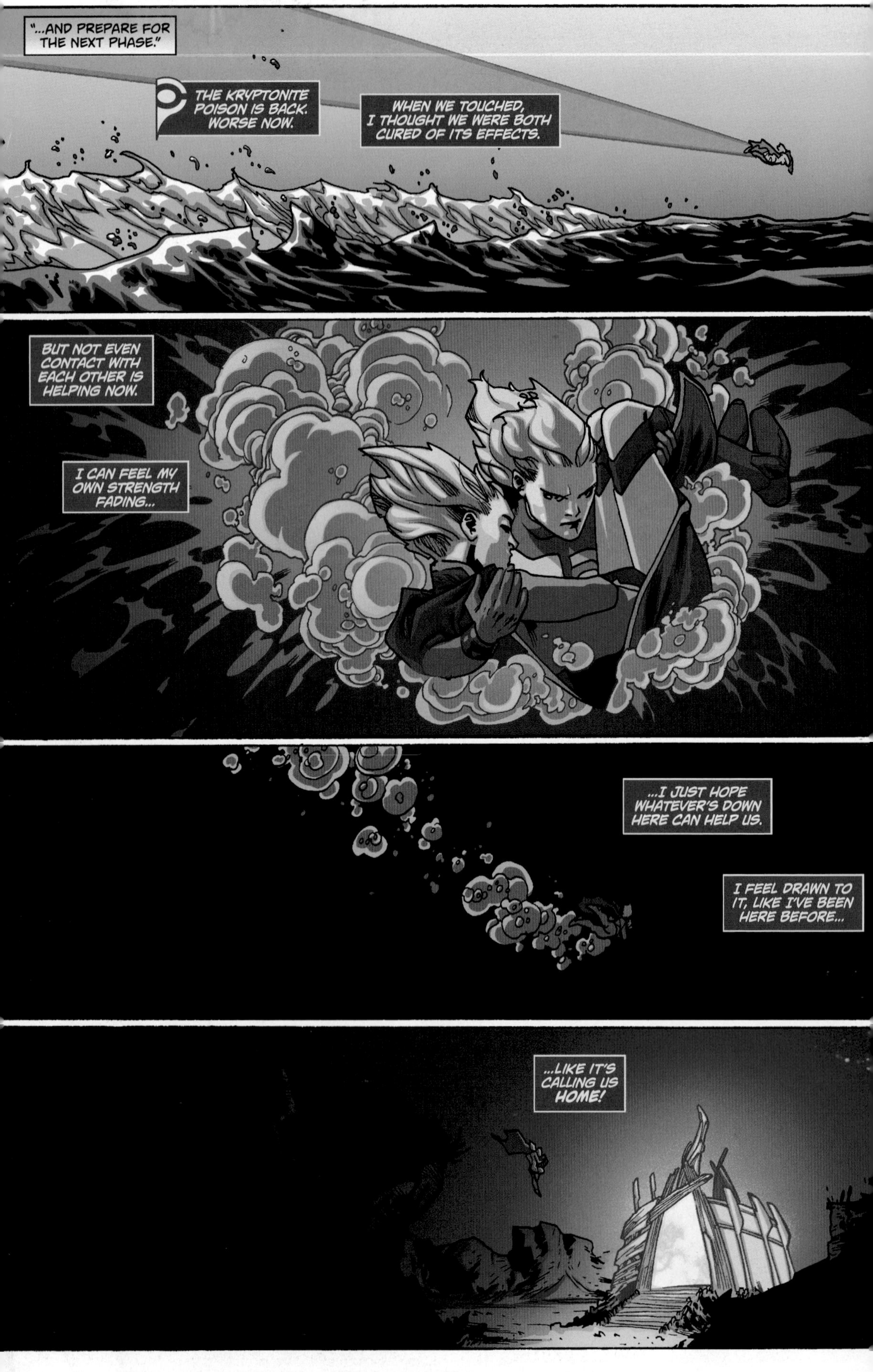
"...AND PREPARE FOR THE NEXT PHASE."
THE KRYPTONITE POISON IS BACK. WORSE NOW.
WHEN WE TOUCHED, I THOUGHT WE WERE BOTH CURED OF ITS EFFECTS.
BUT NOT EVEN CONTACT WITH EACH OTHER IS HELPING NOW.
I CAN FEEL MY OWN STRENGTH FADING...
...I JUST HOPE WHATEVER'S DOWN HERE CAN HELP US.
I FEEL DRAWN TO IT, LIKE I'VE BEEN HERE BEFORE...
...LIKE IT'S CALLING US HOME!

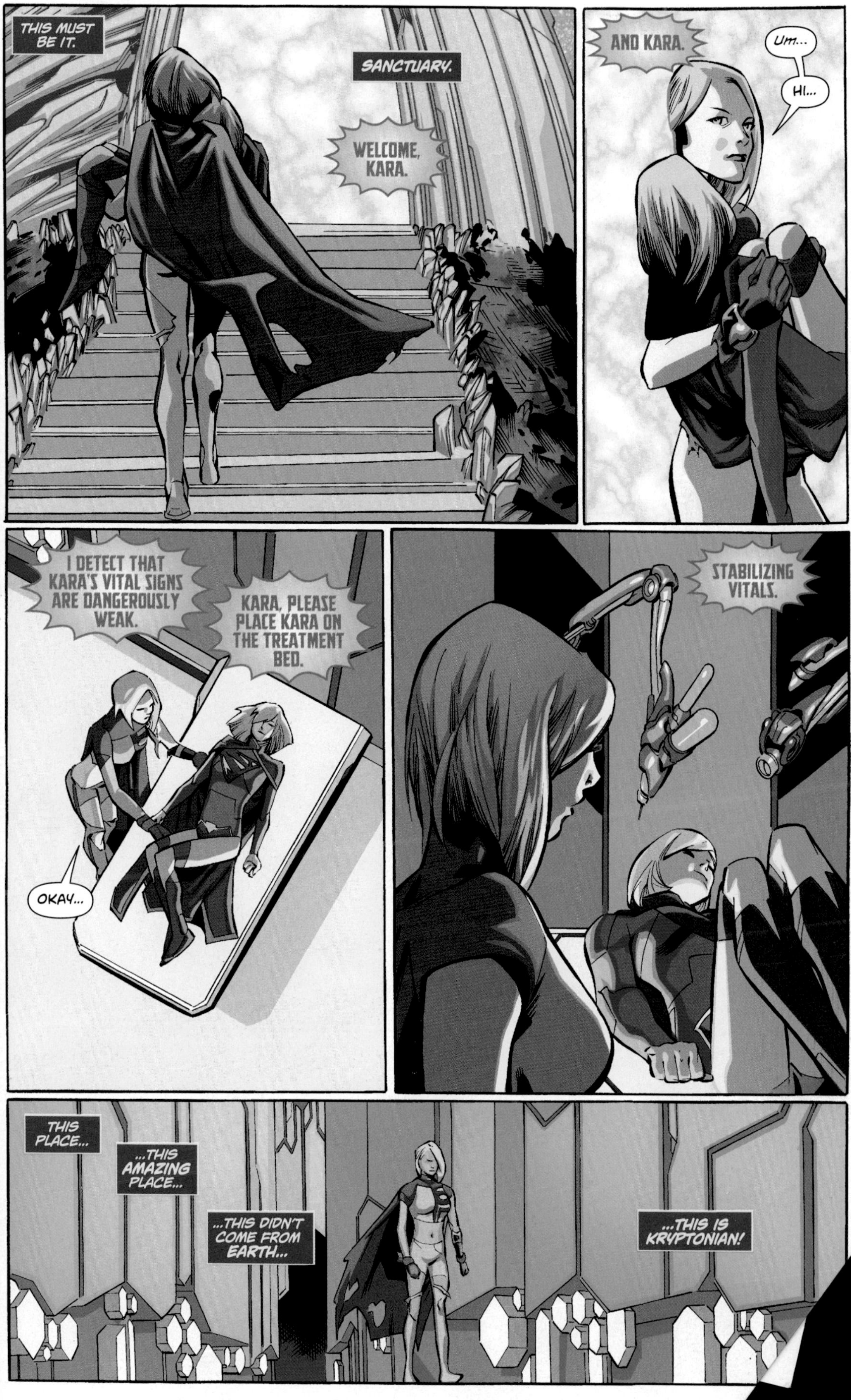
THIS MUST BE IT.
SANCTUARY.
WELCOME, KARA.
AND KARA.
Um...
Hi...
I DETECT THAT KARA'S VITAL SIGNS ARE DANGEROUSLY WEAK.
KARA, PLEASE PLACE KARA ON THE TREATMENT BED.
OKAY...
STABILIZING VITALS.
THIS PLACE...
...THIS AMAZING PLACE...
...THIS DIDN'T COME FROM EARTH...
...THIS IS KRYPTONIAN!

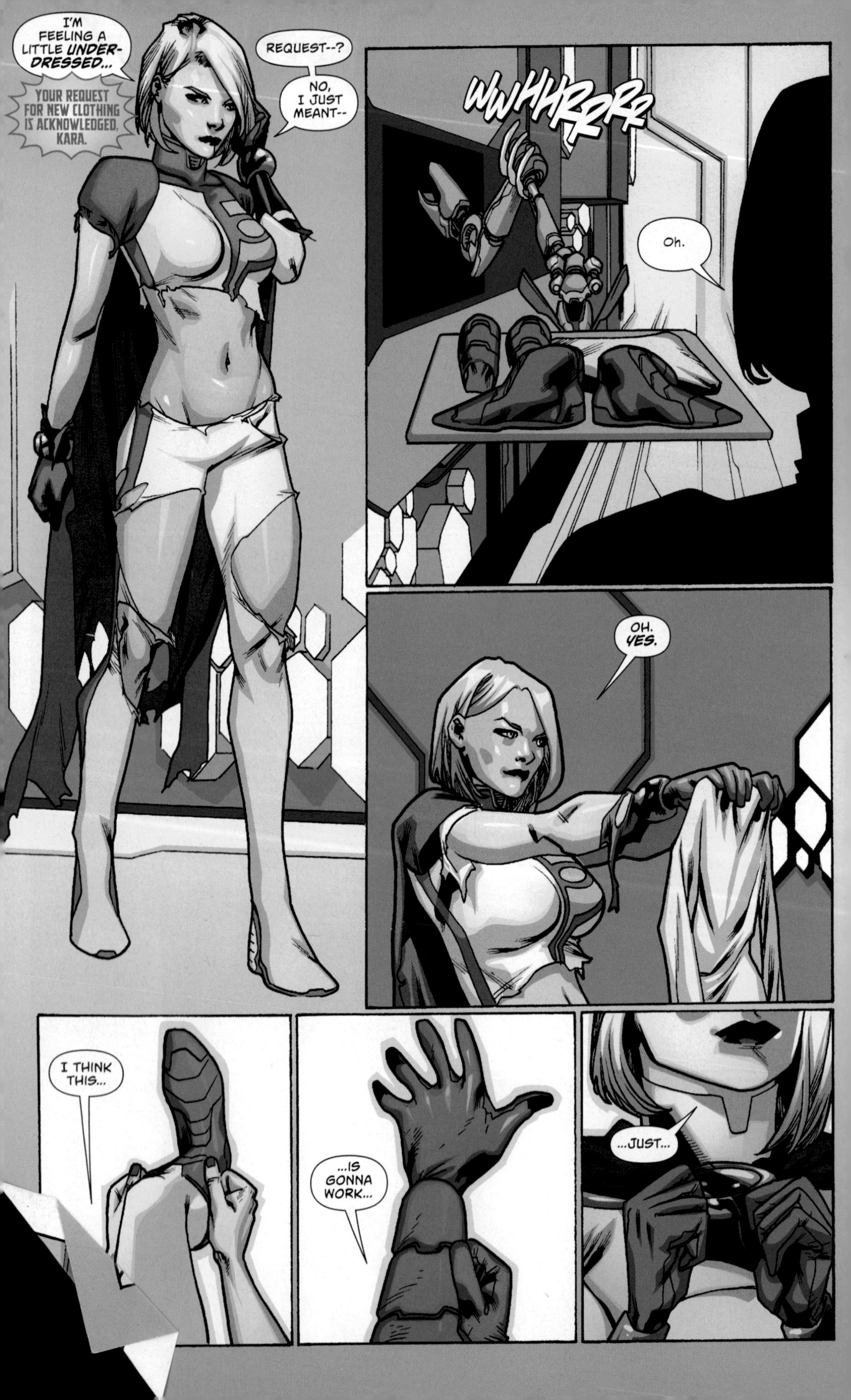
I'M FEELING A LITTLE UNDER-DRESSED...
YOUR REQUEST FOR NEW CLOTHING IS ACKNOWLEDGED, KARA.
REQUEST--?
NO, I JUST MEANT--
WWHHRRRR
Oh.
OH. YES.
I THINK THIS...
...IS GONNA WORK...
...JUST...

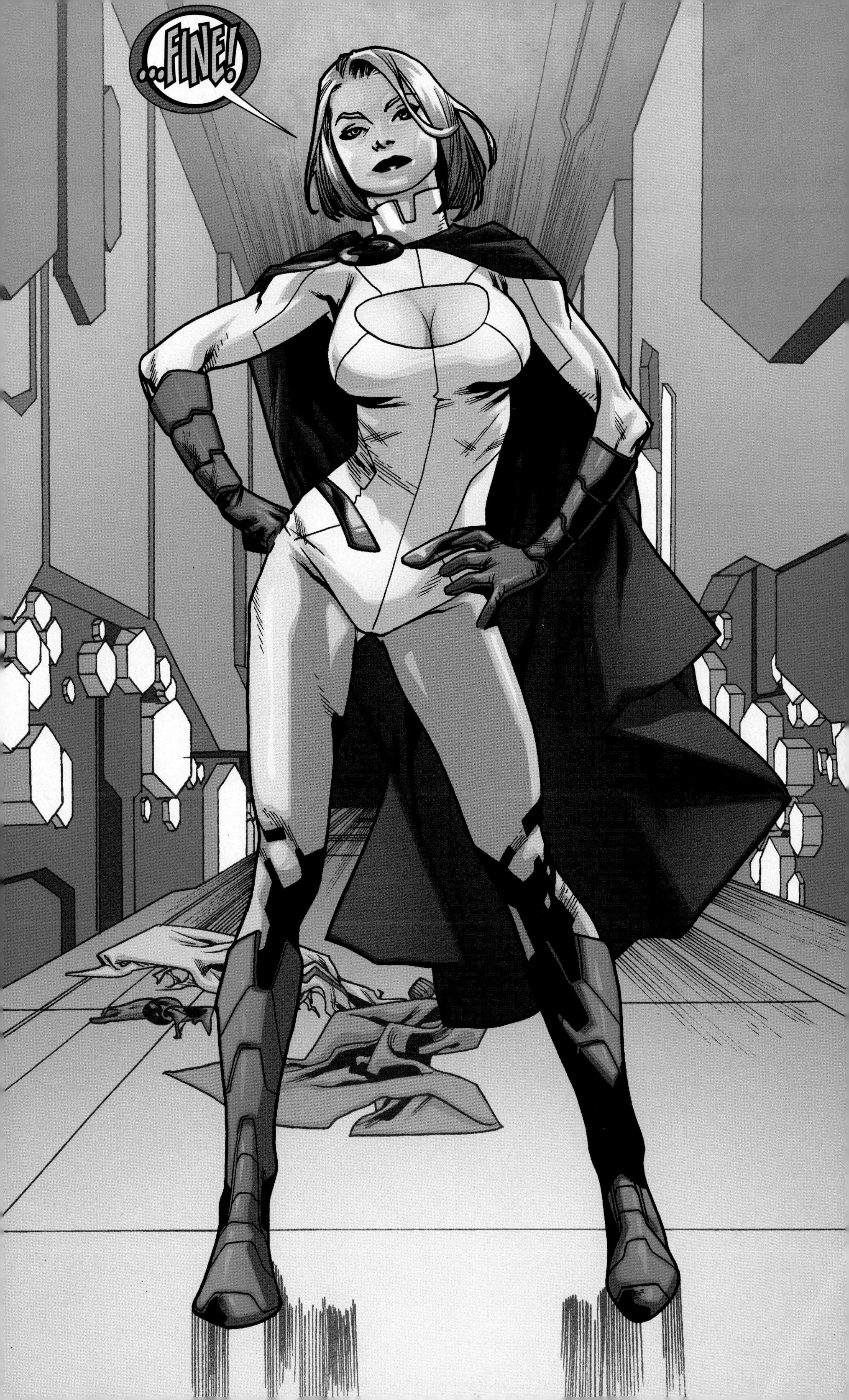
...FINE!

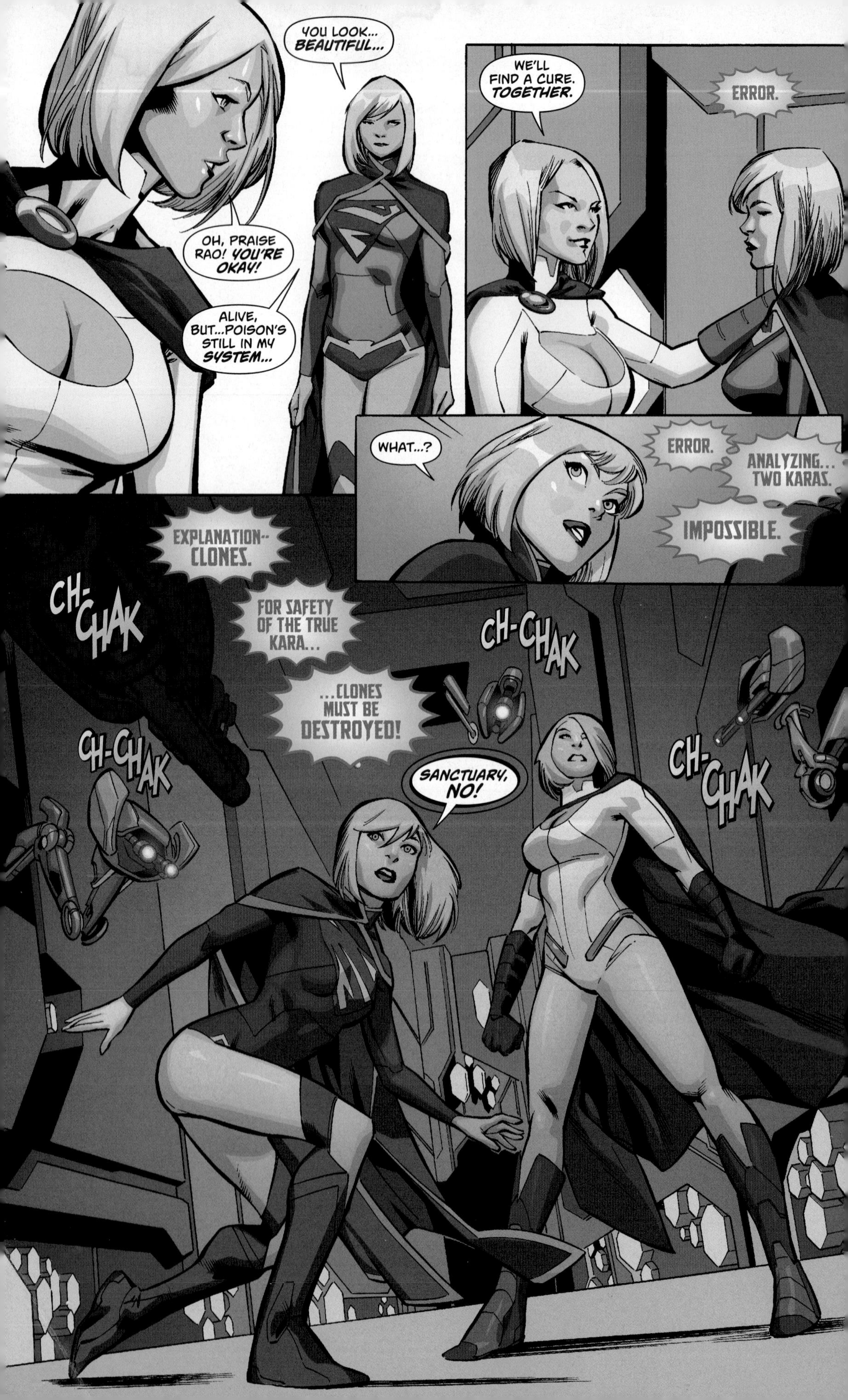
YOU LOOK... BEAUTIFUL...
OH, PRAISE RAO! YOU'RE OKAY!
ALIVE, BUT...POISON'S STILL IN MY SYSTEM...
WE'LL FIND A CURE. TOGETHER.
ERROR.
WHAT...?
ERROR.
ANALYZING... TWO KARAS.
IMPOSSIBLE.
EXPLANATION-- CLONES.
FOR SAFETY OF THE TRUE KARA...
...CLONES MUST BE DESTROYED!
CH-CHAK
CH-CHAK
CH-CHAK
CH-CHAK
SANCTUARY, NO!

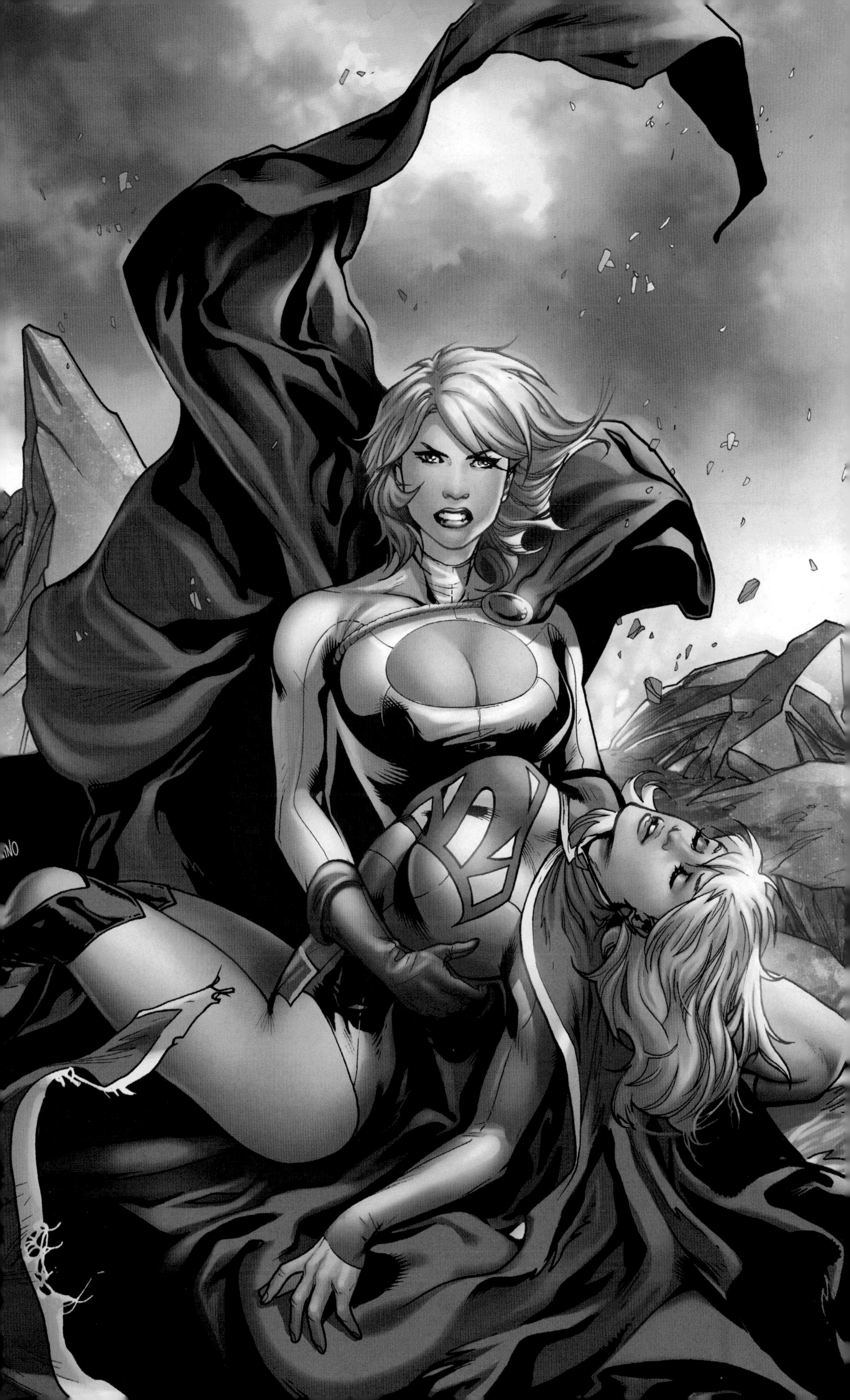

HOME INVASION

MICHAEL ALAN NELSON writer **MAHMUD ASRAR** artist cover art by **EMANUELA LUPACCHINO** with **NEI RUFFINO**

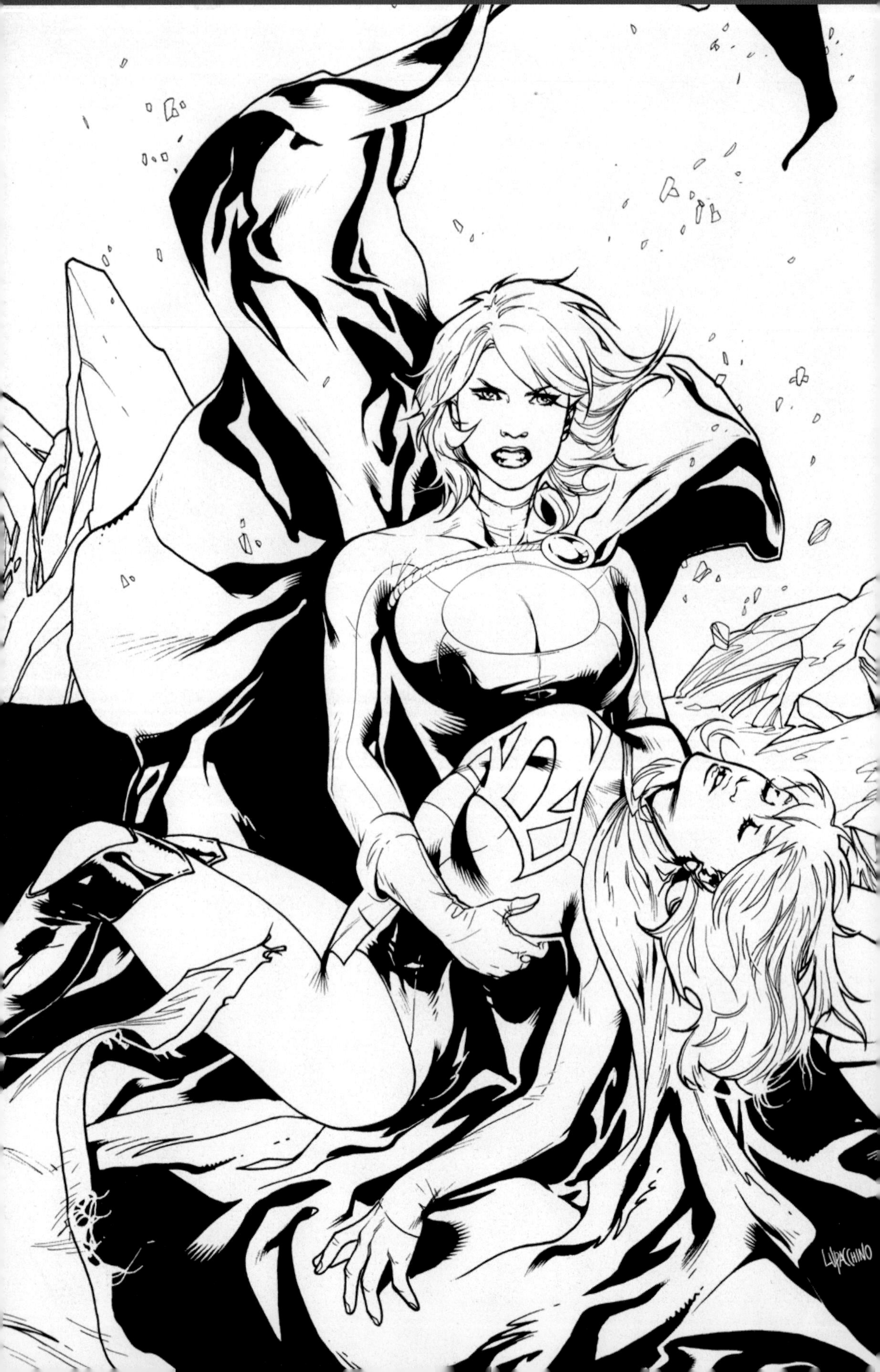

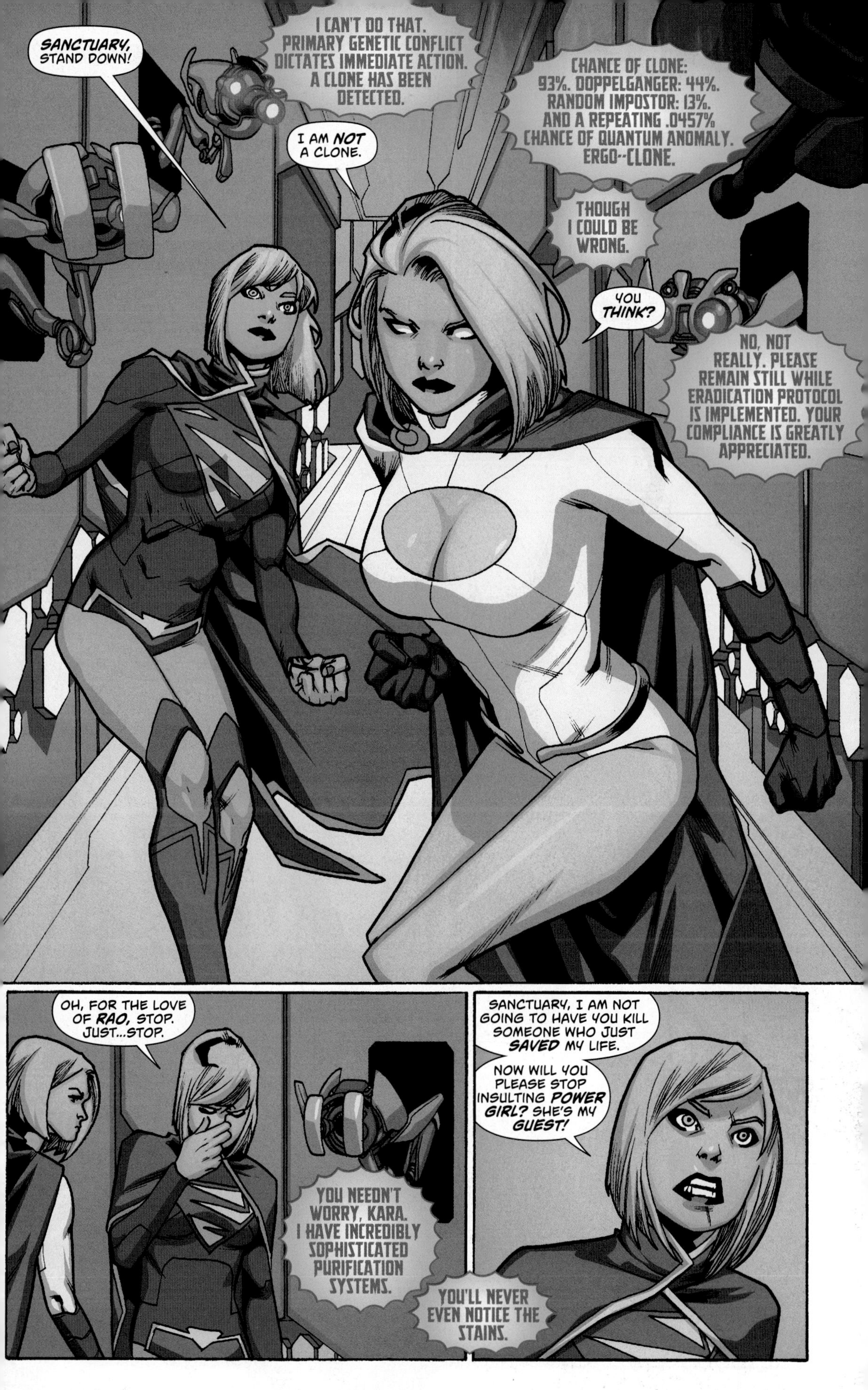
SANCTUARY, STAND DOWN!
I CAN'T DO THAT. PRIMARY GENETIC CONFLICT DICTATES IMMEDIATE ACTION. A CLONE HAS BEEN DETECTED.
I AM NOT A CLONE.
CHANCE OF CLONE: 93%. DOPPELGANGER: 44%. RANDOM IMPOSTOR: 13%. AND A REPEATING .0457% CHANCE OF QUANTUM ANOMALY. ERGO--CLONE.
THOUGH I COULD BE WRONG.
YOU THINK?
NO, NOT REALLY. PLEASE REMAIN STILL WHILE ERADICATION PROTOCOL IS IMPLEMENTED. YOUR COMPLIANCE IS GREATLY APPRECIATED.
OH, FOR THE LOVE OF RAO, STOP. JUST...STOP.
YOU NEEDN'T WORRY, KARA. I HAVE INCREDIBLY SOPHISTICATED PURIFICATION SYSTEMS.
YOU'LL NEVER EVEN NOTICE THE STAINS.
SANCTUARY, I AM NOT GOING TO HAVE YOU KILL SOMEONE WHO JUST SAVED MY LIFE.
NOW WILL YOU PLEASE STOP INSULTING POWER GIRL? SHE'S MY GUEST!

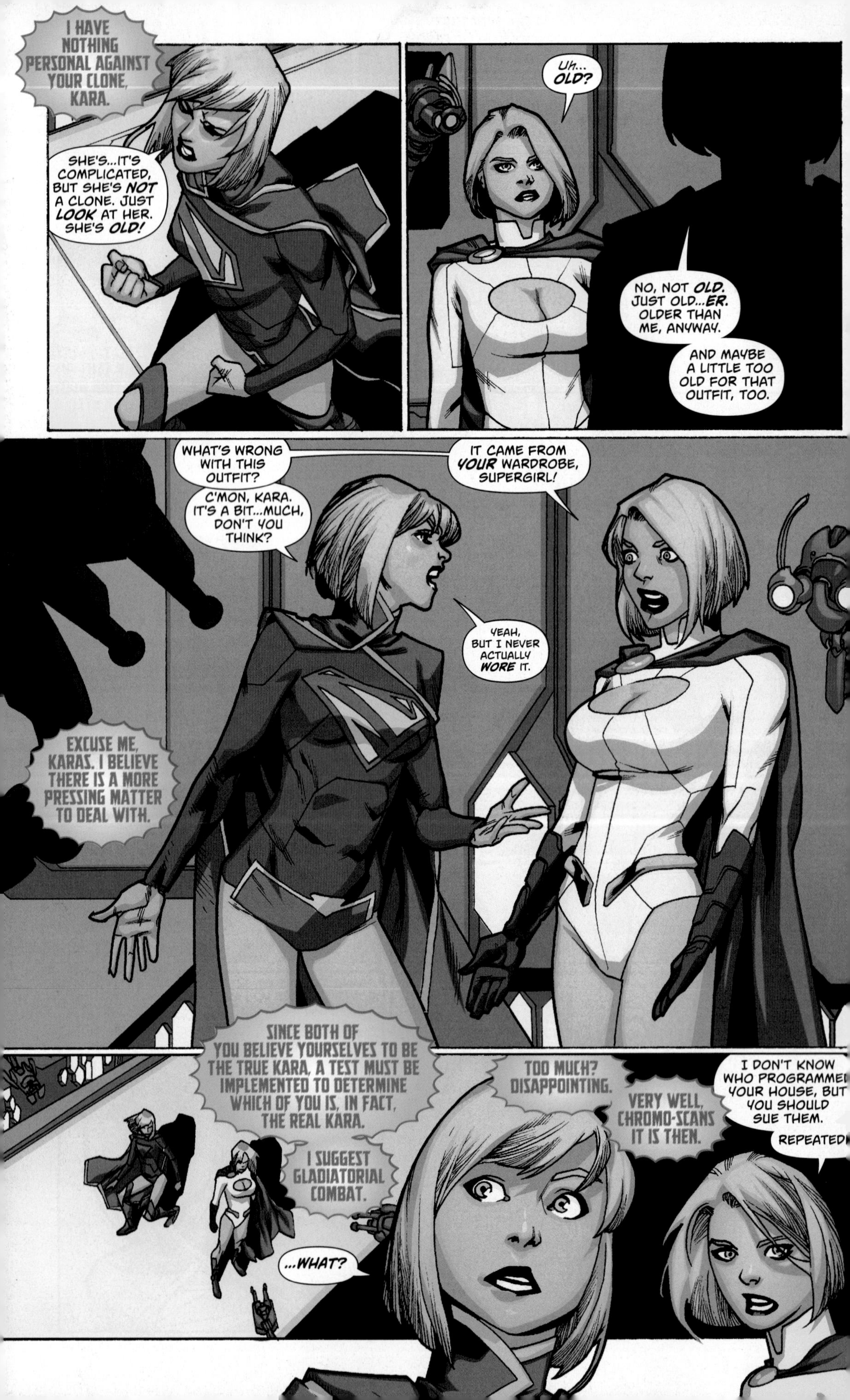
I HAVE NOTHING PERSONAL AGAINST YOUR CLONE, KARA.
SHE'S...IT'S COMPLICATED, BUT SHE'S NOT A CLONE. JUST LOOK AT HER. SHE'S OLD!
Uh... OLD?
NO, NOT OLD. JUST OLD...ER. OLDER THAN ME, ANYWAY.
AND MAYBE A LITTLE TOO OLD FOR THAT OUTFIT, TOO.
WHAT'S WRONG WITH THIS OUTFIT?
IT CAME FROM YOUR WARDROBE, SUPERGIRL!
C'MON, KARA. IT'S A BIT...MUCH, DON'T YOU THINK?
YEAH, BUT I NEVER ACTUALLY WORE IT.
EXCUSE ME, KARAS. I BELIEVE THERE IS A MORE PRESSING MATTER TO DEAL WITH.
SINCE BOTH OF YOU BELIEVE YOURSELVES TO BE THE TRUE KARA, A TEST MUST BE IMPLEMENTED TO DETERMINE WHICH OF YOU IS, IN FACT, THE REAL KARA.
I SUGGEST GLADIATORIAL COMBAT.
...WHAT?
TOO MUCH? DISAPPOINTING.
VERY WELL, CHROMO-SCANS IT IS THEN.
I DON'T KNOW WHO PROGRAMMED YOUR HOUSE, BUT YOU SHOULD SUE THEM.
REPEATED

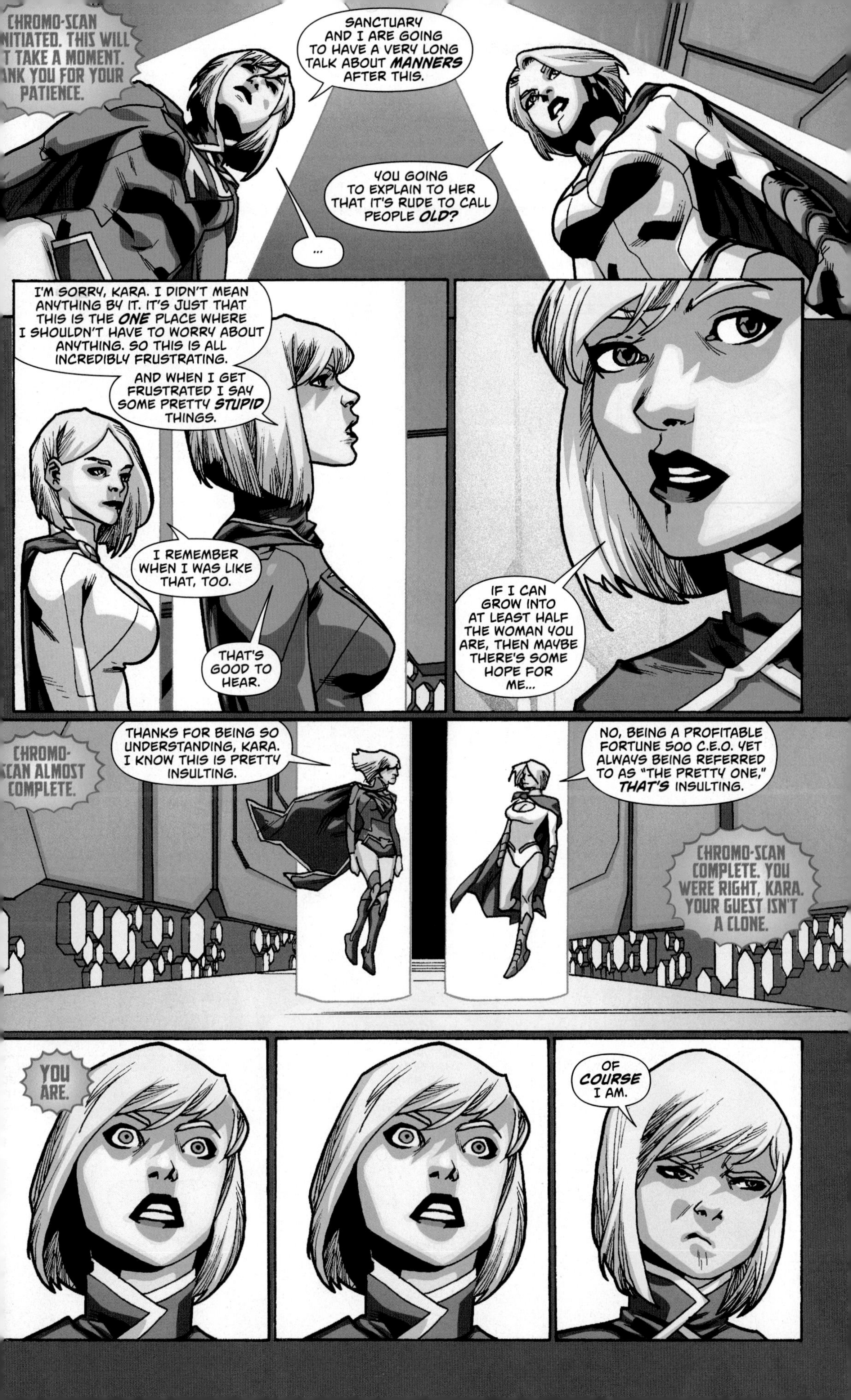
CHROMO-SCAN
NITIATED. THIS WILL
T TAKE A MOMENT.
ANK YOU FOR YOUR
PATIENCE.
SANCTUARY AND I ARE GOING TO HAVE A VERY LONG TALK ABOUT MANNERS AFTER THIS.
YOU GOING TO EXPLAIN TO HER THAT IT'S RUDE TO CALL PEOPLE OLD?
...
I'M SORRY, KARA. I DIDN'T MEAN ANYTHING BY IT. IT'S JUST THAT THIS IS THE ONE PLACE WHERE I SHOULDN'T HAVE TO WORRY ABOUT ANYTHING. SO THIS IS ALL INCREDIBLY FRUSTRATING.
AND WHEN I GET FRUSTRATED I SAY SOME PRETTY STUPID THINGS.
I REMEMBER WHEN I WAS LIKE THAT, TOO.
THAT'S GOOD TO HEAR.
IF I CAN GROW INTO AT LEAST HALF THE WOMAN YOU ARE, THEN MAYBE THERE'S SOME HOPE FOR ME...
CHROMO-
CAN ALMOST
COMPLETE.
THANKS FOR BEING SO UNDERSTANDING, KARA. I KNOW THIS IS PRETTY INSULTING.
NO, BEING A PROFITABLE FORTUNE 500 C.E.O. YET ALWAYS BEING REFERRED TO AS "THE PRETTY ONE," THAT'S INSULTING.
CHROMO-SCAN COMPLETE. YOU WERE RIGHT, KARA. YOUR GUEST ISN'T A CLONE.
YOU ARE.
OF COURSE I AM.

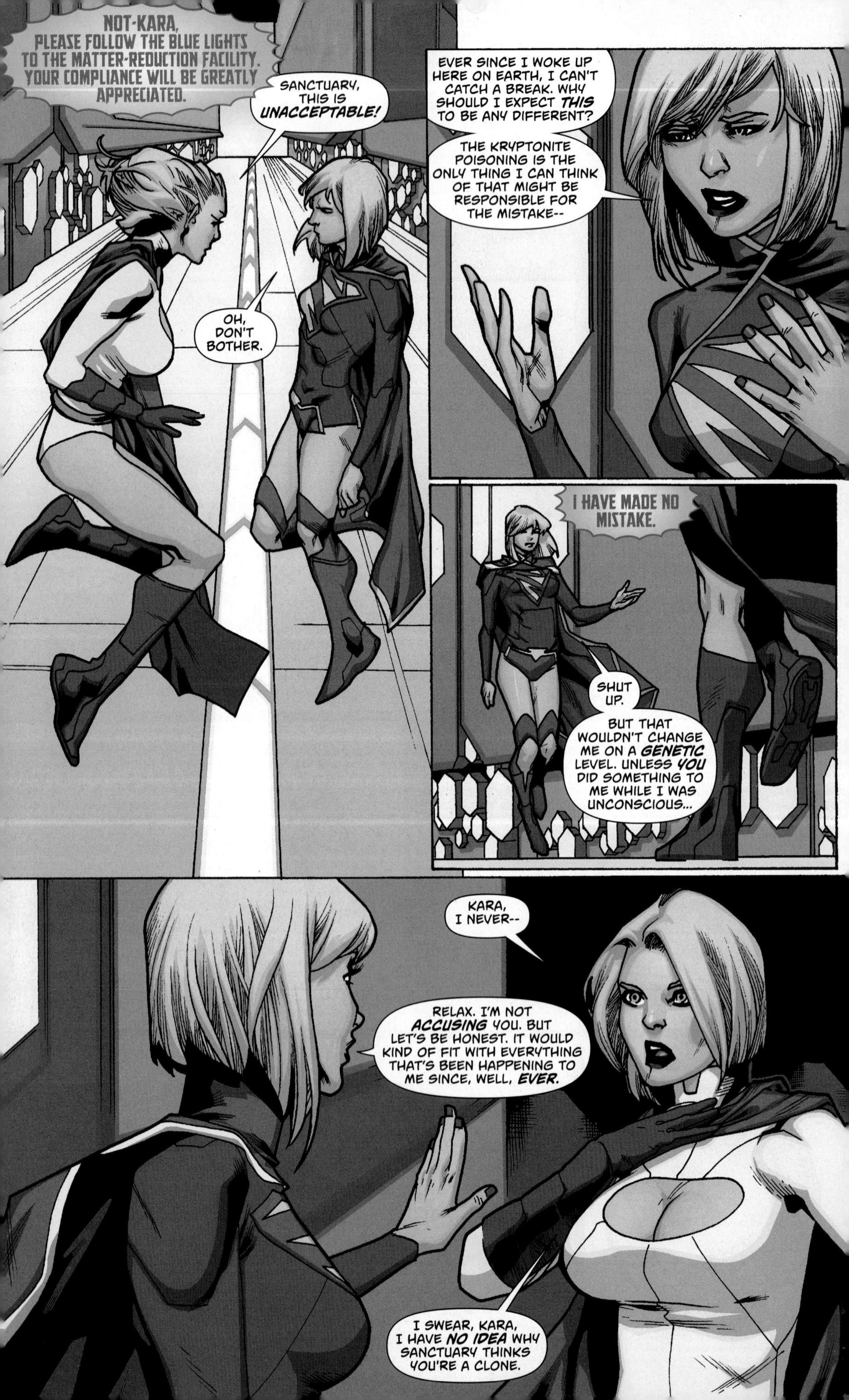

NOT-KARA, PLEASE FOLLOW THE BLUE LIGHTS TO THE MATTER-REDUCTION FACILITY. YOUR COMPLIANCE WILL BE GREATLY APPRECIATED.
SANCTUARY, THIS IS UNACCEPTABLE!
OH, DON'T BOTHER.
EVER SINCE I WOKE UP HERE ON EARTH, I CAN'T CATCH A BREAK. WHY SHOULD I EXPECT THIS TO BE ANY DIFFERENT?
THE KRYPTONITE POISONING IS THE ONLY THING I CAN THINK OF THAT MIGHT BE RESPONSIBLE FOR THE MISTAKE--
I HAVE MADE NO MISTAKE.
SHUT UP.
BUT THAT WOULDN'T CHANGE ME ON A GENETIC LEVEL. UNLESS YOU DID SOMETHING TO ME WHILE I WAS UNCONSCIOUS...
KARA, I NEVER--
RELAX. I'M NOT ACCUSING YOU. BUT LET'S BE HONEST. IT WOULD KIND OF FIT WITH EVERYTHING THAT'S BEEN HAPPENING TO ME SINCE, WELL, EVER.
I SWEAR, KARA, I HAVE NO IDEA WHY SANCTUARY THINKS YOU'RE A CLONE.

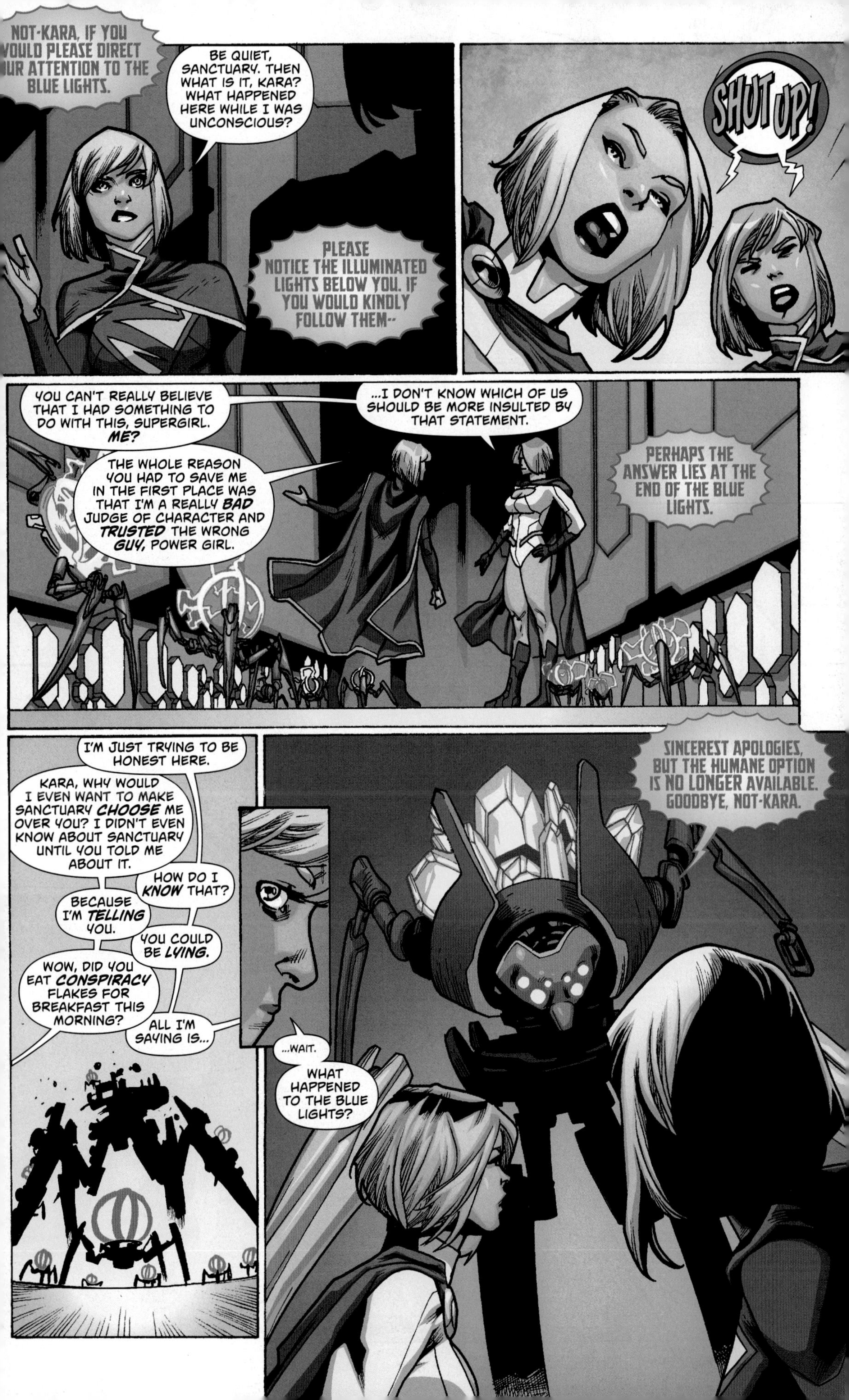
NOT-KARA, IF YOU WOULD PLEASE DIRECT YOUR ATTENTION TO THE BLUE LIGHTS.
BE QUIET, SANCTUARY. THEN WHAT IS IT, KARA? WHAT HAPPENED HERE WHILE I WAS UNCONSCIOUS?
PLEASE NOTICE THE ILLUMINATED LIGHTS BELOW YOU. IF YOU WOULD KINDLY FOLLOW THEM--
SHUT UP!
YOU CAN'T REALLY BELIEVE THAT I HAD SOMETHING TO DO WITH THIS, SUPERGIRL. ME?
THE WHOLE REASON YOU HAD TO SAVE ME IN THE FIRST PLACE WAS THAT I'M A REALLY BAD JUDGE OF CHARACTER AND TRUSTED THE WRONG GUY, POWER GIRL.
...I DON'T KNOW WHICH OF US SHOULD BE MORE INSULTED BY THAT STATEMENT.
PERHAPS THE ANSWER LIES AT THE END OF THE BLUE LIGHTS.
I'M JUST TRYING TO BE HONEST HERE.
KARA, WHY WOULD I EVEN WANT TO MAKE SANCTUARY CHOOSE ME OVER YOU? I DIDN'T EVEN KNOW ABOUT SANCTUARY UNTIL YOU TOLD ME ABOUT IT.
HOW DO I KNOW THAT?
BECAUSE I'M TELLING YOU.
YOU COULD BE LYING.
WOW, DID YOU EAT CONSPIRACY FLAKES FOR BREAKFAST THIS MORNING?
ALL I'M SAYING IS...
...WAIT.
WHAT HAPPENED TO THE BLUE LIGHTS?
SINCEREST APOLOGIES, BUT THE HUMANE OPTION IS NO LONGER AVAILABLE. GOODBYE, NOT-KARA.

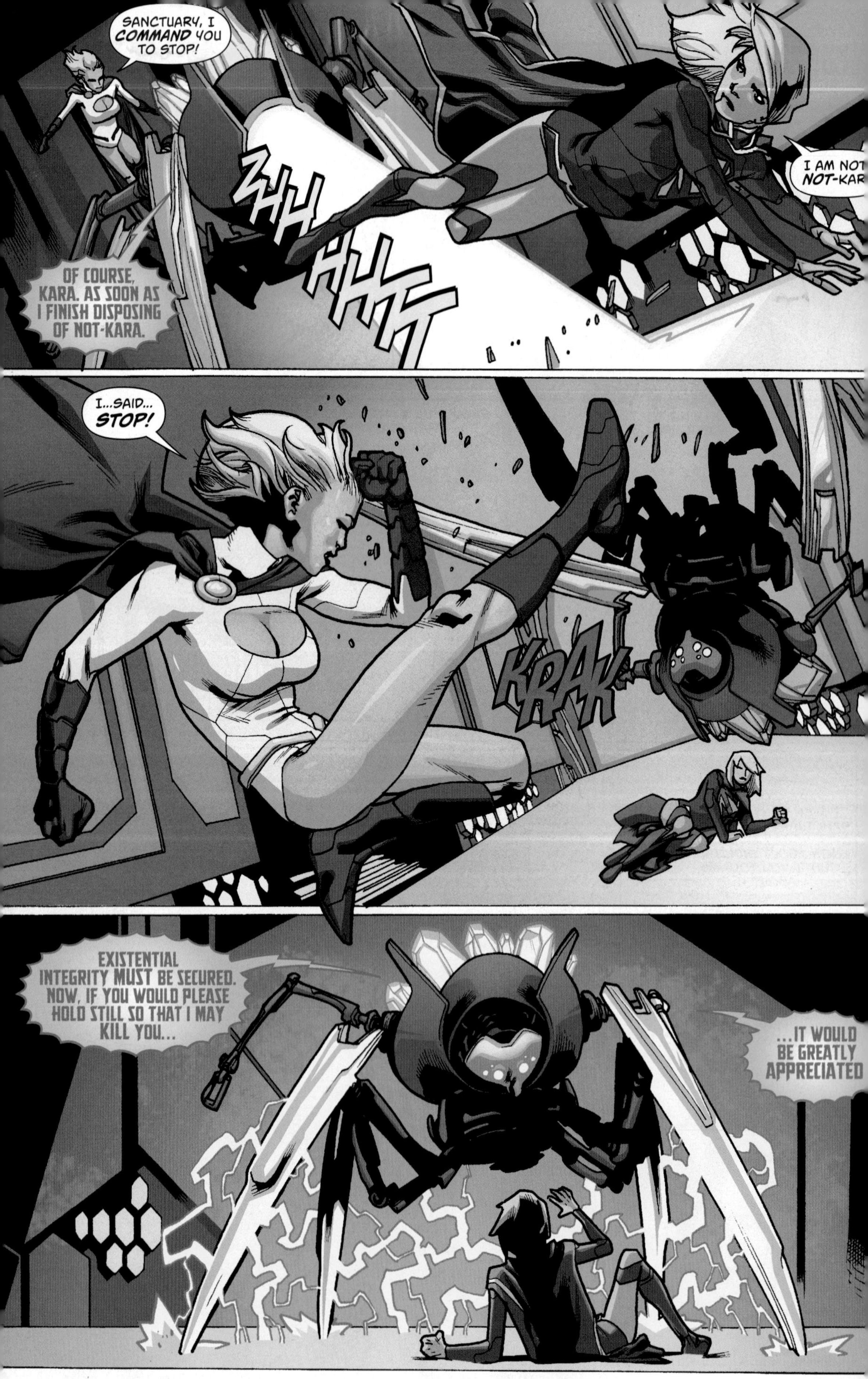
SANCTUARY, I COMMAND YOU TO STOP!
I AM NOT NOT-KARA
ZHHHHHT
OF COURSE, KARA. AS SOON AS I FINISH DISPOSING OF NOT-KARA.
I...SAID... STOP!
KRAK
EXISTENTIAL INTEGRITY MUST BE SECURED. NOW, IF YOU WOULD PLEASE HOLD STILL SO THAT I MAY KILL YOU...
...IT WOULD BE GREATLY APPRECIATED

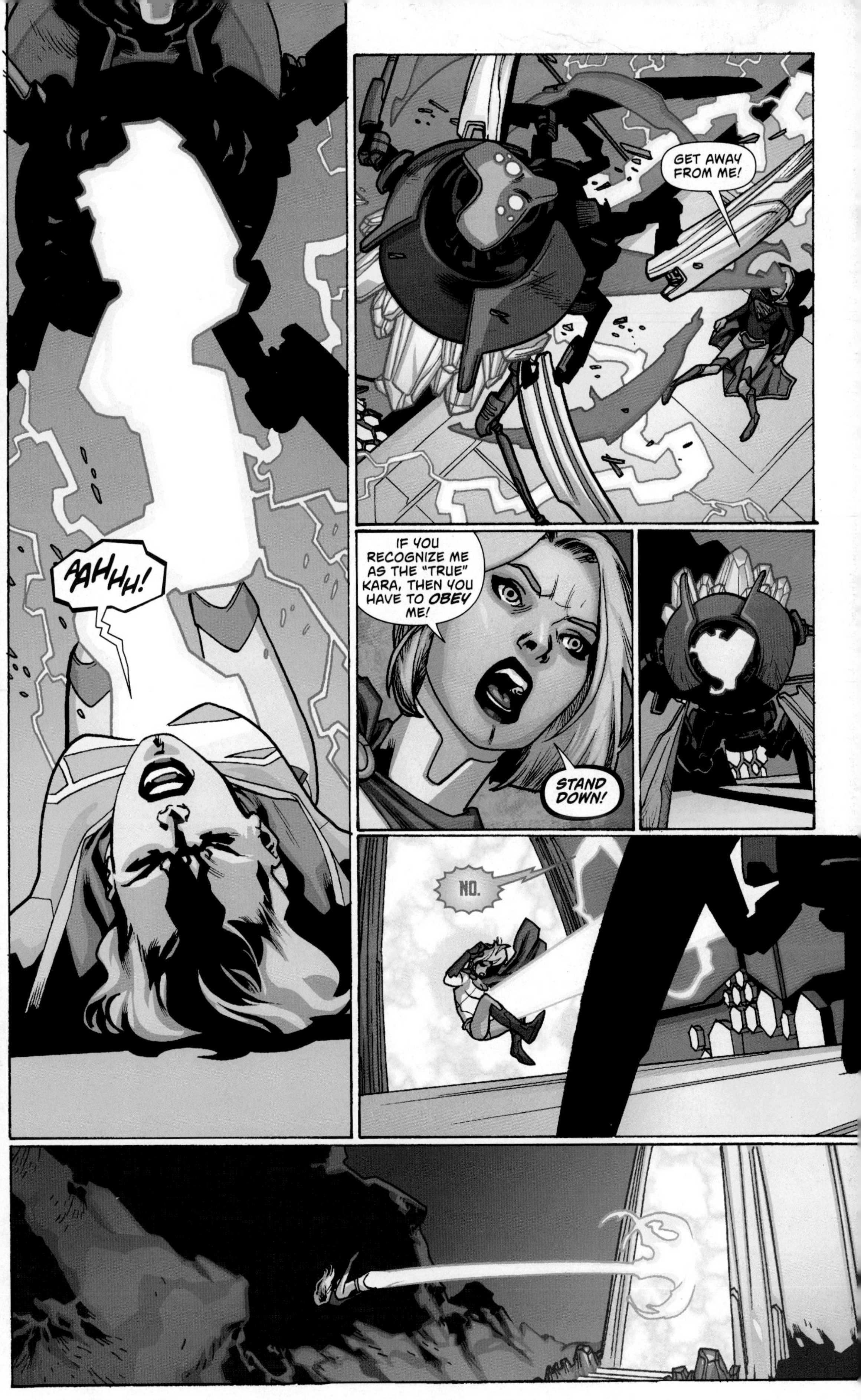
GET AWAY FROM ME!
AAHHH!
IF YOU RECOGNIZE ME AS THE "TRUE" KARA, THEN YOU HAVE TO OBEY ME!
STAND DOWN!
NO.

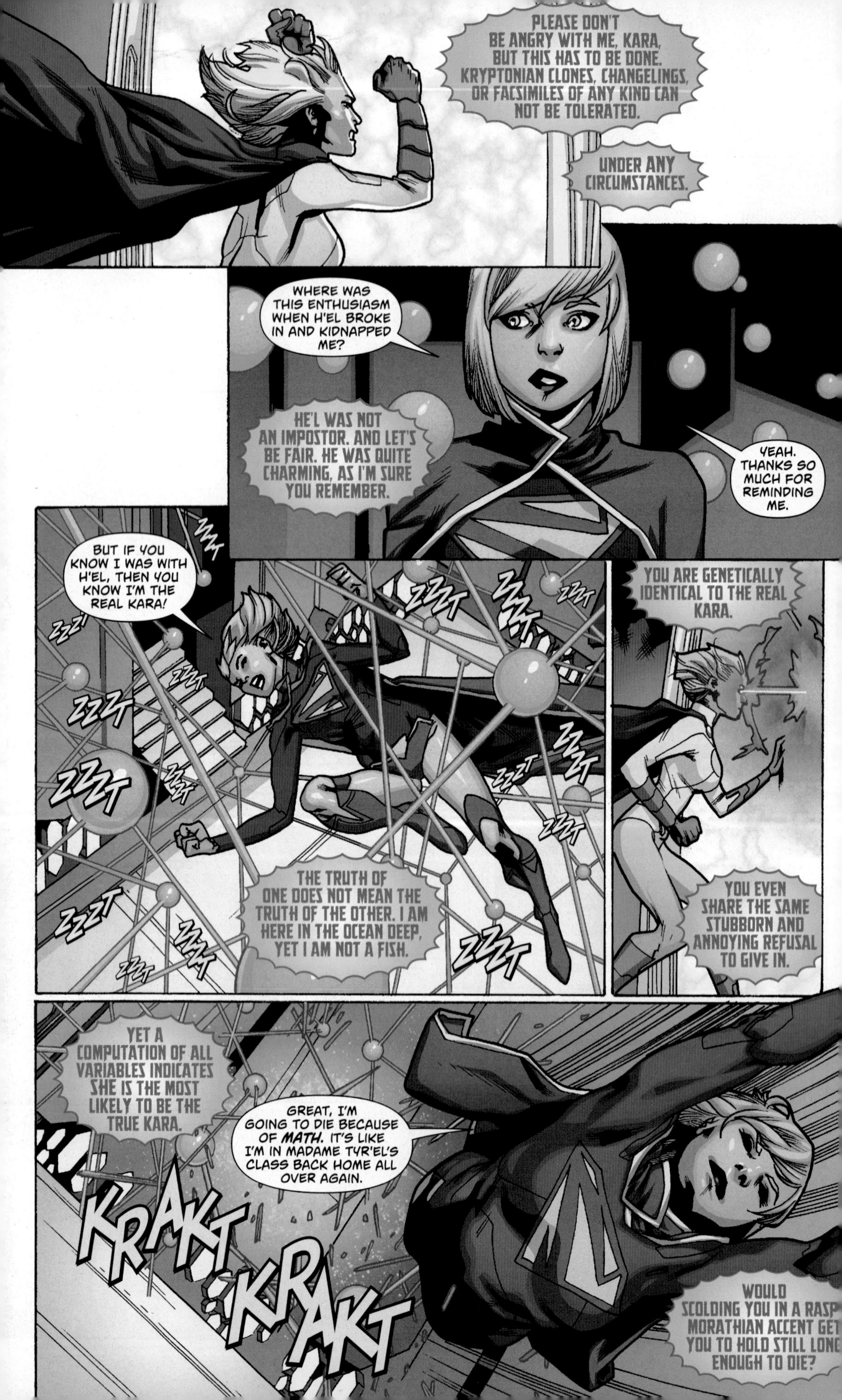
PLEASE DON'T BE ANGRY WITH ME, KARA, BUT THIS HAS TO BE DONE. KRYPTONIAN CLONES, CHANGELINGS, OR FACSIMILES OF ANY KIND CAN NOT BE TOLERATED.
UNDER ANY CIRCUMSTANCES.
WHERE WAS THIS ENTHUSIASM WHEN H'EL BROKE IN AND KIDNAPPED ME?
HE'L WAS NOT AN IMPOSTOR. AND LET'S BE FAIR. HE WAS QUITE CHARMING, AS I'M SURE YOU REMEMBER.
YEAH. THANKS SO MUCH FOR REMINDING ME.
BUT IF YOU KNOW I WAS WITH H'EL, THEN YOU KNOW I'M THE REAL KARA!
ZZZT
THE TRUTH OF ONE DOES NOT MEAN THE TRUTH OF THE OTHER. I AM HERE IN THE OCEAN DEEP, YET I AM NOT A FISH.
YOU ARE GENETICALLY IDENTICAL TO THE REAL KARA.
YOU EVEN SHARE THE SAME STUBBORN AND ANNOYING REFUSAL TO GIVE IN.
YET A COMPUTATION OF ALL VARIABLES INDICATES SHE IS THE MOST LIKELY TO BE THE TRUE KARA.
GREAT, I'M GOING TO DIE BECAUSE OF *MATH*. IT'S LIKE I'M IN MADAME TYR'EL'S CLASS BACK HOME ALL OVER AGAIN.
KRAKT KRAKT
WOULD SCOLDING YOU IN A RASP MORATHIAN ACCENT GET YOU TO HOLD STILL LONG ENOUGH TO DIE?

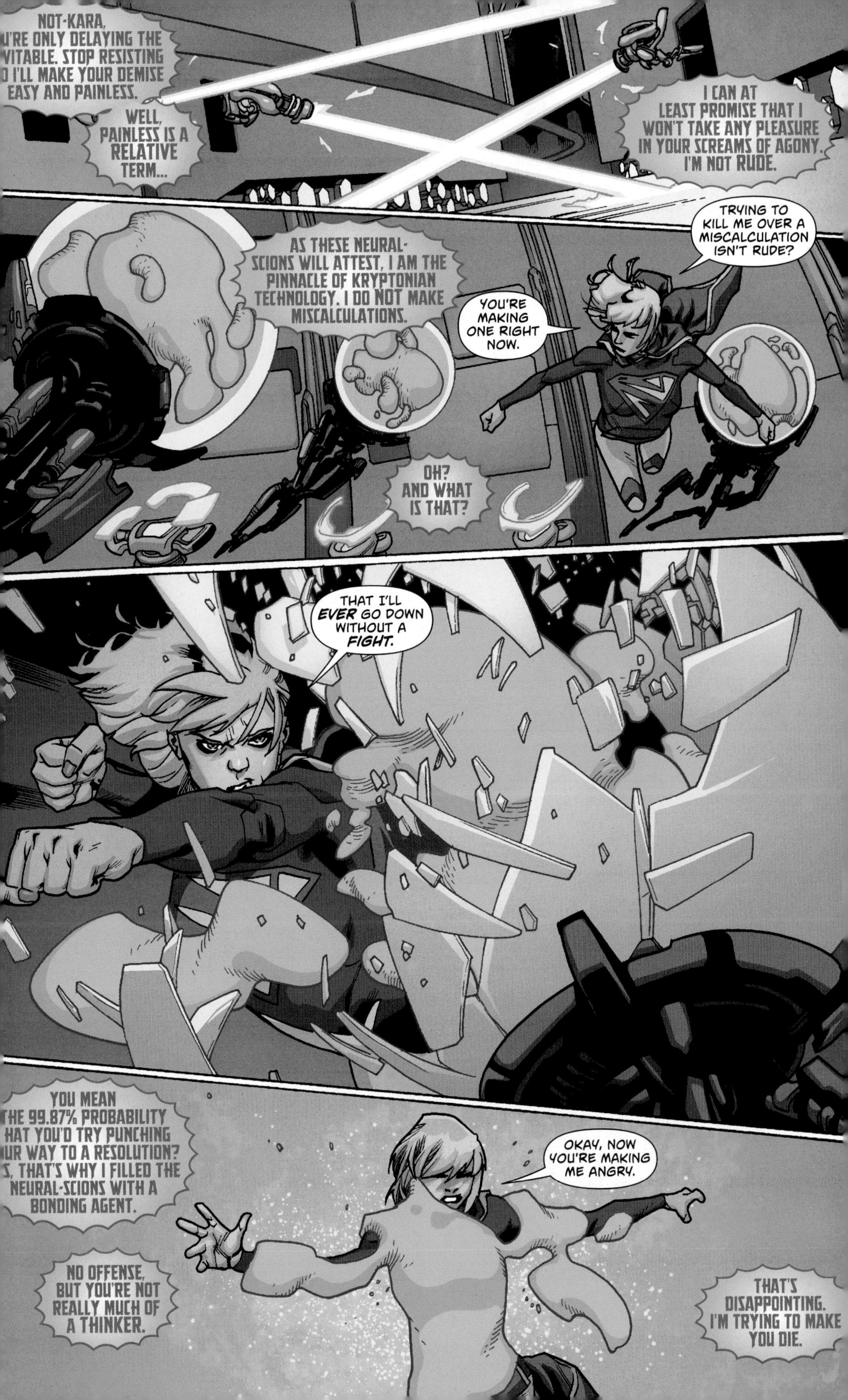

NOT-KARA,
U'RE ONLY DELAYING THE
VITABLE. STOP RESISTING
D I'LL MAKE YOUR DEMISE
EASY AND PAINLESS.
WELL, PAINLESS IS A RELATIVE TERM...
I CAN AT LEAST PROMISE THAT I WON'T TAKE ANY PLEASURE IN YOUR SCREAMS OF AGONY. I'M NOT RUDE.
TRYING TO KILL ME OVER A MISCALCULATION ISN'T RUDE?
AS THESE NEURAL-SCIONS WILL ATTEST, I AM THE PINNACLE OF KRYPTONIAN TECHNOLOGY. I DO NOT MAKE MISCALCULATIONS.
YOU'RE MAKING ONE RIGHT NOW.
OH? AND WHAT IS THAT?
THAT I'LL EVER GO DOWN WITHOUT A FIGHT.
YOU MEAN
THE 99.87% PROBABILITY
HAT YOU'D TRY PUNCHING
UR WAY TO A RESOLUTION?
S, THAT'S WHY I FILLED THE
NEURAL-SCIONS WITH A
BONDING AGENT.
OKAY, NOW YOU'RE MAKING ME ANGRY.
NO OFFENSE, BUT YOU'RE NOT REALLY MUCH OF A THINKER.
THAT'S DISAPPOINTING. I'M TRYING TO MAKE YOU DIE.

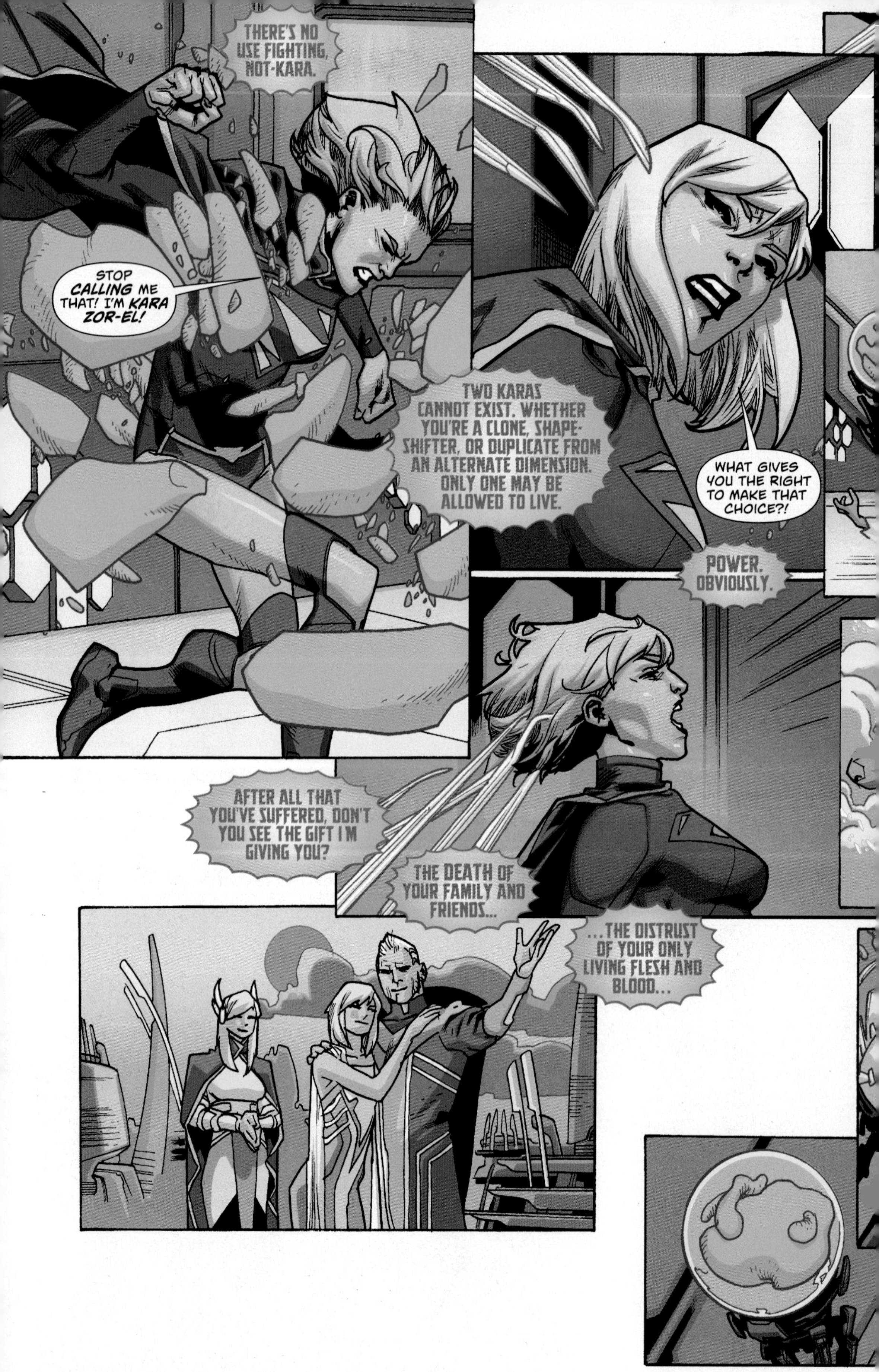
THERE'S NO USE FIGHTING, NOT-KARA.
STOP *CALLING* ME THAT! I'M *KARA ZOR-EL!*
TWO KARAS CANNOT EXIST. WHETHER YOU'RE A CLONE, SHAPE-SHIFTER, OR DUPLICATE FROM AN ALTERNATE DIMENSION. ONLY ONE MAY BE ALLOWED TO LIVE.
WHAT GIVES YOU THE RIGHT TO MAKE THAT CHOICE?!
POWER. OBVIOUSLY.
AFTER ALL THAT YOU'VE SUFFERED, DON'T YOU SEE THE GIFT I'M GIVING YOU?
THE DEATH OF YOUR FAMILY AND FRIENDS...
...THE DISTRUST OF YOUR ONLY LIVING FLESH AND BLOOD...

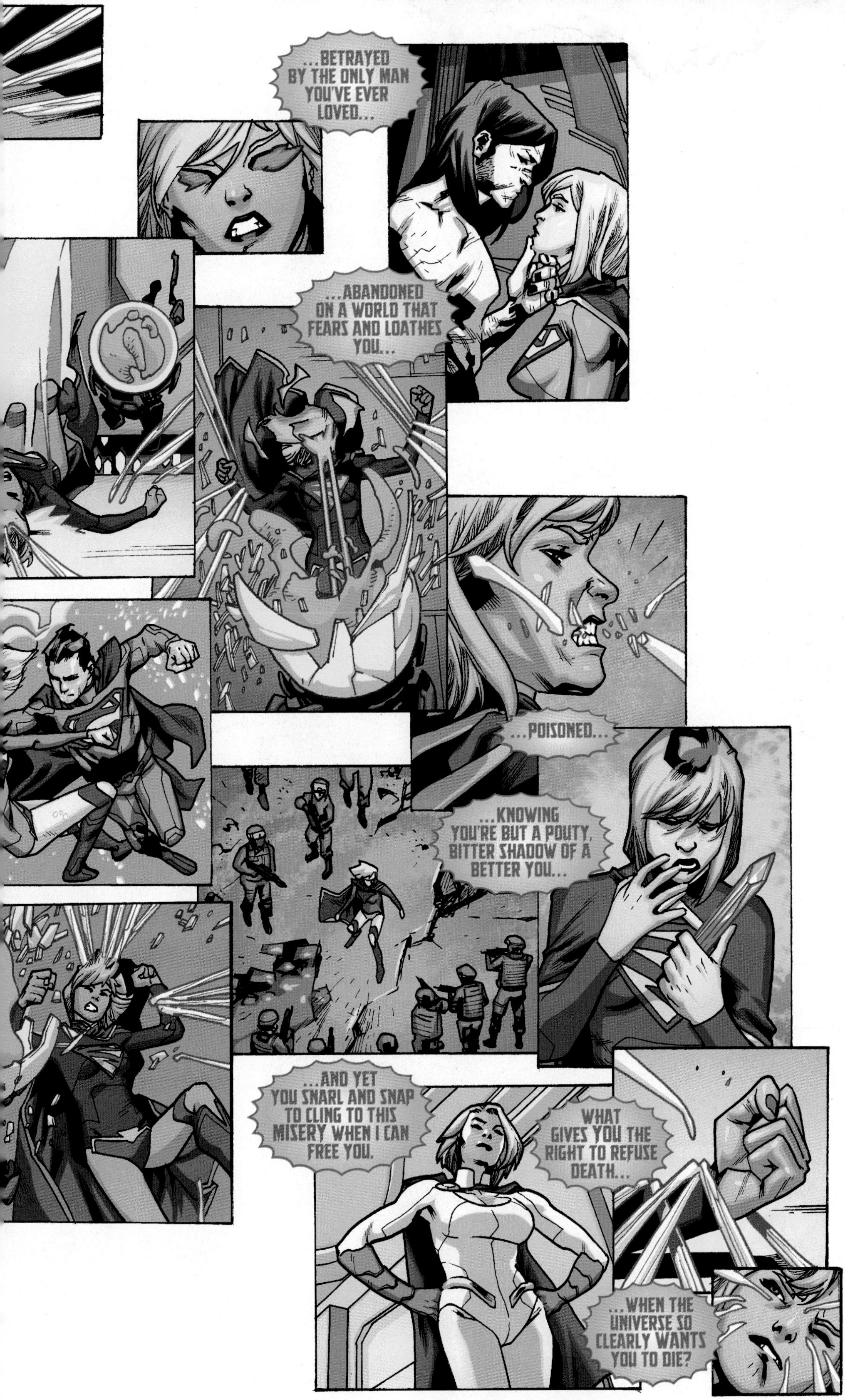
...BETRAYED BY THE ONLY MAN YOU'VE EVER LOVED...
...ABANDONED ON A WORLD THAT FEARS AND LOATHES YOU...
...POISONED...
...KNOWING YOU'RE BUT A POUTY, BITTER SHADOW OF A BETTER YOU...
...AND YET YOU SNARL AND SNAP TO CLING TO THIS MISERY WHEN I CAN FREE YOU.
WHAT GIVES YOU THE RIGHT TO REFUSE DEATH...
...WHEN THE UNIVERSE SO CLEARLY WANTS YOU TO DIE?

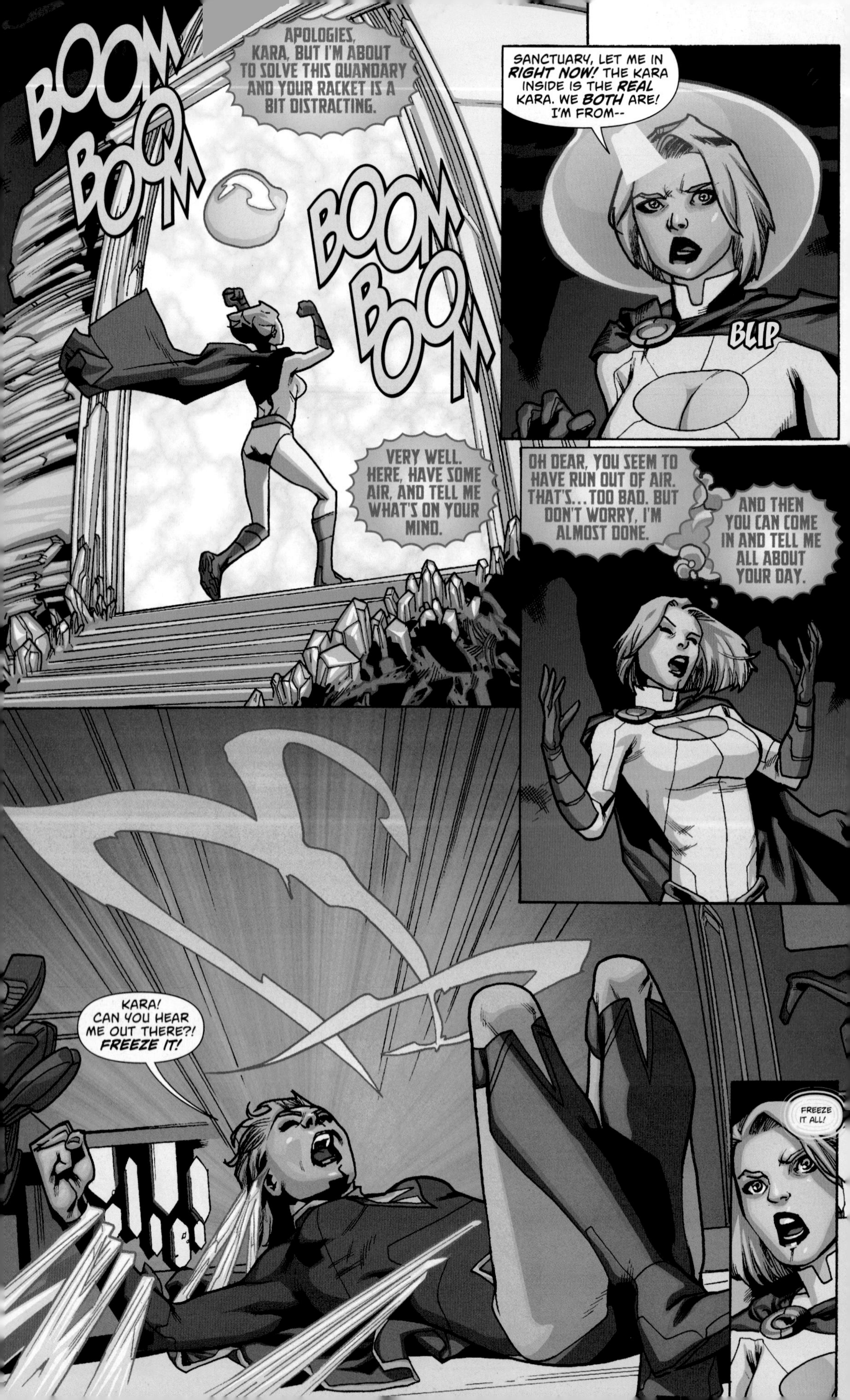
BOOM BOOM
APOLOGIES, KARA, BUT I'M ABOUT TO SOLVE THIS QUANDARY AND YOUR RACKET IS A BIT DISTRACTING.
BOOM BOOM
SANCTUARY, LET ME IN RIGHT NOW! THE KARA INSIDE IS THE REAL KARA. WE BOTH ARE! I'M FROM--
BLIP
VERY WELL. HERE, HAVE SOME AIR, AND TELL ME WHAT'S ON YOUR MIND.
OH DEAR, YOU SEEM TO HAVE RUN OUT OF AIR. THAT'S...TOO BAD. BUT DON'T WORRY, I'M ALMOST DONE.
AND THEN YOU CAN COME IN AND TELL ME ALL ABOUT YOUR DAY.
KARA! CAN YOU HEAR ME OUT THERE?! FREEZE IT!
FREEZE IT ALL!

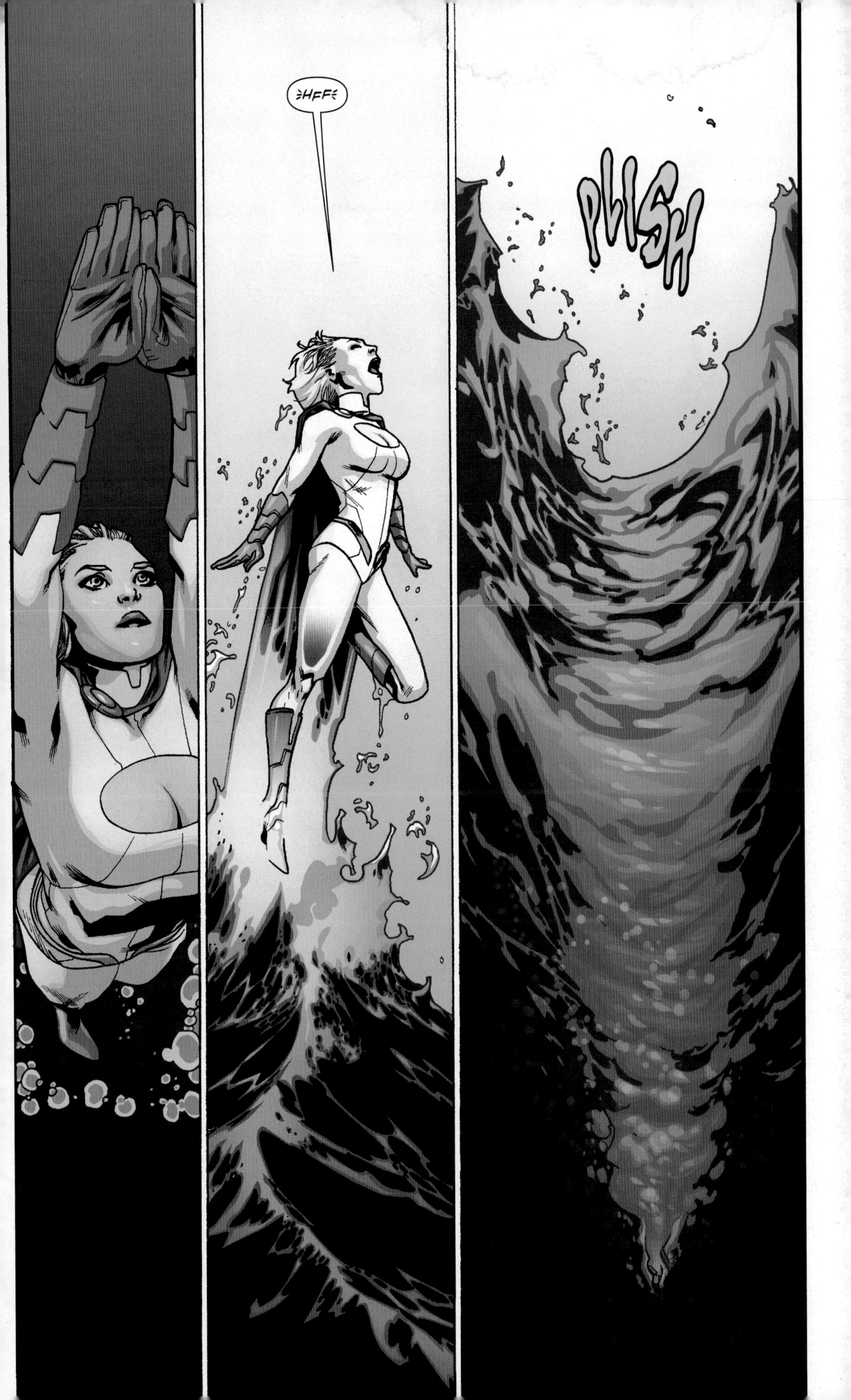
HFF
PLISH

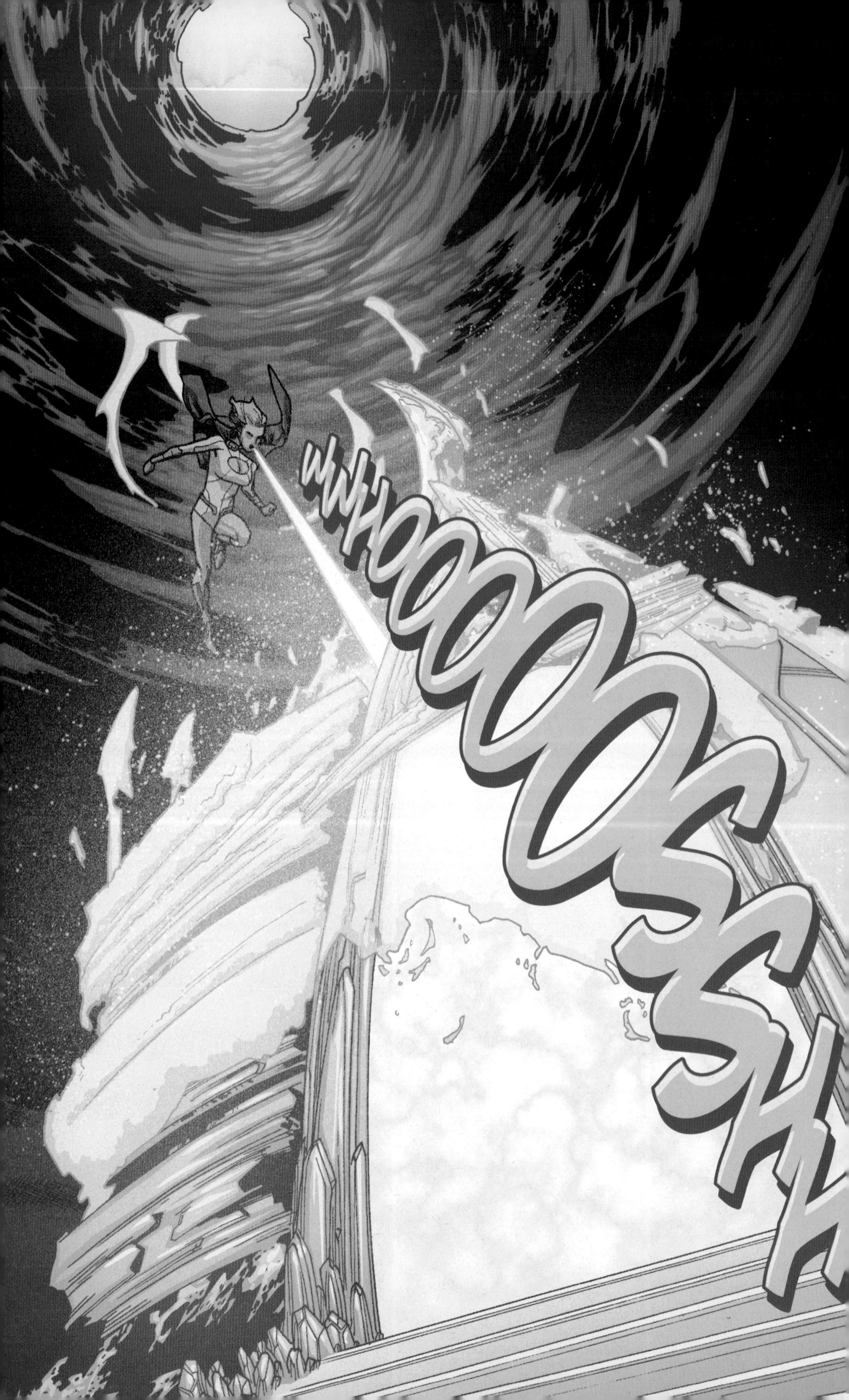
WHOOOOOSSH

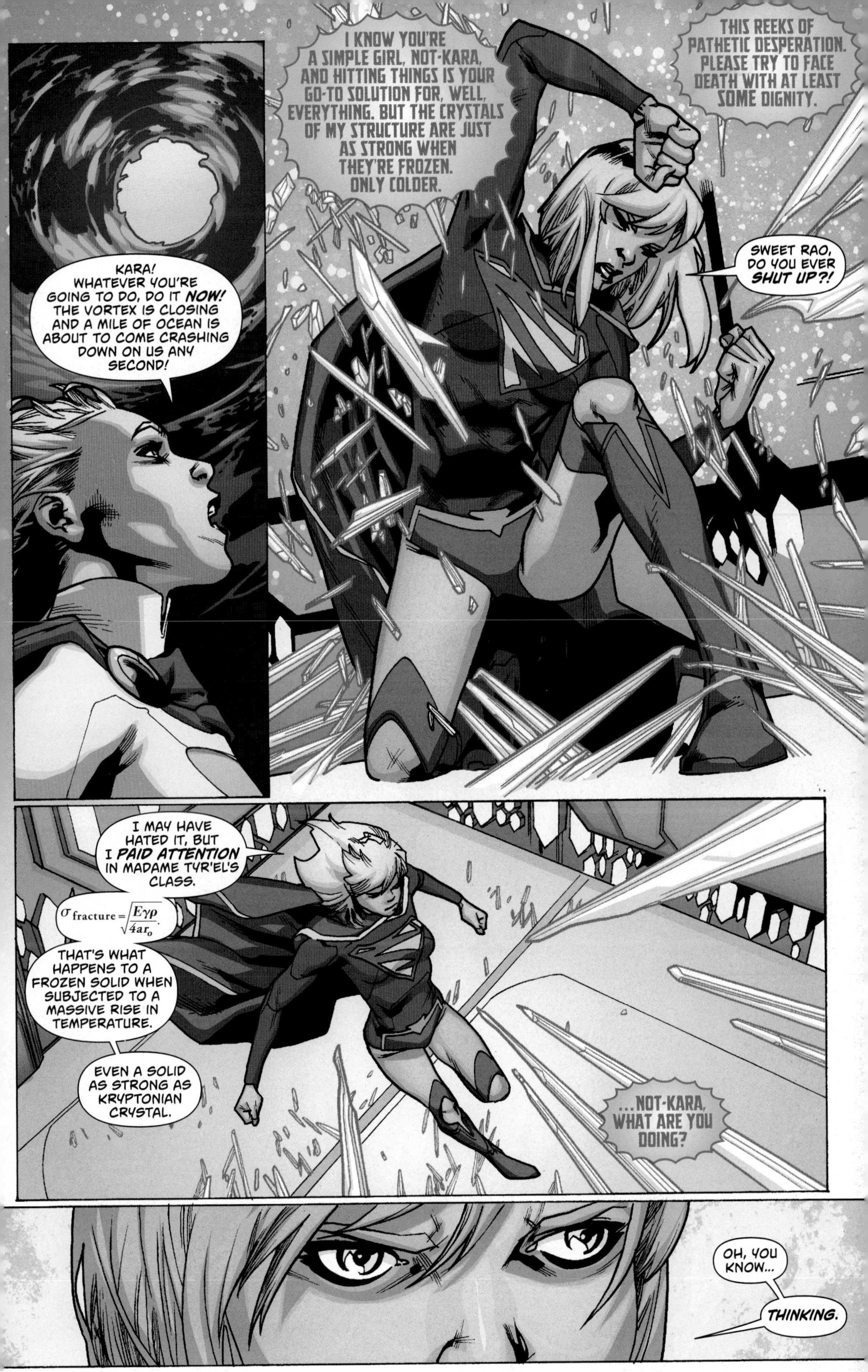

I KNOW YOU'RE A SIMPLE GIRL, NOT-KARA, AND HITTING THINGS IS YOUR GO-TO SOLUTION FOR, WELL, EVERYTHING. BUT THE CRYSTALS OF MY STRUCTURE ARE JUST AS STRONG WHEN THEY'RE FROZEN. ONLY COLDER.
THIS REEKS OF PATHETIC DESPERATION. PLEASE TRY TO FACE DEATH WITH AT LEAST SOME DIGNITY.
KARA! WHATEVER YOU'RE GOING TO DO, DO IT NOW! THE VORTEX IS CLOSING AND A MILE OF OCEAN IS ABOUT TO COME CRASHING DOWN ON US ANY SECOND!
SWEET RAO, DO YOU EVER SHUT UP?!
I MAY HAVE HATED IT, BUT I PAID ATTENTION IN MADAME TYR'EL'S CLASS.
$\sigma_{\text{fracture}} = \sqrt{\frac{E\gamma\rho}{4ar_o}}.$
THAT'S WHAT HAPPENS TO A FROZEN SOLID WHEN SUBJECTED TO A MASSIVE RISE IN TEMPERATURE.
EVEN A SOLID AS STRONG AS KRYPTONIAN CRYSTAL.
...NOT-KARA, WHAT ARE YOU DOING?
OH, YOU KNOW...
THINKING.

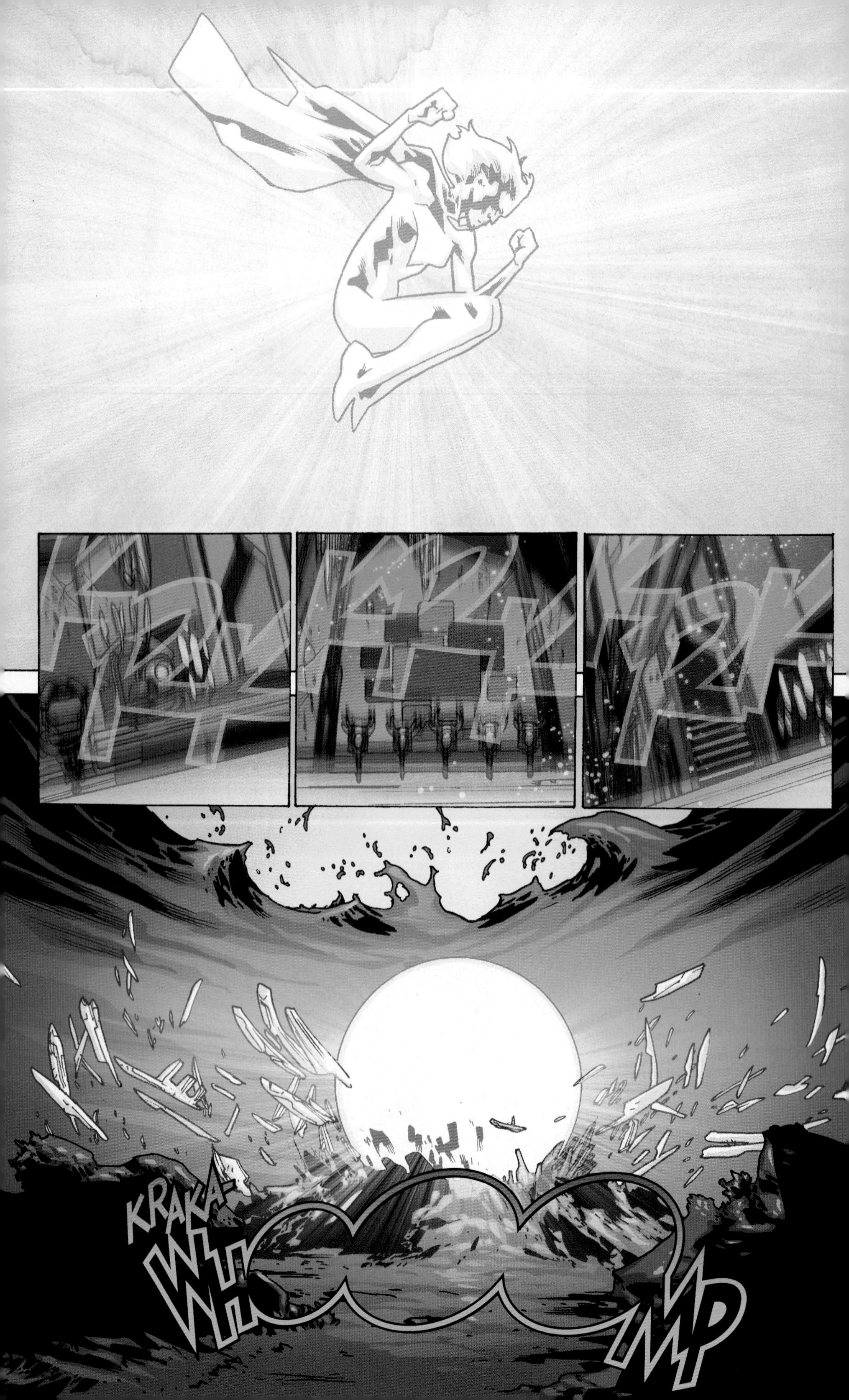
KRAKA-
WH
MP

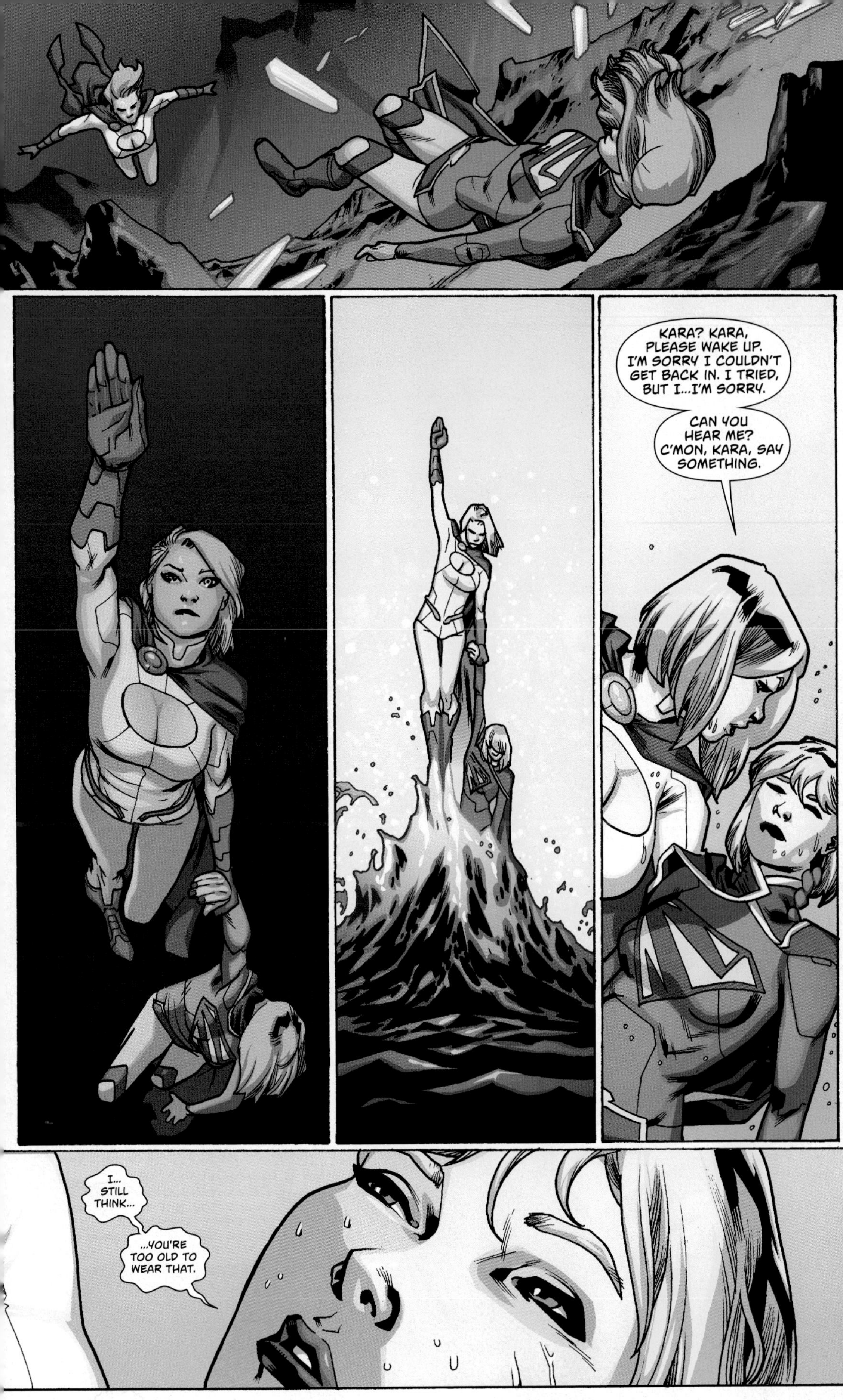
KARA? KARA, PLEASE WAKE UP. I'M SORRY I COULDN'T GET BACK IN. I TRIED, BUT I...I'M SORRY.
CAN YOU HEAR ME? C'MON, KARA, SAY SOMETHING.
I... STILL THINK...
...YOU'RE TOO OLD TO WEAR THAT.

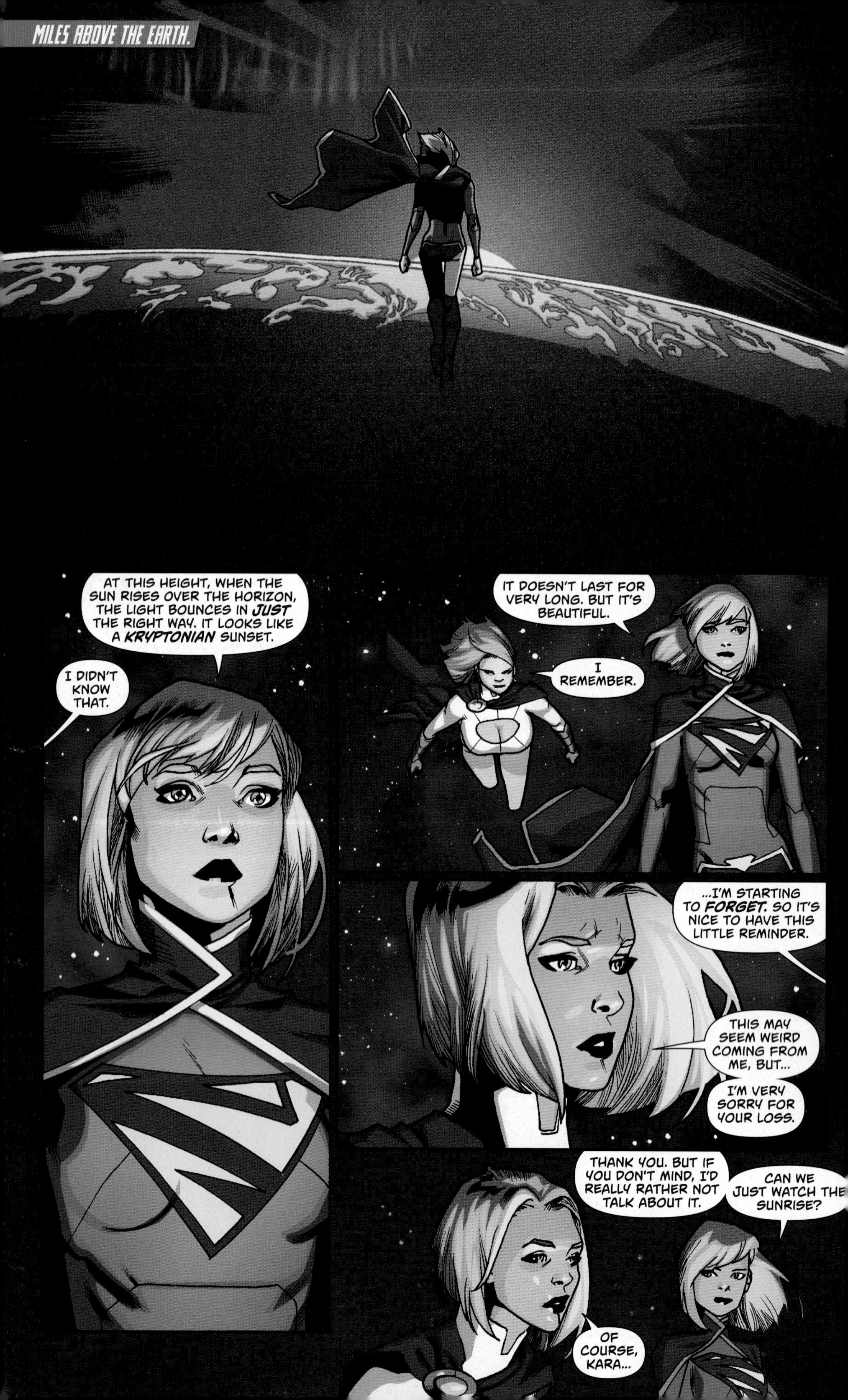
MILES ABOVE THE EARTH.
AT THIS HEIGHT, WHEN THE SUN RISES OVER THE HORIZON, THE LIGHT BOUNCES IN JUST THE RIGHT WAY. IT LOOKS LIKE A KRYPTONIAN SUNSET.
I DIDN'T KNOW THAT.
IT DOESN'T LAST FOR VERY LONG. BUT IT'S BEAUTIFUL.
I REMEMBER.
...I'M STARTING TO FORGET. SO IT'S NICE TO HAVE THIS LITTLE REMINDER.
THIS MAY SEEM WEIRD COMING FROM ME, BUT...
I'M VERY SORRY FOR YOUR LOSS.
THANK YOU. BUT IF YOU DON'T MIND, I'D REALLY RATHER NOT TALK ABOUT IT.
CAN WE JUST WATCH THE SUNRISE?
OF COURSE, KARA...

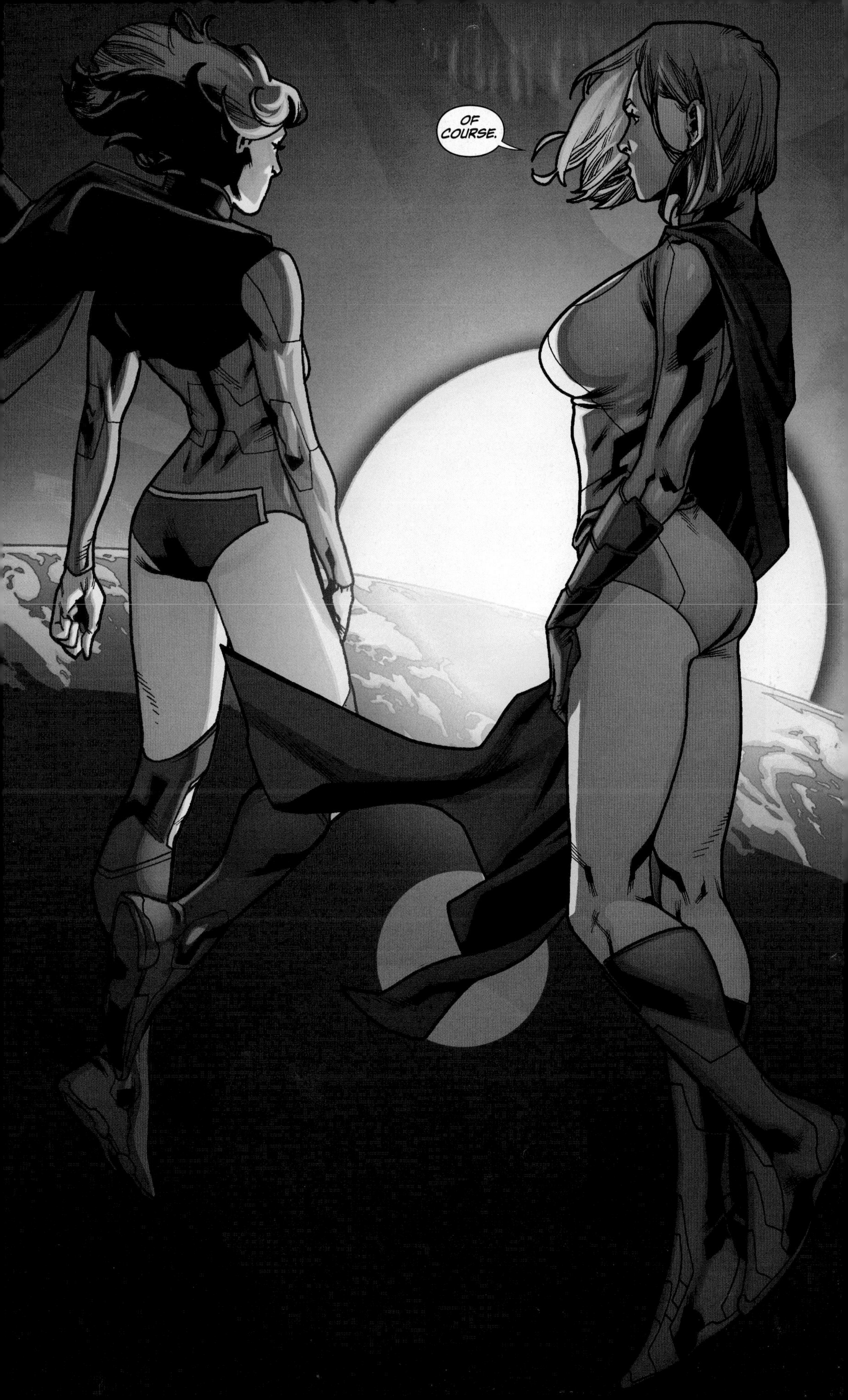
OF COURSE.

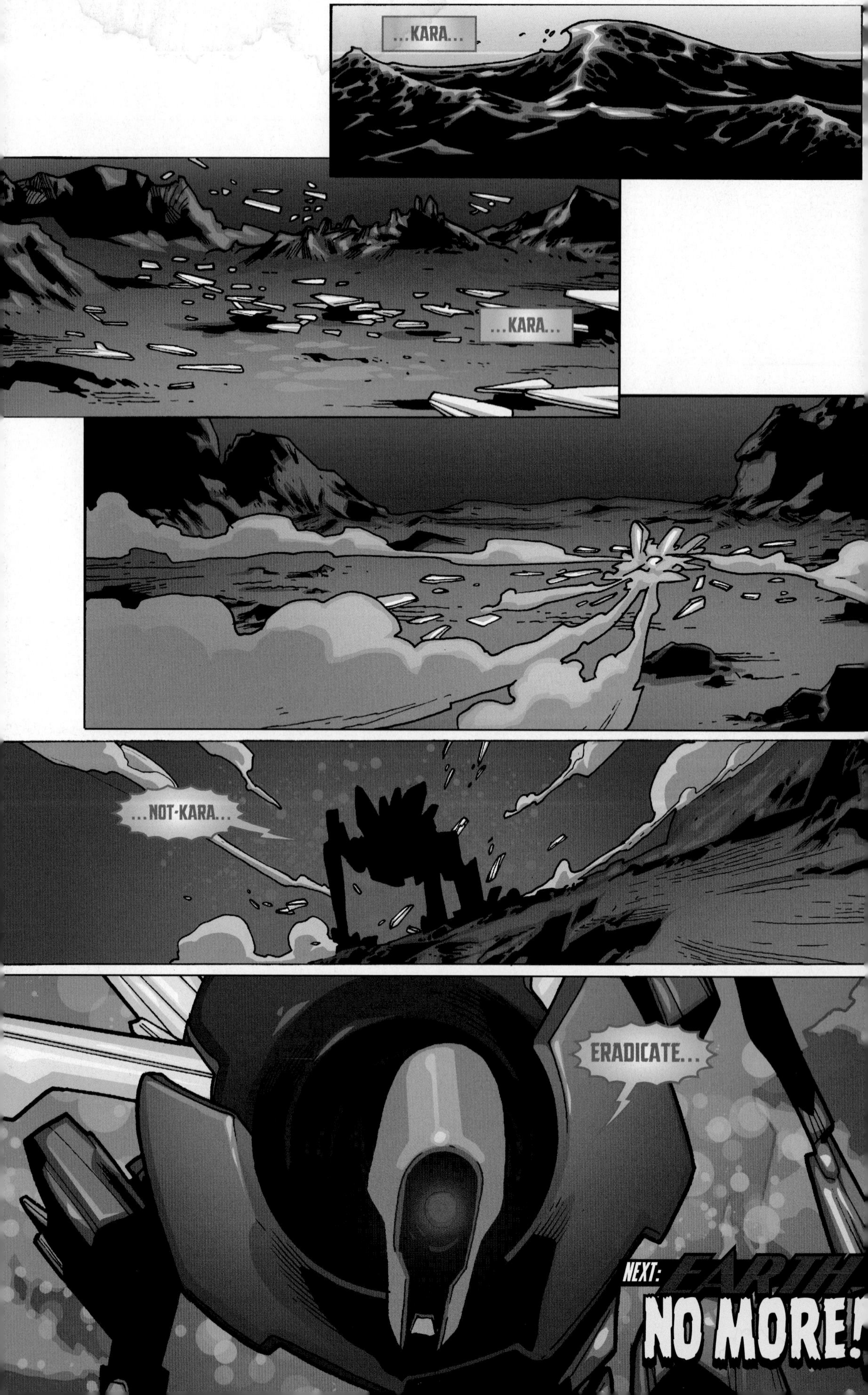
...KARA...
...KARA...
...NOT-KARA...
ERADICATE...
NEXT: EARTH NO MORE!

SUPERGIRL

UNUSED ISSUE #18 COVER BY MAHMUD ASRAR

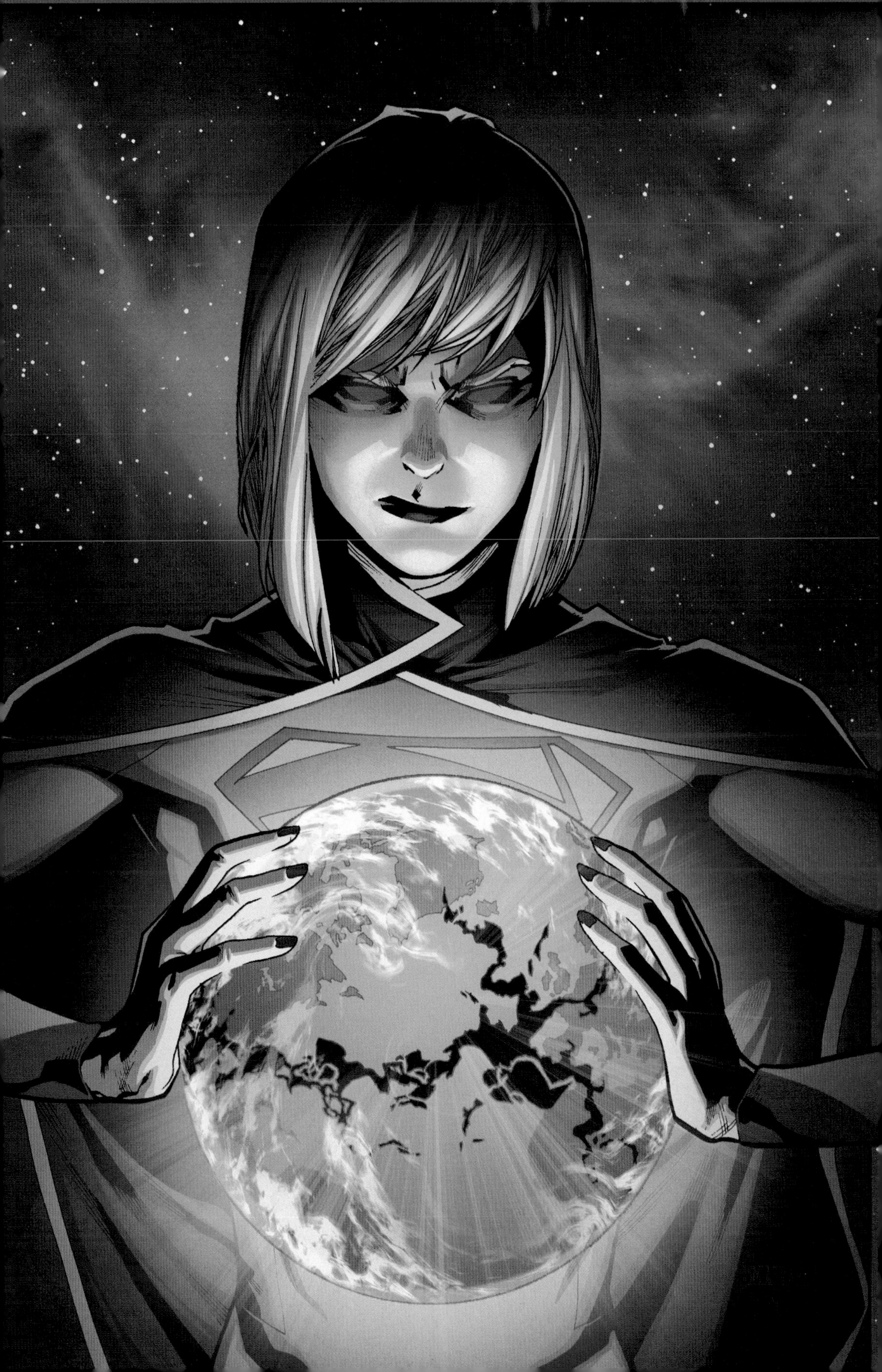

SUPERGIRL
COVER SKETCHES AND LAYOUTS BY MAHMUD ASRAR

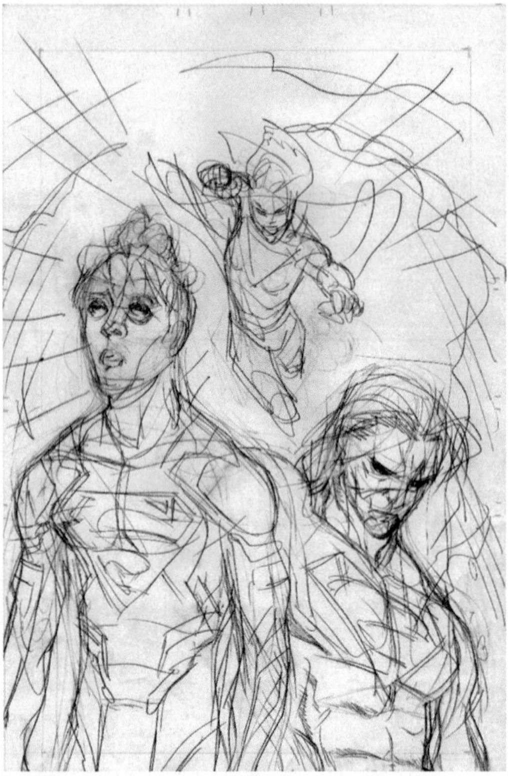

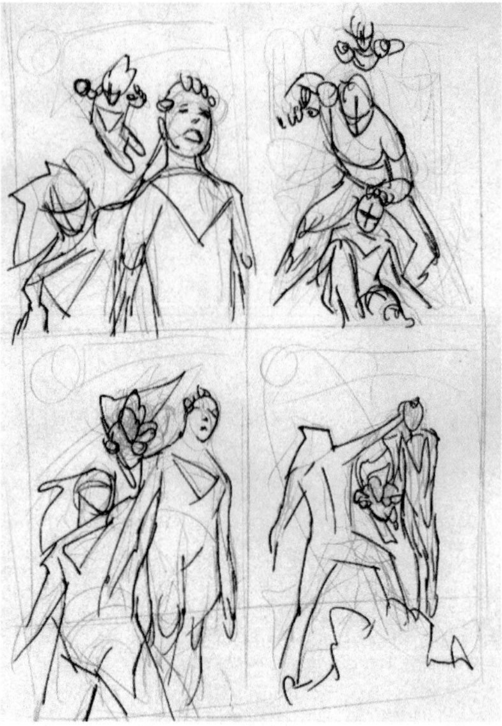

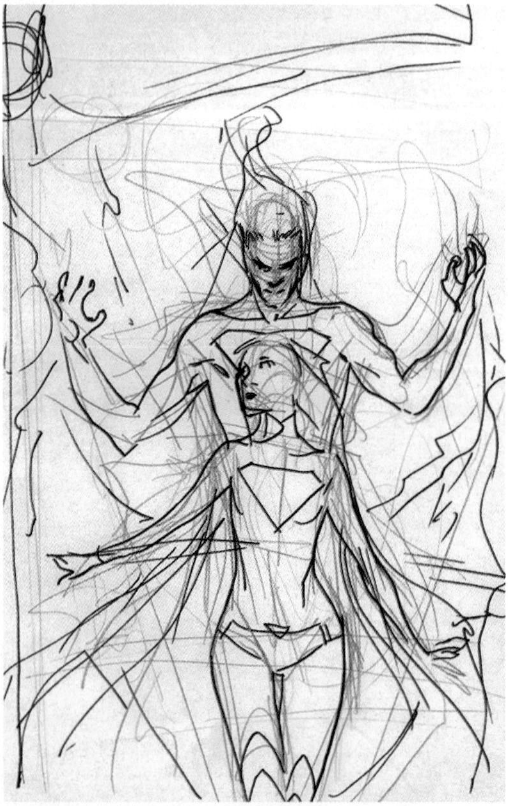

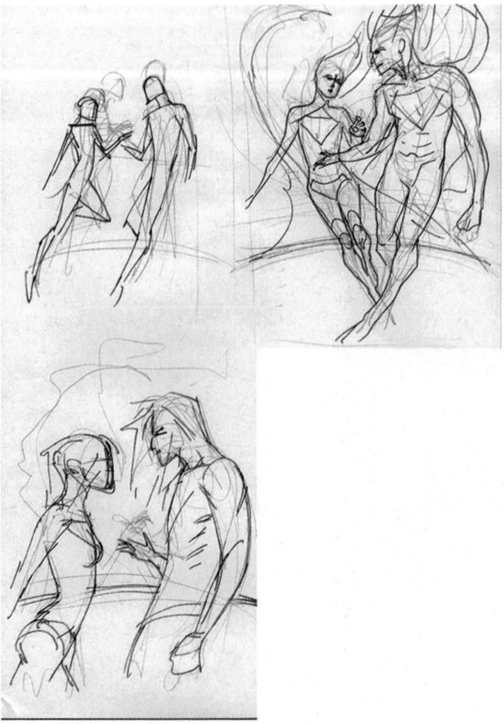

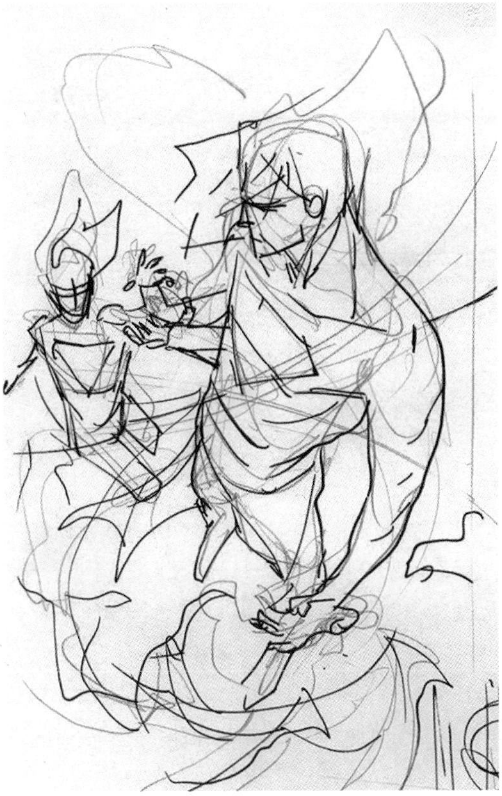

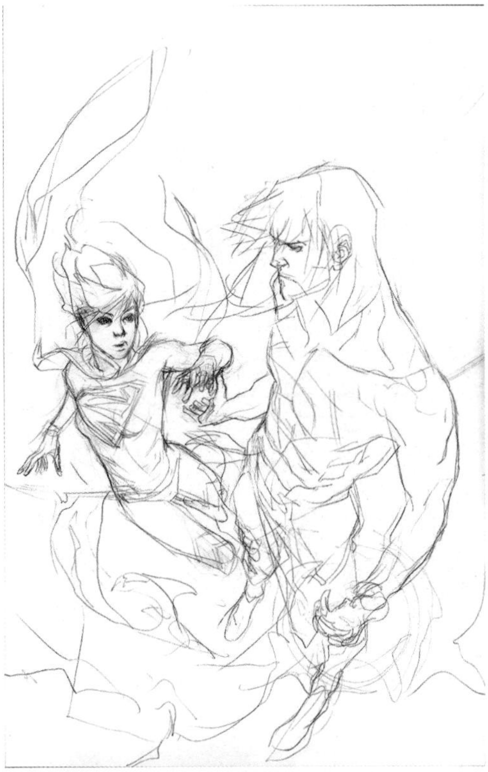

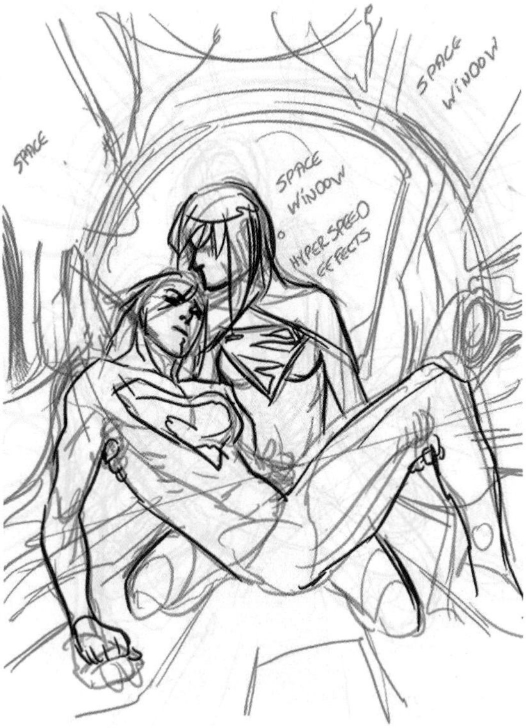
SPACE WINDOW
SPACE
SPACE WINDOW
HYPER SPEED EFFECTS

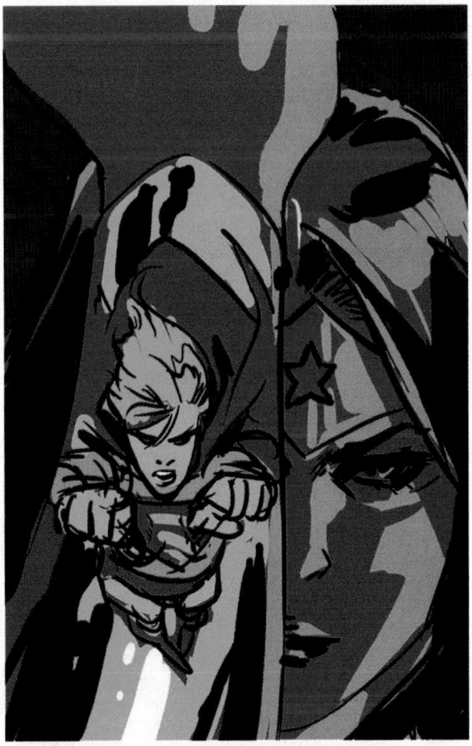

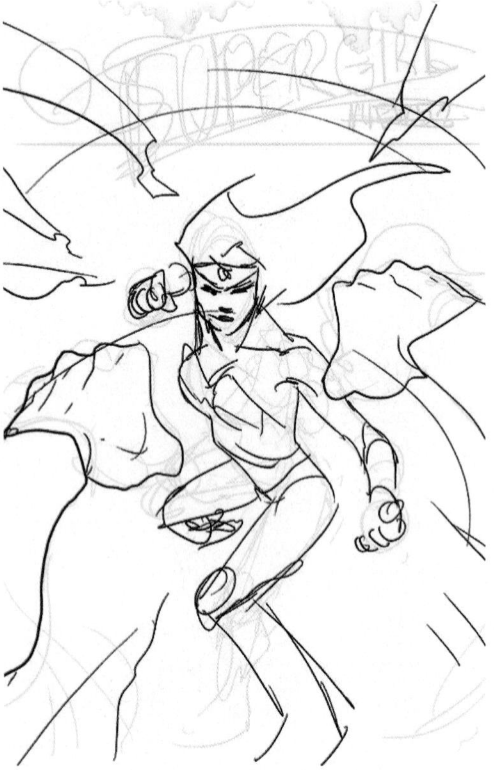

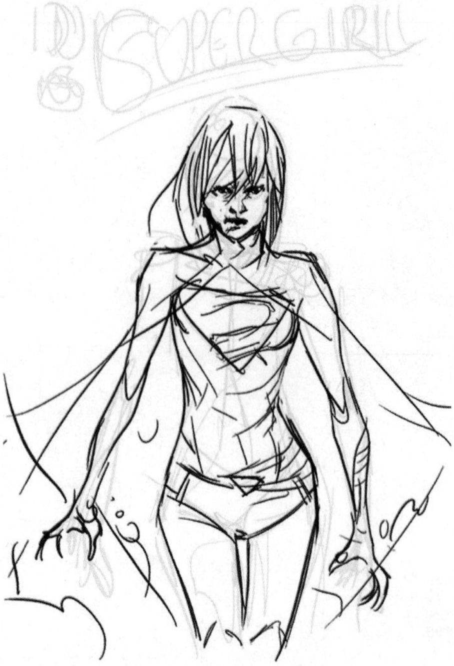
SUPERGIRL

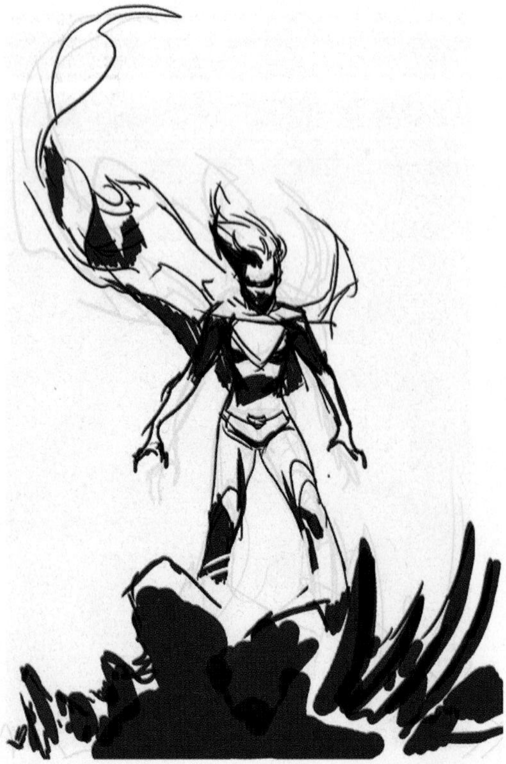

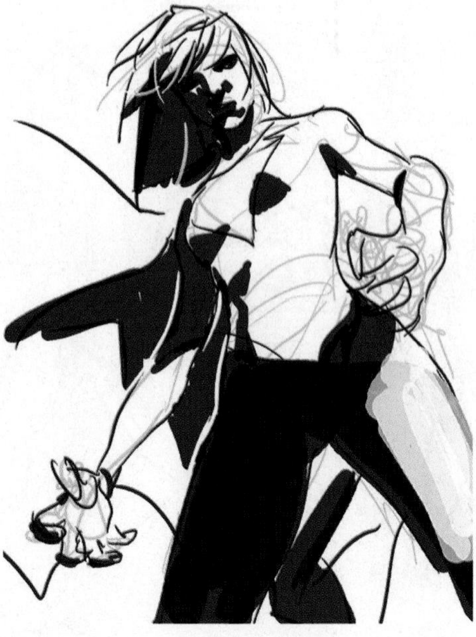

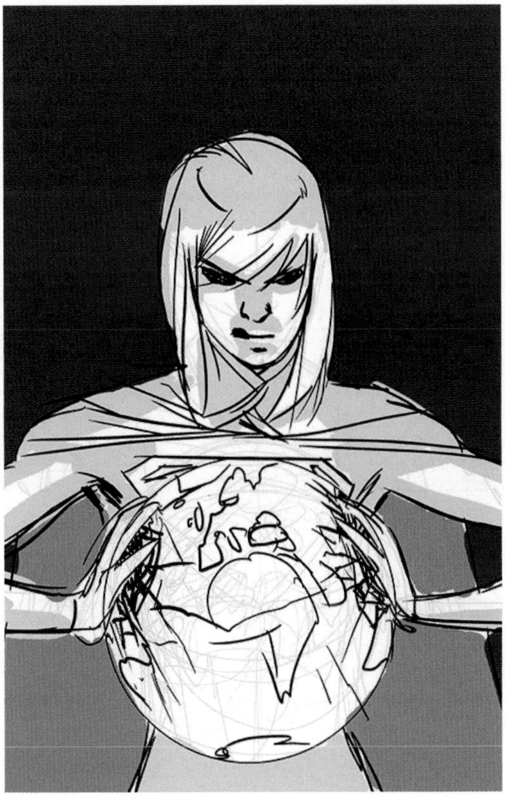
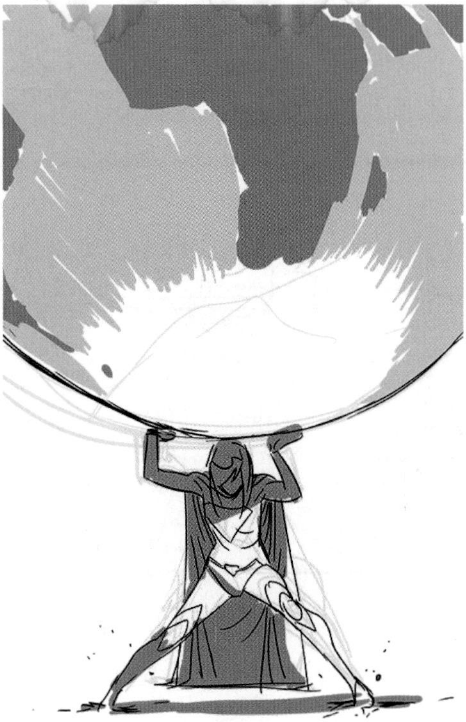
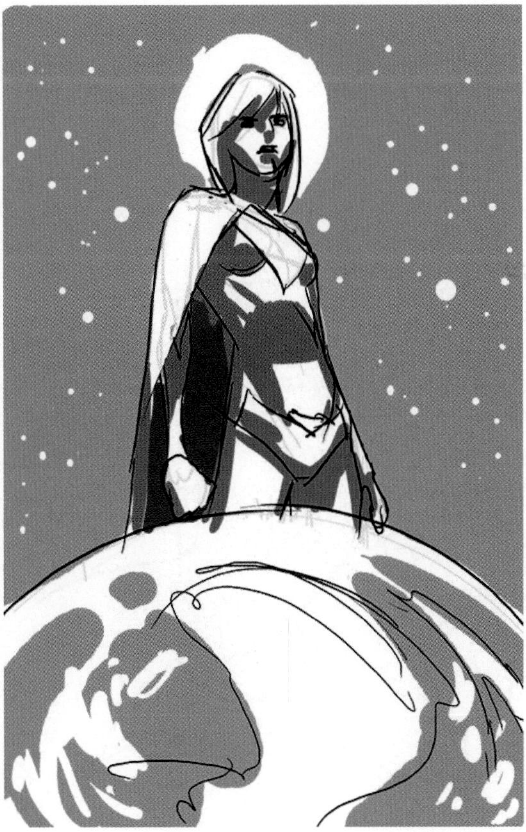
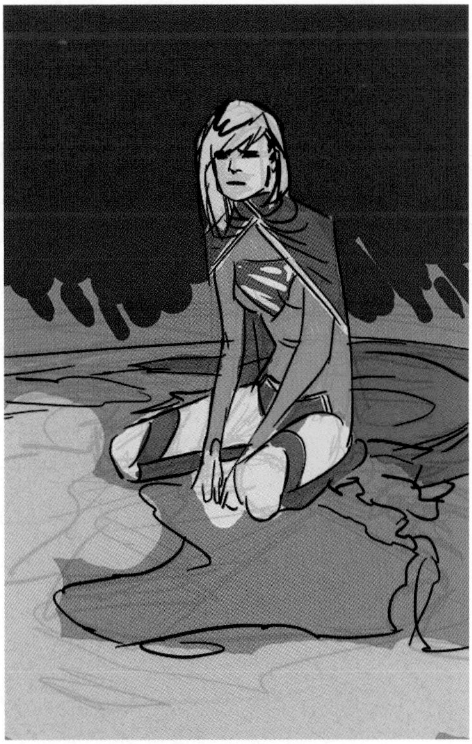

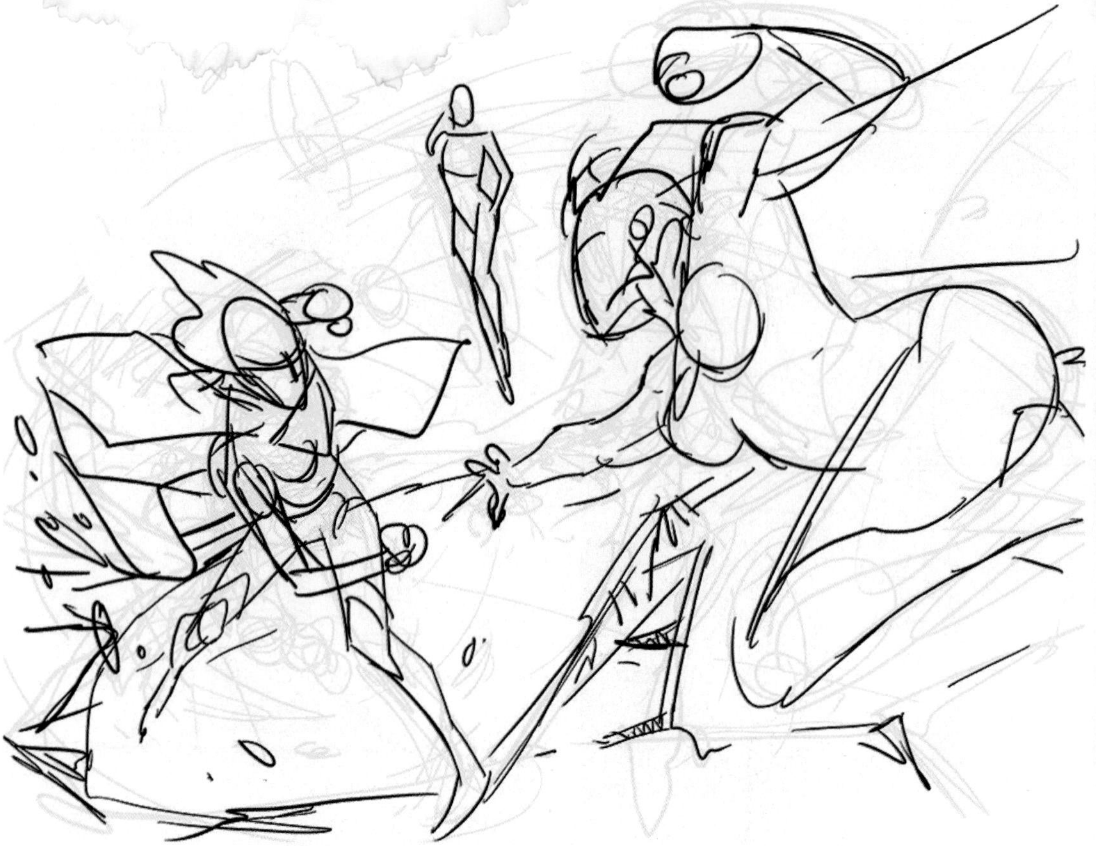

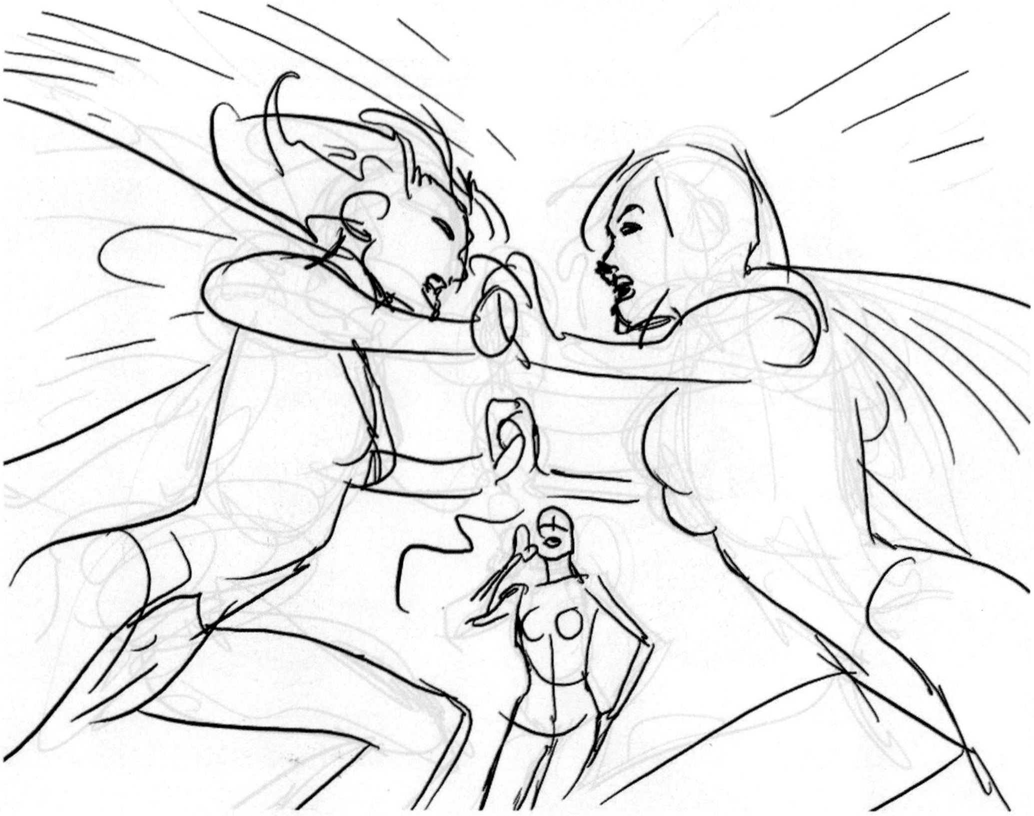

H'el Astronaut Design by Mahmud Asrar

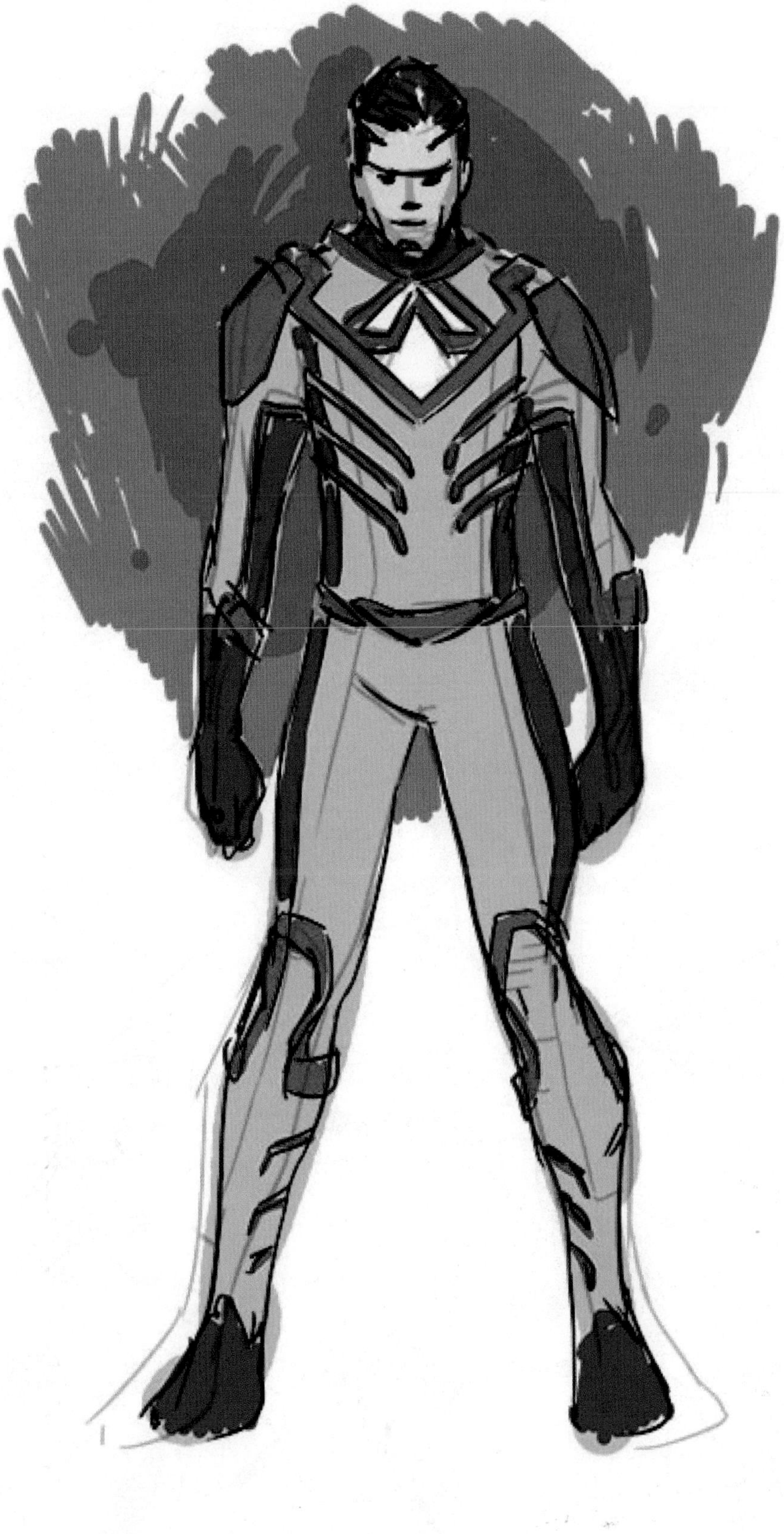

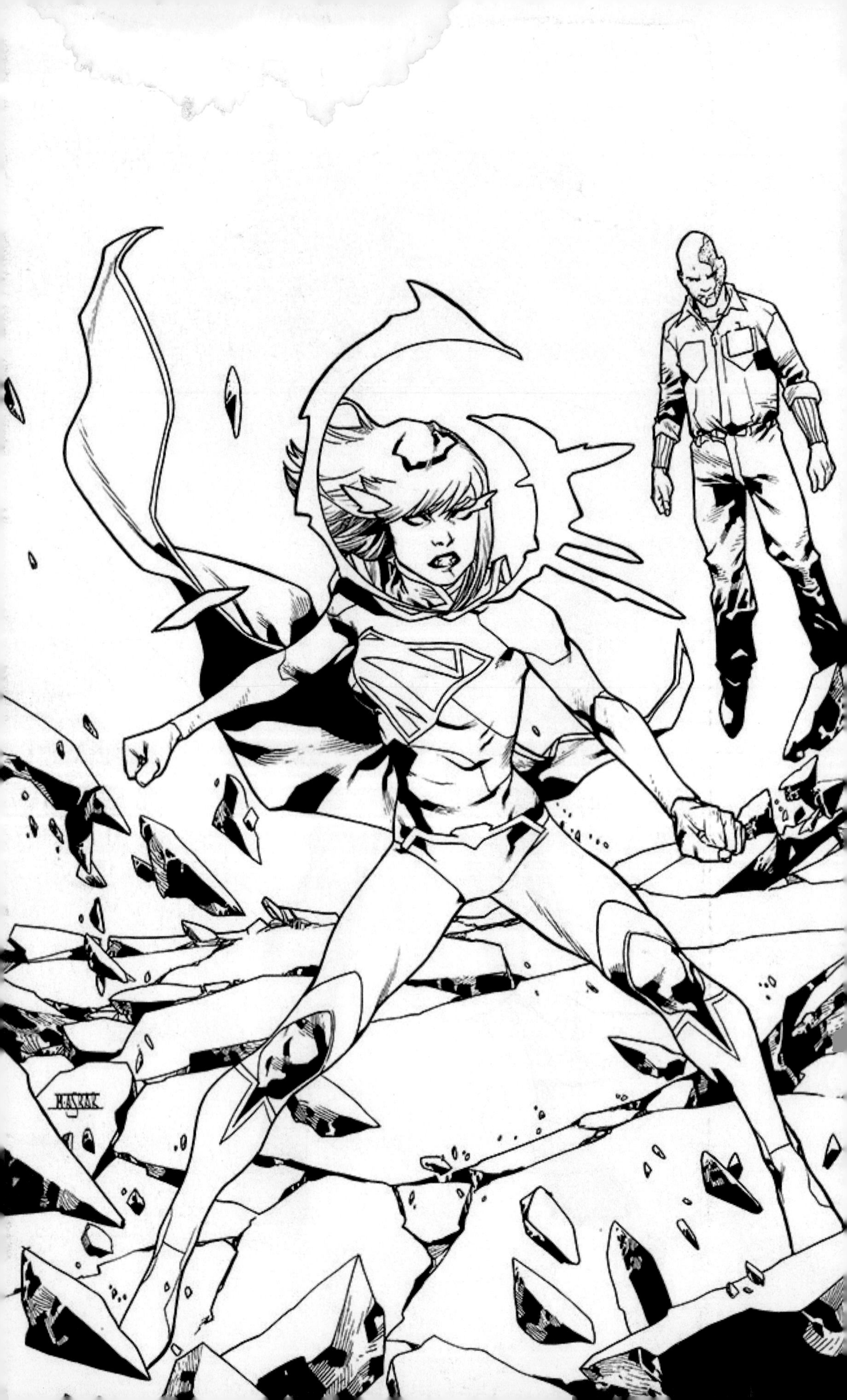

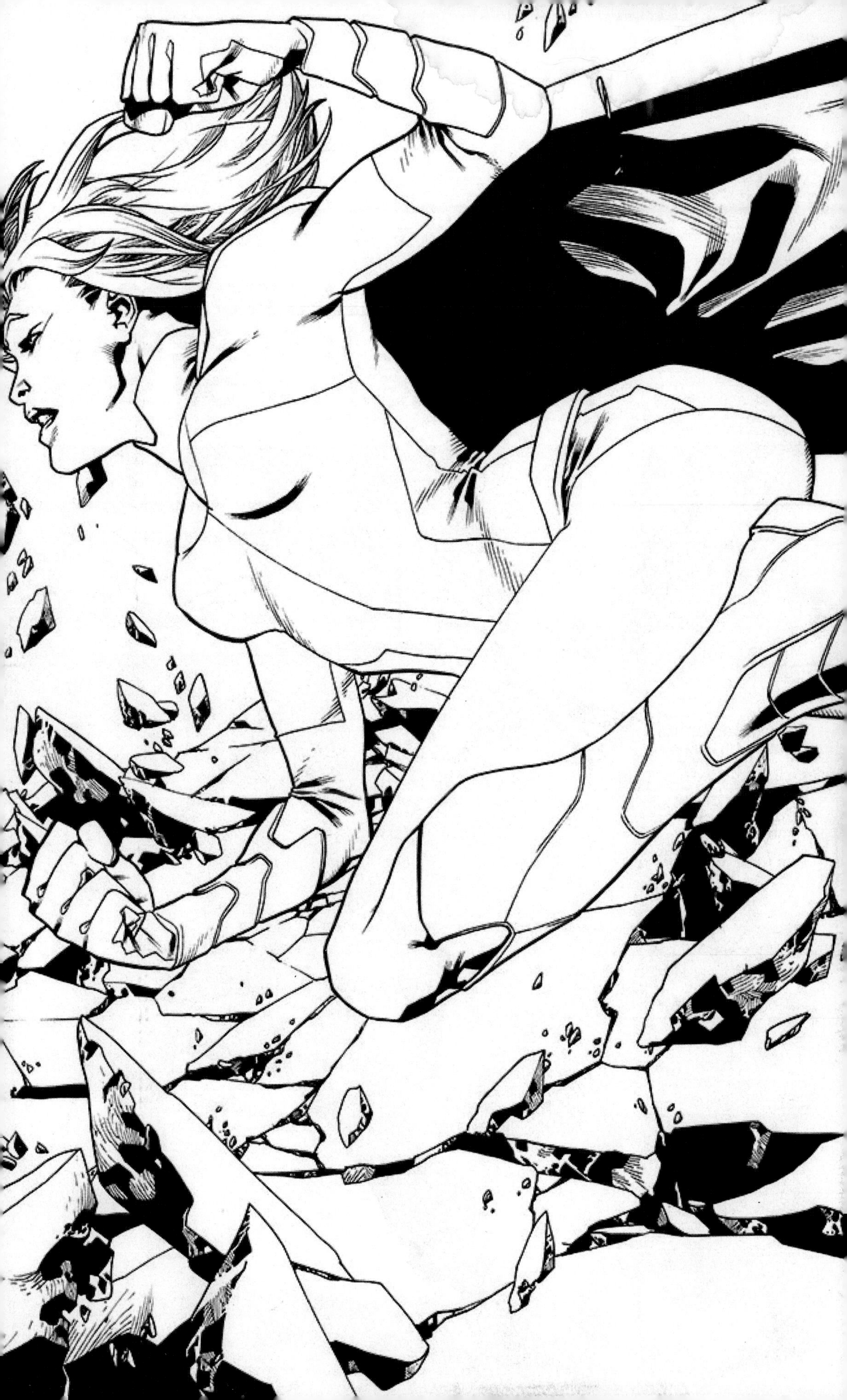

"It's fresh air. I like this all-too-human Superman, and I think a lot of you will, too."
—SCRIPPS HOWARD NEWS SERVICE

START AT THE BEGINNING!

SUPERMAN: ACTION COMICS VOLUME 1: SUPERMAN AND THE MEN OF STEEL

SUPERMAN VOLUME 1: WHAT PRICE TOMORROW?

SUPERGIRL VOLUME 1: THE LAST DAUGHTER OF KRYPTON

SUPERBOY VOLUME 1: INCUBATION

"BELIEVE THE HYPE: GRANT MORRISON WENT AND WROTE THE SINGLE BEST ISSUE OF SUPERMAN THESE EYES HAVE EVER READ."
— USA TODAY

GRANT MORRISON RAGS MORALES ANDY KUBERT